Elizabethan Theater

Dr. Sam Schoenbaum with his cat Sackett. Reproduced courtesy of Peter C. Andrews.

Elizabethan Theater

Essays in Honor
of S. Schoenbaum

Edited by
R. B. Parker and S. P. Zitner

DELAWARE

Newark: University of Delaware Press
London: Associated University Presses

© 1996 by Associated University Presses, Inc.

Associated University Presses
440 Forsgate Drive
Cranbury, NJ 08512

Associated University Presses
16 Barter Street
London WC1A 2AH, England

Associated University Presses
P.O. Box 338, Port Credit
Mississauga, Ontario
Canada L5G 4L8

The paper used in this publication meets the requirements of the American National Standard for Permanence of Paper for Printed Library Materials Z39.48-1984.

Library of Congress Cataloging-in-Publication Data

Elizabethan theater : essays in honor of S. Schoenbaum / edited by R. B. Parker and S. P. Zitner.
    p.   cm.
Includes index.
ISBN 0-87413-587-7 (alk. paper)
    1. English drama—Early modern and Elizabethan, 1500–1600—HIstory and criticism.   2. Shakespeare, William, 1564–1616—Criticisms and interpretation.   3. English drama—17th century—History and criticism.   4. Theater—England—History—16th century.   5. Theater—England—History—17th century.   I. Parker, R. B.   II. Zitner, Sheldon P.
PR653.E67   1996
822'.309—dc20   95-41887
                                                                CIP

PRINTED IN THE UNITED STATES OF AMERICA

Contents

Acknowledgments

OUR most obvious debt as editors is to our contributors, whose eagerness to join in the project, like our aim in undertaking it, reflects the esteem in which all of us hold the recipient of this festschrift. We owe a more than usual debt to the University of Delaware Press, and especially its director, Professor Jay Halio. At Trinity College we have benefited from the material aid and benign interest of Dean Chris McDonough, and from the expert organizational and secretarial skills of Jane Henderson and Herma Joel.

In addition we wish to acknowledge the cooperation of the Associated University Presses, its Director Julien Yoseloff and its Managing Editor Michael Koy. To Dr. Barbara Mowat and the Folger Shakespeare Library we owe thanks for allowing us to use photos of the frontispiece portrait of James I from their copy of James' 1616 *Works*, and of Forrest as Lear from their copy of Gabriel Harrison's 1889 study, *The Actor and the Man*. To the Royal Shakespeare Company we are grateful for permission to use Joe Cock's 1990 production photo of *Lear* 4.6. The frontispiece photo of Samuel Schoenbaum and his familiar spirit was taken by Peter C. Andrews, and the Index was prepared by Ruth Pincoe. Some of the material in "Theatrical Politics and Shakespeare's Comedies, 1590–1600" is taken from Chapter 8 in G. K. Hunter's *The Age of Shakespeare* (The Oxford History of English Literature, vol vi) with permission of the author and the Clarendon Press.

Introduction

A festschrift for Sam Schoenbaum is something of a superfluity. To borrow the observation made about Sir Christopher Wren: if you seek his festschrift, look about you. Much of the current research on Renaissance drama depends, if silently, on foundations solidified by his investigations of Shakespeare's life and theater.

This collection, however, is not the usual arbitrary bouquet. Variety there is—in outlook from Freudian to classically archival, in provenance from Auckland to Toronto—but the collection honors Sam by exemplifying ways that extend his particular contributions. Those contributions focus on the idea of the centrality of the individual—author, actor, entrepreneur—in Renaissance theater.

Nowadays a collection with this theme can hardly claim the innocence of simple scholarly neutrality. Since the eighties there have been, clamorously, a revaluation and shifting of priorities, at least for those who profess to have them. As poststructuralism, historicism, and their offshoots are increasingly contested, refined, or ignored, the role of authorship and the individual contribution becomes increasingly a locus of concern. This collection then is both timely and at times appropriately contentious.

The collection is organized around the four (obviously overlapping) areas that Sam's own work so greatly enhanced: the biographical record, the concept of authorship, evidences of the author in the play, and the multiple contexts in which plays were created and received.

The section on biographical record opens with Stanley Wells's survey of work on Shakespeare's biography since Sam's major contribution, continues with Mary Edmond's demonstration of the possibilities for further digging in the archives, and ends with Brian Gibbons's rethinking of Jonson's self-portraiture as part of the biographical record. Richard Dutton, Barbara Mowat, Ian Donaldson, Sandy Leggatt, and Annabel Patterson provide, not only in the substance of their essays but in their mutual illumination, a serious account of the state of argument on the idea of authorship. In the next section Meredith Skura and Philip Finklepearl consider evidences of the dyer's hand in particular plays. Susan Snyder, Jonas Barish, and Steven Urkowitz continue the argument, using evidence from theme, style, and dramaturgy. Finally, G. K. Hunter gives a sharp account of the theatrical context of Shakespeare's comedy and Arthur Kinney and R. A. Foakes examine historical contexts, as does Michael Neill—for whom the history is contemporary history, an age of cultural transfer and assimilation. The collection ends, as it should, with a checklist of Sam's major publications prepared by Nancy Maguire. Throughout, unless otherwise noted, quotations from Shakespeare's plays have been taken from the Riverside edition of the complete works. Here is scholarship's plenty; Sam deserves no less.

Elizabethan Theater

Part 1
The Biographical Record

Shakespeare's Lives: 1991–1994

STANLEY WELLS

I take as my starting point Sam Schoenbaum's masterly study *Shakespeare's Lives*, which appeared in 1970 and was reissued in revised and updated form in 1991. When it was first published I wrote in a review that "With this book Dr. Schoenbaum joins the ranks of the heroes of Shakespeare scholarship," and I see no reason twenty-odd years later to revise this opinion.[1] No one before him had ever so comprehensively studied attempts to discover the facts about Shakespeare's life and to assemble them into biographical narratives, and no one is ever likely to do so again. Nor can one imagine the task being undertaken with greater learning, humanity, judgment, verve, and wit.

Shakespeare's Lives is an idiosyncratic book, imbued with its author's highly distinctive personality: witty, tolerant, skeptical sometimes to the point of astringency, amused, and, I suspect, fundamentally very conservative. Like any strong personality it is one that can provoke disagreement as well as admiration, but only the most ungenerous of commentators could fail to wonder at the magnitude of the achievement. But, of course, it is bound by the limitations of time. My modest aim in this essay is to continue the story by summarizing and discussing some of the more conspicuous contributions to Shakespearean biography published since Schoenbaum completed his revision in 1991, to the time at which I am writing—summer 1994.[2] I shall not be comprehensive; in particular I shall omit works devoted mainly to demonstrating that Shakespeare did not write Shakespeare— "Deviations," as Schoenbaum calls them—as well as the wholly and avowedly fictional, such as Robert Nye's short novel *Mrs. Shakespeare* (1993). Even without these the bulk is considerable. Nor, of course, shall I make any attempt to imitate the inimitable style of *Shakespeare's Lives*.

The studies that have appeared during the period under review range in scope from brief notes contributed to learned journals to books of three or four hundred pages in length. But this is not an area in which "more" necessarily means "better." Some of the more genuinely original research comes in the less ambitious publications, whereas full-length biographies are more inclined to subsume previously published information, while shaking the kaleidoscope, as it were, in the hope of creating a fresh image. Some "lives" are selective; while most of them draw to some extent on Shakespeare's writings, some are more concerned to use these writings as source for the life; others aim rather to use the life as a framework for discussion of the writings. For example, my own 1994 book *Shakespeare: A Dramatic Life* (of which this will be the only mention) is primarily a critical study of the works, with special emphasis on their theatrical interpretation, which however adopts a broadly narrative framework and includes a couple of chapters, one on Shakespeare's life and personality, the other on his theatrical career, offering a summary and reappraisal of the available evidence. In this essay I shall proceed from writings concerned mainly with original documents, and ones that aim to make fresh contributions to biographical study either by reexamining the existing evidence or by questioning received interpretations, to studies of particular aspects of Shakespeare's career and more broadly based accounts of his life and, sometimes, works.

It is appropriate from time to time that the fundamental sources of our knowledge of Shakespeare's life should be reassessed in the light of changing views and new knowledge about the circumstances of his time. Schoenbaum's *Documentary Life*, published in 1975, is the most recent, and most impressive, major reassessment of the kind.[3] Now Robert Bearman, Senior Archivist of the Shakespeare Birthplace Trust, has taken a fresh look at the thirty (or possibly thirty-one) handwritten documents from Shakespeare's lifetime that mention him by name and that survive in the Stratford records.[4] (Most of the rest are in the Public Record Office in London).[5] Perusal of this short book would be particularly beneficial to writers (such as Graham Phillips and Martin Keatman, whose work is mentioned below), who, as Bearman puts it, express astonishment "that Shakespeare's life is apparently so poorly documented and that this most famous of all writers left behind him virtually nothing in his own handwriting. To archivists," he continues, "this comes as no surprise; to them it would be asking too much to expect anything more" (60). It is true, however, that the documents surviving in Stratford (which do not include the will, with its references to Burbage, Heminges, and Condell) do nothing to remind us that Shakespeare had a career in literature and the theater. Bearman's study shifts a little the focus on Shakespeare's business dealings; he expresses disagreement, for example, with Schoenbaum's view that Shakespeare's sale of twenty bushels of malt in 1604 to the apothecary Philip Rogers was no more than the action of a man "with more than sufficient malt for his domestic brewing" who "sometimes parted with a few bushels of corn on credit." "At the very least," writes Bearman, "it would suggest that Shakespeare had the necessary means to invest in the purchase of quantities of grain well in excess of his needs" (31). Though Bearman's study makes no fresh revelations, it reinforces the growing view, promulgated particularly by Ernst Honigmann, of Shakespeare as a hard-headed business man.[6]

Robert Bearman is able to allude to two fresh discoveries of genuine interest. His assistant archivist, Mairi Macdonald, has found among the archives deposited in the Birthplace a detailed survey of Shakespeare's Old Stratford estate dating from about 1625 that adds considerably to knowledge of precisely which land Shakespeare owned and states that the land had been sold "to William Shakespeare who had one daughter and gave the said land with his daughter in marriage to Mr. Hall of Stratford."[7] Of course, Shakespeare had two daughters; failure to acknowledge the existence of Judith may be an oversight, but could also indicate her ostracism as the result of her ill-judged marriage. And the statement that Shakespeare gave the land to Susanna on her marriage to John Hall in 1607 indicates a generous marriage settlement.

The other recent discovery was made in 1992 by Jeanne Jones, a volunteer worker in the Birthplace Trust's Archive Department, among papers deposited in the Hereford and Worcester County Record Office. It is an inventory of the contents of the Birthplace made on the death in 1627 of Lewis Hiccox, who had taken a long lease of the property in 1605 or 1606.[8] The document tells us much about the layout of the part of the building used as an inn, which had ten rooms along with a kitchen, cellar, and brewhouse, and about its contents at the time its tenant died; it also shows that Shakespeare's sister, Joan Hart, then occupied only a small part of the establishment. These discoveries are not only of interest in themselves; they are also an encouragement, if any were needed, to continuing investigation of the enormous quantities of unexplored archives from Shakespeare's time, among which material of equal or greater value may still await discovery.

Some of the more important investigations of Shakespeare's biography since the publication of Schoenbaum's *Documentary Life* have come from the pen of E. A. J. Honigmann, who can always be relied on for detailed and thorough scholarship, but who also has the courage to propose new or controversial theories on the basis of his investigations. He was engaged for some years, in collaboration with Dr. Susan Brock, Librarian of the Shakespeare Institute, on an edition of wills by theater people of Shakespeare's time, and in a paper originally given to the Fifth World Shakespeare Congress held in Tokyo in 1991, later revised for publication in the *New York Review of Books*, he offered a significant reappraisal of Shakespeare's will.[9] He confirms and emphasizes the general view that Shakespeare was bitterly opposed to his new son-in-law, Thomas Quiney, who married Judith Shakespeare on 10 February 1616 and who confessed to "carnal copulation" with Margaret Wheeler a few weeks later, on 26 March, the day after Shakespeare sent for his lawyer to redraft the will. Honigmann deduces too that Shakespeare intentionally snubbed his brother-in-law, William Hart, by ensuring that a provisional bequest of £50 to Hart's wife, Joan, Shakespeare's sister, should Judith die within three years, was to remain in the hands of Shakespeare's executors—"in other words, was not to go to her husband" (who in the event predeceased Shakespeare). Honigmann's investigations support the well-established view that Shakespeare was "a very sick man" by the time he revised his will; less orthodoxly he suggests that Shakespeare himself, not his lawyer, "was largely responsible for its wording and structure."

The picture of the dying Shakespeare that emerges from this study is of an unforgiving man at odds with his son-in-law, his brother-in-law, and possibly with both the church and his wife. Shakespeare altered his bequest of New Place to Susanna by adding that it was intended "for better enabling of her to perform this my will and towards the performance thereof." Honigmann sees this as an "oblique allusion to Mistress Shakespeare," betraying the fear that she might have interfered in ways that her husband would not have desired. The traditional image of "gentle Shakespeare . . . presents him as he struck others when in congenial company; the will, like the *Sonnets*, gives us glimpses of the solitary inner man, and helps—a little—to explain the sustained rage of a Hamlet or a Prospero."

Complaints about an over-romantic attitude to Shakespeare's life and personality surface again in Eric Sams's "A Documentary Life?"[10] Sams's tone may be gauged from his opening words: "As I have been pointing out for the past ten years, without a word of rational rejoinder, modern Shakespeare scholarship relies on literary fantasy and ignores historical fact." Such sweeping assertiveness does not encourage unimpassioned debate. Sams takes Schoenbaum to task for his attitude towards late seventeenth-century biographical anecdotes. Aubrey reported that Shakespeare's "father was a Butcher, & I have been told heretofore by some of the neighbours, that when he was a boy he exercised his father's Trade, but when he kill'd a Calfe, he would doe it in a *high style*, & make a Speech." The Stratford parish clerk in 1693 also told a visitor that Shakespeare had been apprenticed to a butcher. Schoenbaum is dismissive of the tradition, but Sams argues that, as John Shakespeare is known to have been a farmer, yeoman, glover, wool-dealer, and hide-dresser, he is "very likely indeed to have been a butcher, on all five counts; and eldest sons would naturally give their fathers a hand, at need, then as now." Similarly with the deer-poaching story, which Schoenbaum does not totally dismiss but strongly plays down, and with reports of John Shakespeare's Roman Catholicism and of his son's having served as a lawyer's clerk. Sams judges that Schoenbaum's skepticism derives from the desire to have Shakespeare conform to an over-genteel image: "The Schoenbaum image is the welleducated genteel Shakespeare, a cut above butchery, popery or copy-clerking, who is imagined as a late developer despite his marriage and fatherhood at eighteen." (We might, by the way, ask what is ungenteel about Roman Catholicism.)

Oral tradition is notoriously unreliable, but cannot be definitively disproved; while Schoenbaum may be right to dismiss it, Sams cannot be shown to be wrong to argue that it may reflect truth. What is surely clear is that it belongs to a different category of evidence from that which can be documentarily supported. We know the provisions of Shakespeare's will (even though some of them are subject to variable interpretation) in a way that we do not "know" whether he "died a papist" or held horses' heads outside a London theater. Similarly we know that John Shakespeare was a glover in a way that we do not know he was a butcher. At the best, credence given to anecdotal evidence can be only provisional. And it needs to be assessed in the light of knowledge of the society in which Shakespeare lived. So it is not enough to infer that because Shakespeare's father dealt in wool and used the hides of animals in his trade as a glover it is entirely plausible that he was therefore a butcher as well. The trades were both demanding and distinct, and each appears to have required a full period of apprenticeship as well as very different premises. A maker of violins requires the products of a forester, but does not need to perform this function.

The most painstaking and ambitious recent overall reexamination of Shakespeare's biography has been undertaken by Ian Wilson.[11] Admitting a lack of "formal academic grounding on the literary side of Shakespearean scholarship," he aims "to look dispassionately at all the diverse theories and approaches to the historical Shakespeare as advanced by others, then to steer a sensible middle course among these" (vii). This modestly stated and worthy aim is somewhat belied by the book's presentation as "an enthralling detective story" and by the statements—or rather, questions—on its jacket, which seem intended to whet readers' appetites for sensational challenges to received opinion. "How did William Shakespeare—a humble actor from Stratford-upon-Avon—come to write the greatest plays and sonnets in the English language? Was it indeed Shakespeare who wrote them? If it was, how did he gain from so lowly a background his astonishing insight into the ways of the high and mighty?"

Such sensationalism does less than justice to the earnestness with which Wilson has approached his task. He is a trained historian and has visited many of the places with real or supposed Shakespearean associations as well as consulted original documents. The pity of it is that such diligent and extensive burrowing throws up so little by way of new information or even original hypothesis. Constantly Wilson gives the impression of a man desperately hoping to convince himself, let alone his readers, that he has made sensational discoveries, or at least arrived at a genuinely original point of view, but forced lamely to fall back into the admission that in many respects the truth about Shakespeare's life is unattainable, that such facts as we have cannot be made to yield anything of interest by way of interpretation, and that the only valid response to many of the standard questions is one of agnosticism.

An incisively written, relatively concise survey of the surviving evidence about Shakespeare written by someone with no professional axe to grind might have been worth having, but this long, leaden book, with its profusions of epithets ("Arden *Hamlet* editor Harold Jenkins," "*Faerie Queene* poet Edmund Spenser," and the like) is not it.

Dennis Kay describes his *Shakespeare: His Life, Work and Era* (1992) as an attempt "to tell the story of Shakespeare's life within the context of his age, and to weave into that narrative a chronological study of his writings" (ix).[12] This is an equally written, evenly paced study, careful in its handling of evidence, well-informed about the political and literary history of the period, making no claims to originality in its handling of the biographical evidence. Kay acknowledges that "for the details of the life, I have returned repeatedly to E. K. Chambers, to Samuel Schoenbaum, and to Mark Eccles" (x), but he is more concerned to create a balanced narrative than Chambers, less idiosyncratic in style than Schoenbaum, and more engaging of his readers' attention than Eccles. The tone is expository, kindly, even avuncular; he is a dispassionate guide rather than an incisive commentator, only occasionally committing himself to one biographical theory rather than another. Like Ian Wilson, he categorically denies that what is now known as Mary Arden's House ever belonged to the family. He is tolerantly skeptical about legends of Shakespeare's youth, going so far as to opine that the story about his having been a schoolmaster in the country "merits very serious consideration" but differing from Wilson in finding that the alleged Lancashire connection is inconsistent "with the strongly anti-Catholic sentiments articulated from time to time in the plays" (46).

This is a book that makes a conscious, even self-conscious, effort to wear its learning lightly. Only occasionally could I fault its scholarship. It is not accurate to describe Shylock as a "huge" role, and Kay accepts too easily the assumption that it (and Falstaff) were written for Kemp (184). Though it is true that Marlowe's *The Jew of Malta* was entered in the Stationers' Register in 1594, there is no evidence that it was published then (182). Perhaps it is unwise to assume that Shakespeare was in Stratford for such events as the funeral of his son, Hamnet, in August 1596, and later for the burial of his father in September 1601 and of his mother in September 1608; if their deaths were sudden, they might well have been buried during the time it would have taken for the news to reach London and for Shakespeare to make the return journey. And it is simply not true that Shakespeare left money in his will to set up a monument to himself (349). But this eminently sane and readable book is highly recommendable as a guide to Shakespeare's life and, especially, to his writings.

What I have called "specialized" lives take various forms—I think of studies devoted to particular aspects of Shakespeare's life, such as Mark Eccles's *Shakespeare in Warwickshire* and E. A. J. Honigmann's *Shakespeare: The "Lost Years."* An excellent recent example is Peter Thomson's *Shakespeare's Professional Career*, a biography primarily concerned with Shakespeare as a working man rather than as a private person.[13] It is a handsomely produced, elegantly printed, and sharply written book with enough well-chosen pictures for it to appeal on the coffee-table level but with an informative and well-considered text. Peter Thomson is an acknowledged expert on the theaters of Shakespeare's time and has read widely in the historical background. I admit that as I read I felt at times there was rather too much background and too little foreground. This is a permanent temptation to anyone trying to write at length about Shakespeare's life or career, needing to supplement the meager material in one way or another. Thomson is good on the theaters for which Shakespeare wrote his plays, and is able to draw on recently discovered archaeological evidence in his accounts of the Globe and, especially, the Rose. He treads his way with judicious circumspection among the more speculative highways and byways of Shakespearean biography, inclining to accept Honigmann's account of Shakespeare's "lost years"— that they were spent as a schoolmaster to the Catholic Hoghton family in Lancashire and that this brought him into contact with "the greatest of all the Lancashire families, the Stanleys . . . because it is better argued than any other, and, in many ways, more challenging" (20). This leads to an emphasis on the Stanleys, especially Ferdinando, Lord Strange, as patrons of the drama; but Thomson admits that ultimately "For all Honigmann's exertions, Shakespeare's 'lost years' remain an enigma" (55).

Thomson's reappraisals of the evidence yield some shrewd insights. For example, when Augustine Phillips, the actor, gave evidence about the Chamberlain's Men's performance of *Richard II* on the eve of the Essex rebellion he said that the play was "so old and so long out of use that they should have small or no company at it" but that they were persuaded to put it on by the promise of forty shillings. I have always accepted this statement at face value, while finding it a little strange that a play usually dated around 1595 could have been thought "old" by 1602; Thomson is, astutely, more skeptical, regarding this as a "disingenuous plea": "No one asked him to explain how they could stage, within twenty-four hours, a play that, according to his own deposition, was no longer in the repertoire. His answer to that question would have had to be clever; and it might, furthermore, have provided us with valuable insights (however garbled by special pleading) into playhouse practices" (143).

On a more speculative level, I was interested by Thomson's interpretation of the period in Shakespeare's life when, after the great success of *Hamlet*, he appears to have written in close succession two more recondite plays that seem to have had little commercial appeal: *Troilus and Cressida* and *All's Well That Ends Well*. He suggests that 1601 "was a year in which Shakespeare took stock of his career so far" (144). The death of his father in September "made him rich, by contemporary standards." *Troilus and Cressida*, probably written in 1602 and often thought to have been "prepared specially for performance in one of the inns of court" (the phrasing is careful) may have "failed to attract either the Chamberlain's Men or their audience. It has no easy theatrical charm and few roles for virtuoso actors." "If," writes Thomson, again careful not to overstate his case, "*All's Well That Ends Well* was also in the making in 1602, we can speculate that Shakespeare's usual facility in the penning of plays was temporarily halted." Around this time he moved his living quarters from Bankside to lodge in the northwest part of the city with the Mountjoy family, some considerable distance from the Globe; and in May of 1602 he bought the one hundred acres of arable land in Old Stratford that have recently been identified. This is the basis for Thomson's speculations that it was "at this time that Shakespeare ceased to act, on a regular basis at least," and that he may have been "hoping to spend more time in Stratford now that his elder daughter was well into her marriageable years." Certainly he could have afforded it: Thomson estimates his earnings at not "less than £250 per annum from his income as a sharer in the Globe, a playwright and a property owner," which gives him an income twelve and a half times greater than that of the Stratford schoolmaster so often used as a measuring rod. Well, if Shakespeare did indeed undergo a midcareer crisis he overcame it, happily for us. The possibility that he did so is speculative, depending partly on assumptions about chronology that not everyone would accept—Thomson places *Twelfth Night* in 1600, whereas it is more commonly dated after *Hamlet*, but it is reasoned speculation, intelligently based on knowledge of the facts, and is modestly presented.

The Shakespeare Conspiracy by Graham Phillips and Martin Keatman is easily the worst among the books I have read for this essay, and indeed one of the worst books I have ever read.[14] Such criticism would be indefensible if it were not backed up by hard evidence. This is easy to provide. There are many simple errors of fact. Manningham, we are told, "records seeing a number of Shakespeare plays" (19; in fact, only *Twelfth Night*); a William Condell stands in for William Camden (28) and Thomas for Robert Greene (32); John Hall "had his own books published" (38; not true, though a selection from his casebooks was published posthumously); there are references to "one of . . . Shakespeare's surviving granddaughters" (42; he had only one), to "the *Titus Andronicus* manuscript" (for the quarto, 94 etc.), and to "the dramatist Sir Philip Sidney" (122); and in a notable muddle we learn that "the present bust [in Holy Trinity Church] was made by the theatrical manager John Hall" (43), where the actor-manager John Ward, who organized a benefit performance in support of the restoration, is confused with the "limner of Bristol," John Hall, who effected it.

These are points of detail. More important are the faults of logic and misuse of evidence that pervade the book. The logical gaps in its argument are such that it is not easy to discover the connections between the points the authors make. One implausibility succeeds another as they conjecture that Shakespeare "started life in London, as an apprentice printer working with Richard Field," which, they argue, would have helped him to "gain a wide experience of style, content and grammar, not afforded the academic poets" (130–31). Pointing to the absence of references in Stratford documents to Shakespeare's professional activities (which, as Bearman says, is unsurprising to anyone familiar with local archives), they deduce that Shakespeare deliberately concealed these activities from his townspeople, perhaps because he was involved in espionage associated with Sir Walter Raleigh and the "School of Night."

Finding that "a Secret Service agent known as William Hall appears a number of times in the Secretary of State's records of the 1590s," they conjecture that this was "a cover name used by Shakespeare as a Secret Service operative" that Thomas Thorpe obligingly if cryptically revealed to readers of the dedication of the sonnets. The book reaches a risible climax in speculations about Shakespeare's physical appearance and its effect on his personality. As we know, Heminge and Condell, in their epistle to the First Folio, allude to previously published versions of the plays as "stolen and surreptitious copies, maimed and deformed by the frauds and stealths of injurious impostors that exposed them." Crassly stating that none of the plays had ever appeared "in any way other than they appear in the First Folio," Phillips and Keatman go on to ask, "Were Heminge and Condell making an oblique reference to something about Shakespeare and not the plays? Could the playwright himself have been maimed and deformed?" (191).

They even suggest how it might have happened. Their quotation of Sir Henry Wotton's account of the destruction by fire of the Globe in 1613 omits Wotton's statement that "nothing did perish but wood and straw and a few forsaken cloaks; only one man had his breeches set on fire, that would perhaps have broiled him if he had not by the benefit of a provident wit put it out with bottle ale." This strategic omission leaves the way open for another of their many rhetorical questions: "Had Shakespeare been seriously injured in the Globe fire? Perhaps he had rushed into the flaming theatre, in a desperate attempt to save his precious manuscripts, and instead been terribly burned" (191). And this is "why no one in Stratford appears to have known of Shakespeare's poetry, his plays and his former glory, on his return home" (193). He skulked around licking his wounds until Sir Walter Raleigh, who had been released from imprisonment "just six days before Shakespeare made his will" ("Is this merely coincidence?"), brought about his death by poisoning (196).

When, in a radio broadcast, I challenged Graham Phillips (who happily was in a distant studio) with some of his errors, he offered the excuse that the book was written "for the general reader," as if any old hokum could legitimately be passed off on those who do not know any better. It would have been easier to forgive him and his coauthor for their unscholarly fabrications if these had been presented with verve either as a spoof or as a deliberate fiction.

Fiction is certainly an element in Garry O'Connor's much more genuinely imaginative book straightforwardly called *William Shakespeare: A Life* (1991, paperback 1992).[15] In his introduction O'Connor quotes Schoenbaum as saying, "in his witty and monumental *Shakespeare's Lives*," that the late twentieth century "lacks an authoritative Life conceived in the modern spirit." This is the gap that O'Connor essays to fill in his at-

tempt "to render the whole man in his majestic anonymity and complexity." In some respects his biography follows traditional lines. Admitting that Honigmann's argument that Shakespeare spent time as a tutor in the Lancashire household of Thomas Hoghton "is not conclusively proven" (27), he then goes on to write as if it were: "Shakespeare participated in frequent musical and dramatic entertainments, making contacts that provided openings for his talent later on, particularly with Ferdinando Stanley, Lord Strange, later fifth earl of Derby, who became patron of a leading company of players" (29–30). On the question of religion, O'Connor believes that "Shakespeare retained strong, instinctive sympathy with the old faith of Catholicism ... but he was not really bothered enough to risk offending anyone by insisting on a Catholic priest at his death"(297). His attitude towards the sonnets is somewhat ambivalent: though he is not absolutely convinced that they are autobiographical, he writes of the young man as Southampton: "Shakespeare presented his persona—or the poet's persona, which may not necessarily be that of Shakespeare himself—as deferential, over-awed, devoted, and even both passionately and platonically in love, although never sexually so" (110). Although I can entertain the possibility that the sonnets are wholly fictional, I find it difficult to understand how, if the poet is not Shakespeare, the persons written about can be real people. O'Connor is less confident in the identification of Emilia Lanier as the "dark lady."

Like many modern biographers, O'Connor has a strong psychologizing bent, but while this technique may be fully justified for subjects, modern or even ancient, about whom much personal information survives, for Shakespeare it has to rely entirely on reading between the lines either of the known facts about the life or of the relationships between life and works. Shakespeare "suffered from womb-envy to some degree" so that, "in his later self-projection as the Duke in Measure for Measure ... he thinks, instinctively, in terms of conception and child bearing" (ll); and "through his own sympathetic, feminized nature, he identified strongly with his father: he justified him, took his side" (246).

Presented as theorizing, this kind of thing can be accepted and evaluated for what it is. More ethically debatable are O'Connor's presentations of his own psychologically based interpretations of Shakespeare's life without, as he writes in his introduction, "the hedging qualification ('must have,' 'might') that usually surrounds attempts to describe Shakespeare." (In a somewhat pusillanimous attempt to circumvent criticism he has "printed a table of facts as an appendix," but as this is avowedly a straight crib from William Poel first published in 1919, it is scarcely up to date in scholarship.) The result is that O'Connor appears often to have information about both the outer and inner lives of Shakespeare and of members of his family that could only have been psychically acquired. After Marlowe died, "What the coroner's record did not disclose was that the twenty-nine-year-old Shakespeare called, later that evening, at the house of Eleanor Bull, widow, to seek out his friend Marlowe, and there found him dead, laid out in the garden" (79). "Of Shakespeare's liaisons with other women . . . it can be authoritatively affirmed that these ended in the middle, or towards the end, of the 1590s" (141). After this, "the main task, and the most demanding to which he could apply himself and still discharge his potential for sexual athleticism, was his performance in blank verse" (142). "Shakespeare, writing *Hamlet* at night in the Liberty of the Clink, a frequent user by now of the ever more popular and addictive new American import, tobacco, which cost 3s. per ounce and which he smoked through a pipe, had his own part sheets of *Henry V*—those with only the Chorus speeches written out—on his knee or on the floor beside his table" (187). And at his death, "Shakespeare's body was disembowelled and carefully embalmed for display: led by the High Bailiff, Julius Shaw, perhaps 500 or more people came through the door of New Place to register their grief and pay their respects" (302)—and there follows a touching account of the funeral and its aftermath, for which New Place "was hung with black cloth."

This, of course, is all fiction. It would be perfectly acceptable as such (if still occasionally somewhat preposterous) if it were presented within the context of a novel based on Shakespeare's life; but it sits uneasily with what is offered as "A Life," and might well mislead the uninformed reader.

But for all its extravagances, and in spite of its frequent presentation of guesswork as fact, O'Connor's is an intelligent book with interesting things to say. We may not believe that Shakespeare "felt responsible for Hamnet's death, and *Hamlet* was his attempt at atonement" but the observation that the play "is above all the work of a man who could face pain" (185) was worth making. O'Connor is sensitive to style: in *1 Henry IV* "the rhythm and vocabulary, far from being standardized—so that they become interchangeable between the various acting parts—begin to take on a beat and verbal colour which is specific for each person" (159). He has a proper understanding of Shakespeare's financial prosperity, and does not, as many do, underrate the audiences of Shakespeare's time: "It is a tribute to the Elizabethan age that such a complete, many-layered and many-sided play [as *Hamlet*] should, on its own merits as a piece of entertainment, have become so popular" (195). I can not regard this book as an "authoritative life," whether or not it is "conceived in the modern spirit," and I would not put it in the hands of an innocent reader in search of accurate information, but for one already in possession of the facts it offers the pleasures, both ironical and involved, of watching a cultivated mind tread the tightrope between fact and make-believe.

Studies in Shakespeare's biography in the early 1990s have made a little factual progress in the discoveries relating to Shakespeare's Old Stratford property and to the layout of John Shakespeare's Henley Street property in 1627—by which time, it has to be remembered, it may have undergone changes of layout in conversion into an inn. The authenticity of Mary Arden's House at Wilmcote has come under continued attack. Honigmann's development of earlier arguments for Shakespeare's possible employment during the "lost years" with the Hoghton household (which would confirm Aubrey's claim that he had been "a schoolmaster in the country") have continued to exert an attraction, partly because they would also support the alleged Catholic sympathies, and also because of their links, through the Stanley family, with Strange's Men, named on the title page of the first quarto of *Titus Andronicus* (1594); but they remain unproven. Though the assumption that the sonnets are autobiographical prevails, the possibility that they are fictional remains. Among biographers of Shakespeare there has been a tendency to accept the nonsexual view of Shakespeare's relationship with the young man (in spite of an opposing tendency in more purely literary criticism). More than one writer has claimed that what is seen (and sometimes caricatured) as the conventional view of Shakespeare as a respectable, sweet-natured individual fails to take into account all the relevant evidence; and shifting opinions continue to be expressed about the reliability of anecdotal evidence from writers such as Aubrey and Rowe.

And the saga continues. Park Honan is at work on a full-scale critical biography for the Clarendon Press; and by the time this essay appears in print Yale University Press should have published Eric Sams's *The Real Shakespeare: Retrieving the Early Years, 1564–1594*, revealing how, "in conventional Shakespeare scholarship, the playwright's youth has been concealed within a web of elaborate literary theories which misrepresent his life and work and reject, ignore, or misdate his early plays." Heigh-ho.

NOTES

1. *Notes and Queries*, n.s., 19 (April 1977): 142–43.
2. Among other works concerned with the biographical record published during the period under review are: R. A. Hunt, *The Startup Papers: On Shakespeare's Friend*, (Upton-upon-Severn: Images, 1993): an amateur's attempt to identify Mr. W. H. as William Hole, an engraver; the suggestion had already been advanced by Peter Levi in his *The Life and Times of William Shakespeare* (London: Macmillan, 1988); Russell Fraser, *The Life and Times of William Shakespeare: The Later Years* (New York: Columbia University Press, 1992); the earlier volume, *Young Shakespeare* (1988), of this two-part study is noticed in the revision of *Shakespeare's Lives*. A worthwhile study not mentioned by Schoenbaum is Richard Dutton's *Shakespeare: A Literary Life* (Basingstoke: Macmillan, 1989).
3. S. Schoenbaum, *William Shakespeare: A Documentary Life* (Oxford: Clarendon Press, 1975; compact ed., 1977).
4. Robert Bearman, *Shakespeare in the Stratford Records* (Stratford-upon-Avon: Alan Sutton, for the Shakespeare Birthplace Trust, 1994).
5. These are studied in David Thomas, *Shakespeare in the Public Records* (London: H.M.S.O., 1985).
6. See particularly "'There is a world elsewhere': William Shakespeare, Businessman," in *Images of Shakespeare: Proceedings of the Third Congress of the International Shakespeare Association, 1986*, ed. W. Habicht, D. J. Palmer, and Roger Pringle (Newark: University of Delaware Press, 1988), 40–46.
7. M. Macdonald, "A New Discovery about Shakespeare's Estate in Old Stratford," *Shakespeare Quarterly* 45 (Spring 1994): 87–89.
8. Jeanne Jones, "Lewis Hiccox and Shakespeare's Birthplace," *Notes and Queries* vol. 41 (Dec. 1994), pp. 497–502.
9. E. A. J. Honigmann, "The Second-Best Bed," *New York Review of Books*, 7 November 1991, 27–30.
10. *TLS*, 12 February 1993, 13.
11. Ian Wilson, *Shakespeare, the Evidence: Unlocking the Mysteries of the Man and His Works* (London: Headline Book Publishing, 1993).
12. Dennis Kay, *Shakespeare: His Life, Work and Era* (London: Sidgwick and Jackson, 1992).
13. Peter Thomson, *Shakespeare's Professional Career* (Cambridge: Cambridge University Press, 1992).
14. Graham Phillips and Martin Keatman, *The Shakespeare Conspiracy* (London: Century, 1994).
15. Garry O'Connor, *William Shakespeare: A Life* (London: Hodder and Stoughton, 1991).

Yeomen, Citizens, Gentlemen, and Players: The Burbages and Their Connections

MARY EDMOND

In 1576 James Burbage, then in his forties, and his brother-in-law and financial backer John Brayne, in his thirties, built the Theatre in Shoreditch, just outside the walled city of London to the north. On present evidence, Brayne's Red Lion project in Stepney nine years earlier can hardly be regarded as a serious candidate for "first playhouse," and 1576 remains the date of birth for the London theater as we know it today. Small troupes of players—some of them attached to noble households—had long been providing entertainments away from London; in 1571 Lord Leicester was given permission for his troupe to play in the City, and on 10 May 1574 he secured the first royal patent ever granted to a company of adult actors, permitting them to perform at court, in the City, and throughout the realm. Soon after that the Theatre and other fixed custom-built structures (places "built of purpose" in the language of the day) encouraged the formation of sizable permanent metropolitan companies operating the repertory system; Marlowe and Shakespeare, both born in 1564, provided poetic drama, and Edward Alleyn (born 1566) and Richard Burbage (1568) established the concept of the leading actor as star.

At a time when nearly all secular buildings were of wood, the aristocrats of the woodworking crafts were the carpenters who actually put up the buildings; joiners made the snugly constructed "furniture and fittings"; Shakespeare calls his joiner "Snug" with intent. It seems probable that James Burbage's younger brother Robert, who had completed a seven-year apprenticeship within the Carpenters' Company in June 1573, was the builder of the Theatre; James himself, who had begun his working life as a joiner, was perhaps responsible for the interior. (Robert died in 1584, by then enjoying the status of a house-holder in the parish of St. Giles Cripplegate.)

James Burbage and his family settled in Holywell Street, Shoreditch, between 1574 and 1576, but in earlier years they had been parishioners of St. Stephen Coleman Street, to the east of Guildhall. Addle Street then ran past the north side of St. Mary Aldermanbury, adjoining Guildhall to the west. It then crossed Wood Street and continued as Silver Street, where Shakespeare was later to lodge with the Mountjoys. John Strype, in his 1720 edition of Stow's *Survey*, says that Addle Street was then "yet [still] inhabited by Joiners," which probably explains why James Burbage had begun his working life in the neighbour-hood. Men of the same callings were still tending to congregate in the same parts of the City, as they had done in the Middle Ages. A fellow-parishioner of Burbage was an older man, also a joiner, called John Street; it was his son Peter—the only survivor of a family of eight—whom Burbage's elder son Cuthbert later commissioned to dismantle the Theatre in Shoreditch and use the timber to construct the Globe on Bankside.

Cuthbert and Richard Burbage were baptized at St. Stephen Coleman Street on 15 June 1565 and 7 July 1568. Doubts have been expressed about the baptismal entries because members of the family sometimes appear as "Bridges," "Brigges," and variants, but this is easily explained. Another family, longer-established in the parish than the Burbages and apparently then better off, really were called Brigges; the original will of one of them, dated 1591, survives, and the testator signs himself "Jeames Brigges": the theatrical family always sign "Burbadge". Successive parish clerks no doubt assumed that the two families were one—and by the time the original paper entries were cop-ied into a parchment book in accordance with an injunction of 1598, the Burbages had been gone for nearly a quarter of a cen-tury and would not have been remembered. Some scholars have also been concerned that the baptismal date for Cuthbert Bur-bage is at variance with the fact that when he made a deposition during the Theatre litigation in 1591, he gave his age as about twenty-four. It seems not to be generally realized that in those days people often did not know exactly how old they were (as the cautionary words "or thereabouts" given by deponents in court indicate), so that it is never safe to calculate a date of birth from an age given in later years. Even Sir Edmund Chambers was misled over Cuthbert, declaring—twice—that he "must have" been born in 1566 or 1567.

The first genuine Burbage to appear in the St. Stephen's registers (which begin at 1538) is a Daniel, who married there in 1546; judging by various entries, he was probably James's uncle rather than an elder brother of James, Robert, and another known brother, William. Daniel's eldest son, Lawrence, and James's younger brother, Robert, were apprenticed in the Carpenters' Company on the same day in 1566; Daniel is described in the parish register as a "minstrel," so perhaps it was he who persuaded James to forsake joinery for the entertainment business. James is entered only twice as "joiner," in 1559 (the year of his marriage and the baptism of his first child); it may be more than coincidence that Robert Dudley (created earl of Leicester in 1564) seems to have established his small troupe of players in that year. Burbage, who at some stage became its leader, was perhaps a founder-member. The ensuing years made him very conscious of the pressing need for a permanent playing-place close to the capital. As Robert Miles deposed during the Theatre litigation of the 1590s, he repeatedly told his brother-in-law John Brayne what "contynuall great profitt" they would enjoy by being able to put on plays every week.

Eighteen years after the building of the Theatre, the preeminent London company was established under the patronage of the queen's first cousin, the Lord Chamberlain; and within the next three years its resident dramatist, William Shakespeare, secured the gentlemanly status provided by a country house and a coat of arms (granted in the name of his father, John). What has been described as a "new, experimental social group"[1]—the leading theater men, principally those of Shakespeare's company—was beginning to infiltrate the recognized categories of London society: yeomen—men of some modest substance; citizens—freemen of the City enrolled at Guildhall; and gentlemen. There was of course no actors' guild, but the Chamberlain's/ King's Men, like other business and professional people in the capital, were mostly respectable married householders with children, and sometimes an apprentice living in; exceptions were a few unmarried players and Shakespeare himself. He seems usually to have stayed in lodgings, although he may have had a place of his own when he was in Bishopsgate in the 1590s.

The words "yeoman" and "gentleman" were used imprecisely: James Burbage and his elder son, Cuthbert, appear in records as "yeomen" in their earlier years and later as "gentlemen"; Richard appears as "gentleman" or "player." The word was beginning to acquire respectability because of the exceptional renown of himself and Edward Alleyn. Yet the generality of players, and especially those who had to tour to live, continued to be regarded as of comparatively lowly status, still not far removed from rogues and vagabonds.

The word "citizen" had a precise meaning: citizenship, freedom of the City, was (and is) normally acquired by serving an apprenticeship within a company, by redemption (purchase), or by patrimony. John Heminges, the future coeditor of the First Folio, was baptized on 25 November 1566 at St. Peter Droitwich in Worcestershire and sent by his father, George, to London at the age of eleven. On 2 February 1577/8 (Candlemas), he was apprenticed for nine years to a grocer called James Collins and lodged with him in the tiny parish of Allhallows Honey Lane near Guildhall. Collins (being then a churchwarden) died in 1585, and was buried on 4 August. In his will he bequeathed his apprentice forty shillings "if my wiffe shall thincke good." Heminges completed his service with her and became a freeman on 24 April 1587.[2] The Grocers' Company took, and still takes, precedence over all the Great Twelve except the Mercers': it had evolved from the medieval guild of Pepperers, general traders who bought and sold ("engrossed") all kinds of merchandise in bulk. The commercial practices that young Heminges learned during his apprenticeship no doubt equipped him well for his future role as a business manager of the Chamberlain's/King's Men.

On 5 March 1587/8, Heminges, describing himself as a gentleman of the parish of St. Michael Cornhill, secured a license to marry Rebecca, widow of the player William Knell, the bridegroom then being twenty-one and the bride still only sixteen. The marriage took place at St. Mary Aldermanbury on the tenth of March. Heminges had presumably been moving in theatrical circles during his apprenticeship, and would have become an adult player as soon as he was free. The fourteen children of John and Rebecca were all baptized at St. Mary's—as their mother (née Edwards) had been on 23 December 1571. The powerful magnet of the capital was drawing the ambitious young from all over the realm: while Heminges traveled from Worcestershire, his coeditor of the Folio, Henry Condell, probably came from East Anglia.[3] Both men became pillars of their parish, served as churchwardens, and were buried there. However, as we shall see, they did not spend their whole adult lives there, as is still often supposed.

Cuthbert Burbage came of age in 1586, and it was perhaps then that his father secured employment for him with Walter Cope, Esq., a gentleman usher to the Lord Treasurer. This post introduced young Burbage to Burghley's great house in the Strand. Cope, "my worshipfull frend *M. Walter Cope,*" as Stow calls him, was a considerable figure, closely associated with the Cecils. He was knighted by James I at Worksop on 21 April 1603, during the king's leisurely progress from Edinburgh to London to accede to the English throne, and he held important offices during the new reign. James Burbage's employment by Queen Elizabeth's first and most important favorite, Lord Leicester, and his involvement with the household of her chief minister, Lord Treasurer Burghley, testify to his being held in some regard in high places, and family links with court and aristocracy strengthened during the lifetimes of his two sons. James Burbage is often assumed to have been turbulent, foul-mouthed, and dishonest, but undue weight has perhaps been given to a few depositions in 1592, during the Theatre litigation. John Brayne's widow, Margaret, backed by her friend and executor, Robert Miles, goldsmith of Whitechapel, was continuing to claim half the Theatre profits, and among her witnesses was an undistinguished trio—Nicholas Bishop, soapmaker of Whitechapel, John Alleyn, and Miles's son Raphe. (Bishop gave his age as about thirty-two in January and about thirty in April, a good example of a man who did not know how old he was.) The three were asked about disturbances in the Theatre yard and tiring-house on two days in November 1590. The depositions of Bishop and Alleyn in particular are in the extravagant language typical of litigious Elizabethans. Alleyn, like his famous brother Edward, was a player, and he put his heart and soul into his first performance before the court, telling a tale of his exchanges with James Burbage in the form of dialogue, with interjections of "qd he" and "qd this deponent." Whether his account was truthful or his recollections accurate must be open to doubt; crossexamined later about some of Burbage's alleged outburst (James, deposing in 1591, had of course denied any of the "vnreuerend" words attributed to him), Alleyn replied that he thought they had been "about A yere past"; the incident had in fact been eighteen months earlier.

The stirring episode of Richard Burbage and the broomstick has attracted much attention, but Bishop is the only deponent claiming to have witnessed it, nor did he mention the weapon until his second appearance in court, after Alleyn had mentioned it in his first. On both occasions he said that Richard's mother had joined in the attack on Robert Miles. Alleyn said no more than that he had "found" the actor holding a broomstick and asked him what had been going on. Raphe Miles's evidence is unhelpful, and it is not altogether clear which episode he is talking about. He, too, was a soapmaker—in partnership, he said, with Bishop—but presumably feeling that to describe himself thus might not impress the court, he claimed to be free of the Goldsmiths', one of the leading livery companies. This was a lie. The company's records, still at their hall off Cheapside, show that he did not become a freeman (by patrimony) until five years later, on 18 April 1597.[4] It does not inspire much confidence in his depositions.

Robert Miles himself was not questioned about the events at the Theatre, but only about alleged contempt of court by James and Cuthbert Burbage. He described James as having been "a common player"—omitting to mention that his employer had been Lord Leicester. Some of his other statements are barely credible. For example, he said Brayne (who by the time Miles was testifying had been dead for six years) told him that Burbage had had a secret key made to the "common box" at the Theatre, and over a period of two years had stolen much of the takings, something that Brayne and the players could not have failed to notice. Even less convincing was Miles's assertion that Cuthbert had told him he was "very well contented" that Mrs. Brayne should have half the Theatre profits if his father agreed. Cuthbert himself, deposing in 1591, declared that he had told the Braynes they had no right to the Theatre, since he had "boght it wt his owne proper money as they well knewe." No doubt James was an uninhibited and rumbustious character, but the same could be said of many Elizabethan Londoners, and he was operating in a highly competitive branch of show business.

In spite of the Theatre's popularity, Burbage and Brayne had been constantly in debt in the early years: Brayne had had to borrow just over £125 from a fellow freeman of the Grocers', John Hyde, and Burbage had mortgaged the lease to the same man. When the partners failed to repay within a year, Hyde became the legal owner of the playhouse for a time. In 1589 (as he told the court in 1592), he had reluctantly returned the lease under pressure from the Burbages and Cuthbert's employer, Walter Cope. According to a Shoreditch lawyer, Cuthbert had

had to borrow some money—the lawyer could not remember
how much—to get his father out of trouble.

John Hyde, a native of Wallingford in Berkshire, is usually
referred to as "a grocer," which may give the impression that
he was a shopkeeper. The Grocers' excellent records (now in
Guildhall Library) show that he was a very prominent member
of the company. From 1586 until his death he lived in one of
their most handsome properties in the City, paying the high
rent of £14 a year. It was situated on Thames Street (now Lower
Thames Street, the part below London Bridge) and in the parish
of St. Dunstan-in-the-East. It is a measure of the quality of the
property that in 1567 Alderman James Bacon, brother of Sir
Nicholas the Lord Keeper and uncle of Francis, was seeking a
lease in reversion. At some stage the property, which included
a garden, acquired the name of "The Basket," and on 15 June
1593 the company agreed that their tenant John Hyde should
cause to be set up "the signe of the Baskett paynted vppon a
board and sett forthe in Colors wth oyle, the same to be sett
vpp at the doare."

At this period the company was managed by two wardens
(in 1607 increased to three) with—unusually—an alderman as
Upper Master. On 14 July 1595 Mr. Hyde was elected Second
Warden, and in 1603 he was "put in Eleccon" for First—but it
was the year of his death and the other candidate was chosen.
His will is that of a typical Elizabethan big businessman; he
was a man of property, both in and out of London and made
provision for two of his younger sons (twins) to be maintained
at grammar school and then at Oxford or Cambridge, and left
many charitable bequests. His widow was soon married again,
to Sir James Altham, a Baron of the Exchequer.[5]

If Cuthbert Burbage's remarks in the "Sharers' Papers" in
1634 are to be taken literally, his younger brother began his
illustrious career as an actor in about 1584 at the age of sixteen.
At just that time, a baby who later became Richard's apprentice,
and one of the twenty-six "Principall Actors" named in the First
Folio, was brought to London from Antwerp by his mother. He
was Nicholas Tooley, and it is now possible to construct a biography for him.

The baby's father was William Tooley, freeman of the Leath-
ersellers' Company and a wealthy merchant adventurer. He died
in the large house in Antwerp of his father-in-law, Hans Lan-
quart, between 27 October and 26 November 1583, when his
will was made and proved. He requires his overseers, two other

English merchants in Antwerp with him, to pay from time to time, according to their receipts, "suche portion of money as shalbe for my sonne his parte into the Chamber of the Cittie of London," to be "lette owte by the Lord Maior & Aldermen of the same ... according to theire Lawdable vse and custome." This is a precise description of the system under which the Court of Orphans, which had its origins in the Court of Aldermen, assumed responsibility for orphans of freemen of the City during their minority, and entitled young Nicholas, as an only child, to one-third of his father's estate.[6] Tooley instructed his wife, Susan, to take the baby to England within ten months of his death, and she wasted no time in doing so, for on 14 January 1583/4 she was married in London, at St. Stephen Walbrook, to Thomas Gore, second son of a remarkable family of merchant adventurers. The Gores traded abroad on a very large scale, like Antonios, their minds "tossing on the ocean." They would have known the baby's father well.

During the minority of "orphan Tooley" there are numerous entries about him in the Repertories (minutes) of the Aldermen (now in the Corporation of London Records Office, Guildhall), testifying to the care with which the "laudable custom" was observed. The first is dated 9 January 1583/4, five days before the remarriage of the orphan's mother, when she and one of her late husband's overseers were bound in the sum of £300 to the City Chamberlain (then Robert Brandon, father-in-law of Nicholas Hilliard the miniaturist). On 2 June Thomas Gore was required to nominate "good and sufficient sureties" or recognitors, and on 1 August four of these were bound in the sum of £350 for payment of £300 (figures recurring in later entries). Thereafter payments for the orphan's care were made at irregular intervals, and the distinguished sureties—four at a time— were more often than not members of the Gore family, the most senior being Gerard (d. 1607), and his brother Thomas (d. 1597, a leading member of the Grocers')—described by Stow as "maister *Thomas Gore*, a marchant famous for Hospitality." Thomas was a "friend and cousin" of the father of John Chamberlain the letter-writer and of William Lambarde the historian (letter-writer and historian were both born in the City, sons of aldermen and sheriffs). Five of Gerard Gore's sons—who, like their father, were all freemen of the Merchant Taylors'—acted as sureties for young Tooley at various times, including Richard the eldest, MP for the City, and for many years resident at Hamburg as Deputy for the English merchants trading there; Sir

John, Lord Mayor in 1624–25; and William, alderman and sheriff.

The Gores have strong Shakespearean connections. The London branch of the Davenant family, originally from north Essex, was founded by Raphe (ca. 1504–52), who set up house in the parish of Allhallows Bread Street and was, like the Gores, a freeman of the Merchant Taylors'. He adopted an orphaned niece and nephew, Ellen and John Davenant from Essex, and in 1550 Gerard Gore married Ellen, who became the mother of his eight sons and one daughter. Her brother John (ca. 1540–1606), who was apprenticed to Gore, and his son, also John (1565–1622), became merchant vintners, importing wines from the Continent, and settled on the north bank of the river immediately opposite the playhouses. The younger John (later described by Anthony Wood as "an admirer and lover of plays and playmakers, especially Shakespeare") moved to Oxford in about 1600. He kept the wine tavern in Cornmarket where the poet stayed on his annual visits to Stratford (here the source is Aubrey, who knew the family), and fathered Sir William Davenant, Caroline poet laureate and playwright, and at the Restoration one of only two theater managers licensed for the whole of London. Davenant was largely responsible for restoring Shakespeare's plays to the stage, although sometimes "restoring" them in rather odd forms. It was with the best intentions, since Sir William, supposed godson of the poet, was his devoted admirer.

The marriage of Gerard Gore's son, Thomas, and Nicholas Tooley's mother, Susan, was brief, for on 16 December 1585 Thomas was buried at St. Stephen Walbrook; a year later, on 8 December 1586, Susan was married to Christopher Humfrey, freeman of the Grocers'; her fourth and last husband was Roger Gwyn, a prominent member of the same company and a distinguished apothecary. Roger was a brother of Matthew Gwyn, doctor of medicine, who helped to organize the entertainments at Oxford for Queen Elizabeth in 1592 and for King James and Queen Anne in 1605.[7]

The final entry in the repertories about "orphan Tooley" is dated 9 October 1604. He then appeared before the full Court of Aldermen—Sir Thomas Bennett, Lord Mayor, presiding—was "adjudged by inspection" to be twenty-one "and upwards," and expressed himself satisfied.[8] I think it is not overbold to surmise that his apprenticeship with Richard Burbage had been promoted by Shakespeare. Chambers saw no reason to connect

Nicholas Tooley with a man of the same name in a Warwick-shire muster-roll of 1569, but in fact there is every reason: the elder Nicholas was the actor's grandfather. The Tooleys were landed gentry, settled in the village of Burmington, which is about twelve miles from Stratford on the road to London and only about four miles from Barton-on-the-Heath, where the Lamberts, the poet's uncle and aunt, lived. He would have known the Tooleys from his boyhood. In London young Tooley would normally have lodged in his master's household, but Richard Burbage had as yet no wife to look after the boy. His elder brother Cuthbert *was* married: his employment with Wal-ter Cope had taken him down to the Strand, and I find that on 8 July 1594 he married Elizabeth, daughter of John Cox, gentle-man, by license at the church of St. Mary-le-Strand.[9] Cuthbert and Elizabeth had two sons, Walter and James, who did not sur-vive infancy, and one daughter, also Elizabeth, baptized at Shoreditch on 30 December 1601. Having no son of their own, they were probably glad to take in young Tooley, and in his will years later he thanked Mrs. Burbage for her "motherlie care" of him. He presumably played boys' and/or female parts in the 1590s. He proved his father's will as executor on 25 January 1603/4—perhaps his twenty-first birthday—as a marginal note testifies; and he was adjudged by the aldermen to be over twenty-one in October. It can now be said with confidence that he joined the King's Men as an adult member during the year. It has, of course, long been known that he is named seventh and last of Augustine Phillips's list of fellows in his will dated 4 May 1605. He is named fifth in the company's second license of March 1619, after Heminges, Burbage, Condell, and Lowin—and was in fact fourth, since Burbage had died while the patent was being processed. Tooley was a most unusual recruit to the leading actors' company of the day: Anglo-Flemish, sprung from the English landed gentry, well-to-do and closely connected with wealthy and powerful families in the City of London.[10] The company would have benefited from his money, as he apparently never married.

James Burbage had originally hoped to convert part of the former monastic buildings at Blackfriars into an indoor play-house, and I have assembled evidence showing that, before the plan was thwarted by opposition from residents of the precinct, the Burbages and their master-carpenter, Peter Street, moved down to the river. Street acquired a house and woodyard on the west bank of the Fleet in the precinct of Bridewell, and the

Burbages moved into Blackfriars on the east bank; Shakespeare is known to have moved to Southwark by about 1598–89.[11]

Part of the evidence about the playwright comes from the lay subsidy rolls at the Public Record Office. Subsidies were granted to the Crown by Parliament: the Parliament of 1597–98 assembled on 24 October 1597—close to the end of the queen's thirty-ninth regnal year—and passed an act granting subsidies to be paid in 1598, 1599, and 1600. Mrs. Stopes found, and published in 1913, three entries in Middlesex rolls relating to Shoreditch and the Burbages, but wrongly took the "39 Eliz." endorsements to date the assessments and collections themselves, whereas the dates are usually in their superscriptions. Thus she misdated all three collections and published them out of chronological order; nor did she search any London rolls or go beyond the reign of Elizabeth. Her findings seem not to have been questioned hitherto. The correct details are:

1. Middlesex roll, E179/142/239: Cuthbert Burbage is assessed at £4, tax 10s 8d. Richard is not mentioned and was presumably living with his married brother. The collection was taken on *31 October 1598.*

2. London roll, E179/146/390: Cuthbert is entered under St. Ann Blackfriars, assessed not on "goods" as is customary, but on the property, and is assessed at £20, tax £4. There is an *a* for "affidavit" beside his name, indicating the collectors' report that he was no longer there and had not paid. The collection was taken on *1 October 1599.*

3. Middlesex roll, E179/142/234: Cuthbert is back in Holywell Street, assessed as in 1598. Richard is entered at the nominal sum of £3, tax 8s 0d, but an *a* beside his name indicates that he was elsewhere. The collection was taken on *24 September 1600.*

4. List of Shoreditch defaulters in a Middlesex roll, E179/142/236, endorsed "39 & 40 Eliz." Richard is back and pays his eight shillings on *2 June 1601.*

These newly established dates, showing the Burbage brothers probably away from Shoreditch in 1599, suggest that they had joined their playwright on Bankside to watch day-to-day progress on the building of the Globe.

Richard Burbage was married by 7 October 1601, for when his wife, Winifred, consulted the doctor and astrologer Simon Forman on that date, he entered her in his casebook as "Winfret burbidg," aged twenty-five; her sister-in-law Elizabeth, Cuthbert's wife, aged thirty-two, had been to the doctor on 7 July. Nicholas Tooley consulted him in 1599, when Forman noted his age as seventeen. On 7 July he complained of "melancholy . . . moch gnawing in his stomak & stuffing in his Lungs," and he went again on 1 December.[12]

The Burbage brothers were involved in property deals in Shoreditch from time to time: in April 1608, for example, they bought a house and garden from John and Thomas Austin, of a family then prominent in the parish. This was sold in 1645 by Richard's surviving son and heir, William. In 1617 a wealthy brewer called Henry Hodge, who proves to have been a longtime friend and neighbor, bought a property on the east side of the high street including a brewhouse called the Bell and three acres of land; the brothers signed the indenture as witnesses. Hodge was a leading member of the Brewers' Company (who had their hall in Addle Street), serving as Third Warden in 1613–14, First Warden in 1624–25 and Master in 1626–27.[13] He, like the Grocer John Hyde, owned properties outside as well as in London, and he was a governor of Christ's Hospital. As early as 1610 he had served with Cuthbert Burbage as a principal juryman at Middlesex Sessions.

Richard Burbage died on Saturday 13 March 1618/19, and the burial is recorded in the parish register in especially large writing: "Richard Burbadge Player, was buried the xvjth of Marche." He was in his fifty-first year. His nuncupative will is signed by, among others, his fellow King's Men Nicholas Tooley and Richard Robinson. It was a time of twofold sorrow for the company. As John Chamberlain reported in a letter to Sir Dudley Carleton (ambassador at The Hague) three days after the funeral, the theaters were closed because of the recent death of Queen Anne, and "one speciall man among them Burbage" was lately dead. On 20 May the earl of Pembroke, then Lord Chamberlain, writing a newsletter to Viscount Doncaster (ambassador in Germany), noted that there had been a great supper that night for the French ambassador, and that all the company were now at the play, "wch I being tender harted could not endure to see so soone after the loss of my old acquaintance Burbadg." This was William, third earl of Pembroke, to whom, with his younger brother Philip, Heminges and Condell would dedicate the First Folio four years later.

On the death of Burbage, it was agreed that the Blackfriars playhouse should go to his widow and two surviving children:

William, then not quite three, and the baby, Sara, born posthumously. Under an arrangement dated 4 July 1620, four trustees were appointed, including Henry Hodge the brewer and John Milton, gentleman, probably the poet's father, who was a scrivener by profession.[14]

This year, 1620, also saw the death of Shakespeare's landlord, Christopher Mountjoy, who had moved to the parish of St. Giles Cripplegate. The register entry, on 29 March, is in especially large letters, as Burbage's had been at Shoreditch the year before: "Christopher Mountioye Tyremaker." He was a man of substance, assessed as highly as many of his English neighbors, and describes himself in his will (GL MS 25,626/4, fols. 179–80) as "of London Marchant." His first wife, Marie, had died in 1606— when Shakespeare perhaps moved to other lodgings—and on 21 August 1615 he had married Isabel Dest at St. Olave Hart Street near the Tower. The well-found widow was promptly snapped up: on 17 July 1620, within four months of Mountjoy's death, she was married by license at St. Giles' to William Broxon (Oliver "Crumwell" married Elizabeth Bourchier there, also by license, in the following month). Sixteen-twenty was also the year of marriage of Cuthbert Burbage's daughter and heir: on 8 June Amyas Maxey, described as a gentleman of the parish of St. Margaret Westminster, secured a license (Harleian Soc. 23, p. 26) to marry eighteen-year-old Elizabeth. The marriage was to take place at St. Leonard Foster Lane off Cheapside, but as church and registers were lost in the Fire, there is no means of confirmation. The couple had two children, Elizabeth and James.

Two more subsidy rolls (E179/142/279 and 284), now in a poor state and apparently hitherto unnoticed, supply important information about the Burbages. In the first, dating to 1621–22, Winifred is entered as a householder in place of her late husband, assessed at £5, tax 13s 4d. The names of the Holywell assessors are noted: Cuthbert Burbage, Henry Hodge the brewer, and one other. Burbage and Hodge are both assessed at £4, tax 10s 8d (for Burbage the same sum as in 1598 and 1600). A parishioner called Edmund Turner died intestate in 1622, and letters of administration were granted on 6 August to his daughter Winifred Burbage, with whom he had presumably been living. I find that Winifred was married by license to Richard Robinson on 31 October, at the church of St. Mary Magdalen Old Fish Street, between St. Paul's and the river.[15]

The second subsidy roll dates to 1623–24, and Robinson's name replaces that of his new wife. But the most significant fact about this roll is that Cuthbert is not in it. There was no longer any need for him to remain in the northern suburb in Middlesex "without the walls," as he has always been supposed to have done. The company was playing down by the river, at Blackfriars and the Globe; his brother was dead and his sister-in-law remarried, and his daughter and heir was married. Before the beginning of June 1623 he moved to Redcross Street in the parish of St. Giles Cripplegate. Its site is now covered by the Barbican Centre, but in those days it was a select street, with "fair houses" on both sides and an adjoining large plot of ground with (as both Stow and Strype report) gardens and "summer houses for pleasure." It continued northwards as Golding (now Golden) Lane, where in 1600 Peter Street had built the Fortune for Alleyn and Henslowe. The playhouse was destroyed by fire in 1621 and its successor built in 1623, Burbage presumably arriving in time to watch the work. (There is now a public garden on the site.) Cuthbert was by now of undoubted gentlemanly status: his assessment on goods had gone up from £4 to £5, tax 13s 4d. At some stage he acquired a coat of arms; and in 1630 he paid a fine of £12 as one of those gentlemen who, enjoying an annual income of £40 from lands or rents, had declined to seek knighthoods at the coronation of Charles I in 1626.[16]

Cuthbert's colleague, friend, and longtime lodger, Tooley, had been buried at St. Giles Cripplegate on 5 June 1623, and the entry in the register reads: "Nicholas Tooley Gentleman from the house of Mr Cuthbert Burbidge gentleman." The player's long and meticulous will, made on 3 June, shows that there was something dubious about Cuthbert's son-in-law Maxey: the testator describes him as Elizabeth's "pretended" husband, and a bequest to her of ten pounds is carefully worded to ensure that the money is paid "vnto her owne proper handes," not to her husband, as would normally have been the case. Richard Burbage's daughter, Sara, is bequeathed £29 13s 0d, owed to Tooley by his fellow player Robinson, to be paid on her reaching the age of twenty-one or marrying. Sadly she did neither; she was buried on 29 April 1625 (a bad plague year), leaving William the sole survivor of Richard and Winifred's eight children. In the year of Tooley's death (and publication of the First Folio), Henry Hodge the brewer had a tablet placed on the chancel wall at Shoreditch, bearing the names of principal benefactors of the parish including the actor, who had made a lavish bequest of eighty pounds for bread for the poor "for ever." (The old church was demolished in 1735, and the present one opened in 1740: Mr. Hodge's tablet does not survive.) Hodge himself later made a bequest similar to Tooley's, although somewhat smaller, and the wishes of both men were still being carried out in the 1830s.[17]

Rebecca Heminges had died in 1619 and was buried at St. Mary Aldermanbury on 2 September. No doubt for professional reasons John then moved down to Bankside, to a new house adjoining the second Globe. But at his own request his body was taken back to Aldermanbury for burial—on 12 October 1630. Men who had done well in the City sometimes retained their town houses but also acquired desirable country places not far off, but away from "the hurry and confused bustle of the town" (to quote the Kentish historian Edward Hasted on the delights of his county). Riverside villages upstream from London and Westminster were popular, and Heminges's coeditor of the Folio, Henry Condell, chose Fulham: his body was taken back to Aldermanbury for burial on 29 December 1627 and that of his widow, Elizabeth, on 3 October 1635.[18]

At some stage Cuthbert Burbage adopted his grandson James, thereafter to be known as James Burbage Maxey. The date of death of the boy's father is undiscovered, but on 21 December 1630 his widow was married at St. Giles Cripplegate to George Bingley, Esq., of a family of landed gentry at Blyth in Nottinghamshire. He was much older than his bride and probably a well-to-do widower—the first of his many appearances in the State Papers is in 1606, when Elizabeth was a young child. Bingley became an important figure in the Exchequer at Westminster—a senior Treasury man, as it would be today—and by 1635 he was one of the Auditors of the Imprests (his father-in-law calls him "Kings Auditor"). In the late 1630s he was much involved in planning for resistance to the Scottish Covenanters and the two resulting Bishops' Wars that preceded the outbreak of the English Civil War. One of his important commissions was to recommend appropriate rates of pay and other charges for a "complete army" of twenty-four thousand foot soldiers, six hundred horses, and a train of artillery for six months and for twelve months. Two letters survive among the State Papers, written in his elegant hand to his "much honoured and good ffrende" Secretary of State Edward Nicholas. The first, dated 14 March 1638/9 (CSPD 1638–39, p. 561, 94, SP16/414/94) and despatched "in hast," reports that he will be ready to wait upon King and Council on the following afternoon with some of the required information. The second letter, dated 29 March 1640 (*CSPD 1639–40*, p. 594, 24, SP16/449/24), regrets that he will be unable to report to the Council on the morrow as promised: "I haue a very greate Colde and vehemente Cough wch shatters my heade and bones in peeces." He has not left his chamber and "litle warm parlor" for eight days, and his doctor says that if he ventures out too soon he may endanger his life. This letter is written from his house in Redcross Street.[19]

In the early 1630s Bingley had been involved in further litigation over the Globe, as one of two commissioners appointed to represent Cuthbert Burbage and other plaintiffs during hearings at the Swan on Bankside; a document dated 1647 among the records of the Court of Husting, not hitherto noticed, involves him again and adds a little more information about the Blackfriars properties originally bought by James Burbage. For many years the apothecaries had sought to break away from the Grocers' Company, and eventually King James, on the advice of his law officers, declared: "Grocers are but merchants, the business of an Apothecary is a Mistery [métier, profession], wherefore I think it fitting that they be a Corporation of themselves." The Society was incorporated in 1617 and later secured the former house of Lord Cobham at Blackfriars for its hall. In May 1647 the Society paid eighty pounds for a "litle yarde or peece of void ground with the Brickwall thervnto belonging" adjoining the hall. This is described in detail and can be identified with the little yard in Burbage's indenture of 1596 (the wording has of course been updated, and the original "olde privie" has disappeared). The sellers in 1647 were George Bingley, esq., and his wife, Elizabeth, heir of Cuthbert Burbage, and William Burbage, gentleman, heir of Richard, and the sale was negotiated by Bingley.[20]

This document provided my first clue that Cuthbert had acquired a country house, for the Bingleys are described as "of Hayes in the County of Kent." Hayes is now part of the Greater London borough of Bromley, but in the Burbages' day it was a tiny but very accessible village just south of Bromley, only about twelve miles from London, and close to the highway leading to Sevenoaks and Tonbridge. An eighteenth-century survey shows an idyllic neighborhood of pasture and arable land, woods and commons, with the Ravensbourne brook flowing down between Bromley and Beckenham to enter the Thames at Deptford Creek. Hayes still has the air of a village, and Hayes Common survives.

Cuthbert and Elizabeth died at Hayes in 1636, within a fort-night of each other—Cuthbert having reached the age of seventy-one. A joint entry in the little register reads thus:

Mr Cutbert Burbidg died at haies sept. 15. } but both / buried at /

Mrs [blank] Burbidg died at haies sept 28. } shoreditch in / London.

Cuthbert was buried on 17 September and Elizabeth on 1 Octo-ber. Strype notes that the couple "departed in *September* 1636" and describes their monument in Shoreditch chancel: "On a flat Stone / *Venimus, Vidimus, Redivivimus, Resurgemus.*" Cuth-bert, who died intestate, had apparently retained his town house, for he is described in his letters of administration as of St. Giles Cripplegate.[21]

His son-in-law continued at the Exchequer, and his close col-league in the latter part of his career was another Auditor of the Imprests, Bartholomew Beale, a relative of Pepys who figures in the *Diary*. Bingley retired in 1650, and in 1651 he probably negotiated the sale of the Blackfriars playhouse by William Bur-bage. He died intestate at Hayes in 1652.[22] There were just two houses of consequence in the village: one, Hayes Place, was later acquired and rebuilt by Pitt the Elder, earl of Chatham. His son, the future prime minister, was born there in 1759, and the earl died there in 1778; the other house of consequence was the one acquired by Cuthbert Burbage, which, as his daughter states in her will in 1672, was called "The Heyes." In two hearth-tax lists the names of the Lady Scott and Mistress Bingley head the entries, taxed on fourteen and seven hearths respectively. Elizabeth also owned "a tenement and lands" on Bromley Com-mon. These were probably inherited from her father and "known as the White Lion." In her will she bequeaths to her unmarried daughter, Elizabeth Maxey, all her lands, houses, and tenements in Blackfriars; land and a tenement in Hayes (oc-cupied by a local man called John Ownsted) to her son and daughter-in-law. To the poor of the village she gives 5 pounds and to the poor of Shoreditch twenty shillings, and the rest of her estate to her son. The will was made on 7 January and proved on 29 March, and Elizabeth was buried at Shoreditch on 10 Feb-ruary. Her son, the last of the Burbages, died intestate in 1677, and on 31 October of that year his widow, Elizabeth, was married by license at St. Martin-in-the-Fields to a lawyer, Evan Lloyd, gentleman of Gray's Inn.[23]

Continuing research suggests to me that the forebears of the theatrical Burbage family were inhabitants of Bromley.

NOTES

1. M. C. Bradbrook, *The Rise of the Common Player* (London: Chatto and Windus, 1962), vii.

2. Heminges's apprenticeship, Grocers' wardens' accounts, Guildhall Library (GL) MS 11,571/6, fol. 473v, and freedom, MS 11,571/7, fol. 220v; Collins's will, PROB.11/69/4/, PRO, and burial, GL MS 5022 (the printed transcript of the register, Harleian soc. 44, p. 262, gives the surname as "Dollens"). Heminges's marriage license, Harleian soc. 25, p. 168.

3. David Honneyman, "The Family Origins of Henry Condell," *Notes and Queries*, n.s. 32 (1985): 467–68, and *Closer to Shakespeare* (Braunton: Merlin Books, 1990), 120–21; Mark Eccles, "Elizabethan actors I: A-D," *Notes and Queries*, n.s., 38 (1991): 45, suggests Cambridgeshire. See his p. 43 for James Burbage.

4. Information from the Librarian, Mr. David Beasley.

5. Grocers' wardens' accounts, GL MS 11,571/7, fol. 197 for Hyde taking over the house; for the painted sign, court minutes, GL MS 11,588/2, fol. 20, and election as Second Warden, fol. 40v. Marriage license, Harleian soc. 25, p. 82, and pedigree, *Visitation of London 1633–35*, part 1, Harleian soc. 15, p. 410. Will, PROB.11/102/111 (1603).

6. William Tooley's will, PROB.11/66/10 (1583). Charles Carlton, *The Court of Orphans* (Leicester: Leicester University Press, 1974), chap. 3, 42–55, for the procedures of the court.

7. For more on the Tooley/Gore/Davenant involvements, see Mary Edmond, *Rare Sir William Davenant* (Manchester: Manchester University Press, 1987), chaps. 1 and 2 and notes, and pedigree facing p. 1. The Gwyn brothers were freemen by patrimony of the Grocers' Company.

8. First entry, 9 January 1583/4, Repertory 21, fol. 16; last entry, 9 October 1604, Repertory 26, part 2, fol. 451. Also on 9 October, notes on Tooley's "satisfaction" were added to earlier entries about him (signed by sureties), in Common Council Journals 24, fo. 184 and 25, fol. 43v, and Letter Book Z, fol. 385, and the orphan signed all three "Nicho: Tooley." His naturalization is noted in Huguenot Soc. publications, 8: 233. I am very grateful to the City Archivist, Mr. James Sewell, and his colleague Mrs. Juliet Bankes for advice and help on the orphan.

9. Will of Nicholas Tooley Senior (1582), PROB.11/64/31, and *Victoria County History for Warwickshire*, 5: 26–28 (1949) for the family. The first register of St. Mary-le-Strand is at Victoria library, City of Westminster archives.

10. Mark Eccles, "Elizabethan Actors IV," *Notes and Queries*, n.s., 40 (1993):174, is not aware of the entries in the Aldermen's Repertories about "orphan Tooley," and describes the young man who came of age in 1604 as a "well-to-do Londoner, not the actor," but the two documents he cites are quite appropriate to the actor. The first is a memorandum, Common Council Jour-

nal 28, fol. 201v, and relates to a loan of £100,000 to the Crown in 1610 by all the aldermen, paid in four monthly instalments of £25,000; the memorandum is signed by two of them, Sir John Swinnerton and William Cokayne, who had gone to the Exchequer on 10 May 1611 seeking repayment of one installment plus 10 percent interest. It bears the names of five alleged witnesses including Nicholas Tooley (although the signatures appear to have been written perhaps by a clerk). Swinnerton belonged to the "theatrical" parish of St. Mary Aldermanbury, and was—like the Gore family—a freeman of the Merchant Taylors', and on both counts would have known Tooley personally. The second document, a docket dated 6 September 1619 (SP.38/11, PRO), confirms an earlier grant to Tooley of some old debts to the Crown dating back to "before 31 Eliz." Such debts, while often not worth the trouble and expense of attempted collection by the Crown, were in great demand by individuals, to whom they were sometimes sold, conferring the right to collect; quite often they were conveyed as a gift, from the Crown's point of view a cheap way of rewarding suitors or those whom it wished to honor, and this would apply to men on the fringe of the court like Tooley, a member of the King's Company of players. I am indebted to Professor Robert Ashton, author of *The Crown and the Money Market, 1603–1640* (Oxford: Clarendon Press, 1960), for advice and help.

11. See Mary Edmond, "Peter Street, 1553–1609: Builder of Playhouses," *Shakespeare Survey 45* (1992): 101–14, 105–6. James Burbage's twenty-two-year-old daughter, Ellen, was buried at St. Ann Blackfriars on 13 December 1596 (the page on which the entry appears in the register, GL MS 4510/1, is wrongly headed "1595").

12. Forman casebooks, MS Ashmole 411, fols. 150 and 79 and MS Ashmole 219, fols. 101v and 205, Bodleian Library.

13. *LCC Survey of London, Vol. 8: Parish of St. Leonard Shoreditch* (1922) for some property details. The indenture signed by the Burbage brothers, M457, is now at Hackney archives department. Court minute books of the Brewers' Company, GL MSS 5445/13 and 5445/14 for Henry Hodge's offices.

14. E. A. J. Honigmann and Susan Brock, *Playhouse Wills, 1558–1642* (Manchester: Manchester University Press, 1993), 113–14, and fig. 4, p. 115, for Burbage's will; Herbert Berry, *Shakespeare's Playhouses* (New York: AMS, 1987), 70, for the trusteeship.

15. Letters of administration of Edmund Turner of St. Leonard Shoreditch, Archdeaconry Court, GL MS 9050/5, fol. 153v. Robinson-Burbage marriage, GL MS 11,529.

16. New assessment, entered under St. Giles Cripplegate and dated 6 April 1626, E179/147/553. The coat of arms is depicted in Cuthbert's 1634 entry for the *Visitation of London 1633–35*, p. 121 (in which he enters his late brother as "the famous actor on the stage"); Mr. T. D. Mathew, Windsor Herald, supposes that the boars' heads on the coat of arms are an heraldic pun on the first syllable of the surname. For the £12 fine, Alexandra Mason, "The Social Status of Theatrical People," *Shakespeare Quarterly* 18 (1967): 429–30. These fines were part of Charles I's attempt to raise money, having dissolved Parliament and thus deprived himself of subsidies.

17. Tooley's burial, GL MS 6419/2; will, Honigmann and Brock, *Playhouse Wills*, 124–28—the Wilkinson alias is unexplained. Hodge's burial at Shoreditch, 10 November 1632, will Archdeaconry Court, GL MS 9051/7, fol.

137v; for the Tooley and Hodge bequests, John Ware, *An Account of the Several Charities . . . of the Parish of St Leonard Shoreditch* (London, 1836).

18. Honigmann and Brock, *Playhouse Wills*, 156–60, for Henry Condell, 164–69 for John Heminges, and 182–86 for Elizabeth Condell.

19. A subsidy roll of 1621, E179/147/492, shows that Bingley's house was on the west side of Redcross Street. Half a dozen "auditors clerks," entered nearby, were probably members of his staff.

20. For the Globe litigation, Berry, *Shakespeare's Playhouses*, essay 6. Court of Husting, roll 322, item 22 (25 May 1647), Corporation of London Records Office; Dr. W. S. C. Copeman, *The Worshipful Society of Apothecaries of London* (Oxford: Pergamon, 1967). In the Society's first account book, GL MS 8202/1, p. 242, "wyne for Auditor Bingley" is noted on 28 January and 25 February, and payment for "ye plot of ground" on 13 May.

21. Hayes register at Bromley central library, P180/1/1, microfilm at Centre for Kentish Studies, County Hall, Maidstone; Shoreditch register, GL MS 7499/1, enters Cuthbert as "Burbardge" and Elizabeth as "Burbadge"; Cuthbert's admon., 25 October 1636, PROB.6/16/26. Winifred Robinson buried at Shoreditch 2 May 1642, Richard "a Player" at Blackfriars 23 March 1647/8. Richard Burbage's heir may have been the William Burbage who died intestate in 1654, *PCC Admons. vol. 1, 1649–54*, British Record Soc. (1944), p. 55.

22. Last State Paper appearance, *CSPD 1650*, p. 415, SP18/11/76; Berry on the 1651 sale, *Shakespeare's Playhouses*, 70–71; Bingley's admon., 16 June 1652, PROB.6/27/101.

23. Hearth-tax lists for Hayes, E179/249/25/4 (1662) and E179/249/36/4 (1664); for the property on Bromley Common, Chancery suit, C6/171/13 (1661); Elizabeth Bingley's will, PROB.11/338/25 (1672); James Burbage Maxey's admon., PROB.6/52/123.

Jonson and Reflection

BRIAN GIBBONS

No glass renders a man's form, or likeness, so true as his
speech.
—Ben Jonson, *Discoveries*

JOHN Marston is typically Elizabethan in his gusto for caricature. His *Satire VII* begins with a parody of Richard III:

A man, a man, a kingdom for a man!

Marston has the caricaturist's confidence in selective distortion
to expose the truth, and he arrogantly expects that we will discern his own sharply positive self-portrait through his negative
images of other people. He proceeds to inspect and dismiss a
series of figures, every one too ludicrous to deserve the name
of man:

These are no men but apparitions,
Ignes fatui, glowworms, fictions,
Meteors, rats of Nilus, fantasies,
Colosses, pictures, shades, resemblances.

The short-lived theatrical fashion for inductions was in fact to
give John Webster a chance to make portraits of some famous
shadows—in his added induction to *The Malcontent* he presents
in propria persona the actors Condell, Sly, Lowin, Sinklo, Burbage—but the result is rather tame; ultimately the inductions
yield only one memorable portrait, and that one is in Ben Jonson's *Every Man Out Of His Humour*—a self-portrait conceived
as a series of sketches from different (and ironically calculated)
angles, by the Presenter, his friends Cordatus and Mitis, and by
Carlo Buffone.

50

This experiment by Jonson in the use of diverse points of view to create a dialectical or dynamic portrait may be a bit unwieldy, but it does at least demonstrate the principle of transferring techniques of caricature and portraiture to the drama. What is also remarkable is Jonson's interest in self-assertion, his demand that the spectators remain conscious that this is not just a play but a Ben Jonson play. Awareness of his authorial presence is to be a part of the dramatic experience; we are to perceive elements of the poet dispersed wittily among his creations, like fragments of a mirror that always reflect an incomplete image.

There is always a doubt in the case of Jonson's more teasing poetic self-portraits, *My Picture Left in Scotland, The Poet to the Painter, An Epistle Mendicant 1631,* whether in the end we can perceive what is constant behind the changing self-caricatures unless it be a kind of nothing, the nothing we are left to contemplate in Sir Epicure Mammon (in *The Alchemist*) when the great works fly *"in fumo"* and he goes to mount a turnip cart and preach the end of the world, or in the revelations from Morose in *Epicoene* that begin with his horror that the woman is not silent—"Why?" she asks, "did you think you had married a statue?"—and end, after his own confession that he is "no man," in the discovery that Epicoene is just a name and a costume, an impersonation by a boy: she does not exist. So Jonson's self-caricature in *My Picture Left in Scotland* is as a rocky face above a mountain belly—a fantastic half-Atlas, half-Parnassus, a truly unfathomable if genial source of inspiration and fertility, though forbiddingly aged and gigantic, and not a little ridiculous too. Here there is an allusion also to the man-mountain painted on the back scene in the masque *Pleasure Reconciled to Virtue.* It had a huge head, with hair and beard all covered with frost, and rolled its eyes and moved itself with wonderful cunning. In the masque this was half-Jonson, a poetic conceit, half-Inigo, an object painted and carpentered; but in his poem it is undividedly Jonson's, a purely verbal entity, and, he would claim, all the better for it.

In his poem *The Poet to the Painter* Jonson assures Burlase that a portrait of him is possible, that even though he is grown into a round lump, "there are lines wherewith I might be embraced." Yet the supposedly helpful suggestions are pure Rabelais—if not the art of portraiture, suggests Jonson, then perhaps carpentry—a great wine-tun? Or architecture—an amphitheatre? Or, "if in the compass of no art it came," then, simpler still, just a random flick of the pen at the paper and

With one great blot you had formed me as I am.

In the *Epistle Mendicant 1631* Jonson caricatures himself, a bed-rid wit, as a besieged town, again emphasizing the gaping space within by describing the outer bounding line, this time imagined as the fortifications of a beleaguered town, a line full of squiggles and flourishes,

> faussebraies,
> Redoubts, half-moons, horn-works, and such close ways,
> The muse not peeps out one of hundred days.

Here the wordplay (doubt in "redoubts," lunacy in "half moon," sexual innuendo in "horn-works" and "close ways") hints equivocally at dark shades in the negative casting of the conceit. It is worth recalling, too, that the seventeenth-century caricature was defined as a portrait in which no single feature corresponds but the whole represents a recognizable likeness.

The sense of instability is vital to the creation of a lifelike impression in a portrait, according to the art historian E. H. Gombrich: "A surpassing masterpiece, such as Velasquez's great portrait of Pope Innocent X, never looks arrested in one pose, it seems to change in front of our eyes. . . . And yet this refusal to freeze into a mask and settle into one rigid reading is not purchased at the expense of definition."[1] Inside every fat man, it is said, there is a thin man trying to get out. Jonson's brilliant short lyric, *My Picture Left in Scotland*, merits more than a glance in this connection.[2]

> I now think Love is rather deaf than blind,
> For else it could not be
> That she
> Whom I adore so much, should so slight me,
> And cast my love behind;
> I'm sure my language to her was as sweet,
> And every close did meet
> In sentence of as subtle feet,
> As hath the youngest he
> That sits in shadow of Apollo's tree.
>
> Oh, but my conscious fears,
> That fly my thoughts between,
> Tell me that she hath seen
> My hundred of grey hairs,
> Told seven-and-forty years,

> Read so much waste, as she cannot embrace
> My mountain belly and my rocky face;
> And all these through her eyes have stopped her ears.

As the title indicates, Jonson is intent on a self-portrait, though the poem is placed in a sequence of love poems and at a particular point when anxiety and jealousy are in question. This then is the portrait of the poet as forty-seven-year-old frustrated lover, and it opens abruptly, the voice breaking in with exasperation:

> I now think Love is rather deaf than blind

Yet this impression alters as soon as it is received, for the next three lines unexpectedly falter, piteous in their triplet rhymes; they enact the poet's almost speechless dismay:

> For else it could not be
> That she . . .

Should we grant this new emotion our sympathy? The last line focuses his sense of absurd injustice at nature's unfairness:

> And all these through her eyes have stopped her ears.

We may feel an impulse to be moved but we should not let the old rogue con us: some lines of W. B. Yeats bring out by contrast what real poignancy is like:

> Words I have that can pierce the heart.
> What can he do but touch?

Jonson's mercurial humor and nimble wit allow the nineteen stone, forty-seven-year-old to dance like Nijinsky. The role of lovelorn poet is one he can certainly dance out brilliantly, but does a man deserve a lady's love just because his sentences are so sweet and his poetic feet so nimble? This version of Jonson knows perfectly well that he will survive unrequited love, that "men have died from time to time and worms have eaten them, but not for love"; he even lets us see him admiring himself, a preposterous and therefore disarming strategy. The elusive playfulness creates a space for maneuvre and conjecture for the reader/auditor on one side, as much as for the poet on the other. The counterpoint between the studied elegance of its design and its impulsive, intimate voice is perfectly equal. The poem's climax is a grotesque sketch that is mournful but at the same time funny. The poet gives himself fantastic features, a "mountain belly" and "rocky face." That such sweetness of the language is somehow owed to the monstrous weight of his belly is a pretty paradox, as odd in Falstaff as in Pavarotti.

In Renaissance English drama the verbal text is so important that there is overlap with portrait techniques in nondramatic texts. *Twelfth Night* offers an instance:

> *Olivia.* . . . we will draw the curtain, and show you the picture.
> Look you, sir, such a one I was this present. [*Unveiling*] Is't not well done?
> *Cesario [Viola].* Excellently done, if God did all.
> *Olivia.* 'Tis in grain, sir, 'twill endure wind and weather.
> *Cesario [Viola].* 'Tis beauty truly blent, whose red and white
> Nature's own sweet and cunning hand laid on.
> Lady, you are the cruell'st she alive
> If you will lead these graces to the grave,
> And leave the world no copy.
>
> (1.5.233–43)

In Shakespeare's theater Olivia and "Cesario" would have been boy actors, so that theatrical makeup, face-paint, laid on with a "cunning hand," would have contributed to the impressions of beauty and femininity—an irony that an alert audience might savor. Olivia finds this handsome newcomer, "Cesario", attractive, though Orsino's long-drawn-out poetical courtship has been a bore. Nevertheless when Olivia speaks, sonneteering habits come automatically:

> *Olivia.* O, sir, I will not be so hard-hearted; I will give out divers schedules of my beauty. It shall be inventoried, and every particle and utensil labell'd to my will, as, *item*, two lips, indifferent red; *item*, two grey eyes, with lids to them; *item*, one neck, one chin, and so forth.
>
> (1.5.244–49)

Evidently Orsino's barrages of sonnets (though he may not know her eyebrow from her elbow) have, after all, left their mark on her mind. Hers is a witty piece of parody: in this sonneteer's catalogue her facial features, itemized separately, are defamiliarized.[3] Without the schema of the face to provide a context, there is absurdly no scale by which to read them: the eyes might be as large as linen chests ("with lids to them"), and the neck and chin transposed.[4] Yet aiming to dismantle the tropes, she finds herself, as female wooer, only reversing them. Olivia does have a trump card, though: she is safe in the knowledge that this is not writing but theater, that she can send Cesario an extra message that is nonverbal. She lifts her veil to give him the full effect of her beautiful gaze. It is entertaining that she chooses Cesario, the only man in the play (as the spectators know) certain to be unmoved by this display.

In the earlier comedy *Much Ado About Nothing* the villain Don John makes the bridegroom Claudio suspicious that his bride-to-be, Hero, is unchaste, and offers Claudio ocular proof: "you shall see her chamber window entered," he says. Though at a distance and at midnight Claudio persuades himself the figure he sees at a window is Hero. Shakespeare uses the social gatherings at the beginning of the play to suggest a society in which people rely on fixed images. Benedick and Beatrice at first appear to be intent on living down to the mocking labels "Signior Mountanto" and "Lady Disdain." Even when masked for the ball everyone finds that his or her fixed image betrays them: old Antonio is instantly recognized by the "waggling" of his head. For Benedick, ironically, becoming a lover at first seems to be a matter of exchanging one set of conventional signs for another, now dressing smartly, brushing his hat, and even having a shave. Only further developments make demands on him for a mobile, changing, more flexible self, and force both him and Beatrice to the final point where they communicate while negating all conventional expressive means, particularly language. Thus the "much ado" brings them to a kind of silence, a kind of "nothing," and to the inner self, true but an essence and therefore another kind of nothing. It may be inferred but cannot be shown.

The nature of personal identity in Shakespeare's plays is inseparable from the means of representation, and the impressions of a person reflected by others make an important contribution, sometimes perhaps even more than the impressions projected by the individual in question. In Shakespeare propositions about identity being a matter of reflection are very useful to devious politicians. For instance in *Troilus and Cressida* Ulysses and Achilles develop these propositions in 3.3, Achilles observing

>   nor doth the eye itself,
> That most pure spirit of sense, behold itself,

Not going from itself; but eye to eye oppposed,
Salutes each other with each other's form;
For speculation turns not to itself,
Till it hath travell'd and is mirror'd there
Where it may see itself.

Ulysses answers that

>   no man is the lord of anything,
> . . . .
> Till he communicate his parts to others;
> Nor doth he of himself know them for aught,
> Till he behold them formed in th' applause
> Where th' are extended.

(3.3.105–20)

These ideas about the reflexive condition of identity are directly applicable to Ben Jonson's mature poetic portraits as displayed in the collection "The Forest," from his 1616 Folio *Works*. In these poetic portraits emphasis falls on the occasion, which is a public commendation of a great name; yet these portraits are also emphatically concerned to advance the famous name of Ben Jonson. The declared lofty aim of the poems is to affirm moral ideals, and such eulogy traditionally involves stiff, ideal images, the obverse of satiric caricature;[5] yet the relation between eulogy and satire in these poems is unstable because the stance of the poet himself is palpably (though not always consciously) ambivalent. On the one hand Jonson strives to portray his patrons as superior to venal worldly concerns and his own role of poet as sacred; on the other hand his patrons' value is inseparable from their riches and good connections, and his own career as court poet depends on these, too. The lifelike quality of these poems is in their instability, generated by the irresistible intrusions, the self-dramatizing, the presence in the portraits of Jonson himself.

Jonson's *Epistle to Katherine Lady Aubigny* (1611–12) is a particularly interesting example of this and repays some closer examination. It is a kind of double portrait. Indeed the poet himself, not the lady, is the first to attract our attention, right in the foreground. Jonson places us as witnesses to this conversation piece.

Lady Aubigny is invited to "see / In my character what your features be." Now "character" means "a graphic sign," "a distinctive style of writing or drawing," as well as "personal ap-

pearance," "reputation," and "moral constitution." Jonson
offers to restrict the sense of "character." In lines 30–36 he
dismissively remarks that the lady's physical beauty is obvious:
any man can tell of it in simple, plain words on which the
poet cannot improve—"perfect, proper, pure and natural." His
concern is however to make a portrait of her mind, something
demanding a language capable of laying hold on "more removed
mysteries" (to use Jonson's own phrase for his Neoplatonic
ideals in the masque *Hymenaei*) Yet in fact the poem's vitality
consists in representing "character" in its full diversity of meaning. His bragging, her vanity, coexist with the genuine virtue
deserving celebration, so "character" and "features" are ambivalent. The lines are inscribed by his own hand on paper, and they
reflect the minds of both the lady and himself. More interestingly, they identify two opposed kinds of ancestral line—hers
from great families, his deriving from great poets. Jonson had
recently treated the topic in burlesque terms in *The Alchemist*,
with Mammon's hyperbolic courtship of Dol:

> *Mammon.* There is a strange nobility, i' your eye,
>   This lip, that chin! Methinks you do resemble
>   One o' the Austriac princes.
> *Face.*   (Very like,
>   Her father was an Irish costermonger.)
>
> (4.1.55)

One wonders whether Lady Aubigny had the wit to see that
Jonson's claim to nobility, as an artist, involved the implicit
challenge: which kind of ancestral line is superior?

His opening phrase breaks in rather abruptly, as if from the
submerged current of his thoughts as he contemplates his sitter:

> 'Tis grown almost a danger to speak true
> Of any good mind now, there are so few.

We, as readers, are included in his suspicions as he ironically
shares with Lady Aubigny his doubts about everyone else's
moral and political integrity. The poet tells Lady Aubigny that
while he commends her great name and fortune, the portrait
will be no routine Elizabethan canvas, will include no armorial
bearings and "gifts of chance" that "raise not virtue." Right
away Jonson stresses that his purpose is defiantly unfashionable
if not downright impossible: to refine away from his subject,
Lady Aubigny, and himself, the dross of worldly context and (as

the poem's alchemical language suggests) to represent them in terms of spirit—to make a portrait of minds in language, not of appearance in paint:

My mirror is more subtle, clear, refined,
And takes and gives the beauties of the mind

Jonson asserts that she deserves praise for choosing to live a life apart, and that he is a true mirror for the lady because he too has independence, that of the artist. Yet Aubigny was his most important patron at the time, and the poem does appear to have had an immediate practical relevance to his career. Jonson went to live in the Aubigny household the next year, 1613, and he is believed to have still been there in 1616, when this poem was published in "The Forest."[6]

In the second part of the poem (53–92) the poet commends the lady (who was only twenty years old at the time) for having already chosen a life of retirement from court and Society:

This makes, that wisely you decline your life
Far from the maze of custom, error, strife,
And keep an even and unaltered gait,
Not looking by, or back (like those, that wait
Times and occasions, to start forth and seem)

(59–63)

What were the facts here? Lady Katherine Aubigny (D'Aubigny) née Clifton, had married Esme Aubigny in 1609 when she was seventeen. Their first child was a daughter, Elizabeth, born on 17 July 1610. When Jonson wrote the poem she was awaiting the birth of her second child, a son, born in the family mansion in Blackfriars in April 1612. This child was christened in the presence of the king at Whitehall a few weeks later and named James in his honor.

Now these facts, especially the king's presence at the christening in Whitehall, suggest that Jonson was stretching a point in claiming Lady Aubigny had retired from court and Society on moral grounds. As J. C. A. Rathmell has pointed out to me,[7] Lady Aubigny went on to have eight children altogether, "which means she must have been pregnant for most of the time in what otherwise might have been her dancing years." It is clear that Jonson's choice of metaphor—"you . . . keep an even and unaltered gait"—is intended to compliment the lady on her firmness of stoical purpose, yet, quite simply, one thing one cannot say about a woman during her pregnancy is that her gait remains unaltered. Either this is a private joke or it is an artistic mistake, as if Jonson's subconscious rebelled at the tedium of eulogy. In any case the result is to expose the eulogy to momentary bathos.

Jonson's alchemic efforts to exalt and sublimate these mundane circumstances might seem strained, and in view of Lady Aubigny's home being in Blackfriars, one may also note that only a year or so earlier, in 1610, it had been Blackfriars that Jonson had chosen for Lovewit's house in *The Alchemist*. Jonson's Blackfriars was, then, all too clearly a "maze of custom, error, strife"—no place for a lady—but his great comedy is serious in its concern with blasphemy and the perversion of spiritual values, and it takes the degradation of alchemy as a metaphor seriously. It is possible that Jonson himself thought of *The Epistle to Lady Aubigny* as another attempt, this time serious, at poetical alchemy. Towards the end of the poem an element of self-mockery seems to creep in when the poet catches himself out trying to prophesy, perhaps too much like Dr. Subtle for comfort (106–7).

When Jonson commends Lady Aubigny's retirement from the "turning world" (64) that "studies spectacles and shows," he is also thinking about himself; the metaphor seems clearly to be an allusion to the "mikrokosmos or globe" that "turned softly" to discover the first masque in his *Hymenaei*. A pattern of acute tension, reflecting that in the present poem, is apparent in Jonson's divided attitude to masque-theater, as soul or as body. In the printed text of *Hymenaei* (1606) Jonson had justified the scenic spectacle by reference to its "more removed mysteries," although his description is rapturous:

> a microkosmos or globe, filled with countries, and those gilded: where the sea was expressed, heightened with silver waves. This stood, or rather hung (for no axle was seen to support it), and turning softly, discovered the first masque ... which was of the men, sitting in fair composition within a mine of several metals; to which the lights were so placed as no one was seen, but seemed as if only Reason with the splendour of her own illumined the whole grot.

Nor does Jonson fail to allude with sensuous approval to the fashions and attires of the ladies in the masque:

> ... their hair being carelessly (but yet with more art than if more affected) bound under the circle of a rare and rich coronet adorned

with all variety and choice of jewels . . . their shoes were azure and gold set with rubies and diamonds; so were all their garments, and every part abounding in ornament.

Jonson was especially sensitive to the reactions of court spectators who, he said, had "little or (let me not wrong 'em) no brain at all," could not read the complex harmonies of masque dances, and judged such spectacles as *Hymenaei* only a mirror of their own empty, tinsel, "turning world".[8] Being thus "Giddy with change" they could not read Jonson's masques as mirrors of moral idealism; they did not "see / Right the right way" (67–68). Jonson later blamed Inigo Jones for giving his serious masque allegories unintelligible visual representation, attiring the persons "as no thought can teach / Sense what they are" and thus contributing to the degradation of occasions at which some were only too ready in any case to behave disgracefully.

Because of his ambivalent attitude to excess, he was a master of its poetic evocation. Jonson is therefore warning himself, as maker of masques, as much as addressing Lady Aubigny, whose pregnancy prevented her dancing, when he recalls that to have true understanding is to be lonely:

> . . . yet must your comfort be
> Your conscience; and not wonder if none asks
> For truth's complexion, where they all wear masks.

(68–70)

The next lines (70–87) associate costume, cosmetics, jewelery, and portraits as branches of the art of disguise (itself an older word for court masquing). Opposed terms, of encrusted surfaces and fluid deliquescences, are applied to the court, seen as a body whose brittle paint crazes and gapes in response to the flux and decomposition ceaselessly working within. It was a Jacobean commonplace to notice that country estates and with them rural communities were being dissolved to pay for the ruinous costs of court life. This ironically complicates the attitude to the paint-and-canvas landscapes of Inigo Jones's masque scenery, to those landscape backgrounds to Jacobean portraits or to those hunting scenes in silk, gold, and silver thread fantastically embroidered on courtiers' costumes or their gloves and shoes, or wrought in precious metals for jeweled brooches.

Jonson insists at the poem's beginning on the "danger" of speaking true "now," in 1611–12, and to this person, Lady Aubigny. He declares

> as I am at feud
> With sin and vice, though with a throne endued,
> And in this name am given out dangerous
> By arts and practice of the vicious,
> Such as suspect themselves, and think it fit
> For their own capital crimes t'indict my wit;
>
> (9–14)

Is there some particular reason for Jonson to speak like this—to darken the tone of the double-portrait right at the beginning? Would Lady Aubigny have known what he was talking about? The answer seems to be decidedly yes. Jonson was a Catholic for nearly the whole time he had known Aubigny, a period of great tension for all English recusants. In 1603 Jonson had in fact been charged with the "capital crime" of treason—actually "popery and treason"—by Northampton for writing the play *Sejanus.* Jonson began a sojourn as a guest in Aubigny's house later in 1604. The next year, 1605, Jonson certainly received Aubigny's support when imprisoned over the scandalous remarks about King James I in the play *Eastward Ho.* The year after that Jonson was marginally involved in helping to confound the Gunpowder Plot and thereby showed himself a patriot though a Catholic. He returned to the English church in 1610. Now in 1612, a few months after the failure of his play *Catiline* had opened the old wounds over *Sejanus* and added fresh hurts, it might be natural for Jonson to invite approbation of the new play *Catiline* because it heroizes the loyal informer Cicero, condemns "capital crimes," and makes the assertion very relevant to English recusants, "no religion binds men to be traitors." Thus, signaled in the phrase "capital crimes," Jonson alludes to difficulties in his career and public reputation and to the patronage of the Aubignys, giving himself a somewhat saturnine complexion, a suitable foil to his fair partner in the double portrait.

Jonson declares (16) he has not "altered" his "look." His poet's eye (also his "look") is sharp; his philosophical outlook constant; indeed everything the spectator can see in his attitude and expression is recognizably "Jonsonian," and so are his mind and ideals. His "look" is both how he looks to others and how as portrait painter he looks at his sitter.

As artist he insists that he will not fear to "draw true lines 'cause others paint." There is a punning allusion here to the lines of the portrait (brush strokes or verse-lines) but also to the Aubigny family's ancestral line (Elizabethans often did not distinguish between painters of portraits and painters of heraldic arms, applying the term *painter* to both). The stress on the inserted word "true" yields the further innuendo that associates "painting" with face-painting[9] and the false arts of cosmetics and disguise. Only the poet makes portraits with words and in that sense his truth is abstract, held on a higher plane than that of the senses. But Jonson did in fact sit for at least one surviving portrait, although he obstinately and obtusely slighted the art of the portrait painter, as we see in the poems to Venetia Digby (Underwood, 84, iii and iv) *To Burlase, To the Reader of Shakespeare's First Folio* ("reader, look / Not on his picture but his book") and *To Weston, Lord Treasurer* (Underwood, 77), where Jonson acknowledges that "Romano, Tintoret, / Titian, or Raphael, Michelangelo" may have equaled or outdone "the old Greek hands in picture" but nevertheless that was in an art "wherein the judge is wise / As far as sense, and only by the eyes." He commends Weston's study of the superior arts of life, which leads to his brag

> though I cannot as an architect
> In glorious piles or pyramids erect
> Unto your honour: I can tune a song
> Aloud; and (haply) it may last as long.
>
> (P. 251)

A spirit of self-assertive rivalry informs Jonson's attitude to visual art and is vigorously made part of his own self-portrait, and this identification of painting with cosmetic arts immediately precedes the announcement to Lady Aubigny

> I, madam, am become your praiser.

He invites her to share his sense of the equivocal nature of the activity, and teases her urbanely:

> If it may stand with your soft blush to hear
> Yourself but untold unto yourself, and see
> In my character what your features be,
> You will not from the paper slightly pass;
> No lady but, at some time, loves her glass.
> And this shall be no false one, but as much
> Removed, as you from need to have it such.
> Look then, and see yourself. I will not say
> Your beauty,
>
> (22–30)

An ordinary portrait painter would give the lady a blushing cheek as a matter of routine, whether she has one in reality or not; Jonson first records his lady's "soft blush" as a mark of beauty, but then goes on to redefine its value as signifying an absence of cosmetic paint and a true indication of modesty.

Yet Jonson's efforts to cleanse his poem of irony by openly admitting the problem cannot succeed, given the rigidity of this poem's decorum. Panegyric or satire—whichever is uppermost—we are made conscious of the presence of the obverse. This division gives Jonson's tone at times an air of inescapable ambivalence, and it is really disconcerting to notice how the tone of lines 22–30 is indistinguishable from that of Shakespeare's smoothly mendacious Cassius, going to work on Brutus in *Julius Caesar:*

> Cassius.   since you know you cannot see yourself
>   So well as by reflection, I, your glass,
>   Will modestly discover to yourself
>   That of yourself which you yet know not of.
>
> (1.2.67–70)

Jonson's is a portraiture in which the sitter is partly a creation of the beholder; these are poetic voice-portraits in which the portrait is a double image mirroring painter and subject. These concerns with reflected identity are deployed to complex effect, for there is tension between Jonson's contradictory perceptions of his subjects, as creatures of flesh and creatures of spirit. Some of the flattery in the Aubigny poem risks comic or farcical bathos, as if Jonson's imaginative interest in human weakness was just too strong for him to suppress, and it is relevant to recall what he wrote in the preface to *Hymenaei*, especially his admission that in courtly art the artist's voice must "be taught to sound to present occasions":

> So short lived are the bodies of all things in comparison of their souls. And though bodies oft times have the ill luck to be sensually preferred, they find afterwards the good fortune, when souls live, to be utterly forgotten. This it is hath made the most royal princes . . . who are commonly the personators of these actions [*sc.* masques] not only studious of riches and magnificence in the outward celebration or show, which rightly becomes them, but curious after the most high and hearty inventions to furnish the inward parts, and those grounded upon antiquity and solid learnings; which, though their voice be taught to sound to present occasions, their sense or doth or should always lay hold on more removed mysteries.

The idea of being an unwilling subject to social pressure is conveyed by the negative turn of phrase—"though their voice be
taught to sound"—and this gives the equivocal suggestion of
emptiness and vanity in "sound" (as in the biblical "sounding
brass" or *Measure for Measure* 1.2.56: "so sound as things that
are hollow"). Jonson is saying not just that a masque is to be
read topically as well as allegorically, but that he does accept
the yoke of fashionable court decorum: his artist's voice, he
equivocally concedes, is bound to sound false notes, so that artistic integrity can only be preserved at another level, that of
"more removed mysteries."

In the *Epistle to Lady Aubigny,* therefore, Jonson stresses the
need to use a restricted, metaphysical language, one begot
through negatives to compose a negative image: "not-saying":

> . . . this shall be no false one, but as much
> Removed, as you from need to have it such.
> Look then, and see yourself. I will not say
> Your beauty . . .
>
> (27–30)

The portrait is to reveal the mind, something that poetry can
do while paint cannot. Any actual mirror must, like any portrait
done with real paint, eventually cause the lady to reflect on sad
or cruel signs of her decay and age. In Congreve's *The Way of
the World* Lady Wishfort's maid Foible puts it in terms that
contrive to be at once more candid and more soothing: "A little
art at once made your picture like you; and now a little of the
same art must make you like your picture. Your picture must
sit for you, madam." Jonson by contrast offers a poetical portrait, fixed at a specific time in script and then in print, but
abstract and incorporeal—the lady's good mind reflected in his
art. In analogy to alchemy, the poem represents the completion
of a process of exaltation for her mind. Still, such a sublime
process of purification is a kind of annihilation, and the Lady
Aubigny whom Jonson's praise exalts is one whose human identity it annihilates and reconstitutes, and whose mortality it
aims to outlive.

> as long years do pass,
> Madam, be bold to use this truest glass,
> Wherein your form you still the same shall find,
> Because nor it can change, nor such a mind.
>
> (121–24)

Lady Aubigny is commemorated for *not being*, in important senses, a great lady. It is finally, at the most serious level, a picture of nobody. There was a challenge in Jonson's attaching such poetry of idealization to real names and to Jonson's contemporary England. In lines 38–42 Jonson had filled in the picture with specific, disconcerting instances of the foul ways to riches and great place—if the Aubignys did get and keep their fortune by no "indirect, crook'd ways," if no alderman or "cozening farmer of the customs" can be found in their family history, they are certainly extremely exceptional. But in 1616 the Aubignys, at any rate, were still flourishing. Not so with the countess of Rutland, Sir Philip Sidney's sister. Jonson's *Epistle to Elizabeth Countess of Rutland* was originally a present to the countess on New Year's Day 1600. Jonson eloquently celebrates the power of poetry to perpetuate a virtuous name, like a "rich and golden pyramid / Borne up by statues," whereas mere sculptors and architects work in stone that, crumbling to dust, takes the names with it to oblivion; yet in fact this poem itself had become a broken column within a year of its completion, its final lines looking forward to the birth of the countess's first child having been canceled by Jonson once it became public that her husband, the earl of Rutland, was impotent.

Perhaps the best known poem in "The Forest," published in the Folio *Works* in 1616, is *To Penshurst*. That poem is a monument to the Sidneys, who were important to Jonson as patrons; brilliant as it is, there is a somber aspect to it—it stresses the scarcity of subjects for praise among the nobility, it commemorates the loss of Sir Philip Sidney, and it illustrates his dictum that only poets can deliver a golden world. A shadow was cast over the poem addressed to Sir Robert Sidney's son-in-law, *To Sir Robert Wroth*, when he died in 1614, and also over the penultimate poem in "The Forest," that to Sir Robert's son, William: it was written for the boy's coming-of-age, but he died in 1612 at only twenty-two.

Such marks of the passage of time on Jonson's monuments of praise to named, great contemporaries are to be seen in other revisions he made for the 1616 *Works*. Jonson had written the masque *Hymenaei* to celebrate the Howard-Essex marriage in 1606, and published a quarto text with the names of the participants prominently displayed, including two ladies celebrated in Jonson's poetry, Lucy Countess of Bedford and Elizabeth Countess of Rutland. The scandal in 1613 surrounding the Howard-Essex divorce led Jonson to remove the names of the participants and the occasion from the Folio text of *Hymenaei*. The dedication of *The Masque of Queens* to the young heir to the throne, Prince Henry, had been printed in the 1609 quarto. Jonson had to remove the dedication in the 1616 folio because the prince had died in 1612. It was a death widely felt as a dark augury for the second decade of the Jacobean age.

When in 1612 Jonson gravely began the *Epistle to Lady Aubigny* with the lines

'Tis grown almost a danger to speak true
Of any good mind now, there are so few

he was anxiously meditating on his own life as reflected in the fortunes of his patrons, and in Lady Aubigny he saw reflected the social and moral contradictions of his situation, the exactions on his conscience in trying to follow the heroic example of Horace, and the cost of trying imaginatively to transform James I into Augustus. Somber though these prospects evidently were in 1612, it may have been more chilling only four years later to realize how few of those good minds were still alive when his poems to them were published in his 1616 *Works*. The political dangers he had personally encountered convinced him of the value of having friends among the Great, no matter how defiantly he might insist on his independence. Patrons had constituted both an ideal and a means of survival, but now they were becoming rather a *memento mori*. Pursuing several parallel careers in the uncertain seas of the court and the public theater took its toll. His ambition as a playwright was clearly huge, and he made his frustration, exasperation, and bitterness when rejected part of his self-dramatization, his creation of the public persona Ben Jonson. In this sense he is one of the first modern artists in English.

Jonson upholds Sir Philip Sidney's dictum that the end of all earthly learning should be virtuous action, but he is often forced to declare that the world deserves only derision. He is a lofty artist, but like his best comic characters he always keeps one eye on the main chance. He has a wonderful gift for caricature, but his portraits reveal a deep longing for the purely spiritual. His poetry aspires to austere purity of mind, but his invective is pungently personal. It is the continuous movement between such contraries that characterizes his portraits, that makes them so . . . Jonsonian.

Notes

1. E. H. Gombrich, "The Mask and the Face," in *Art, Perception and Reality*, ed. Gombrich, Julian Hochberg, and Max Black (Baltimore: Johns Hopkins University, 1972), 42–46.

2. I quote from Ian Donaldson's edition of *The Poems* (London: Oxford University Press, 1975) and, later, from Stephen Orgel's edition of *The Complete Masques* (New Haven: Yale University Press, 1969).

3. Similar mock blazons can be found in Donne's *Elegy II* (lines 3, 7, 15–16), Shakespeare's sonnet 130 ("My mistress' eyes are nothing like the sun"), and Pyramus's lament over Thisbe ("These lily lips,/ This cherry nose . . ."; *A Midsummer Night's Dream*, 5.1.324–45); while in *The Garden* Marvell gives the traditional lilies-and-roses trope an almost postimpressionist twist: "No white nor red was ever seen / So amorous as this lovely green."

4. Compare Magritte's famous portrait in which a female torso is substituted for the face, or "Lydia the Tattooed Lady" or Groucho Marx's song from *The Marx Brothers at the Circus* (1939):

Lydia, oh! Lydia, that "Enclopedia,"
Oh! Lydia, the Queen of Tattoo.
On her back is the battle of Waterloo,
Beside the wreck of the Hesperus too,
And proudly above waves the Red, White, and Blue,
You can learn a lot from Lydia.

5. O. B. Hardison considers that the inherent difficulties of *epideictic* poetry—poetry concerned with actual events or persons—can be resolved in *pictura*, poetry that uses specific persons or events selectively to create a pattern intended to arouse emulation or aversion (*The Enduring Monument* [Chapel Hill: University of North Carolina Press, 1962], passim).

6. David Riggs, *Ben Jonson: A Life* (Cambridge: Harvard University Press, 1989), thus offers to reinterpret the evidence about the dates of Jonson's five-year stay in the Aubigny household. Mark Eccles ("Jonson's Marriage," *RES* 12 [1936]: 269–71) claimed 1613–18; Herford and Simpson, *Ben Jonson*, proposed 1602–7, later modified to 1603–7 (11: 576–77) or 1604 plus a stay at a later period.

7. Private letter, 1982. I am grateful to John Rathmell for this advance information from his forthcoming book.

8. Further significances of the idea of "turning" in Jonson's poetry are discussed by Richard S. Peterson, *Imitation and Praise in the Poems of Ben Jonson* (New Haven: Yale University Press, 1981).

9. Act 2, scene 1, of *Catiline* is a memorable instance of Jonson's use of face-painting in the plays as an image of fraud and corruption.

Part 2
The Idea of Authorship

The Birth of the Author

RICHARD DUTTON

WHY did Shakespeare not print his own plays? There is a fair
consensus that he did not, though thirteen of them were printed
in his own lifetime, in texts that seem based on the author's
papers or a good playhouse copy.[1] Yet hardly anyone has supposed that Shakespeare actively saw them into print. This is
one of those "facts" about Shakespeare's career usually taken
quietly for granted. In the course of this paper I shall review a
number of these, arguing that they need to be reassessed in the
light of recent thinking about early modern culture and the
place of Shakespeare's career within it. He clearly was responsible for the publication of *Venus and Adonis* (1593) and *The
Rape of Lucrece* (1594), both of which carried signed dedications
to the earl of Southampton and were printed by his fellow Strat-
fordian, Richard Field. Yet Field had no hand in the printing of
any of the plays; none of the play texts until *Love's Labor's
Lost* (1598) even had an indication of authorship; and none in
Shakespeare's lifetime carried an author's preface or commenda-
tions from friends, the usual marks of the writer's personal
involvement. Shakespeare was not shy of print, it seems, only
of printing plays (and sonnets).[2]

Why this should be so is still a subject of conjecture. For some
scholars, only staging appears to have mattered to Shakespeare;
Leeds Barroll, for instance, argues that Shakespeare wrote plays
only when he could anticipate immediate performance: "Denied the visual and auditory realization of his plays on stage,
Shakespeare's creative drive for drama seems to have faltered."[3]
For others, legal and practical restraints also deflected Shakespeare from print,[4] with most of the relevant evidence revolving
around these commonly agreed facts: copyright belonged to the
acting companies, not to the author; and though the companies
condoned the printing of many of their plays,[5] others they were
clearly reluctant to have published.[6]

71

G. E. Bentley seeks to order this evidence by suggesting that the actors had different contractual arrangements with writers who were retained as "ordinary poets" and those who wrote for them only on an occasional basis. Shakespeare's understanding with the King's Men, he argues, is likely to have concurred with the stipulation in the one contract for an "ordinary poet" of which we have documentary evidence (Richard Brome's with Salisbury Court), which states that the author "should not suffer any play made or to be made or composed by him" for the company to be printed with his consent or knowledge, "without the license from the said company or the major part of them."[7] Other writers, who had no such contractual relationships, seem to have suffered few restrictions on their rights to sell their scripts to a printer (though it is not impossible that they had to agree to a lower fee in return); and though they may have been expected to observe some delay between first performance and publication, even this is doubtful in many instances. The obvious question, therefore, is why the actors should expect some of their writers to observe this restraint and others not. A play was just a play, and its commercial value was never more than marginally related to the person who actually wrote it.

We may deduce that freelance authors had permission to print from the fact that they frequently wrote again for companies whose plays they had published. Jonson, for example, printed *Every Man out of His Humour* in 1600 and *Every Man in His Humour* in 1601, but was employed again by the King's Men for *Sejanus, The Alchemist,* and *Catiline,* all published within two years of their performance, then republished in Jonson's 1616 *Works.* While *Sejanus* and *Catiline* were failures in the theater, and so might not have been regarded as "viable" stage pieces, this is not true of the majority. Both *Every Man* plays were in the King's Men repertoire in 1605 and performed at court, with *Every Man in* revived as late as 1631. This suggests that the companies thought them valuable stage properties and calls into question the common explanation that actors were reluctant to have plays printed that were still successful on stage.

This view was championed by E. K. Chambers, citing the Epistle to *The English Traveller* (1633), where Heywood observes that some of his plays "are still retained in the hands of some actors, who think it against their peculiar profit to have them come in print."[8] Heywood's wording here suggests that only some, and not all, actors took this view of the matter, which possibly reflects his different contractual experiences as a free-lance and "ordinary poet." Chambers, however, goes on to speculate: "Presumably the danger was not so much that readers would not become spectators, as that other companies might buy the plays and act them," a supposition that the subsequent stage history of Jonson's printed plays belies completely.[9] With one exception (a Dublin performance of *The Alchemist* between 1637 and 1640), there is no evidence that any acting company other than the King's Men attempted to stage them, even though they were in print, and no commercial rival exploited their availability in London, where it really mattered. The same is true of plays by Shakespeare, which were all in print by 1623. There are records of amateur and provincial performances of *Richard II* and *Hamlet* in 1607/8 by the company of the *Dragon* off the coast of Sierra Leone, and of *Pericles* and *King Lear* by Sir Richard Cholmeley's players in Yorkshire in 1610, and possibly of *Hamlet* by Queen Anne's Men in Oxford in 1607, and by a group at Newcastle in the same year. But none challenges the King's Men's exclusive right to profitable London performances.

Such challenges were rare, I would argue, because the danger Chambers presumed did not exist. When the Master of the Revels granted a license to perform a play, it was specific to the companies that acquired it and could only be passed on to others with their consent. In granting a license Sir Henry Herbert always records the name of the company or, occasionally, of the theater where that company performed (for example, "1623, August. For the Company at the Curtain; a Tragedy of *the Plantation of Virginia*"[10]). Herbert was not issuing a general license for the play: he was conferring on a known company, with a known playhouse, the exclusive right of performance—at least in the London region—and any deviation from this understanding would be an affront to his authority. The few surviving office-book entries by Herbert's predecessor, Sir John Astley, are less consistent in format but at times even more conclusive in wording.[11]

Herbert's papers also demonstrate how the passing on of performance rights was regulated. Several circumstances required further clearance from the Master of the Revels, of plays already licensed, as when a company wished to adopt a play formerly licensed to someone else.[12] An office-book entry for 21 August 1623 records: "For the Lady Elizabeth's Servants of the Cockpit; An Old Play, called, *Match me in London*, which had been formerly allowed by Sir George Bucke."[13] This records a transfer of performing rights, since the play, written by Dekker around 1612 and performed by the Queen Anne's Men (defunct by 1623), was not printed until 1631. A similar process presumably governed boy company plays that passed into the adult repertoire, though no records have survived. Fletcher's *The Scornful Lady* and Jonson's *The Silent Woman* were both first printed in 1616. The former had passed to the King's Men by 1625, when a reprint announced them on the title page as the acting company. *The Silent Woman* had probably passed to the King's Men when it was considered for performance at court in 1619/20, and certainly had done so when it was performed there twice in 1636.[14] Both works demonstrate that a play was not liable to unlicensed appropriation simply because it was in print, even when the original licensees were defunct: they both passed in an orderly way to a new license-holder. They also demonstrate that publication need not diminish commercial viability in the theater.

One notorious instance of a company appearing not to respect licensed performing rights and seeming to take advantage of the fact that a rival company's plays were in print is the King's Men's performance of Marston's *The Malcontent*. This was apparently after the first of its three printings in 1604, since Webster's "additions acted by the King's Majesty's Servants" were not available to the press until the third edition. Webster's dialogue for the actors "playing" themselves is quite unabashed about what had happened:

> *Sly.* . . . I would know how you came by this play.
> *Condell.* Faith, sir, the book was lost; and, because 'twas pity so good a play should be lost, we found it, and play it.
> *Sly.* I wonder you would play it, another company having interest in it.
> *Condell.* Why not Malevole in folio with us, as Jeronimo in decimo-sexto with them? They taught us a name for our play: we call it *One for another.*
>
> *Induction, 72–80*[15]

As Sly points out, the performing rights to the play still reside with the Blackfriars company, by now the Children of the Queen's Revels. Condell makes light of this, implying that it is a quid-pro-quo for that troupe having played "Jeronimo," presumably—since they did not own *The Spanish Tragedy*—a lost King's Men's play on a related theme. What Condell does not make clear is whether these appropriations were by mutual consent or were forms of piracy.

If the former, my case about the protection of performing right is not affected. If the latter, it is the dating that provides the likeliest explanation for the irregularity. The Children of the Chapel Royal were reincorporated in February 1604 as the Children of the Queen's Revels, at which point they left the control of the Master of the Revels and were given their own licenser. Their patent specifies "that noe such playes or Shewes shalbee presented . . . or by them any where publiqelie acted but by the approbacion and allowaunce of Samuell Danyell."[16] As I have argued elsewhere, this division of the authority for dramatic licensing in part explains the controversial theatrical activity early in the reign of James I, so much of it centering upon the Blackfriars company in its various guises.[17] Thus, the circumstances in which the King's Men appropriated *The Malcontent* were so unusual as to be exceptional, with a real possibility of friction between the licensing authorities themselves, which the actors may have exploited. The case is an exception that proves the rule, significant in its rarity, not as evidence of what was commonly likely to befall plays appearing in print.

Given the evidence that printing plays did not make them more liable to piracy by rival companies and did not necessarily reduce their audience appeal, we can understand E. M. Albright's conclusion that "the probability is, that there was no such widespread and constant objection to publication as has been supposed."[18] Yet Heywood *did* observe that "some actors . . . think it against their peculiar profit to have them come in print." It is possible that those who had paid good money for a play were less certain than I can now be that publication would not reduce its value. After all, the late revivals of the Jonson plays I have mentioned may have been undertaken to cash in on the afterlife created by their circulation in print—but no one could have predicted such an outcome when they first released the copyright. More compelling, however, is Bentley's evidence that it was the works of contracted "ordinary poets" that companies were particularly anxious to keep out of print. It is clear that this was due to the companies, rather than to the writers concerned, since men like Fletcher, Heywood, and Brome were quite willing to help plays into print (as we see from their signed prefaces) that were *not* the product of their work under retained contracts, in those instances behaving exactly like freelancers such as Jonson.[19] Shakespeare, however—always the exception—never seems to have been other than a retained author in the period from 1594 when we can really trace his career.

Reviewing the total picture of which plays got into print and when, one is almost drawn to the conclusion—contrary to the received wisdom—that the plays of such authors were the only ones to which the companies held a copyright respected by the Stationers' Company and the licensers for the press, since there is no apparent consistency to the way in which plays by other authors were or were not allowed into print. (This could never be gauged accurately, anyway, since there is no telling how many plays would never have been printed simply because there was no demand for them.) The evidence, however, will not sustain so categorical a conclusion, though it does seem that the works of "ordinary poets" were more rigorously denied the press than those of other authors. In 1600 the almost systematic piracy of playbooks by unscrupulous printers was a possibility, and the principal companies of the day, the Lord Admiral's and Lord Chamberlain's Men, took steps to forestall it. On 28 March Henslowe put up for the former the not inconsiderable sum of two pounds for the "stayinge of printinge" of *Patient Grissell*, while the Lord Chamberlain's Men had "staying" entries in the Stationers' Register on 27 May and 4 August.[20] There is no evidence that the companies were resisting print per se; it seems likely that they were trying to preclude unauthorized publication by establishing prior copyright. My point is that the Lord Chamberlain's Men acted to protect plays written by Jonson (*Every Man in His Humour*) and two anonymous authors, as well as recent work by their "ordinary poet," Shakespeare (*Much Ado About Nothing* and *Henry V*). Henslowe's papers reveal no individual enjoying the special position reflected in the Brome contract, and apparently enjoyed by Shakespeare, but he was still prepared to protect copyrights.[21]

The fact that the Henslowe papers, our fullest information about the business of play-writing in the period, contain no examples of anyone employed on this exclusive basis doubtless colors our sense of what was normal. Part of the continuing success of the Lord Chamberlain's/King's Men, however—answerable to no entrepreneur like Henslowe—must be ascribed to their shrewd retention of one popular and proficient "ordinary poet" after another, a practice that subtly must have colored their corporate ethos. Though a more convenient and assured way of acquiring suitable plays than ad hoc commissioning, it perhaps led to payments above the market rate. It is difficult to be sure of this, since our knowledge of the going rate for plays throughout the period is patchy, and the relativities of the figures we do have must be heavily distorted by inflation.[22] Moreover, retained authors were not paid by the play but mainly by a weekly wage, in return for which they undertook to produce a specified number of plays annually (in Brome's case three, in Shakespeare's probably two). This makes real comparisons all but impossible.

But it must be significant (a point overlooked by Bentley) that it was when Brome's contract was renegotiated in 1638, and the salary was raised from fifteen to twenty shillings a week, that the injunction against him printing the plays without permission, noted above, entered their agreement. This suggests that such injunctions were not always a feature of the contracts of "ordinary poets" but that it may have been so when it was linked to a salary above the market rate. In Brome's case this seems to have followed what amounts to an initial trial period with the company. In 1594 Shakespeare was already a very well established dramatist, by some way the most successful of those who continued to write for the theaters after the plague of 1593/94, following the deaths of Greene, Marlowe, and Kyd and other defections. It would have been shrewd sense for the Lord Chamberlain's Men to retain his services on the most attractive terms they could muster. Even so, in such a context it might seem reasonable to exact print rights in return for secure and relatively handsome remuneration.

Perhaps more important than the strict financial implications of a copyright was how it related to the cooperative structure of the acting company. Andrew Gurr observes, "The London companies after about 1580 consisted of a core of between eight and twelve co-owning players, 'sharers' in both profits and costs."[23] Verbal agreements became more formalized, carrying stipulations such as those agreed to by the actor Robert Dawes and Henslowe: penalties for turning up late or missing rehearsals or performances or being drunk when he should be performing. Penalties were measured in pence or shillings, rising to a maximum of a pound, save for a forty-pound penalty for absconding with costumes or props.[24] This particular agreement says nothing about playbooks and their copyright, though these may have been classed as "propertie." The contract for the sharers in the King's Revels company (10 March 1608) is more explicit. The specific prohibition against putting the company's plays into print without permission is part of a much wider set

of understandings about its property.[25] The swingeing penalties—forty pounds or loss of the entire share—were clearly not
ways of dealing with minor infringements such as turning up
drunk. They were part of a wider attempt to define the company
and its standards, exercises in corporate bonding.

It is important to bear in mind that these agreements cited
relate to sharers in an acting and/or theater company, often—
though not always—actors themselves, and not specifically to
the writers of their plays, who would not normally be members
of the company in anything like the same sense. Brome, for
example, was never a sharer in Salisbury Court, only an em-
ployee. The most he stood to lose, if he broke his agreement,
was employment—unless (as actually happened) he was sued for
breach of contract, where the issue was putative loss of earnings
to the company through dereliction and bad faith, not a penalty
for breaching the company's own code of conduct.[26] This was
presumably also true of other "ordinary poets" like Fletcher and
Massinger. But Shakespeare was significantly different, since
from the inception of the Lord Chamberlain's Men in 1594 he
was a shareholder—and sufficiently senior to be trusted, along
with Richard Burbage and Will Kempe, to receive payment from
court on the company's behalf. In due course he was also a
shareholder in the Globe and Blackfriars' theaters, companies
whose membership significantly overlapped with that of the acting company that performed in them. Of those who signed the
syndicate agreement for the Globe of 21 February 1599, five
besides Shakespeare were actors.

We do not know precisely what constraints any "sharing"
agreements placed on Shakespeare. But if we compare the
Whitefriars theater contract, Henslowe's agreement with
Dawes, and the Brome contract, we conclude that he was bound
by constraints of corporate bonding virtually unparalleled in the
period. Since these constraints commonly seem to have put an
embargo on the printing of corporately owned playbooks for
both shareholders and "ordinary poets," Shakespeare must have
felt massively restricted. As I have argued, there is little evidence that the printing of plays did actually reduce their value
as theater pieces. But we see in the Whitefriars contract concerns that run deeper. Draconian penalties awaiting anyone
who, without common consent, removed company property
"exceeding the value of two shillings" bespeak a need to put
corporate interests above individual desires. In such a context
the inviolability of the "ordinary poet's" plays might take on an

almost fetishistic significance, disproportionate to their strict commercial value. They were, so to speak, the company's family silver, not to be traded in by any of the sharers, even the author. Works commissioned from freelancers such as Jonson would never have the same value to the corporate psyche, even though it would be prudent (as in 1600) to guard such properties against outright piracy.

The short answer, then, to why Shakespeare never published his own plays is quite likely to be that he was a company man, too identified with an ethos in which any removal of company property warranted expulsion from its ranks, too bound to a small group by ties that went beyond a mere contractual framework, if the bequests in his will to Burbage, Heminge, and Condell of money to buy rings denote real friendship. Perhaps the strongest corroboration we can find for the strength of company affiliations comes from the only other man in the period to occupy anything like the same position, Thomas Heywood. The Queen's Men copied the Globe arrangements; some of the actor-shareholders also became sharers in "the house," the Red Bull. Heywood was one of these, and also their "ordinary poet." Throughout a long career, in which he famously claimed to have written or "had a main finger" in 220 plays (address to the readers in *The English Traveller*), barely twenty found their way into print.

The 1608 quarto of *The Rape of Lucrece* stands out because, as Heywood was aware, it is the one instance where publication cut across his contractual status at the time as an "ordinary poet."

> Though some have used a double sale of their labors, first to the stage and after to the press, for my own part I here proclaim myself ever faithful to the first [i.e. Queen Anne's company] and never guilty of the last.[27]

Yet because of the threatened illicit publication of a mangled version of the play, Heywood was willing to print it correctly, with the permission of the rightful owners, Queen Anne's company. There is an element of disingenuousness about this disclaimer. If Heywood truly discovered that it was "accidentally" coming into the hands of the printers (along, apparently, with others not contractually bound), he could, with the rest of the company, assert their true copyright with the Stationers' Company. Nonetheless, Heywood feels it necessary to assert publicly that his decision to supply an accurate copy has the full "consent" of other members of the company, to which he himself has been "ever faithful."

Since Shakespeare never even condescended to supply prefaces of this nature, we cannot be certain that he did not actually cooperate with the printers in this way, only that he never advertised the fact. Yet the history of Shakespearean editing is littered with suggestions that some of the quartos (such as *2 Henry 1V, Much Ado About Nothing,* the 1599 *Romeo and Juliet*) are based on the author's "foul papers," though no one has squared this with the orthodox view that he played no part in their publication. If Shakespeare's "foul papers" found their way to the printshops, the supposition seems to be, it must be from the playhouse, not from his study and not by his hand. The very fact that "foul papers" or prompt-copies of so many reputable texts reached the printers challenges the assumption that the Lord Chamberlain's Men were implacably opposed to their "ordinary poet's" work appearing in print. There have been numerous explanations for certain specific "breaches." Andrew Gurr has argued persuasively that the shareholders might have released *Richard III, Love's Labor's Lost,* and *1 Henry IV* for print in 1597/98 only because they faced a financial crisis when unable to use either the Burbages' new Blackfriars venue or the Theater.[28] And it has been suggested more than once that the appearance of a "good" quarto in the wake of a "bad" one (the 1599 *Romeo and Juliet* and the 1604/5 *Hamlet* are examples) may reflect the company's preference, once the issue had been forced, to sanction respectable texts rather than let their own and their poet's reputation be sullied by the travesties already in print. (If so, we have to ask why they did not also do so in the case of, say, *Henry V* and *The Merry Wives of Windsor.* Or did not do so until the 1623 folio). All in all, however, too many reputable Shakespeare texts found their way into print for it to be entirely credible that they did so as a result of ad hoc company decisions, contravening their apparent general policy.

Even if we accept that there were compelling corporate pressures against Shakespeare as an individual going into print (whatever the company as a whole may, from time to time, have decided), that is not evidence that he was indifferent to his plays as works to be read. I am thinking here of the circulation of plays in manuscript. This, again, is supposed not to have happened. As Leeds Barroll puts it: "Before Shakespeare's death, public stage plays were seldom composed to be circulated in manuscripts or in printed books as was, say, Sir Philip Sidney's *Arcadia* or Edmund Spenser's *Faerie Queene*."[29] But if much of the evidence for this practice applies to plays dating from after Shakespeare's death, it is only because theatrical documentation is much fuller for the later period, and more manuscripts of all sorts found their way into collections, where they were respected and preserved. There is no real reason to suppose that the circulation of commercial playscripts changed significantly between, say, 1590 and 1642.

We know, of course, that it happened with *A Game at Chess*. No fewer than six manuscripts of that play have survived, none of them the licensed playhouse copy. The existence of so may copies of the play may, of course, be ascribed to the phenomenal interest it aroused. Yet if the scandal over the play prompted manuscripts in unusual numbers (how many were lost if six actually survive?), it does not follow that it was unusual per se for transcripts to be made in this way. Beaumont and Fletcher's *A King and No King*, dating from 1611 when Shakespeare was still active, was printed in 1619, apparently from a manuscript copy supplied by Sir Thomas Neville. Similarly, Ralph Crane copied both Middleton's *The Witch* (ca. 1609–16) and Fletcher's popular *Demetrius and Enanthe* as presentation copies. As F. P. Wilson observed, "it is curious that so notable a get-penny as *Demetrius and Enanthe* should have been allowed to stray outside the playhouse, and should have existed in a private transcript twenty-two years before it got into print."[30]

But is it really so curious? Humphrey Moseley's preface to his monumental first folio of Beaumont and Fletcher (1647) contains two remarkable admissions: that *The Wilde-goose Chase* was lost when "a Person of Quality borrowed it from the Actours," and that the actors commonly omitted passages of plays for performance—but that when "private friends desir'd a Copy, they then (and justly too) transcribed what they *Acted*."[31] This suggests practices that were relatively commonplace and of long standing, and implies an altogether more relaxed attitude than is commonly supposed to the distribution of manuscript copies of even the most popular plays, though they were still barred from print. More important, it also suggests that there was an understanding that the text supplied by the author and that performed by the actors (which would be the one licensed by the Master of the Revels) enjoyed a different status. Moseley actually makes a selling point of this care to print complete texts, perhaps implying that these always enjoyed more cachet with

discerning readers: "the *Care & Pains* was wholly mine, which
I found to be more then you'l easily imagine, unless you knew
into how many hands the Originalls were dispersed" (xiv). The
actors, then, were quite careless about preserving the texts as
they were originally written, but fairly ready to supply copies
of what they actually performed (which was commonly different). Six Beaumont and Fletcher manuscripts seem to have survived only because copies were made in this way. Moseley's
defensive "and justly too" even suggests that it would have been
improper of the actors to circulate more than the acting text,
that the originals still belonged in some way (presumably) to
their authors.

It will be objected that all this was years after Shakespeare's
death, when stage plays supposedly enjoyed a social cachet un-
imaginable earlier. Besides, no texts by Shakespeare or his immediate contemporaries have survived in the same way. But the
survival of any theatrical manuscript from the late sixteenth or
early seventeenth century, as I have argued, is rare and fortu-
itous. Of the 280 plays mentioned in Henslowe's diary only
thirty have survived in print, and perhaps one in manuscript.[32]
In the case of Shakespeare, the 1623 folio must have made the
manuscripts of his plays seem redundant. His daughter, Susanna
Hall, still had some "play-writings" by her father at the time
Queen Henrietta Maria stayed at New Place during the Civil
War, but there is no evidence that she appreciated their value.[33]
Probably no one did until it was too late. Apart from the Fletcher
examples I mentioned earlier, none of the apparently numerous
copies to which Moseley refers seems to have survived either.

But it will still be objected that in Shakespeare's day playscripts simply did not have the cachet with readers that Moseley
seems to imply, so that there would not have been a demand
for copies. This seems to me, to say the least, questionable. We
know from Francis Meres's *Palladis Tamia* (1598) that Shakespeare circulated his "sugared sonnets among his private
friends." Might he not have done the same with his plays, as
the actors were to do later with those of Beaumont and Fletcher?
One of the strongest arguments for at least taking this possibility seriously is the sheer length of so many of the surviving
texts. I quote here from Philip Edwards on this point, though
to draw very different conclusions: "Why is it that nearly all
[Shakespeare's] tragedies were far too long to be performed in
full on his stage? The average length of Elizabethan plays was
under 2,500 lines, allowing two to two-and-a-half hours' playing

time. . . . Only three or four of Shakespeare's plays are within that limit" and five are over 3,500 lines each.[34]

But Edwards continues: "I can see only one solution to this problem [texts too long to be acted.] Everything that Shakespeare wrote, he wrote in terms of the stage. . . . At the same time, those long, brilliant, unwieldy texts which have come down to us witness to an ideal theater in Shakespeare's imagination. He wrote for himself perhaps" (22). There is indeed "only one solution" if one starts convinced that Shakespeare never wrote with a readership in mind. But Edwards's perplexities disappear if we entertain the possibility that some of Shakespeare's plays have survived in versions that reflect his expectation that they would be read as well as acted. Edwards argues: "The only other dramatist who persistently wrote overlength plays was Ben Jonson. Jonson most certainly regarded his plays as literature to be read and pondered, and he carefully published the full texts as literary texts" (21). *Every Man out of His Humour* (1600) was published "As It Was First Composed by the Author B.J. / Containing more than hath been Publicly Spoken or Acted," something we may suspect of many if not all of his printed plays. It may be, however, that Edwards is too categorical in describing Jonson as "the only other dramatist" persistently to *write* overlength plays. Jonson, it is true, was the author who made a point of seeing the fullest, most "readerly" versions of his play into print. Yet Webster advertised the same of *The Duchess of Malfi* (1623), declaring it to be "The perfect and exact Copy, with diverse things Printed, that the length of the play would not beare in the Presentment." And again we know from Moseley that the writers of the Beaumont and Fletcher canon regularly wrote more than the actors could use—and that there was a demand from readers for that fuller version. How many other plays of the period may similarly have been written overlength, but only survive (like those of the Beaumont and Fletcher works for which Moseley could not recover the originals) in the cut-down acting versions?

Jonson, Webster, and "Beaumont and Fletcher" all wrote overlength plays, either with the expectation of a print readership, or knowing that they would be circulated in manuscript. There is no reason in principle to suppose that Shakespeare might not have done the same, though—for the reasons I have reviewed (and others I shall suggest later)—print was not an option for him. Indeed, there is every reason to suppose that, like Jonson, he had a sense of them as "literary texts," albeit not the same sense that Jonson had, and not one that envisaged the same (print) readership. Many features of Shakespeare's work (including "authorial revision") appear in a new light once such a possibility is entertained, but I shall confine myself to one broad and one specific observation. First, it would help to explain just how so many quartos based on "foul papers" (not playhouse versions) found their way into print, if there were multiple copies of his unadapted manuscripts, and those not under the control of the actors. Second, it would provide an intelligible explanation for the notorious conundrum of the two states of the 1609 quarto of *Troilus and Cressida* (third longest of all Shakespeare's plays). The first of these announces the play as "The Historie of Troylus and Cresseida. As it was acted by the Kings Majesties servants at the Globe. Written by William Shakespeare." The second omits all mention of performance, describing it as "a new play, never staled with the stage, never clapper-clawed with the palms of the vulgar," and concludes with an apparent sideswipe at the King's Men as the jealous copyright holders. The text has been conjectured to be "printed from a private transcript of Shakespeare's own draft made by himself or a scribe," with little or no evidence of playhouse adaption.[35]

Explanations for these discrepancies range from publishers' hype to suggestions that the play had been performed only at some private venue, and in that sense it was never demeaned by "the smoky breath of the multitude." Special performances were not unknown, but plays written by a professional dramatist exclusively for private performance are. There is a more logical explanation, and Sam Schoenbaum grasps half the nettle: "The play could have been 'new' only to readers. ... Had the publishers got hold of a transcript in private hands?"[36] But he still rehearses the private performance theory to explain references to "the multitude." Surely the point of the epistle is that it is announcing a *reading version* of the play, new to a print readership and superior to what had doubtless been performed in a cut text by the King's Men at the Globe. Indeed, the difference may well have been what got the publishers their license. As early as 7 February 1603 the play had been entered in the Stationers' Register for "Master Robertes" ("The book of Troilus and Cresseda as yt is acted by my Lord Chamberlens men"— further proof of actual performance, almost certainly on the public stage) but "stayed" until "he hath gotten sufficient authority for it." The 1609 entry says nothing of Robertes, but grants a license jointly to Richard Bonian and Henry Walley, who may well have convinced the licenser, William Segar, that what they were printing was different in kind from the acting version. All of this foreshadows the situation Moseley describes in respect to the Beaumont and Fletcher texts, where the acting versions were popularly known (and indeed often available in manuscript copies), but a particular cachet attached to what the authors had originally written: that was what Moseley wanted to make a selling point of his edition, though the carelessness of the actors with the originals made his task difficult. Bonian and Walley first advertised their text as something it was not, an acting version, and then haughtily changed their tune in trumpeting a text unsullied by the common stage.

I conclude my argument with two familiar comments by contemporaries that seem to me far more intelligible if Shakespeare were indeed writing for readers. The first of these is Henry Chettle's defense, in *Kind-Heart's Dream* (1592/3), of his own role in the printing of Robert Greene's *Groatsworth of Wit, bought with a Million of Repentance*, with its bitter deathbed denunciation of fellow playwrights. This is, of course, a notorious minefield.[37] I want to draw attention only to the curiously oblique commendation of Shakespeare's writing, at the end of the passage: "divers of worship have reported, his uprightness of dealing which argues his honesty, and his facetious grace in writing, that approves his art." The passage as a whole, with its references to Shakespeare's civil demeanor, his "uprightness of dealing" and "honesty," is an attempt to convince "Gentlemen Readers" that Shakespeare was every inch a gentleman himself, presumably to repudiate Greene's slurs ("upstart crow," "absolute Johannes Factotum") on an actor/artisan with pretensions. What Chettle cannot vouch for personally he takes from the report of other gentlemen ("divers of worship"), and this includes "his facetious grace in writing, that approves his art." This is an oddly precise phrase, "facetious grace" apparently echoing Cicero's praise of Plautus in *De Officiis*.[38] But to what does it refer? What had the "divers of worship" actually seen to warrant this praise? There was certainly nothing then in print. Shakespeare's first published work, *Venus and Adonis*, was entered in the Stationers' Register 18 April 1593, some months after *Kind-Heart's Dream*. To be sure, it might already have been circulating in manuscript, as might some of the sonnets. But if the phrase really does echo Cicero on Plautus, it must relate to Shakespeare's plays—and all the more so, since it was those that Greene had scorned. Chettle could have heard these in the theater, as could anyone else. What Chettle implies, however, is that "divers of worship" have access to written texts, where "facetious grace"—the mark of a polished, gentleman writer—will be more apparent than in performance.

This stray remark is given substantial corroboration by those who ought to be the most authoritative of sources, the actors with whom Shakespeare worked. In prefacing the 1623 folio, Heminge and Condell pay homage to a Shakespeare "Who, as he was a happie imitator of Nature, was a most gentle expresser of it. His mind and hand went together: And what he thought, he uttered with that easinesse, that wee have scarse received from him a blot in his papers" (A3r). It was the "gentle . . . easinesse" of the gentleman writer, though an "easinesse" that they do not scruple to polish by imposing on the plays a five-act structure in imitation of classical precedents, notably Terence, though this was almost certainly alien to Shakespeare's writing practice.[39] But they also declare themselves "so to have publish'd [the plays] as where (before) you were abus'd with diverse stolne, and surreptitious copies, maimed, and deformed by the frauds and stealthes of injurious impostors, that exposed them: even those, are now offer'd to your view cur'd, and perfect of their limbes . . . as he conceived them." As a blanket dismissal of all the earlier quartos this is less than candid. It is entirely possible that all were indeed "stolne and surreptitious," but were they "maimed, and deformed" in the process? As we have observed, the latter may be true of the 1603 *Hamlet*; it is certainly not true of the 1604 *Hamlet* and the 1609 *Troilus and Cressida*, which modern scholars regard as at least as good as the versions in the folio.

Ironically, what tends to make them "superior" is precisely the quality that Heminge and Condell single out for praise, the "easiness" of expression that characteristically produced texts which, while intensely theatrical, were (if we follow Edwards) too long to use. Some folio texts—*Macbeth* and *The Tempest* for example, (significantly lacking quarto versions)—seem to reproduce what might practicably have been staged, showing distinct signs of having been cut down from longer originals. W. W. Greg long ago observed of *Macbeth* that "there is clear evidence of cutting at some points in short abrupt lines accompanied by textual obscurities."[40] In *The Tempest*—in so many ways admirably edited—a "ghost" (Antonio's son) and undeveloped characters (Adrian) also suggest cutting rather than carelessness. In short, Heminge and Condell praise a quality in Shakespeare's writing that their own texts tend rather to diminish than to enhance: it is better preserved in the "good" quartos. It may be true that the "foul papers" they received from him contained "scarce . . . a blot." But they say nothing about the blots needed to reduce them to playing form. As with Beaumont and Fletcher, "When these *Comedies* and *Tragedies* were presented on the Stage, the *Actours* omitted some *Scenes* and Passages (with the *Author's* consent) as occasion led them." In the case of Shakespeare it is usually assumed that there is no real distinction between "actors" and "author" in this way, because he was indeed an all-round man of the theater. The issues I have raised here call that into question. We have no way of knowing what part Shakespeare had in preparing what he wrote for the stage. It may have been a considerable one, and there are no grounds finally for believing that anything in the 1623 folio was not in some sense sanctioned by him.

But it also seems clear that the process was not as simple as Heminge and Condell imply, or as later ages have often taken on trust. There is substantial evidence of a Shakespeare who regularly wrote, with some facility, plays too long and complex to be staged in the theater of his day, plays for which the only plausible audience was one of readers. The "good" quartos provide us with the clearest evidence of what those plays were like, and the sheer number of them suggest that manuscript copies were in circulation, making it possible for printers eventually to obtain them—as, without question, they did the "sugared sonnets."

What I have argued here calls into question the primacy increasingly often accorded performance as the only true, or at least most authentic, manifestation of the Shakespeare text. The most distinguished recent contribution to that school of thought is the *Complete Oxford Shakespeare* (1986), whose general editors were Stanley Wells and Gary Taylor. The guiding principle throughout the volume was to reproduce as nearly as possible the state of the plays as they were performed in Shakespeare's lifetime. To take only one example, this resulted in a preference for the folio *A Midsummer Night's Dream* as copy text over the almost universal use of the 1600 quarto by earlier editors. As the general editors argued in the *Textual Companion* to the edition, "we have found no reason to doubt that the bulk of the Folio directions represents the play as originally and authoritatively staged. Those directions which clearly envisage a different staging from that implied in Q seem to us dramatic improvements for which Shakespeare was probably responsible."[41] Elsewhere other editors have accorded significantly more authority than has traditionally been allowed to the so-called bad quartos, even where their printers patently did not have access to authoritative texts, on the grounds that they nevertheless embody actual stage practice, however crudely.

These are entirely legitimate and defensible editorial practices, but they are not definitive ones. What Chettle, Heminge, and Condell and the evidence of the "good" quartos tell us is that Shakespeare had readers in mind, too, however much practical theatrical applications must also have shaped his thoughts. The habit of reading Shakespeare as much as we play him is not a modern, or academic, perversity. This is indirectly acknowledged in Ben Jonson's riposte to Heminge and Condell in *Discoveries:* "I remember the players have often mentioned as an honour to Shakespeare, that in his writing, whatsoever he penned, he never blotted out line. My answer hath been, 'Would he had blotted a thousand'; which they thought a malevolent speech. . . . [He] had an excellent fantasy, brave notions, and gentle expression; wherein he flowed with that facility that sometime it was necessary he should be stopped. His wit was in his own power; would the rule of it had been so too."[42] What grates with Jonson is the adoration of a Shakespeare who wrote like a gentleman amateur ("gentle expressions"), giving every impression that it was effortless ("flowed with . . . facility") and, what was more, that he did not give what he wrote a second thought ("never blotted out line")—as much because he did not care as because he got it right instinctively. This is a Shakespeare who affects a *sprezzatura,* a dismissive nonchalance like that of Sir Philip Sidney commending as he devalues the *Arcadia* to his sister with the kind of self-deprecation that traditionally constitutes boasting in the English upper classes.[43] And it smacks much more of a man writing for "gentle readers" than of one crafting texts for the stage.

It is an image of authorship that Jonson very much resisted because it was so much at odds with his own, that of the self-made man of letters, proud of his "laborious" art and determined to make his mark in public print. For another notable aristocratic mark was the aversion to print, with its connotation of artisan labor and writing for money.[44] Jonson does not, however, deny that Shakespeare wrote as Heminge and Condell implied; on the contrary, he confirms that they were only too right—even if their edition of the plays is not the best reflection of the qualities they claim. Between them, Chettle, Heminge and Condell, and Jonson all associate Shakespeare with this tradition—all but Jonson doing so with awed respect. So we cannot rule out the possibility that Shakespeare's apparent lack of involvement in the printing of his plays also derives from a sense of the associated social stigma (an embarrassment we repeatedly find in writers with social pretensions, like Samuel Daniel). If so, Shakespeare's lack of inhibition in printing *Venus and Adonis* and *The Rape of Lucrece,* quasi-classical epyllia demonstrating "facetious grace" in writing but in no way associated with artisan labor, suggests that different social nuances were at work there, possibly deriving from their association with a bid for Southampton's patronage. In the case of the plays, written primarily for money rather than status, social pretensions and the pressures of corporate bonding may mutually have reinforced one another.

It is unusual, to say the least, to link together *sprezzatura* (generally associated with courtly lyrics, sonnets, and romances) with writing for the public playhouse. But Shakespeare's career crossed many of the fault lines of writing in early modern culture, to which Michel Foucault refers when he writes that the "coming into being of the notion of the 'author' constitutes the privileged moment of 'individualization' in the history of ideas, knowledge, literature, philosophy, and the sciences."[45] Such a development was neither spontaneous, nor did it occur in a single, definitive form. The competition between the old world of courtly letters, largely wedded to manuscript culture, and the new world of commercial print played itself out over several generations. It has always been apparent that Shakespeare straddled these divides. What I have argued here is that the two sides of his career were less clearly demarcated than is usually supposed, that in writing plays which were in some respects unplayable (albeit perfect raw material for his actor colleagues) he was effectively writing for a readership no different in essence from that of his sonnets. Heminge and Condell knew this in commending his plays to a wider readership, "To the Great Variety of Readers," but they blurred the message—perhaps, like Moseley, finding it difficult to recover some originals—in favoring texts that spoke more of the playhouse than they did of unblotted lines. Thus they gave (new) birth to an author of mixed authority, to a hybrid poet-playwright, who speaks simultaneously the different languages of which he was composed.

This has important implications for our editing and reading practices. If Wells and Taylor, for example, have gone to one extreme of the spectrum of Shakespearean language, that located as comprehensively as possible in theatrical practice, it is only fair to observe that they did so at least partly in response to centuries of editorial practice that silently privileged the "writerly" end of the spectrum, the Shakespeare who "never blotted line." It has been usual, at least this century, to pay lip service to the idea of Shakespeare as "a man of the theater" but at the same time to make editorial judgments on what were essentially aesthetic rather that theatrical grounds, measuring the options against an elusive ideal text, usually characterized by "fulness" and "facility." Whether consciously or not, this has actually favored the "writerly" Shakespeare, who remains the dominant voice in the English-speaking world's construction of its definitive author—a voice essentially of preprint culture, of closet or privileged readership, of (to a degree) social snobbery. That is not to say that the other, "theatrical" Shakespeare is necessarily in any real sense more modern or democratic or egalitarian. But he is different, and he speaks with a different voice, attuned to a different audience. And one of our duties as modern readers (or practitioners) of Shakespeare is to recognize the fact of multiple voices and to discriminate between them as best we can.

NOTES

1. *Titus Andronicus* (1594); *Richard II* (1597): *Love's Labor's Lost* (1598); *I Henry IV* (1598); *Romeo and Juliet* (1599); *A Midsummer Night's Dream* (1600); *2 Henry IV* (1600); *The Merchant of Venice* (1600); *Much Ado about Nothing* (1600); *Hamlet* (1604); *King Lear* (1608); *Troilus and Cressida* (1609); and *Othello* (1622); while *Richard III* (1597) is not far behind the standard of these thirteen. Dates are those of publication. I omit palpably unsatisfactory texts such as the 1600 *Henry V* and 1603 *Hamlet* from this list, as well as the problematic *Pericles* (1609).

2. See, for example, George Walton Williams, "The Publishing and Editing of Shakespeare's Plays," in *William Shakespeare: His World, His Work, His Influence*, ed. John F. Andrews, 3 vols. (New York: Charles Scribner's Sons, 1985), 3: 589–601, 589–90; Fredson Bowers, "The Publication of English Renaissance Plays" in *Elizabethan Dramatists*, ed. Bowers, *Dictionary of Literary Biography* (Detroit: Gale Research Co., 1987), 62: 406–16, 414.

3. Leeds Barroll, *Politics, Plagues, and Shakespeare's Theater* (Ithaca and London: Cornell University Press, 1991), 17.

4. See E. K. Chambers, *The Elizabethan Stage*, 4 vols. (Oxford: Clarendon Press, 1923), 3: 177–92; E. M. Albright, *Dramatic Publication in England 1589–1640* (1927; reprint, New York: Gordian Press, 1971), esp. 217–61; and

G. E. Bentley, *The Profession of Dramatist in Shakespeare's Time, 1590–1642* (Princeton: Princeton University Press, 1971), chap. 10.

5. Prolonged plague and the Civil War closure of the theaters are most often cited as occasioning the sale of playbooks the actors would otherwise have preferred to retain.

6. See Bentley, *Profession of Dramatist*, 266–67.

7. Ann Haaker, "The Plague, the Theater, and the Poet," *Renaissance Drama*, n.s., 1 (1968): 283–306. Text modernized.

8. See Chambers, *Elizabethan Stage*, 3: 183, 339.

9. In support of Chambers on this, see S. Schoenbaum, *William Shakespeare: A Compact Documentary Life*, rev. ed. (New York and Oxford: Oxford University Press, 1987), 159, and Barroll, *Politics, Plagues, and Shakespeare's Theater*, 16–17.

10. Cited from Joseph Quincy Adams, ed., *The Dramatic Records of Sir Henry Herbert* (New Haven: Yale University Press, 1917), 24. On the state of the papers left by the Masters of the Revels, see Richard Dutton, *Mastering the Revels: The Regulation and Censorship of English Renaissance Drama* (London and Basingstoke: Macmillan, 1991), 15–16; on Herbert's distinctive form of entry, see 223.

11. See Adams, ed., *Dramatic Records of Sir Henry Herbert*, 23.

12. See Dutton, *Mastering the Revels*, 94–96.

13. See Adams, ed., *Dramatic Records of Sir Henry Herbert*, 25.

14. Ibid., 55, 75.

15. References are to John Marston, *The Malcontent*, ed. George K. Hunter (London: Methuen, 1975).

16. Quoted in Chambers, *Elizabethan Stage*, 2: 49.

17. See Dutton, *Mastering the Revels*, chap. 7, on the licensing of the boy companies early in the reign of James I. On tensions between actual and potential licensers, see 47–49, 115–16, 148–55.

18. Albright, *Dramatic Publication in England 1580–1640*, 283.

19. See Bentley, *Profession of Dramatist*, 267–68, 227, 281–84.

20. See Edward Arber, ed., *A Transcript of the Registers of the Company of Stationers of London 1554–1646*, 5 vols. (London: Privately printed, 1875–94; reprinted New York: P. Smith, 1950), 3: 36, 37, 167.

21. The Lord Admiral's Men did finally in 1602 come to an arrangement with Henry Chettle (their most prolific writer for some time). But since that arrangement was directly with the company, rather than their financier, we know nothing of the details from Henslowe.

22. See Bentley, *Profession of Dramatist*, chap. 5, esp. 97–108, for a full analysis of the evidence on payment.

23. Andrew Gurr, *The Shakespearean Stage 1574–1642* (Cambridge: Cambridge University Press, 1970), 46.

24. See Chambers, *Elizabethan Stage*, 2: 256–71.

25. On the King's Revels company's Articles of Agreement, see Chambers, *Elizabethan Stage*, 2: 65.

26. See Haaker, "The Plague, the Theater, and the Poet."

27. Quoted from Bentley, *Profession of Dramatist*, 282. The gloss in square brackets is Bentley's. Details of the Queen's Men actors becoming sharers in the Red Bull are given in Chambers, *Elizabethan Stage*, 1: 357.

28. See Andrew Gurr, "Money or Audiences: The Impact of Shakespeare's Globe," *Theatre Notebook* (1988): 3–14.

29. Barroll, *Politics, Plagues, and Shakespeare's Theater*, 16.

30. See F.P. Wilson, "Ralph Crane, Scrivener to the King's Players," reprinted in *The Seventeenth Century Stage*, ed. G. E. Bentley (Chicago: University of Chicago Press, 1968), 137–55, 149.

31. Cited from *The Works of Francis Beaumont and John Fletcher*, ed. Arnold Glover, 10 vols. (Cambridge: Cambridge University Press, 1905), 1: xiii.

32. The figures are based on Neil Carson, *A Companion to Henslowe's Diary* (Cambridge: Cambridge University Press, 1988), 82–84. The one manuscript play would be Munday's *John a Kent and John a Cumber*, but only if that is a version of what Henslowe refers to as *The Wise Man of West Chester*.

33. See S. Schoenbaum, *Shakepeare's Lives* (Oxford: Clarendon Press, 1970), 125–26; Richard Wilson, *Will Power: Essays on Shakespearean Authority* (Detroit: Wayne State University Press, 1993), 183.

34. Philip Edwards, *Shakespeare: A Writer's Progress* (Oxford: Oxford University Press, 1987), 21–22. Alfred Hart computed that the average length of a Globe play ca. 1594–1603 (omitting Jonson and Shakespeare) was 2,494 lines: "The Length of Elizabethan and Jacobean Plays," *RES* 8 (1932): 139–54.

35. Virgil K. Whitaker, "Note on the Text" in his Pelican Shakespeare edition of the play, in *William Shakespeare: The Complete Works*, gen. ed. Alfred Harbage, rev. ed. (Baltimore: Johns Hopkins University Press, 1969), 979.

36. Schoenbaum, *Shakespeare: Compact Documentary Life*, 267–68.

37. See my earlier comments on the passage in *William Shakespeare: A Literary Life* (London: Macmillan, 1989), 17–20, and "Shakespeare and Marlowe: Censorship and Construction," *Yearbook of English Studies* 23 (1993): 1–29, 6–8. See also Schoenbaum, *Shakespeare: Compact Documentary Life*, 154–57.

38. See Schoenbaum, *Shakespeare: Compact Documentary Life*, 155 and note.

39. See T.H. Howard-Hill, "The Evolution of the Form of Plays in English During the Renaissance," *Renaissance Quarterly* 43 (1990): 112–45.

40. W. W. Greg, *The Editorial Problem in Shakespeare* (Oxford: Clarendon Press, 1942), 147.

41. Stanley Wells and Gary Taylor, *William Shakespeare: A Textual Companion* (Oxford and New York: Oxford University Press, 1987), 280.

42. "Timber, or Discoveries," in *Ben Jonson*, ed. Ian Donaldson (Oxford: Oxford University Press, 1985), 521–94, lines 658–73.

43. See the letter of Sir Philip Sidney to the countess of Pembroke, prefacing *The Arcadia*, ed. Maurice Evans (Harmondsworth: Penguin Books, 1977), 57.

44. See J. W. Saunders, "The Stigma of Print: A Note on the Social Bases of Tudor Poetry," *Essays in Criticism* 1 (1951): 139–59.

45. Michel Foucault, "What is an Author?," in *The Foucault Reader*, ed. Paul Rabinow (New York: Pantheon Books, 1984), 101.

Constructing the Author

BARBARA A. MOWAT

Sʜᴏʀᴛʟʏ after 1349, Richard FitzRalph, formerly Chancellor of Oxford, addressed the following authorship problem: If Moses is accepted as the author *(auctor)* of the books of the Pentateuch, as was traditional, then "it would appear that Moses was the *auctor* of lies and falsehoods."[1] When, for example, the serpent says to Eve, "You shall not die," that statement is a lie; when Jacob says to Isaac, "I am your son Esau," yet another lie. Who is speaking here? FitzRalph asks. If Moses is speaking, he is the author of lies. If the serpent and Jacob are the authors of their statements, then the text has several authors, an untenable conclusion for a medieval scholar; or—equally untenable—if neither Moses nor the serpent nor Jacob "possess[es] authorship" of these untrue statements, then the passages are unauthored. FitzRalph's solution—setting up a distinction between "asserters," "compilers," and "authors," who both compile and assert—is less interesting to me than is the ghostly resonance between FitzRalph's question about who is speaking and its echo in Roland Barthes' "Death of the Author" some six hundred years later.[2]

Barthes' interrogation of the voice speaking in Balzac's *Sarrasine* is, of course, differently grounded than FitzRalph's. Instead of assuming that authorship matters, that we as readers should care "who is speaking thus," Barthes announces that "We shall never know, for the good reason that writing is the destruction of every voice, of every point of origin. Writing is that neutral, composite, oblique space where. . . all identity is lost, starting with the very identity of the body writing" (142). FitzRalph pondered authorship at a time when "the body writing" had become newly interesting, when, that is, the human scriptor of biblical

An early version of this paper was presented at the 1993 annual meting of the Shakespeare Association of America.

texts was emerging as a figure no longer dismissable as simply
God's amanuensis; Barthes pondered authorship after, as Michael Bristol puts it, "'the author' was itself already a pathetic
and overwrought metaphysical category," at a time when Foucault, quoting Beckett, would ask, "what does it matter who is
speaking?"[3] Between these moments lie six centuries in which
the Author as a category was variously constructed and in which
the name of Author was variously bestowed.

My interest in these pages is in exploring the parameters of
the Author category as it was constructed in England during the
early modern period.[4] We know that the beginning of this period
saw a shift away from one major mode of Author-construction,
that of the medieval *auctor*. According to A. J. Minnis, the *auctor* had emerged through the work of theological and biblical
scholars who found human *auctores* implicated in the writing
of sacred Scripture. As the human qualities of these *auctores*
began to receive more attention, the term *auctor* took on meaning in a literary context, where "it denoted someone who was
at once a writer and an authority, someone not merely to be
read but also to be respected and believed" (10), "a writer" (to
quote Thomas Greene) "whose work had commanded respect
for so many centuries as to have become an authority . . . to be
read as an *authentic* source of knowledge."[5] By the late sixteenth century, this medieval concept of the *auctor* was considered outmoded, so much so that John Guillory can describe
Spenser's citation of his *auctores* as "already . . . an archaic gesture," and so much so that Shakespeare can, in *Pericles*, use
Gower's "I tell you what mine authors say" as a way of placing
Gower as a revenant come from "ashes" to sing to those "born
in these latter times" (1. Chorus 20, 1–2, 11).[6]

We also know that the end of the early modern period in
England saw the beginning of a new mode of Author-
construction, a mode that Mark Rose calls the "proprietary
author."[7] The signal date for this new construct is 1709, the
year that saw the passage of the statute first allowing the author
to hold copyright. What seems unclear is just how the Author
category was constructed in the intervening years, the years
between the fading out of the *auctor* and the rise of the modern
proprietary author. Indeed, following on Barthes' and Foucault's
seminal essays, there prevails today a widespread assumption
that, as Barthes put it, "the author is a modern figure" (142)—
that is, an eighteenth-century invention, a character not yet

present in the early modern period and one that we read back into that period to our peril (or, at least, to our embarrassment).[8]

In the following pages I will try to show that, in fact, the category of Author was alive and robust in Renaissance England. While at no time is Author-construction a uniform process—while, that is, it is as hard to periodize the processes of Author-construction as it is to periodize the Authors so constructed—I will suggest that there existed in early modern England a category of Author not totally unlike that described by Barthes and Foucault, though certainly not identical to what they describe. This category, as I see it, was constructed in ways reminiscent of Author-constructs from the classical period as perpetuated by scholastics and humanists, but with characteristics of its own that emerged as the construct of the classical Author was appropriated by current cultural needs and desires. I will suggest further that those who published Shakespeare's "Works" in the 1623 Folio constructed Shakespeare as Author in much the way other authors at the time were constructed. The Author of the "Works" collected in the 1623 Folio is not what Roger Chartier describes as "the sovereign author," the "superb and solitary romantic figure . . . whose primary or final intention contains *the* meaning of the work and whose biography commands its writing with transparent immediacy" (28). But he is an Author nonetheless, as Elizabethan-Jacobean England constructed and recognized such imposing figures.

No one, I think, would argue that the word *author* was unavailable in Elizabethan-Jacobean England. Shakespeare's plays alone contain numerous examples of *author* used as Cotgrave's 1611 dictionary defines *autheur*—to mean the "causer, founder; th' original inventor, the first deviser of a thing; also, an author or writer of books."[9] None of these definitions, however, gets even close to what Barthes means by *author* in his "The Death of the Author" (1968) or his "From Work to Text" (1971),[10] or to what Foucault means when, in his 1969 "What Is an Author?" he discusses author-construction and describes discourses containing "the author-function." For these theorists, the Author, while obviously being what Cotgrave calls "a writer of books," is more importantly a Creator of Works. For Barthes, an Author "is in the same relation of antecedence to his work as a father to his child" (145). For Foucault, an Author is "a historical figure at the crossroads of a certain number of events"; he is at the same time "defined as a constant level of value," "a field of conceptual or theoretical coherence," a "stylistic unity," "a point where contradictions [in his works] are resolved."[11] This is the Author whom Barthes vividly depicts as, beginning with Mallarmé, "diminishing like a [figure] at the far end of the literary stage" (145).

It is easy to read Barthes and Foucault as saying that this figure first appears on the literary stage in the eighteenth century and to accept the obvious corollary that the Author-as-creator-of-Works did not exist in sixteenth- and seventeenth-century discourse or culture.[12] In some respects (which I will mention later) this formulation is accurate—that is, some attributes of the posteighteenth-century Author-construct do not seem to apply to the early modern Author. But one finds, for example, in works published in folio in Elizabethan-Jacobean England a panoply of front and back matter that constructs the writer of the work as an Author who shares many attributes with the modern Author whose demise Barthes and Foucault celebrate. Whether in the Englished works of such classical *auctors* as Homer, Virgil, Plutarch, and Livy; of translations of such vernacular writers as Ariosto, Boccaccio, and Montaigne; or the folio editions of, for example, the works of Chaucer and James I, the Author is presented as (in Foucault's language) "a historical figure at the crossroads of a certain number of events"; his biography places him interestingly in his time and is generally placed in connection with the Work it introduces; and his Work is set forth with the editorial attention and discussion due authoritative discourse. Further, the very iconography of the tomes themselves seems a conscious effort to produce Works that will in turn construct the Work's Author as having what Foucault calls "a certain status" (147). Bibliographical descendant of the massive codices of Greek and Latin manuscripts and of the great printed editions that followed, the early modern English folio constructs an Author who seems larger than life, and the folio itself seems physically the monument to the Author's fame that it so often claims to be. The entire package—the life, the elaborate table of contents, the letters to readers, the eulogies, the indices and glossaries, and the elaborately printed text itself—seems designed to bring to life the writer of the text as a powerful presence, a Creator of a Work, almost as if while the scriptors of the books of the Bible were beginning to be constructed as human, the authors of the *Iliad*, the *Aeneid*, the *Orlando Furioso*, and *The Canterbury Tales* were being raised to near-divinity.

The early modern construction of the Author-as-massive-presence can in part be traced back to the earliest days of humanist scholarship in Italy; one can find its antecedents in Greek and Roman statements about authors and can see this very author-construction as underlying the meticulous textual work undertaken in the great early libraries.[13] Even the historicizing, the personalizing, of the Author, descends in a direct line from the first century AD.—that is, from *De viris illustribus*, as Seutonius called his biographies of Latin literary figures. This influential work—the model for Saint Jerome's "lives" of Christian saints—provided both the material and the form for the "lives" that Donatus and others used to preface the great codices of Terence and Virgil. Indeed, it is Suetonius's "Life of Virgil" as presented by Donatus that appears in Twine's English edition of the *Aeneid*.[14] Authors constructed in Elizabethan and Jacobean folios are thus descended in more than bibliographical ways from classical figures. But they are also endowed with features that mark them as creations of the early modern English culture in which and for which they were produced. They are, for example, placed in specific relation with the English language and/or the English nation; they are described in language that distances them (or that acknowledges their distance) from the present moment of publication; and authors in the vernacular, such as Montaigne and James I, are imaged in the very language of filiation that Barthes uses to characterize the modern Author.

The several editions of Homer published between 1581 and 1616 illustrate the gradual construction of a great Author in England's early modern period. Homer, already the author of authors for many centuries, is presented to English readers by Arthur Hall in quarto in his 1581 translation of ten books of the *Iliad* as "My Author that most famous Poet," with the reminder that "That happie conquerour Alexander the great, would not sleepe without [Homer] under his beddes head," and with the lament that it had been "poore blind Homers case . . . to fall to me, poore blinde soule, poorely and blindly to learne him to talke our mother Tongue."[15] Hall's trope constructs a Homer who is like Shakespeare's Gower, come from the past to "sing a song that old was sung," or like the Virgil who "dumbly crosses [Dante's] path" at the beginning of *The Inferno*, "as though grown voiceless from long lack of speech." Thomas Greene points to Dante's description of "Virgil as hoarse from long silence" as revealing an emerging European sensitivity "to the fact of radical cultural change" (17). Hall's trope of teaching poor blind Homer to speak English seems to signal an awareness of hermeneutic anachronism more poignant even than Dante's. And such an awareness pervades the letters and poems in the front matter of the folios that construct Authors at this time and place, whether it be Livy presented "in English habit," his "spirit (which yet liveth in his writings)" having "made a voyage" across the centuries and into the present-day "courts of emperours and kings,"[16] or whether it be Chaucer, whose "ancientness" is stressed in references to the misty times in which he lived, in explanations and defenses of his obscure words, and in the very title given his collected works (*The Workes of our antient and lerned English Poet*). Hall's trope of teaching Homer to speak English also gestures toward another feature that tends to characterize Authors as constructed in early modern England: namely, as writers whose eloquence in English—whether as a native speaker or in translation—can be presented as contributing to the glory of the English tongue and the English nation.

The next edition of Homer in English—Chapman's 1598 translation of seven books of the *Iliad*[17]—is prefaced by a letter, "To the Reader," that touches on a different set of Author-related issues. Chapman's first concern is with defending his presentation of the Author's Work, aware that he will be criticized for "disordering" Homer's text by omitting several books of the *Iliad* while numbering the published books as if they comprised a single continuous Work. He answers such putative critics by distinguishing between the Work as "ordred" by the Author and as it has survived in its "common received forme":

> I haue good authoritie that the bookes were not set together by Homer himselfe, Licurgus first bringing them out of Ionia in Greece as an entire Poeme, before whose time his verses were sung disseuered into many workes . . .: and if those were ordred by others why may not I chalenge as much authority. . . . ? But . . . in the next edition when they come out by the dosen, I will reserue the ancient and common receiued forme; in the meane time do me the encouragement to confer [compare] that which I haue translated with the same in Homer and . . . let this first edition passe: so shall you . . . make me take paines to giue you this Emperor of all wisedome (for so Plato will allow him) in your owne language. . . . (A6-A6v)

Chapman then promises his readers a future volume that will provide the appropriate accouterments for an Author published in England and in English:

You shall in the next edition have the life of Homer, a table [a table of contents], a prettie comment, true printing [a text that is accurate and error-free], the due praise of your mother tongue aboue all others, for Poesie; and . . . demonstratiue proofe of our english wits aboue beyond sea-muses. . . . (A6v)

Chapman's promised "next edition"—the 1610 translation of the *Iliad*, when the books came out, as he said, "by the dosen"[18]—was missing several of the promised items, but it did contain the promised "prettie comment" in two poems by Chapman, one addressed to Prince Henry and one "To the Reader."[19] In both poems Homer is compared to God the creator, is praised for having made live eternally the hosts of Greece and Troy, is marveled at for virtually creating "the actual rage of war / With only the divine strains of his pen" (A3v), is celebrated through a recounting of Pliny's story about Alexander's treasuring of Homer's books, and, finally, is credited with having given "Antiquitie her living fire" (A4). Captured in these poems is the accolade traditionally given a major Poet: namely, comparison of the poet to God the creator, an accolade that recurs in one of the dedicatory poems affixed to the end of the work, where Chapman claims that ". . . none like Homer hath the world enspherde; / Earth, Seas, and Heauen, fixt in his verse, and mouing" (Dd2). Captured as well are characteristics that, in Elizabethan and Jacobean presentations, define the classical Author: namely, admiration from other worthies and credit for having given immortality to the age in which the author lived.

This 1610 edition also constructs Homer (a Homer who "well deserved to be / Esteemed a God" and whose "books" are "the most precious worke of all mens mindes") as vital to English culture. As Chapman explains to Prince Henry in his "Epistle Dedicatorie": "How much . . . were this kingdome's maine soule maim'd / To want this great inflamer of all powers / That moue in human soules?" Homer's Englished works are constructed by Chapman as themselves necessary to the English state: "All Realmes but yours," he writes to Prince Henry, "Are honord with him; and hold blest that State / That haue his workes to read and contemplate"(sig. π2v).

In 1611, with the publication of the complete *Iliades*, Chapman moved yet closer to fully monumentalizing Homer in folio. In this edition, the verse letter "To the Reader" has acquired explanatory sidenotes and the text throughout is provided with marginal commentary and, at the end of each of several of the

"Bookes," a variorumlike commentary on specific passages. The volume also contains a prose "Preface to the Reader," which includes a biography of the poet featuring largely what we can gather about him from his no longer extant statues.[20] In 1612 Chapman's translation of the *Odysses* was given comparable form, and in 1616 the two sets of translations were joined in the folio edition of *The Whole Works of Homer*.[21]

These Elizabethan-Jacobean constructions of Homer as an Author-now-speaking-English are paralleled in contemporaneous publications of the Englished works of other classical authors, whose authorly status is constructed around their lives, the excellence of their works, the admiration of other worthy authors or rulers, the immortality they have given to their long-dead countrymen, and the fame accruing to them as Authors through their Works (which are sometimes imaged as a monument, sometimes as the container of their yet-living spirit). Philemon Holland, for instance, presents Livy in terms of the Author's "unequaled" "exquisite eloquence," gives a Life of "this T. Livius" (complete with "the portraict of his visage" from his tomb at Padua), writes that he knows not whether the Paduans were more fortunate in having Aeneas as "the author of their beginning & admirable greatnes" or in having "this writer Livie who commended their deeds to everlasting fame," cites the admiration of "good and approved authors," and writes that "no Epitaph nor inscription either enchased in stone or cut in brasse, is there left, better than the monuments of his owne writings."[22]

Holland is like Hall, Chapman, and the translators of other classical authors in commenting at some length on textual matters. He writes that the more he commends Livy, the more the learned will grieve over

> the piteous maime and defect of that notable peece of worke and uniforme composition which hee left unto posteritie. . . . Bookes of farre lesse moment and importance, yea and those of greater antiquitie, have been spared and remaine safe: but of that work of his, one fourth part hath not escaped the envie of fortune: and that which now is extant, hath been delivered unto us either by fragments of old copies unperfect, or by the over-curious medling of some busie Aristarches of late daies depraved, who with their correcting have corrupted, & in stead of reforming words, have deformed the natural sense. . . . ([A5])

"In making [Livy] english," Holland writes, "endevoring by conference [comparison] especially of the select copies in Latin, yet not rejecting other translations (such as I had some little skil in)," he has tried "to come as neere as possibly I could, to the true meaning of the Author ([A5v])." Amyot's preface to Plutarch's *Lives* (in Thomas North's translation) similarly laments lost authorial matter, for which he "used all the diligence that [he] could in serching the chiefe Libraries of Venice and Rome," to no avail, and, like Holland, Amyot describes his collation of extant manuscripts and printed books.[23]

For presenters of more recent authors, authors writing in the vernacular—Montaigne, say, or Ariosto, or James I—the worthiness of the writer being constructed as Author must itself be established or defended. Harington constructs Ariosto by setting him above Virgil: "whatsoeuer is prayseworthy in Virgill is plentifully to be found in Ariosto, and some things that Virgill could not haue, for the ignoraunce of the age he liued in, you finde, in my author sprinckled ouer all his worke."[24] Florio grounds his claim for Montaigne's worth on Montaigne's own account of the "letters testimonial" granted him by the Senate and the City of Rome.[25] James I needed little by way of commendation to prove his worthiness, but his editor did feel the need to answer those who affirm that "it had beene better his Majestie had neuer written any Bookes at all." If the king must write, they say, let him write proclamations. The editor answers with an account of kings who have been authors, beginning with God, who wrote, first, the laws of Moses on stone, then wrote on the hearts of man, and then wrote the books of the Bible, which he dictated to the prophets and apostles (a late return to biblical authors as God's amanuenses).[26]

Discussion of textual matters, too, is different for editors or translators of the more recent writers, tending to focus more on attribution—where (in Foucault's language) the Author functions as "a stylistic unity" and "a constant level of value"—or on complaints about the printers of the author's "originals." Harington, for instance, writes that "as for the five Cantos that follow *Furioso*, I am partly of opinion they were not his [Ariosto's], both because me thinke they differ in sweetnesse of stile from the other, and beside it is not likely, that a man of his judgement having made so absolute a peece of worke, as his *Furioso* is, and having brought every matter to a good and well pleasing conclusion, would, as it were mar all agayne, and set them all by the eares. . . ."[27] And Florio explains errors in his translation on "the falseness of the French prints, the diversitie of copies, editions and volumes (some whereof have more or less than others) and I in London having followed some, and in the countrie others; now those in folio, now those in octavo, yet," he promises, "in this last survay reconciled all" ([A6]).

The relationship between Author and Work is also figured differently in these editions of writers in the vernacular, where the work is described not (as is usually the case with classical authors) as a monument but instead as the author's child. The prefatory material to the 1593 *Countess of Pembroke's Arcadia* depends heavily on the filiation trope, both in Sidney's letter to his sister, which begins with his claiming that "(as the cruell fathers among the Greekes, were woont to doe to the babes they would not foster) I could well finde in my heart, to cast out in some desert of forgetfulnesse this childe, which I am loath to father" and continues with his hope that, "for the fathers sake, it will be pardoned, perchaunce made much of, though in it selfe it haue deformities"—a trope that is picked up by the book's editor, who begs its readers to lovingly "entertaine it, as well for affinity with themselves, as being child to such a father. Whom albeit it do not exactly and in every lineament represent; yet considering the fathers untimely death prevented the timely birth of the childe ... yet the greatest unlikenes is rather in defect then in deformity."[28] The Author as father to the Work is also the trope chosen by the editor of the Works of James I, who defends the collection of an Author's Works on the grounds that such collections allow us to see "what divers Off-springs have proceeded from one braine" (sigs. bv–b2). And Florio weaves elaborate figurations around the filiation trope in his dedicatory letter to Lucy Countess of Bedford and Lady Ann Harrington. To Florio's "last Birth" [the publication of his own most recent book], he claims, "I the indulgent father invited two right Honorable Godfathers," since the child was "masculine, as are all mens conceipts that are their owne." Montaigne's *Essais* themselves, for example, were, "to Montaigne like Bacchus, closed in, or loosed from his great Jupiters thigh." The current volume, however, as a translation, is a "defective edition (since all translations are reputed femalls, delivered at second hand; and I in this serve but as Vulcan to hatchet this Minerva from that Jupiters bigge braine) I yet at least a fondling foster-father, having transported it from France to England; put it in English clothes; taught it to talk our tongue ... [and] would set it forth to the best service I might" (sig. A2). Hence his calling on two distinguished ladies to take "her" under their charge.

Florio might well have been spurred to this flight of fancy by Montaigne himself, who, in his essay "Of the affection of fathers to their children" (an essay to which Florio directs the reader for evidence of how rightly this volume is Montaigne's beloved offspring [sig. A2]), compares the begetting of children and the begetting of books, much preferring "the fruits of his minde" (the "far more noble part") to "the issue of his loins." "I wot not well," he writes, "whether my selfe should not much rather desire to beget and produce a perfectly-well-shaped, and excellently-qualitied infant, by the acquaintance of the Muses, than by the copulation of my wife. . . . There are few men given unto Poesie, that would not esteeme it for a greater honor, to be the fathers of *Virgils Aeneidos,* than of the goodliest boy in Rome, and that would not rather endure the losse of the one than the perishing of the other" (233.)

The filiation trope does not loom large in the construction of Chaucer as England's own Author, but this century-long construction in all other respects follows the familiar pattern. In the 1602 edition of his works, Chaucer is pronounced the glory of England:

What Pallas citie owes the heavenly mind
Of prudent Socrates, wise Greeces glorie

. . . .

The same, and more, fair England challenge may,
By that rare wit and art [that Chaucer] doest display.[29]

But Chaucer's construction as Author began a century earlier. Throughout the sixteenth century, as Derek Brewer points out, Chaucer's works "appeared in a series of volumes which . . . were not so very unlike, in size, appearance, and content, the great manuscript volumes of the fifteenth century."[30] Following early printings of *The Canterbury Tales* and separate printed editions of other of his writings, the collected *Workes* appeared in 1532 as edited by William Thynne.[31] The dedicatory letter to Henry VIII places the writings of Chaucer in the context of the history of language—from speech to writing among the Phoenicians, thence to Greek and Latin, thence to the romance languages and German, and finally to English. The letter makes it clear that the wonder of Chaucer is not so much "his excellent

lernyng in all kyndes of doctrynes & sciences" as it is his remarkable "frutefulness in wordes wel accordynge to the mater
and purpose" and his "so swete and plesaunt sentences"—the
wonder, that is, that at a time when "all good letters were layde
a slepe throughout the worlde . . . suche an excellent poete in
our tonge shulde . . . spryng and aryse."[32] This 1532 edition of
Chaucer's works contains several features listed by Chapman
as necessary for presenting a proper Author: a table of contents,
a "prettie comment" (in the form of a Latin elegy on Chaucer
first printed by Caxton in his edition of the Boethius[33]), an "attempt at a true printing," and much praise of Chaucer as an
English-speaking poet. As the writings of an author who
"framed a tonge before so rude and imperfite to suche a swete
ornature and composicion," Chaucer's works merited the editor's "collacion" of "divers imprintes of [Chaucer's] bokes" and
his "dilygent sertch" for "trewe copies or exemplaries" of
"those workes of Geffray Chaucer whiche before had ben put
in printe" and for "dyvers other never tyll now imprinted but
remaynyng almost unknowen and in oblyvion" (sig. Aiiv).

This is Chaucer as constructed in 1532 and presented in three
subsequent sixteenth-century editions of the *Works*. With the
1598 edition, however, Chaucer as Author is given new dimensions. The 1598 edition is worth pausing over, since both its
commentary matter and its printing history can contribute to
our understanding of the period's own sense of author-
construction. The volume opens with an elaborate title page, a
dedicatory letter, a letter "To the Readers," and a letter from
Francis Beaumont to Thomas Speght, the work's editor, in praise
of Chaucer as an Author superior to such precursors as Virgil.
Next comes a full-page picture of the Author (taken from Oc-
cleve) surrounded by an elaborate family tree showing Chaucer's
links to John of Gaunt and delineating Chaucer's progeny. The
emphasis on the person of Chaucer and his family and on Chaucer as a figure carefully placed in English history continues in
the biography that follows, with its repeated marginal and internal references to documents that Speght had consulted in "the
Guild Hall in London," the "office of the Heralds," the "Book
of Fees and Sergiancies in the Exchequer," and "the Tour of
London." This obtrusive insistence on extant records of the life
of Chaucer-as-Londoner keeps reminding the reader of Chaucer's Englishness—as does Speght's frequent citing of biographies of Chaucer by Gower, Leland, and Bale; the
accumulation of purported historical detail (including such

items as "it seemeth that [Chaucer was] of the inner Temple: for not many yeeres since, Master Buckley did see a Record in the same house, where Geoffrey Chaucer was fined two shillings for beating a Franciscane fryer in Fleetstreete") serve to bring Chaucer to life as someone not so far away, in effect countervailing the very cultural distance created by emphasis elsewhere on Chaucer's "ancientness."[34] That such an effect was desirable— that it was at least a part of the period's sense of author-construction—seems implied in the prefatory letter to Speght from Beaumont in which he writes: "in the paines and diligence you haue used in collecting [Chaucer's] life, mee thinks you haue bestowed upon him more favorable graces than Medea did upon Pelias, for you have restored us Chaucer both alive again and yong again" ([aiiv]–[aiii]).

The printing history of the 1598 edition also yields insights, suggesting that author-construction and presentation were serious business in late-sixteenth-century England. When one pieces together the story of the work's publication, combining Thomas Speght's narration with the traces left in the records of the Stationers' Company and with Katherine Panzer's construction in the Short Title Catalogue, one sees two lines of activity converging to produce this impressive, newly constructed complete *Workes* reauthorizing Chaucer as England's Poet. One line of activity centers on Speght, who, during the 1590s at the instigation of friends, prepared for their reading a newly corrected text of Chaucer's works and elaborate scholarly commentary material.[35]

While this was going on and in seeming ignorance of Speght's project, the Stationers' Company decided to publish a new edition of Chaucer's works, presumably based on that of 1561. The copy was first entered to Abell Jeffes in 1592 "to Print for the companye," then transferred in 1594 to Adam Islip—again, "to printe for the companye"—an extremely rare formula, according to Peter W. M. Blayney—with the following even rarer formulation: if "hereafter there be any Comentary or other thinge written uppon the same booke, then the same Adam shall have the offer of the same, either to take it, or refuse yt," a proviso that may indicate that the Company was trying to find, or to have someone write, such a commentary.[36] In any case, Islip seems to have proceeded with the printing, because, according to Speght, "so it fell out of late, that Chaucers Works being in the Presse, and three parts thereof alreadie printed, not only these friends [who had urged Speght to edit Chaucer's works] did by their Letters sollicit me, but certaine also of the best in the Companie of Stationers hearing of these Collections, came unto me, and for better or worse would have something done in this Impression" ([aiiiv]). Speght writes that he gave in to the "importunitie" of his friends and the members of the Company of Stationers, did what he could with the text (which he had already begun to "correct" by "old written Copies"), and allowed them to print his "life" of the Author, his annotated bibliography of Chaucer's sources, his glossary defining Chaucer's obscure words, and his other commentary matter. The STC reveals that the printing of this massive folio edition was jointly funded by three very wealthy stationers[37]—G. Bishop, B. Norton, and T. Wight—and that the edition sold out quickly, the works being reedited by Speght and published in a new edition only four years later, in 1602.

Judging by such volumes as the 1598 Chaucer, it would appear that the Author in early modern England was constructed as an historical figure complete with parents, children, and a career, and, at the same time and more importantly, as a larger-than-life Creator of Works, monumentalized in and made immortal by these works, and available for appropriation by the patriotic and the powerful. This is an Author-construct that both is and is not that of Foucault and Barthes. The ways in which this Author is like theirs should by now be clear. The differences lie primarily in those features that the Author later accrued, features that one does not find in Speght's Chaucer or Holland's Livy or Harington's Ariosto—that is, the Author defined as "a field of conceptual or theoretical coherence" or as "the point where contradictions [among his writings] are resolved." In other words, the sixteenth-and seventeenth-century Author was not constructed as a consciousness or a set of beliefs or desires in which texts find coherence and organic integrity. While these are aspects that will, in general, attach to the Author at a later time, one can argue that, in the early modern period, Ben Jonson did so define *himself* as Author.[38] One can argue further that Jonson's publication of himself as an Author of Works was derided at the time not only because he included plays in the volume of *Workes*, but also because a writer who published his own authorial tome would have been seen by his contemporaries as arrogating to himself the larger-than-life semimythical aspect of the Author as constructed at that time and place.[39]

Shakespeare did not, of course, so publish himself. Those who did publish his Works in folio[40]—and the plays are, in fact, announced as "Works" more than once in the Folio front matter—constructed him as Author in much the same way other authors at the time were constructed. As with other folios commemorating living or recently dead Authors (Montaigne, for example), there is no "Life." But the other requisites are in place. There is the portrait, the standard discussion about the reliability of the manuscripts behind the printing, the appropriate letters to readers and to patrons, the requisite commendatory poems, and the elaborate table of contents. There is, in the Dedicatory Epistle, the familiar filiation trope; there is, in Jonson's poem, the conventional touting of England's best in Jonson's "Triumph, my Britaine, thou hast one to showe / To whom all Scenes of Europe homage owe"; there is the standard cliché in Jonson's "Thou art a Moniment without a tombe, / And art alive still, while thy Booke doth live"; there is the hint of a constructed cultural distance in Jonson's mention of the good old days when Shakespeare delighted "Eliza, and our James"; and there is the utterly familiar in Leonard Digges's poem "To The Memorie of the deceased Authour," in which Shakespeare is promised that his Works will make his name outlive his tomb and that his Book, "When Brasse and Marble fade, shall make thee looke / Fresh to all Ages."

It is possible to read these commentary materials—as Margreta de Grazia does—as signaling the presence in the Folio of the various agencies that collaborated in staging and printing plays (21–22). In the context of the other tomes produced at the time, however, it is also possible to read them as standard Author-construction material—not the Author that Malone created of Shakespeare, nor the Shakespeare that has been culturally dominant following on Malone's work, but an Author nonetheless, constructed on a then-quite-fashionable model. If the modern Author of Barthes and Foucault is disappearing, "diminishing like a figure at the far end of the literary stage," then *this* Author—this descendant of classical and humanist constructs, appropriated by an England intent on aggrandizing itself—is dead indeed. But we should, I think, at least say "hail" before we say "farewell."

NOTES

1. In this paragraph I am drawing on A. J. Minnis's paraphrase of FitzRalph. See A. J. Minnis, *Medieval Theory of Authorship* (London: Scolar Press, 1984), 100–103.

2. Barthes, "The Death of the Author" (1968), in *Image-Music-Text*, trans. Stephen Heath (New York: Hill and Wang, 1977), 142–48. Barthes asks the same question—i.e., "Who is speaking?"—of Balzac's *Sarrasine* in his *S/Z: An Essay*, trans. Richard Miller (New York: Hill and Wang, 1974), 41. All quotations from Barthes refer to "The Death of the Author" and will be cited parenthetically in the text.

3. For the late-medieval interest in the human scriptor of biblical texts, see Minnis, *Medieval Theory of Authorship*, 39ff. See also Michael Bristol, *Shakespeare's America, America's Shakespeare* (London: Routledge, 1990), 115, and Michel Foucault, "What Is an Author?" in *Textual Strategies: Perspectives in Post-structuralist Criticism*, ed. Josue V. Herari (Ithaca: Cornell University Press, 1979), 141–60, esp. 141.

4. I am indebted to those who have raised questions about the construction of authorship in Shakespeare's England and who have thus made it possible for me to frame my own questions on the topic. These include Margreta de Grazia, *Shakespeare Verbatim: The Reproduction of Authenticity and the 1790 Apparatus* (Oxford: Clarendon Press, 1991); Jonathan Goldberg, *Voice Terminal Echo: Postmodernism and English Renaissance Texts* (London: Methuen, 1986), esp. 100–110, and "Textual Properties," *Shakespeare Quarterly* 37 (1986): 213–17; and Stephen Orgel, "What Is a Text?" *Research Opportunities in Renaissance Drama* 24 (1981): 3–6, and "The Authentic Shakespeare," *Representations* 21 (1988): 1–26. I am also indebted to the work of Roger Chartier, whose *The Order of Books: Readers, Authors, and Libraries in Europe between the Fourteenth and Eighteenth Centuries*, trans. Lydia G. Cochrane (Stanford: Stanford University Press, 1994) appeared too late for me to use in the shaping of my argument, but whose conclusions seem to accord with my own.

5. Thomas M. Greene, *The Light in Troy: Imitation and Discovery in Renaissance Poetry* (New Haven: Yale University Press, 1982), 12; emphasis mine.)

6. John Guillory, *Poetic Authority: Spenser, Milton, and Literary History* (New York: Columbia University Press, 1983), 64.

7. "The Author as Proprietor: *Donaldson v. Becket* and the Genealogy of Modern Authorship," *Representations* 23 (1988): 51–85. See also David Saunders and Ian Hunter, "Lessons from the 'Literatory': How to Historicise Authorship," *Critical Inquiry* 17 (1991): 479–509; and Chartier, *The Order of Books*, 25–58, esp. 36–38.

8. Chartier helpfully shows how Foucault's essay does, in fact, allow for a construction of the Author in earlier periods (see 31–32). Jonathan Goldberg also suggests as much in differentiating Barthes' discussion of the Author from that of Foucault. (See *Voice Terminal Echo*, 107.)

9. Randle Cotgrave, *A Dictionarie of the French and English Tongues* (London: Adam Islip, 1611).

10. "From Work to Text," in *Textual Strategies*, ed. Herari, 73–81.

11. These characteristics of the Author are given by Foucault in his discussion of Saint Jerome's criteria for legitimate authorship of sacred works. But Foucault ends this discussion by writing that "Clearly, Saint Jerome's four criteria of authenticity (criteria which seem totally insufficient for today's exegetes) do define the four modalities according to which modern criticism brings the author-function into play" (151).

12. Indeed, some of Foucault's followers suggest that only beginning in the

eighteenth century is the Author historicized and periodized, and that only then are the Author's writings and life records treated as historical documents. See, for example, de Grazia's chapters "Situating Shakespeare in an Historical Period" and "Individuating Shakespeare's Experience," 94–176.

13. For early statements about authors, see, e.g., Ovid's remarks about himself and his work in Book 15 of the *Metamorphoses*, lines 984ff. On the work of the great libraries, see Anthony Grafton, "The Vatican and Its Library," in *Rome Reborn: The Vatican Library and Renaissance Culture*, ed. Grafton (Washington, D.C.: Library of Congress, 1993), 3–86, esp. 34–45.

14. See J. C. Rolfe, "Prefatory Note," Seutonius's *The Lives of Illustrious Men*, in *Seutonius* (Loeb ed.), 2 vols. (Cambridge: Harvard University Press, 1914), 2: 388–93, esp. 389 n. 3 and 390–91. See also the title page of Twine's 1573 *Aeneid:* "There is added moreover to this edition Virgils life out of Donatus." *The whole xii Bookes of the Aeneidos of Virgill,* ed. Thomas Twyne (London: Wyllyam How, 1573).

15. Arthur Hall, "The Epistle Dedicatorie," *Ten Books of Homers Iliades,* translated from the French by Arthur Hall (London, 1581), Aiii–Aiiiiv, esp. Aiiii and Aiiiv.

16. Philemon Holland, "To the Reader," *The Romane Historie written by T. Livivs of Padva,* trans. Philemon Holland (London: Adam Islip, 1600), sigs. [A4]–[A6], esp. [A6]. Holland's dedicatory letter to Queen Elizabeth (sig. [A3]) describes Livy as "having arrived long since and conversed as a meere stranger in this your famous Iland, and now for love thereof learned in some sort the language."

17. *Seaven Bookes of the Iliades of Homere, Prince of Poets,* trans. George Chapman (London, 1598).

18. *Homer, Prince of Poets: Translated according to the Greeke, in twelve Bookes of his Iliads by Geo. Chapman* (London, [1610?]). This volume is technically in folio, though so small a book that it is easy to mistake it for a quarto. It thus stands interestingly—both in its contents and its physical appearance—between the 1581 and 1598 quarto editions of Homer in English and the next translation, the 1611 folio edition of the *Iliad.*

19. A third poem in the front matter, addressed to Queen Anne, is simply a short dedicatory poem, much like the set of dedicatory poems printed at the end of the volume.

20. According to the incorporated "biography," "What Kind of Person Homer was . . . his statue teacheth, which Cedrenus describeth," a statue which stood in Constantinople but since destroyed by fire. . . . "Another renowned statue of his (saith Lucian) stood in the temple of Ptolomy." *The Iliads of Homer Prince of Poets . . . with a comment on some of his chiefe places. Donne according to the Greeke by Geo. Chapman.* (London, 1611), sig. [A5].

21. *The Whole Works of Homer, Prince of Poetts, In his Iliads and Odyses,* trans. Geo. Chapman (London, 1616).

22. "To the Reader," [A4]–[A6], esp. [A4], [A5].

23. "Amiot to the Readers," *The Lives of the Noble Grecians and Romanes, compared together by . . . Plutarke of Chaeronea: Translated out of Greeke into French by James Amyot . . . and out of French into English, by Thomas North* (London, 1579), sigs. 3v–[7], esp. [7].

24. John Harington, "A Preface, or Rather a Briefe Apologie of Poetrie," *Orlando Furioso in English Heroical Verse [translated] by John Harington* (London: Richard Field, 1591), iiv–[viiiv], esp. [viv].

25. "How nobly [this book] is descended, let the father in the ninth Chapter of his third booke by letters testimoniall of the Roman Senate and Citty beare record," *The Essayes or Morall, Politike and Millitarie Discourses of Lo. Michaell de Montaigne,* trans. John Florio (London: Val. Sims, 1603), sig. A2.

26. James, Bishop of Winton, "The Preface to the Reader," *The Workes of the most high and mightie Prince, James* (London: Robert Barker and John Bill, 1616), b–e2v, esp. b2v.

27. "The Life of Ariosto," 414–23, esp. 422.

28. *The Countesse of Pembrokes Arcadia. Written by Sir Philip Sidney Knight. Now . . . augmented and ended* (London: William Ponsonbie, 1593), sigs. ¶3, ¶4v.

29. "Upon the picture of Chaucer," *The Workes of our Ancient and learned English Poet, Geffrey Chaucer, newly Printed* (London: Adam Islip, 1602), sig. bi.

30. Derek Brewer, ed., *Geoffrey Chaucer: The Works, 1532* (Menton, Yorkshire: Scholar Press, 1969), [i].

31. *The Workes of Geffray Chaucer* (London, 1532).

32. "The Preface. To the kynges hygnesse," sigs. Aii–Aiii, esp. Aiiv. For the evidence that the letter was written not by Thynne, as the Preface claims (Aiiv) but by Sir Bryan Tuke (secretary to Henry VIII and a patron of learning), see Brewer, *The Works, 1532,* [i].

33. See Derek Brewer, *The Works, 1532,* [iv]. The elegy is printed at the close of the work on fol. 383.

34. Thomas Speght, "The Life of our Learned English Poet, Geffrey Chaucer," in *The Workes of our Antient and lerned English Poet, Geffrey Chaucer* (London: 1598), bi–ciiiv, esp. biii–biiiv.

35. Speght describes these activities in his "To the Readers," sigs. [aiiiv]–[aiiii].

36. Edward Arber, ed., *A Transcript of the Registers of the Company of Stationers of London: 1554–1640,* 10 vols. (London, 1875), 2:621, 2:667. The rare 20 December 1574 record of entrance of "Chawcers *workes*" to Adam Islip carries the acknowledging signature of Abell Jeffes. I am very grateful to Peter Blayney for generously sharing with me his expertise in these matters.

37. Again I express my gratitude to Peter Blayney, as well as to T. L. Berger and Paul Werstine, all of whom generously helped with the reconstruction of this story.

38. For a reading of Jonson that supports this position, see Sara van den Berg, "Ben Jonson and the Ideology of Authorship," in *Ben Jonson's 1616 Folio,* ed. Jennifer Brady and W. H. Herendeen (Newark: University of Delaware, 1991), 111–37. See also Timothy Murray, *Theatrical Legitimation: Allegories of Genius in Seventeenth-Century England and France* (New York and Oxford: Oxford University Press, 1987), and Richard Helgerson, *Self-Crowned Laureates* (Berkeley and Los Angeles: University of California Press, 1983).

39. For some of the contemporary attacks on Jonson's 1616 folio, see C. H. Herford and Percy and Evelyn Simpson, *Ben Jonson,* 9 vols. (Oxford: Clarendon Press, 1950), 9:13.

40. *Mr. William Shakespeares Comedies, Histories, & Tragedies,* (London: Isaac Jaggard and Ed. Blount, 1623).

Jonson and the Tother Youth

IAN DONALDSON

Since the early romantic period Shakespeare has commonly been regarded as a towering figure in the English cultural landscape, "Out-topping knowledge," as Matthew Arnold put it, "Making the heaven of heavens his dwelling place." Shakespeare is up there on his own in that heaven of heavens, beyond comparison (it would seem) with other, lesser writers. Throughout the seventeenth and much of the eighteenth centuries, however, Shakespeare was seen in a rather different way: as one of a group, or, more pointedly, one of a pair of celebrated English writers whose qualities came gradually to be defined through a series of formal and, eventually, much-repeated contrasts. It was indeed, as I want to argue, through this very process of comparison that Shakespeare's modern reputation was established. The writer with whom Shakespeare was regularly compared was Ben Jonson, who was regarded by many good judges in the seventeenth century as the supreme genius of his age. The comparisons begin early, in the lifetime of the writers themselves, being encouraged at first by Jonson himself, who was however destined in due course to fall victim to a process he had, ironically, helped to initiate. The formal opposition of the two writers encouraged an imaginative reconstruction of their lives, which in turn affected the reading and interpretation of their texts. This circular and incremental process might fairly be called "the invention of Shakespeare and Jonson."[1]

Ben Jonson's comedy *Epicoene, or The Silent Woman* is about a man who hates noise and women yet marries a supposedly silent wife in order to beget an heir and disinherit his troublesome nephew. In the second act of the play this disagreeable character is visited on the eve of his wedding by one of his nephew's friends, who, in a lengthy tirade fulfilling and exceeding Morose's wildest nightmares, warns him of the many

111

perils of marriage. All women, argues Truewit, bring noise, terror, and tribulation to a household, but one kind of woman is to be avoided above all others, and that is the female critic: the sort who will "censure poets, and authors, and stiles, and compare 'hem, Daniel with Spenser, Jonson with the tother youth, and so foorth" (2.2.115–19).[2]

Scholars have long wondered who this "tother youth" could be. Upton in the eighteenth century suggested he was Thomas Dekker; Gifford in the nineteenth century proposed John Marston; Herford and Simpson in this century confidently declared him to be Samuel Daniel, an identification accepted by most modern editors of the play.[3] Mulling over the significance of the phrase, Gifford conceded that it was "more easy to say who is not meant than who is," and who in his opinion the tother youth most definitely was not was William Shakespeare. Gifford was determined to head off an unwelcome identification proposed by his old adversary, Edmond Malone, who had incautiously written, "In the *Silent Woman* the author perhaps pointed at Shakespeare, as one whom he viewed with fearful, yet with jealous eyes." Gifford was scornful: "A more improbable conceit has rarely been hazarded." Eager to dispose once and for all of the myth of Jonson's supposed malignity towards Shakespeare, Gifford could not contemplate the possibility of Jonson's making even a light-hearted allusion to the existence of his great rival or the possibility of public debate concerning their respective merits. "With what propriety," labored Gifford, "could Shakespeare be called "the t'other *youth?* He was now in his 46th year, a time of life to which such an expression can scarcely be applied."[4]

I believe Jonson's reference in *The Silent Woman* is indeed to Shakespeare, who (it is certainly true) was scarcely a youth in 1609. But then neither was Jonson himself, who was by then a highly successful writer in his late thirties: and that of course is the humorous point. "The tother youth," with its Falstaffian casualness, wittily rejuvenates both men, while dispatching the older, more celebrated dramatist, young whatsisname, to anonymous obscurity. "Jealousy," "malignity," "fearfulness" seem hardly the appropriate terms to invoke in relation to such a quip, but some sort of friendly contestation between the two men (we might think) is afoot.

Truewit's catalogue of the perils of marriage in *The Silent Woman* is freely adapted from Juvenal's even more deeply misogynistic sixth satire. Juvenal's female critic, the moment she sits down to dinner, "commends Virgil, pardons the dying Dido, and pits the poets against each other, putting Virgil in one scale and Homer in the other": "committit vates et comparat, inde Maronem / atque alia parte in trutina suspendit Homerum" (lines 436–37). If Homer and Virgil are balanced in one set of classical scales, Jonson would surely have been choosy about the poet measured against him in the English heavyweight contest; and in 1609 Shakespeare was the obvious choice. *Committit vates et comparat:* to "commit" poets against each other, bringing them together like gladiators or fighting cocks, was a well-established classical exercise. Homer and Virgil were regularly paired in this manner for formal comparison, a habit encouraged by Virgil's own contestive practice. Juvenal himself compares Homer and Virgil in his eleventh satire (lines 180–81), and Juvenal was to find himself in turn matched against Martial, who wrote an indignant epigram (7.24) against the impertinent critic who attempted this feat, beginning "Cum Iuvenale meo quae me committere temptas." "When you try to commit me against my Juvenal," says Martial, you might as well suggest that Orestes and Pylades, Castor and Pollux, were not devoted friends and brothers, but envious and jealous rivals. "Iuvenale meo"—"my Juvenal"—writes Martial affectionately, staving off the very notion of possible envy existing between himself and his fellow poet.[5]

This habit of assessing authors (or people) comparatively in pairs formed the basis of a well-known rhetorical exercise known to the ancient Greeks as *syncrisis*. This was an exercise in persuasion, intended to demonstrate the superiority of one author or one individual over another; it was widely practiced in classical times by Longinus, Quintilian, and Cicero, for example, and by Homer himself in book 3 of *The Iliad*.[6] Syncrisis was also practiced by critics in England from the Renaissance period well into the eighteenth century: Dryden's comparative evaluation of Horace and Juvenal in his *Discourse Concerning the Original and Progress of Satire* and Dr. Johnson's extended analysis of the merits of Dryden himself in relation to those of Pope in *The Lives of the Poets* are obvious examples of the art.[7]

One needs no special rhetorical training, however, to grasp the basic point in Jonson's comedy, which I have seen conveyed in one modern production of *The Silent Woman* by a pair of familiar Jacobean portraits of bearded men—one bald, the other plump—hung on either side of the stage; at the line "the tother youth," the actor gestured absent-mindedly towards the man with the big bald head. This is a device that, interestingly enough, was actually used on the Elizabethan stage, in the final act of Thomas Dekker's *Satiromastix*. Wanting to deflate Ben Jonson's pretensions in identifying himself with the Roman poet Horace, Dekker has his character Captain Tucca produce two portraits—one of Horace, the other of Ben Jonson—and triumphantly demonstrate the superiority of the Roman poet over his presumptuous English imitator.[8] Shakespeare allowed Hamlet to practice the art of syncrisis in a similar manner and with similar visual aids in conversation with his mother.

> Look here upon this picture, and on this,
> The counterfeit presentment of two brothers.
> See what a grace was seated on this brow:
>
> . . . .
>
> This was your husband. Look you now what follows.
>
> (3.4.53–55, 63)

To "commit" poets formally against each other is to imply— and it is precisely this implication that Martial in the epigram just quoted is determined to resist—that they are somehow naturally at enmity with each other or mutually envious or engaged in some kind of bitter flyting in the manner of Kennedy and Dunbar. It is not therefore surprising to find a legend developing in the seventeenth century about a warfare that existed between Jonson and Shakespeare—a merry warfare, perhaps, but a warfare none the less. Thomas Fuller was to give this legend its classic shape in his *History of the Worthies of England* in 1662, when he wrote about Shakespeare as follows:

> Many were the *wit-combats* between him and *Ben Johnson*, which two I behold like a Spanish great Gallion, and an *English man o' War*; Master *Johnson* (like the former) was built far higher in Learning; *Solid*, but *Slow*, in his performances. Shake-spear, with the *English man of War*, lesser in *Bulk*, but lighter in *sailing*, could turn with all tides, tack about and take advantage of all winds, by the quickness of his Wit and Invention.[9]

Fuller presents these celebrated wit-combats as a replay of the Spanish Armada, in which the heavy Spanish galleons were repeatedly outmaneuvred by the lighter, faster English vessels. Shakespeare is thus cast as a national hero, a Sir Francis Drake of the realm of letters, while Jonson's role is that of the bungling foreign invader. This vivid and seemingly firsthand account was to have a powerful effect on subsequent perceptions of the entire relationship between Shakespeare and Jonson. Well into the nineteenth century it continues to shape (for example) Carlyle's view of the two writers:

> And there are Ben and William Shakespeare in wit-combat, sure enough: Ben bearing down like a mighty Spanish Warship, fraught with all learning and artillery; Shakespeare whisking away from him,—whisking right through him, athwart the big bulk and timbers of him; like a miraculous Celestial Lightship, woven all of sheet-lightning and sunbeams![10]

Fuller's account is the starting point and seeming validation of such indefatigable works of Victorian scholarship as Robert Cartwright's *Shakespeare and Jonson: Dramatic, versus Wit-Combats* (1864), a book that sets out to demonstrate the existence of a long-standing feud whose progress (so Cartwright believes) can be clearly read in almost every play that the two dramatists wrote.

But as Samuel Schoenbaum has pointed out, Fuller's *History of the Worthies of England* was written a quarter of a century after Jonson's death and nearly half a century after the death of Shakespeare. Fuller himself was eight years of age and living in Northamptonshire when Shakespeare died in Stratford-upon-Avon, where he had been living in retirement for several years. When Fuller says that he *beholds* the wit-combats of Jonson and Shakespeare at the Mermaid Tavern in London he is not speaking as an old drinking companion who once witnessed such scenes; he beholds them rather in his mind's eye; he makes them up. There is in fact no evidence that Shakespeare ever drank at the Mermaid Tavern or that these wit-combats ever occurred.[11] They are invented, I believe, in the spirit of the rhetorical exercise of formal comparison that I have just described.

Dryden's *Essay of Dramatic Poesy*, written six years after the publication of *The History of the Worthies of England*, begins with the invocation of another sea battle, not this time from England's glorious past but from the historical present: Dryden sets his literary debate on "that memorable day, in the first summer of the late war, when our navy engaged the Dutch: a day wherein the two most mighty and best appointed fleets which any age had ever seen disputed the command of the greater half of the globe, the commerce of nations, and the riches of the universe." The sea battle of 3 June 1665 forms the fitting

background of a debate in which the two great English dramatists, Shakespeare and Jonson, are also brought into comparison.
"If I would compare him with Shakespeare," says Neander of
Ben Jonson, "I must acknowledge him the more correct poet,
but Shakespeare the greater wit. Shakespeare was the Homer,
or father of our dramatic poets; Jonson was the Virgil, the pattern of elaborate writing; I admire him, but I love Shakespeare."
Skilled in the art of syncrisis—the comparison of Homer and
Virgil is one which he develops more fully elsewhere, along
with the comparison between Horace and Juvenal—Dryden for-
malizes the contrast of Shakespeare and Jonson, tipping his
thumb finally on the balance in favor of Shakespeare. Dryden
extends this comparison in other essays and prologues over a
period of years; and as G. E. Bentley has shown in detail, it was
through Dryden's decisive influence that Shakespeare's literary
reputation began in the last decade of the seventeenth century
finally to outstrip that of Jonson.[12]

While Dryden was attempting these serious exercises in literary assessment, another more frivolous kind of comparative narrative involving Shakespeare and Ben Jonson was developing—
namely, the popular anecdote. Most of the anecdotes about
Shakespeare and Jonson that survive from the late seventeenth
century are set in taverns, and most turn upon strikingly feeble
pieces of wordplay. They memorialize Jonson's remarks on tum-
bling downstairs at the Feathers Tavern after a bout of drinking
("Gentlemen, since I am so luckily fallen into your company, I
will drink with you before I go"), and on finding a familiar entry
to the Half-Moon Tavern unexpectedly closed: "Since that the
Moon was so unkind to make me go about, / The *Sun* henceforth
shall take my coin, the *Moon* shall go without." One persistent
story is that of Shakespeare standing as godfather to one of Jonson's children, and resolving to give the child "a dozen good
latten [brass] spoons," quipping to Jonson as he does so, "and
thou shall translate them."[13] Many of these distressing anecdotes are solemnly recorded in a recent biography of Ben Jonson
on the grounds that they accord with "Jonson's own precept and
practice in following the principle of classical historians that
the gossip, rumour, and anecdote surrounding a great life are as
informative as the facts about him."[14] Yet unless some effort is
made to sift such stories it is not easy to see in what sense they
can ever be regarded as "informative." Jonson and Shakespeare
appear in these stories as pedantic buffoons, trading labored
jokes in the manner of Holofernes and Sir Nathaniel in *Love's*

Labor's Lost, or a couple of characters from the Elizabethan jest books. And it is indeed from the jest books, as one scholar has pointed out, that many of these anecdotes derive.[15] They are preexisting stories about a pair of clowns, to which in the course of the seventeenth century the names of Jonson and Shakespeare are simply attached. The stories are "informative," then, not on account of their content, but in what they imply about the semilegendary status of Jonson and Shakespeare in the period, considered as a famous pair; and about the wider process of folkloric transmission, adaptation, and attribution.

Towards the end of the seventeenth century, at the very time when the oral tradition to which an appeal is made can no longer reliably be verified, another and more interesting kind of biographical narrative about Jonson and Shakespeare begins to show itself. In this narrative, the focus is no longer upon the witty quips of the two dramatists, but upon their inner character, their basic temperament and disposition. This new curiosity about the inner life of Shakespeare and Jonson develops at much the same time that critics begin to interest themselves in the interior life of Shakespeare's dramatic characters, and to speculate imaginatively about those aspects of their existence that the dramatist chose not to describe. A loosely ruminative, quasi-fictionalizing approach to Shakespeare's dramatic characters was to develop particular momentum throughout the eighteenth and nineteenth centuries, giving rise to such studies as *The Girlhood of Shakespeare's Heroines,* and meeting its Waterloo only in the 1930s (if then) with L. C. Knights's influential essay "How Many Children Had Lady Macbeth?"[16] During the same long period literary biography perfected much the same loosely ruminative, quasi-fictionalizing mode that might enable a novelistic scholar (or scholarly novelist) to write, for example, a three-volume work entitled *Judith Shakespeare.* (Not a great deal is known about Shakespeare's daughter, but this did not deter William Black, who published such a work in 1884.)[17]

From the late seventeenth century onwards, biographical and literary interpretations of Shakespeare and Ben Jonson became intriguingly confused, as writers attempted to deduce the personal characters of both men from the dramatic characters they created. As both Shakespeare and Ben Jonson created a very large number of dramatic characters, the choice of character is clearly crucial. Which of Shakepeare's characters could be said to typify the author's temperament and genius? By the mid-eighteenth century there was a measure of agreement on this

question: it was Falstaff.[18] Not the Falstaff whom Hal describes
as a "bolting-hutch of beastliness," or whom Jeremy Collier
declared had been "thrown out of favour as being a *Rake*" to
die "like a Rat behind the Hangings," but an altogether more
benign and well-behaved character who was carefully laundered
and presented through the writings of such scholars as Corbyn
Morris, William Guthrie, and Maurice Morgann.[19] Sir John Falstaff, wrote Corbyn Morris in 1744,

> possesses Generosity, Chearfulness, Alacrity, Invention, Frolic and
> Fancy superior to all other Men;—The *Figure* of his *Person* is the
> Picture of Jollity, Mirth and Good-nature, and banishes at once all
> other ideas from your Breast; He is happy himself, and makes you
> happy.—If you examine him further, he has no Fierceness, Reserve,
> Malice or Peevishness lurking in his Heart; his Intentions are all
> pointed at innocent Riot and Merriment; nor has the Knight any
> inveterate Design, except against *Sack*, and that too he *loves*.[20]

Notice the variations Morris plays on Shakespeare's language:
Falstaff's "I am not only witty in myself, but the cause that wit
is in other men" (*2 Henry IV* 1.2.9–10) becomes "he is happy in
himself, and makes you happy." Happiness replaces wit as the
cardinal comic virtue, and Falstaff's amiability is thought to
derive more or less directly from the good-natured temperament
of the author who created him. It is hardly necessary to point
out that the character of Falstaff is open to other constructions,
and that a very different picture of Shakespeare's temperament
might in any case have been drawn if the concentration had
been upon other dramatic characters, such as Edmund or Titus
Andronicus or Lady Macbeth.

Ben Jonson's personality, it was agreed, was quite contrary to
that of Shakespeare and was not amiable at all. The contrast
was sometimes expressed in relation to the two dramatists'
characteristic comic techniques, which were explained by reference not primarily to dramatic or generic convention but rather
to authorial temperament. Here again is Corbyn Morris.

> *Johnson* by pursuing the most useful Intention of *Comedy*, is in
> Justice oblig'd to *hunt down* and *demolish* his own Characters.
> Upon this plan he must necessarily expose them to your *Hatred*,
> and of course can never bring out an amiable Person. . . . But *Shake-*
> *spear*, with happier insight, always supports his Characters in
> your *Favour*.[21]

Jonson's compulsion to hunt down and demolish his own dramatic characters seems, in this analysis, attributable as much to authorial temperament as to the demands of dramatic convention. Shakespeare is perceived as having quite another nature, happily sustaining his dramatic characters as he no doubt in real life sustained his friends and colleagues. "One exalted, the other debased, the human species," declared "Horatio" (significantly so-called) in *The Gentleman's Magazine* in 1772, speaking of the qualities of Shakespeare and Jonson. "You despise Bobadil, though he makes you laugh. You wish to spend a jolly evening with Falstaff, tho' you cannot esteem him."[22]

The character and disposition of the two playwrights themselves had long been the subject of confident speculation. "He was a Man of very free Temper, and withal blunt, and somewhat haughty to those, that were either Rivals in *Fame*, or Enemies to his Writings," wrote Gerard Langbaine of Ben Jonson in 1691, "otherwise of good Sociable Humour, when amongst his Sons and Friends in the *Apollo*."[23] The adjectives favoured by Langbaine are worth pondering. "Haughty": none of Jonson's contemporaries, so far as I am aware, ever used this word (at least in print) to describe him, but from the 1690s "haughty" is used repeatedly in relation to Jonson's character, being joined before long by another tenacious adjective, "morose." Sir Thomas Blount liked Langbaine's description of Jonson well enough to repeat it verbatim in 1694.[24] Now Jonson has a female character called Haughty in his comedy *The Silent Woman*, whose protagonist is named, of course, Morose. Dryden's Neander in the *Essay of Dramatic Poesy* declared that he had been assured "from divers persons that Ben Jonson was actually acquainted with such a man" as Morose, "one altogether as ridiculous as he is here represented." By the 1750s this story has changed: W. R. Chetwood now affirmed that Jonson had modeled the character of Morose on himself and had actually played the part in the theater. This identification of the temperament of the author with that of his own dramatic creation survives into modern times in Edmund Wilson's Freudian essay of 1948 entitled "Morose Ben Jonson."[25]

By the eighteenth century the contrastive epithets are well in place: Jonson is not merely haughty and morose, but crabbed, pedantic, slow, grudging, sour, saturnine, envious, and splenetic. Shakespeare was regularly seen as generous, loving, open, quick, and amiable: not merely as a national genius, but also as a thoroughly nice man. "It is highly gratifying to an Englishman," declared a writer in the *European Magazine* in 1793, "to ob-serve, that every new discovery tends to confirm the opinion that Shakespeare was as estimable for the goodness of his private life, as he was superior in genius to every one of his contempo-raries."[26] The two portraits were mutually dependent and mutu-ally sustaining, the view of Shakespeare's character being elaborated in contradistinction to that of Jonson, like Henry Fielding's contrastive portraits of Tom Jones and Bliful, or Sheri-dan's of Charles and Joseph Surface, in *The School for Scandal.* How did these largely fictitious portraits of Shakespeare and Jonson ever develop, and how were they made plausible?

Part of the answer lies in the remarkable publishing history of that enigmatic text which came to be known as Jonson's *Conversations with William Drummond of Hawthornden.*[27] These are the notes made by the Scottish poet William Drum-mond of remarks that Ben Jonson had made when he stayed with Drummond in Scotland over the winter of 1618–19. These frequently cryptic, telegrammatic, asyntactical jottings were quite clearly not intended for publication, but as rudimentary aides-memoires, to remind Drummond of some of the gossip and literary opinions that his famous and at times perturbing houseguest had voiced in his cups at Hawthornden. We cannot judge the tone, we do not know the context, of Jonson's seem-ingly laconic verdicts upon Shakespeare that Drummond scrib-bled down—"That Shakesperr wanted Arte"; "Sheakspear in a play brought in a number of men saying they had suffered Ship-wrack in Bohemia, wher yr is no Sea neer by some 100 Miles" (lines 50, 208–10)—but for eighteenth-century readers they were sufficient to establish the fact of Jonson's malevolence towards his great contemporary. It is important to realize that Drum-mond appears to have made no attempt to publish these notes, which did not see the light of day until 1711, nearly a century after Jonson's walk to Scotland. Drummond's editor, Bishop Sage, took some liberties with the text he chose to publish, running together, for example, the two quite separate comments about Shakespeare just quoted, and adding a few words of his own: "He said, Shakespear wanted Art, *and sometimes Sense;* for in one of his Plays he brought in a Number of Men, saying they had suffered Ship-wrack in Bohemia, where is no Sea near by 100 Miles."[28]

This, however, was a trifling amendment compared with that which was made in 1753 in a volume entitled *The Lives of the Poets of Great Britain and Ireland* attributed to Theophilus

Cibber but actually the work of a literary hack named Robert Shiels, who had worked as an amanuensis for Dr. Johnson in the preparation of his *Dictionary.* In composing *The Lives of the Poets* Shiels simply took over material from wherever he could find it, plundering the work of earlier literary historians and adding certain flourishes of his own. In his chapter on Ben Jonson, Robert Shiels quotes the passage that Drummond writes towards the end of the *Conversations,* after Jonson has finally left Hawthornden and is heading back to London.

> He is a great lover and praiser of himself, a contemner and Scorner of others, given rather to lose a friend, than a Jest, jealous of every word and action of those about him (especiallie after drink which is one of the Elements in which he liveth) a dissembler of ill parts which raigne in him, a bragger of some good that he wanteth, thinketh nothing well bot what either he himself, or some of his friends and Countrymen hath said or done. he is passionately kynde and angry, carelesse either to gain or keepe, Vindicative, but if he be well answered, at himself. (680–89).

This is the most detailed and suggestive account of Ben Jonson's personality that has come down to us. To interpret the passage one needs to remember the somewhat prim character of William Drummond himself and the occasion of the two men's encounter; it is necessary also to observe the fine balance of Drummond's reckoning, what is reluctantly admired, not merely deplored, in that "passionately kynde and angry, careless either to gaine or keepe, Vindicative, but if he be well answered, at himself." Overriding this balance, Shiels chooses to add a few words of his own, keeping the passage still within quotation marks, as though he were still simply relaying Drummond's firsthand observations:

> In short, he was in his personal character the very reverse of Shakespear, as surly, ill-natured, proud and disagreeable, as Shakespear with ten times his merit was gentle, good-natured, easy and amiable.[29]

How did Shiels know, or imagine he knew, that Shakespeare had these qualities? Why is Shakespeare invented after this fashion in the eighteenth century? Very little in fact is known about the personality of William Shakespeare, and it is precisely this absence of information that has traditionally prompted conjecture of every variety, from the radically skeptical to the way-

wardly anecdotal and the romantically novelistic. It is one of
the more curious ironies of literary history that the fullest, most
plausible, and most heavily relied-upon references to Shakespeare's personality are made by Ben Jonson himself; and that
the greatest stumbling block to those who wish to argue that
"Shakespeare" was not really Shakespeare but Bacon or Oxford
has always been the clear and unambiguous testimony of his
friend and colleague Ben Jonson.[30] One clue to the eighteenth-
century interpretation of Shakespeare may lie in that passage
from Jonson's *Discoveries* that, for its incidentally critical remarks, was often quoted as evidence of Jonson's malevolence
towards Shakespeare: "He was (indeed) honest, and of an open,
and free nature: had an excellent *Phantasie;* brave notions, and
gentle expressions: wherein hee flow'd with that facility, that
sometime it was necessary he should be stop'd" . . . (655–59).
"Gentle" is a word that Jonson uses repeatedly of Shakespeare,
as in his verses designed to accompany the frontispiece of
Shakespeare's First Folio in 1623:

> This Figure, that thou here seest put,
> It was for gentle Shakespeare cut.
>
> (*Ungathered Verse,* 25.1–2)

The word occurs again in Jonson's poem "To the Memory of My
Beloved, The Author, Mr William Shakespeare, and What he
Hath Left Us" (*Ungathered Verse,* 26), which stands at the head
of the commemorative poems in the same Folio: "Yet must I
not give Nature all: Thy Art, / My gentle *Shakespeare,* must
enjoy a part" (55–56). The word appears once more in the pre-
liminary pages of the Folio in the address "To the Great Variety
of Readers," signed by John Heminge and Henry Condell, but
as Steevens first suspected, possibly drafted in part by Jonson
himself: Shakespeare, "as he was a happie imitator of Nature,
was a most gentle expresser of it. His mind and hand went together. . . ."[31] Thus launched into the critical vocabulary, the
word "gentle" recurs repeatedly in later tributes to Shakespeare
and forms an important ingredient in the eighteenth-century
concoction of the dramatist's personality. It is perhaps worth
pausing, however, to ask what Jonson may have meant when
he called Shakespeare "gentle," for I suspect that the primary
reference is not to Shakespeare's mildness of manner (as the
eighteenth century believed) or to his station in life, but rather
to his fluency of composition. The word "gentle" in the seven-

teenth century was commonly used of a river that was neither torpid nor in torrent, but that flowed steadily. Shakespeare himself uses the word in this way in *Lucrece:* "Deep woes roll forward like a gentle flood" (1118). One of the commonest remarks made about Shakespeare in the seventeenth century was that his writings flowed with miraculous fluency; and it is this point that I believe Ben Jonson, like other seventeenth-century commentators, is primarily intending when he uses the word "gentle" in relation to his beloved friend.[32]

In eighteenth-century appropriations of the adjective by Shakespearian admirers, the Jonsonian origins and inflections of the word are quite ignored, as are the obvious warmth and affection with which Ben Jonson customarily speaks of his great contemporary: "for I lov'd the man, and doe honour his memory (on this side Idolatory) as much as any" (*Discoveries*, 654–55). That warmth is clearly apparent in Jonson's poem to the memory of Shakespeare that stands at the head of the 1623 folio, a poem that was widely read in the seventeenth and eighteenth centuries and was deeply influential in shaping opinion about the nature of Shakespeare's genius.[33]

It is a poem that employs the comparative and contrastive methods of syncrisis on a grand and generous scale, ranking Shakespeare against a whole series of possible rivals, past and present, English and classical, allowing him to emerge triumphant as a writer second to none, a single star blazing in the literary firmament. The poem begins in deliberate hesitation, registering suspicion of both indiscriminate praise and comparative judgment. A minor Oxfordshire poet named William Basse had written a memorial elegy for Shakespeare in which he called upon learned Chaucer and rare Beaumont "to lie / A little nearer Spenser, to make room, / For Shakespeare in your threefold, fourfold tomb." Jonson ridicules this bid to make the English poets roll over in the great bed of fame to make room for Shakespeare, whom he sees instead as a living author: "My Shakespeare, rise." Like Martial hailing Juvenal as *Iuvenale meo*, Jonson subtly implies an intimacy with his fellow poet beyond the reach of envy, beyond the need for comparison. The poem constantly denies the comparisons that it seems to propose.

> That I not mixe thee so, my braine excuses;
>   I meane with great, but disproportion'd *Muses:*
> For, if I thought my judgement were of yeeres,
>   I should commit thee surely with thy peeres,

And tell, how farre thou didst our *Lily* out-shine,
  Or sporting *Kid*, or *Marlowes* mighty line.
And though thou hadst small *Latine*, and lesse *Greeke*,
  From thence to honour thee, I would not seeke
For names; but call forth thund'ring *AEschilus*,
  Euripides and *Sophocles* to us,
Paccuvius, Accius, him of Cordova dead,
  To life againe, to heare thy Buskin tread,
And shake a Stage: Or, when thy Sockes were on,
  Leave thee alone, for the comparison
Of all, that insolent *Greece*, or haughtie *Rome*
  Sent forth, or since did from the ashes come.
                              (*Ungathered Verse*, 26. 25–40)

Modern readers may wonder why Jonson selected the not-very-well-known names of the Roman tragedians Pacuvius and Accius in this passage. Jonson would have remembered that Pacuvius and Accius are formally compared by Quintilian in a chapter in the *Institutes of Oratory* in which Quintilian practices syncrisis extensively, bringing several pairs of authors together for comparative assessment; and that the comparison of Pacuvius and Accius had subsequently become a commonplace of classical criticism.[34] Syncrisis is the art that Jonson recalls, and despite his apparent diffidence ("if I thought my judgement were of yeeres, / I should commit thee surely with thy peeres"), practices throughout this passage, moving through a series of witty and generous comparisons to his supreme tribute: "He was not of an age, but for all time!" (1.43). No one in 1623 had ever praised Shakespeare in those terms, declaring him so firmly to be a writer equal or superior to any of the ancients, a writer "for all time."[35]

By the Restoration, however, Dryden could characterize this poem as "an insolent, sparing, and invidious panegyric."[36] Always ready to commit Shakespeare and Jonson against each other, Dryden helped through this verdict to perpetuate the notion of a warfare between the two poets that existed even after Shakespeare's death. Those lines about Shakespeare's small Latin and less Greek were seen in the eighteenth century as clinching evidence of Jonson's malevolence in disparaging Shakespeare's gifts in order to brag about his own, and they helped in turn to fashion a further contrast, between the formidably learned Jonson and the untutored genius, Shakespeare—a contrast we now know to have been greatly exaggerated.[37] Jonson in writing these lines may have remembered Quintilian's advice about how to praise another person: begin (says Quintilian) by mentioning the person's disadvantages, then go on to say how he overcame them: as for example, he was a small man, but very brave.[38] Jonson is saying: Shakespeare was not a classical scholar, did not aim to outgo the ancients, but despite this, he exceeded them all. It is a serious and profound tribute. During Shakespeare's lifetime, as I have already suggested, Jonson was ready in some sense to vie with his rival, to test, sometimes humorously, his practice against that of Shakespeare. Jonson's memorial poem is deeply marked by Jonson's own ways of thinking about literature, and by his authorial presence. But it is not, as Dryden thought, a contestive poem. It is instead, ironically, the very cornerstone upon which the eighteenth-century construction of Shakespeare was to proceed.

The anxiety of influence is often thought to flow from the past, imposing a burden upon the present. The Bloomian model is patrilinear: sons fret about the great achievements of their fathers, which they can surely never hope to match. Feminists have looked quizzically at this model; Virginia Blain once suggested, only half-humorously, that women writers might find encouragement in the example of their aunts.[39] The sketch I have drawn of the evolving reputations of Jonson and Shakespeare raises another sort of question about the model that Bloom and Bate propose, for the present, as well as the past, imposes its burdens. Sons may struggle against the achievements of their fathers, but siblings also contest with one another. Martial and Juvenal, Jonson and Shakespeare, Dryden and Milton, Fielding and Richardson, Browning and Tennyson, Auden and Eliot, Murdoch and Lessing, such pairs of authors write in the knowledge that, whether they wish it or not, their work may be comparatively judged and they themselves may be viewed as eager or hostile competitors. Sometimes these pressures lead to friendship and sometimes not. In France, the relationships of Racine and Corneille, Rousseau and Voltaire, Sartre and Camus—writers whose work was routinely contrasted and compared—were marked by genuine tension and mutual dislike. In England, James Fenton, Professor of Poetry at Oxford, was formally challenged in 1994 by Adrian Mitchell to a Public Poetry Bout: a two-hour contest, beginning with a twenty-five-minute reading by each poet, followed by some "shorter, wilder bouts . . . culminating in a flying exchange of insulting couplets and a farewell exchange by each fighter." "Shake hands and come out reciting," cried the challenger ringingly.[40] Such bardic postures may or may not be rooted in personal antagonism; they have their rhetorical precedents and their own opportunities for self-advertisement and fun.

Jonson's relationship with Shakespeare was no doubt complex and at times uneasy. He was an independent and opinionated writer, and in his prologues and epilogues, inductions and choruses, he commented freely on the practice of his great contemporary. Some of Jonson's allusions to Shakespeare, "the tother youth," are teasing; others seriously assert his own contrastive beliefs and principles, clearing a space for his own creative work. The notion of Jonson's warfare with Shakespeare and of his moroseness, malignity, and envy, was (however) an eighteenth-century invention, an intrinsic part of the simultaneous construction of the modern idea of "Shakespeare." Vigorously denied by Gifford, the mythology continued to flourish throughout the nineteenth century, forming an aspect of the burdensome past with which modern criticism has had to contend.[41]

NOTES

1. "Shakespeare," in *The Poems of Matthew Arnold*, ed. Kenneth Allott (London: Longmans, 1965), 49. This essay builds on the arguments of Samuel Schoenbaum in *Shakespeare's Lives* (Oxford and New York: Clarendon Press, 1970), and "Shakespeare and Jonson: Fact and Myth," in *Elizabethan Theatre*, ed. David Galloway (Hamden, Conn.: Archon Books, 1970), 5:1–19.

2. C. H. Herford and P. and E. Simpson, eds., *Ben Jonson*, 11 vols. (Oxford: Clarendon Press, 1925–52); u/v and i/j spellings and u.c./l.c. regularized. All references are to this edition.

3. *The Works of Ben Jonson*, ed. William Gifford and Francis Cunningham, 3 vols. (London, 1904), 1:415; *Ben Jonson*, ed. Herford and Simpson, 10:17. The best modern edition of *Epicoene*, by R. V. Holdsworth, New Mermaids (1979; reprint, New York: W. W. Norton, 1990), identifies "the tother youth" as Shakespeare.

4. *Works*, ed. Gifford and Cunningham, 1:415.

5. *Juvenal and Persius*, trans. G. G. Ramsay, Loeb edition (London and New York: Harvard University Press, 1930); Martial, *Epigrams*, trans. Walter C. A. Ker, Loeb Classical Library, 2 vols. (London and Cambridge: Harvard University Press, 1968). On the verb "commit," used in its Latin sense, see *OED*, 9.

6. *"Longinus" on the Sublime*, ed. D. A. Russell (Oxford: Clarendon Press, 1964), 12.2–13 (Plato and Demosthenes, Demosthenes and Cicero), 32.8 (Lysias and Plato); Quintilian *Institutes of Oratory* 10.1.93, 98, 101, 105; Cicero *Brutus* 43. At Christ's Hospital the young Coleridge was taught by the Reverend James Bowyer to discriminate in this way: "He early moulded my taste to the preference of Demosthenes to Cicero, of Homer and Theocritus to

Virgil, and again of Virgil to Ovid": *Biographia Literaria*, chap. 1. Plutarch's "Parallel Lives" of Greeks and Romans further encouraged the comparative habit. See Friedrich Focke, "Synkrisis," *Hermes* 58 (1923): 327–68. (I am grateful to Dr. Gordon Howie and Professor Peter France for advice about this figure.)

7. John Dryden, *Of Dramatic Poesy and Other Critical Essays*, ed. George Watson, 2 vols. (London: J. M. Dent, 1962), 2 : 71–155; Samuel Johnson, "Pope," *The Lives of the English Poets*, ed. George Birkbeck Hill, 3 vols. (Oxford: Clarendon Press, 1905), 3 : 220–23. Pope himself was to reflect shrewdly on the critical custom of matching Shakespeare against Jonson in the preface to his edition of *The Works of Shakespeare*, 6 vols. (1725), 1 : xi.

8. Thomas Dekker, *Satiromastix*, ed. Josiah H. Penniman (Boston and London: D.C. Heath and Co., 1913), 5.2.163ff.

9. Thomas Fuller, *The History of the Worthies of England* (1662), "Warwickshire," 126.

10. Thomas Carlyle, *Historical Sketches of Notable Persons and Events in the Reigns of James I and Charles I* (London: Chapman and Hall, 1902), 77.

11. Schoenbaum, *Shakespeare's Lives*, 294–96; I. A. Shapiro, "The Mermaid Club," *Modern Language Review* 45 (1950): 6–17.

12. Dryden, *On Dramatic Poesy*, ed. Watson, 1 : 70. For the comparison between Homer and Virgil see ibid., 2 : 36, 144, 166–67, 186, 204, 274–77; between Virgil and Ovid, 2 : 21f.; between Horace and Juvenal (and Persius), *Discourse Concerning the Original and Progress of Satire*, ibid., 2 : 71–155, passim. G. E. Bentley, *Shakespeare and Jonson: Their Reputations in the Seventeenth Century Compared*, 2 vols. (Chicago: University of Chicago Press, 1945). See also D. H. Craig, ed., *Ben Jonson: The Critical Heritage* (London and New York: Routledge, 1990).

13. J. F. Bradley and J. Q. Adams, *The Jonson Allusion-Book* (1922; reprint, New York: Russell and Russell, 1971), 412, 415, 91; Sir Nicholas Le Strange, *Merry Passages and Jeasts: A Manuscript Jestbook*, ed. H. F. Lippincott (Salzburg: English Language and Literature Institute,, 1974), 19.

14. Rosalind Miles, *Ben Jonson: His Life and Work* (London and New York: Routledge and Kegan Paul, 1986), x.

15. Thornton S. Graves, "Jonson in the Jest Books," in *Manly Anniversary Studies in Language and Literature* (Chicago: University of Chicago Press, 1923), 127–39.

16. L. C. Knights, *Explorations* (New York: Stewart, 1947), 1–39.

17. For different rhetorical purposes, Virginia Woolf was later to wonder, "what would have happened had Shakespeare had a wonderfully gifted sister, called Judith, let us say": *A Room of One's Own* (1928), chap. 3.

18. Stuart Tave, *The Amiable Humorist* (Chicago: University of Chicago Press, 1960), chap. 6; R. W. Babcock, *The Genesis of Shakespeare Idolatory, 1766–1799* (Chapel Hill: University of North Carolina Press, 1931).

19. *I Henry IV* 2.4.450; Jeremy Collier, *A Short View of the Immorality and Profaneness of the English Stage* (London, 1698), 154.

20. Corbyn Morris, *An Essay Towards Fixing the True Standards of Wit, Humour, Raillery, Satire, and Ridicule* (London, 1744), 26–27.

21. Ibid., 33–34.

22. *The Gentleman's Magazine*, 42 (1772): 522.

23. *An Account of the English Dramatic Poets* (Oxford, 1691); see Bradley and Adams, *The Jonson Allusion-Book*, 431.

24. *De Re Poetica* (1694): *The Jonson Allusion-Book*, 444.

25. Dryden, *Of Dramatic Poesy*, ed. Watson, 1:71; [W. R. Chetwood], *The British Theatre* (Dublin, 1750), 26; Edmund Wilson, *The Triple Thinkers* (Harmondsworth: Penguin Books, 1962), 240–61.

26. *The European Magazine*, xxiv (1793), 185.

27. Part, but not all. The contrasts are already apparent in Nicholas Rowe's "Some Account of the Life &c. of Mr William Shakespear" in his edition of *The Works of William Shakespear*, 6 vols. (London, 1709), volume 1.

28. William Drummond of Hawthornden, *Works* [ed. J. Sage and T. Ruddiman] (Edinburgh, 1711), 225 (emphasis mine).

29. Theophilus Cibber [Robert Shiels], *The Lives of the Poets of Great Britain and Ireland* (London, 1753), 1:241.

30. For some characteristic wrestling with this problem, see Sir George Greenwood, *Ben Jonson and Shakespeare* (London: C. Palmer, 1921) (Jonson's poem to Shakespeare celebrates not Shakespeare but the syndicate of unnamed learned men, including Bacon, who wrote his works); Gerald H. Rendall, *Ben Jonson and the First Folio Edition of Shakespeare's Plays* (Colchester: Benham and Co., 1939) (the earl of Oxford wrote Shakespeare's plays, as Jonson well knew, and the folio verses are lapwing); and Alden Brooks, *This Side of Shakespeare* (New York: Vantage Press, 1964) (Shakespeare merely polished the plays of others and got them performed; Jonson's verses are trying to tell us as much).

31. *The First Folio Edition of Shakespeare*, prepared by Charlton Hinman, The Norton Facsimile (New York: W. W. Norton, 1968). Schoenbaum is dismissive of Steevens' theory: *Shakespeare's Lives*, 278. But there are several markedly Jonsonian turns of phrase in the address "To the Great Variety of Readers": compare in particular Jonson's *Epigrams* 1, 3, 18; *Bartholomew Fair*, Ind. 85–112; "Ode, to Himself" ("Come leave the lothed stage," Herford and Simpson, 6:492–94), 1–6; *Ungathered Verse*, 8 ("To the Worthy Author, Mr John Fletcher"). The imagery of (textual) dismemberment and reimbodiment is paralleled in Jonson's dedication of *Sejanus* to Esmé Stuart, Lord Aubigny, in the 1616 folio. Jonson's famously dissenting views on Shakespeare's scarcely blotted papers are registered in *Discoveries*, 647ff.

32. See *OED*, "gentle" 6b. Cf. Suckling, *Fragmenta Aurea, &c.*, 1646: "The sweat of learned *Johnson's* brain, / And gentle *Shakespear's* eas'er strain"; Sir John Denham, commendatory verses on John Fletcher, 1647: "Yet what from *Johnsons* oyle and sweat did flow, / Or what more easie nature did bestow / On *Shakespears* gentler Muse" (cf. Denham's wish that his own writing emulate the passage of the Thames: "Though deep, yet clear, though gentle, yet not dull," *Cooper's Hill*, 189ff.): Margaret Cavendish, Duchess of Newcastle, "General Prologue to All My Playes," *Playes* (1662): "Yet Gentle *Shakespear* had a fluent Wit, / Although less Learning, yet full well he writ"; Richard Flecknoe, *A Short Discourse*, 1664: "Comparing [Jonson] with *Shakespear*, you shall see the difference betwixt Nature and Art; and with *Fletcher*, the difference betwixt Wit and Judgement: Wit being an exuberant thing, like *Nilus*, never more commendable than when it overflowes; but Judgement, a stayed and reposed thing, always containing it self within its bounds and limits." See *The Shakespere Allusion-Book*, comp. C. M. Ingleby, L. Toulmin Smith, P. J. Furnivall, ed. John Munro, 2 vols. (London: Oxford University Press, 1932), 1:407, 504; 2:134, 85. "Sweet," another standard epithet in later

tributes to Shakespeare, may owe its currency to Jonson's "Sweet Swan of Avon!" (line 26)—a phrase directly echoed by subsequent writers.

33. The best accounts of the poem are those of T. J. B. Spencer in *The Elizabethan Theatre IV*, ed. G. R. Hibbard (London and Basingstoke: Macmillan, 1974), 22–40; Richard S. Peterson, *Imitation and Praise in the Poems of Ben Jonson* (New Haven: Yale University Press, 1981), chap. 4; Lawrence Lipking, *The Life of the Poet* (Chicago: University of Chicago Press, 1981), chap. 3; Sara van den Berg, *The Action of Ben Jonson's Poetry* (Newark: University of Delaware Press, 1987), chap. 6.

34. Quintilian *Institutes of Oratory* 10.1.97; Horace *Epistles* 2.1.56.

35. See my essay "Not of an Age': Jonson, Shakespeare, and the Verdicts of Posterity," *Georgia State Literary Studies* 14 (1995):

36. "A Discourse Concerning the Original and Progress of Satire," in *Of Dramatic Poesy*, ed. Watson, 2:75.

37. T. W. Baldwin, *Shakespere's Small Latine and Lesse Greeke*, 2 vols. (Urbana: University of Illinois Press, 1944); Emrys Jones, *The Origins of Shakespeare* (Oxford: Oxford University Press, 1977).

38. Quintilian *Institutes of Oratory* 3.7.10.

39. Harold Bloom, *The Anxiety of Influence: A Theory of Poetry* (New York: Oxford University Press, 1973); W. Jackson Bate, *The Burden of the Past and the English Poet* (Cambridge, Mass.: Belnap Press, 1971); Virginia Blain, "'Thinking Back Through Our Aunts': Harriet Martineau and the Female Tradition," *Women: A Cultural Review* 1 (1990): 223–39. See also Christopher Ricks's critique of these theories, "Allusion: The Poet as Heir," *Studies in the Eighteenth Century, III*, ed. R. F. Brissenden and J. C. Eade (Toronto: University of Toronto Press, 1976), 209–40.

40. *The Independent* (London) 20 August 1994, 1.

41. Octavius Gilchrist's temperate and well-reasoned essay of 1808, "An Examination of the Charges Maintained by Messrs Malone, Chalmers, and Others, of Ben Jonson's Enmity, &c. Towards Shakespeare," was followed by Gifford's acerbic essay ironically entitled "Proofs of Ben Jonson's Malignity, From the Commentators on Shakespeare," prefixed to his edition of the *Works of Ben Jonson* in 1816. Gifford was an unfortunate champion of Jonson. He invented an absurd theory about Drummond's "treachery" in luring Jonson to Hawthornden and then betraying his confidential remarks about Shakespeare. Critics such as Hazlitt appear to have disliked Ben Jonson partly at least because they could not abide his editor: see "Mr. Gifford" in *The Spirit of the Age*, in William Hazlitt, *Complete Works*, ed. P. P. Howe, after the edition of A. R. Waller and Arnold Glover (London: J. M. Dent and Sons, 1931), 11:114, 115, 125; "On Shakspeare and Ben Jonson," *Complete Works*, 6:30–49. For modern reassessments of the relationship between the two dramatists, see S. Musgrove *Shakespeare and Jonson*, The Macmillan Brown Lectures (1957; reprint, Folcroft, Penn., Folcroft Library Editions, 1975); Jonas A. Barish, ed., *Ben Jonson: A Collection of Critical Essays* (Englewood Cliffs, N.J., 1963); introduction, Ian Donaldson, ed., *Jonson and Shakespeare* (London and Basingstoke; Macmillan, 1983); Anne Barton, *Ben Jonson: Dramatist* (Cambridge: Cambridge University Press, 1984); Russ McDonald, *Shakespeare and Jonson: Jonson and Shakespeare* (Lincoln: University of Nebraska Press, 1988); and of course Schoenbaum (note 1, above).

The Presence of the Playwright, 1580–1640

ALEXANDER LEGGATT

On the opening night of Noel Coward's *Home Chat* in 1927 the play was booed. Coward leapt to the stage and confronted the audience. A voice came out of the auditorium—"We expected a better play"—to which Coward retorted, "And I expected better manners."[1] The story illustrates not just the vagaries of fame but the strong presence of the playwright in twentieth-century theater. The custom of the playwright's facing public judgment on opening night was well established. Coward was known to his audience, and the responsibility for the play's failure was laid on his shoulders: he had established a reputation and was expected to live up to it. The importance of playwrights can be seen in other ways as well. Adjectives like Shavian, Chekhovian and Pinteresque show how firmly certain writers set their distinctive marks on the theatrical occasion. Did the playwrights in what we now think of as the Age of Shakespeare have anything like this presence? They were evidently not expected to face the public directly, as Coward was. In the prologue to his *If This Be Not a Good Play, the Devil Is In It*, Thomas Dekker suggests that it might be a good idea if they were:

> Would t'were a Custome that at all New-playes
> *The Makers* sat o'th'*Stage*, either with *Bayes*
> To haue their Workes Crownd, or beaten in with *Hissing*.
>
> (1–3)[2]

He goes on to claim that this would weed out the second-raters. In a letter of 1699 John Dryden describes the listing of Congreve's name on the playbill of *The Double Dealer* as unprecedented. No playbills for the period before the closing of the theaters have survived, but Gerald Eades Bentley has suggested that—given Dryden's long experience and the institutional con-

130

servatism of theater—on those playbills too the author's name was probably omitted.[3] Thomas Nashe's tribute to the emotional impact of the death of Talbot in *1 Henry VI* credits "the tragedian that represents his person" but makes no mention of the author who wrote the scene.[4] That very author, in prologues and epilogues, puts the onus on the actors for the success or failure of the piece; they, not the playwright, are in the front line: "What here shall miss, our toil shall strive to mend" (*Romeo* prologue, 14); "If we shadows have offended" (*Midsummer Night's Dream* epilogue, 1); "We'll strive to please you every day" (*Twelfth Night* 5.1.408). Throughout *Henry V* the Chorus sees the play as a collaboration between the actors' efforts and the audience's imagination. Only in the epilogue does the "bending author" (2)—bowing to the public, bent over his manuscript, or just keeping his head down?—emerge as the party responsible. He does not appear and he is never named. When we turn to the printed drama, we find—especially in the period before 1600—many title pages that reproduce what must have been the audience's sense of the play in performance: they name the acting company but not the author. This way of seeing the performance can be roughly equated to the perceptions of the twentieth-century moviegoer: anyone who follows the movies can name the stars of a popular big-studio picture; only a few specialists can say who wrote the screenplay.

Around the turn of the century, however, we see a change in the printed drama, and given the likelihood of a certain overlap between playreaders and playgoers this may reflect a change in audience perception as well. On title pages, which booksellers would have used to entice purchasers, the names of playwrights become increasingly common. Between 1591 and 1600 fifty-five plays are published with no reference to the author on the title page, seven identify the author only by initials, and twenty-three identify him by name. Between 1601 and 1610 the number of title pages that omit the author's name holds fairly steady at fifty-eight; title pages giving only the author's initials drop to three; while title pages that name the author leap to sixty-five, almost treble the number for the previous decade.[5] *Tamburlaine the Great*, first published in 1590, is, strictly speaking, an anonymous play. Shakespeare's earliest published plays are anonymous, but his name starts to appear on title pages in 1598. In fact, it appears on three title pages in that year, the same year as Francis Meres's tribute in *Palladis Tamia*. By 1608, on the title page of the Quarto of *King Lear*, Shakespeare gets star bill-ing: the largest print is reserved for his name, which appears over the title of the play. Ben Jonson receives similar treatment on the title pages of *Volpone* (1607) and the first version of the 1609 Quarto of *The Case is Altered.*

In the early years of the new century, the awareness of playwrights, not just as a growing collection of names that will sell books, but as a community of writers who know each other's work and are prepared to support each other, emerges in the growing custom of affixing commendatory verses to printed plays. The custom implies an assumption that endorsement from a colleague means something, not just to the recipient but to the reading public as well. Bentley assumes that commendatory verses were normally not freewill offerings but were solicited by the authors.[6] Webster's claim, prefixed to the 1623 Quarto of *The Devil's Law-Case*, that several of his friends have offered him verses that he has turned down, may be evidence to the contrary, or it may be corroborating evidence if we take it that Webster is boasting of an unusual kind of support. As we get into the later Jacobean and Caroline periods, commendatory verses become to a great extent a matter of routine. In the earlier years, however, they emerge at points of crisis, when a playwright has had a serious failure and needs his colleagues to rally round in support against the common enemy, the audience. Coward, flinging his counterattack into the auditorium, was following an old tradition; these playwrights go one stage further, taking the reader as a final court of appeal before whom the author's colleagues will plead his case. The 1605 Quarto of Jonson's *Sejanus* has seven commendatory poems, whose authors include George Chapman and John Marston. Chapman glances at the play's failure with the audience but does not dwell on it; instead he praises the play, in lofty terms and at length, as a poem. Marston, in a six-line tribute, praises the style in particular: *"For neuer English shall, or hath before / Spoake fuller grac'd."*[7] Both endorse Jonson's sense of himself as a literary artist. The 1611 Quarto of *Catiline* has three commendatory poems, all by playwrights: Beaumont, Fletcher, and Nathan Field. Field's support is predictable; he was a Son of Ben and an actor in some of his plays. Beaumont and Fletcher are more surprising, and their presence suggests that patterns of loyalty within the community do not always depend on affinities of style. (Jonson himself could make common cause with a puppet show if a Puritan attacked it.) In this case there is a stronger sense of a group of playwrights who appreciate that one of their number is trying to set standards, even at the cost of popular failure. Beaumont writes,

If thou had'st itch'd after the wild applause
Of common people, and had'st made thy Lawes
In writing, such as catch'd at present voyce,
I should commend the thing, but not thy choyse.
But thou hast squar'd thy rules, by what is good;
And art three Ages yet, from understood.

(1–6)

"I should commend the thing": Beaumont admits that he appreciates a popular success written to a formula (he and Fletcher are beginning a string of such successes) but he is glad that Jonson aims higher. Fletcher and Field do Jonson the compliment of borrowing one of his poses, expressing contempt for the vulgar taste of the audience.

Jonson, together with Field, Beaumont, and Chapman, had already performed the same service for Fletcher in the Quarto of *The Faithful Shepherdess* (undated, but likely between 1608 and 1610). This has been described as "the only play of nearly seventy in the Fletcher canon which shows clearly that the author was concerned in its publication."[8] He saw himself as setting literary standards: his epistle to the reader offers instruction in the principles of pastoral tragicomedy, prefaced by the warning, "If you be not reasonably assurde of your knowledge in this kinde of Poeme, lay downe the booke or read this, which I would wish had bene the prologue."[9] You can't understand the play without the theory. Of the playwrights who support Fletcher, it is Chapman who recognizes this literary ambition most clearly: "A Poeme and a play too! why tis like / A scholler that's a Poet." The audience is of course unworthy—"This Iron age that eates it selfe, will never / Bite at your golden world"— but his fellow writers appreciate what he is trying to do: "Your poeme onely hath by us applause" (3–4, 27–28, 20). Beaumont concentrates on the stupidity of the audience, joining with Fletcher against the common enemy. Given the tensions and frustrations of performance, there are times when any artist, however successful, hates the audience, and Beaumont's verse has the effect of settling a number of old scores:

One company knowing they judgement lacke,
Ground their beliefe on the next man in blacke:
Others, on him that makes signes, and is mute,

Some like as he does in the fairest sute,
He as his mistress doth, and she by chance,
Nor wants there those, who as the boy doth dance
Betweene the actes, will censure the whole play:
Some like if the wax lights be new that day:
But multitudes there are whose judgments goes
Headlong according to the actors clothes.

(19–28)

Jonson too would complain, in the induction to *Bartholomew
Fair*, about the audience's tendency to take their opinions from
each other; but Beaumont, defending a fellow playwright who
is trying to create a literary drama, is particularly nettled by the
way they look for things other than the script. Jonson not only
castigates the audience but does so in terms that suggest he was
present, or at least heard reports: the audience "had, before /
They saw it halfe, damnd thy whole play" (7–8). He then adopts
the ceremonial role of priest of the muses, promising that the
play's martyrdom will secure its lasting fame. Field presents
himself in a more informal role, as a beginning playwright
whose "muse (in swathing clowtes) / Is not yet growne to
strength" (2–3) but whose ambition is

To live to perfect such a work, as this,
Clad in such elegant proprietie
Of words, including a morallitie
So sweete and profitable. . . .

(10–13)

In contrast to Jonson's formality, Field presents his verse as public confirmation of what he has already said to Fletcher in private (7–8).

Webster, so far as the public record shows, faced the failure
of *The White Devil* alone. But his "Epistle to the Reader," with
its claim that he has "truly cherish'd my good opinions of other
men's worthy labours" and its listing of other playwrights, may
have purposes that run deeper than the ostensible one of proving
that Webster himself is not given to detraction. Webster praises
"the full and height'ned style of Master Chapman, the labour'd
and understanding works of Master Jonson: the no less worthy
composures of the both worthily excellent Master Beaumont,
and Master Fletcher: and lastly (without wrong last to be named)
the right happy and copious industry of Master Shakespeare,
Master Dekker, and Master Heywood. . . ."[10] He is trying, I

think, to evoke the community of playwrights, to gather himself into their company, showing he has studied his fellows' work and can discriminate among their different types of achievement. He knows a thing or two about playwriting, and the failure of *The White Devil* is not to be laid at his door. Beneath the assertion we may detect another feeling: at this time of failure, he needs company. Company emerges to celebrate the success of *The Duchess of Malfi*, which has commendatory verses by Middleton, Rowley, and Ford. As John Russell Brown notes, while Ford commended other plays, Middleton and Rowley appear in this role nowhere else.[11]

The titles of poems commonly address the recipient, with variations, as "dear friend." We may suspect a routine courtesy, like the modern "let's do lunch." But sometimes relationships are established in a more particular and discriminating way. In commendatory verses to Richard Brome's *The Northern Lass* (1632), John Ford calls himself "the *Authors* very Friend" but Dekker makes a deeper claim, addressing "my Sonne BROME."[12] Dekker and Jonson were on bad terms, and part of Dekker's way of dealing with this seems to have been to strike Jonsonesque poses; here he claims Brome as one of the Tribe of Tom. Jonson tops this with a more particular claim: "I had you for a Seruant, once, *Dick Brome*" (1). He goes on to praise Brome for rising to the rank of fellow playwright "By observation of those Comick Lawes / Which I, your *Master*, first did teach the Age" (7–8).

The authors also present themselves as playgoers, interested in each other's work in performance. John Ford, whose commendatory verses are usually so general that they pass through the reader's mind without leaving any residue, takes extra trouble over Massinger, praising the power of *The Roman Actor* to inspire the reader's theatrical imagination—"Hee may become an Actor that but Reades" (14)—and the ability of *The Great Duke of Florence* to inspire the actors: "Action *gives many Poems right to live,* / This Piece *gave life to* Action" (1–2).[13] (In the ongoing reassessment of Massinger's work, Ford's tribute to his ability to write for actors deserves special consideration.) Commending *Women Beware Women*, the minor playwright Nathaniel Richards, having agreed with the sentiments expressed in the title, adds, "I that have seen't can say, having just cause, / Never came tragedy off with more applause" (11–12).[14] Middleton pays tribute to the emotional impact of *The Duchess of Malfi* in performance: "For who e'er saw this Duchess live,

and die, / That could get off under a bleeding eye?" (17–18).
Rowley's tribute to the heroine's eloquence seems likewise
based on performance: "I never saw thy duchess till the day /
That she was lively body'd in thy play" (25–26). This may mean
that Rowley saw the play before he read it; and since Rowley
makes a point of this, a fair inference would be that writers
commonly read each other's work before it was performed.

Some writers impose their own identities on the routine of
commendatory verses, revealing more about themselves than
they say about the work in question. Jonson, characteristically,
presents himself as a judicious and critical reader of Joseph Rut-
ter's pastoral tragicomedy *The Shepherds Holy-day:*

> I have read,
> And weigh'd your *Play:* untwisted ev'ry thread,
> And know the woofe, and warpe thereof. . . .
>
> (13–15)

Chapman imposes himself in a different way, offering Jonson
incongruous praise for *Volpone:* "Thou hast no earth; thou
hunt'st the *Milke-white way;* / And, through th'*Elisian* fields,
dost make thy traine" (7–8). The image sits oddly on Jonson's
comic villain-hero, who is so at home in his earth; but it would
suit the aspiring heroes of Chapman's own tragedies. It may
even be that Chapman has seen a quality in the play that eludes
most of us.

For those of us who have in our heads a twentieth-century
pecking order for these playwrights, there are other surprises in
the ways they view each other. We would not lump Shakespeare
with Dekker and Heywood so casually as Webster does, and
we wonder about his omission of Middleton and Marston. (Did
private-theater specialists belong to a different club?) Jonson sin-
gles out Beaumont as the only playwright among the named
good people addressed in the *Epigrams,* and gives him a special
place in the memorial ode to Shakespeare:

> I will not lodge thee by
> *Chaucer,* or *Spenser,* or bid *Beaumont* lie
> A little further, to make thee a roome. . . .
>
> (19–21)

Other playwrights are listed as Shakespeare's beaten rivals; only
Beaumont is put in such august company. That this high valua-
tion of Beaumont was not just a peculiarity of Jonson's is indi-

cated by Humphrey Moseley's "The Stationer to the Readers," prefixed to the 1647 Beaumont and Fletcher Folio, where the praise lavished on Beaumont is significantly warmer than that reserved for his colleague.[15] Beaumont's high standing may explain the otherwise curious designation of the plays in this collection as "Beaumont and Fletcher," when his own contribution was relatively small. Fletcher's standing, too, was higher than it is now. His death in 1625 does not seem to us a major event; but several writers refer to it with a sharp sense of loss that appears to go beyond the conventional routine of commemoration.[16]

Phoebe Sheavyn has issued a proper warning about commendatory verses, and it applies also to the prologues and epistles into which our discussion has strayed: "The custom of writing commendatory verses to be prefixed to one another's works was a matter of fashion rather than evidence of genuine literary approval. They served the purpose nowadays filled by excerpts from critical reviews appended to dust jackets and advertisements."[17] Nevertheless, this material does create the sense of a community of authors, presenting themselves to the public *as* a community, expecting their names to mean something. Within this community we glimpse networks of relationship and patterns of judgment that are occasionally surprising. What cannot always be taken at face value, of course, is the constant expression of mutual esteem. It is not just in contemporary showbusiness (or academe) that "let's do lunch" is the prelude to a knife under the fifth rib. Communities have their tensions, and these too can surface in print—as they do early in the period, in Greene's notorious attack on the upstart crow Shakespeare. Jonson aimed at the same target, good-humoredly enough, in the prologue to the revised *Every Man in His Humour*, with its jibes at *Henry V* and "*Yorke*, and *Lancasters* long iarres" (11), and in the promise that there will be no servant-monster in *Bartholomew Fair*. The ode to himself on the failure of *The New Inn* is closer to Greene's bitterness in its complaint that the public prefers "some mouldy tale, / Like *Pericles*" (21–22). Jonson himself comes in for some teasing. Marston assures the readers of *Sophonisba* (1606) that "To transcribe authors, quote authorities, and translate Latin prose orations into English blank verse, hath, in this subject, been the least aim of my studies."[18] The 1605 Quarto of *Sejanus* would be fresh in memory; Marston had contributed verses to it, but relations with Jonson had evidently soured—or were about to. Jonson's pretension (as it seemed) in publishing his "Works" in the Folio of 1616 was still an issue when Heywood wrote the epistle "To the Reader" for *The English Traveller* (1633): "True it is, that my plays are not exposed unto the world in volumes, to bear the title of works, (as others); one reason is, that many of them by shifting and change of companies have been negligently lost; others of them are still retained in the hands of such actors, who think it against their peculiar profit to have them come in print; and a third, that it never was any great ambition in me, to be in this kind voluminously read."[19] Heywood claims to think of his plays as scripts for a working theater, not as literature. Much recent twentieth-century criticism of the drama of this period echoes this view. We have seen, however, that Jonson was not alone in resisting it. The support he got from Chapman, Marston, Beaumont, Fletcher, and Field, and Fletcher's own ambitions for *The Faithful Shepherdess*, suggest a group effort to raise drama to the ranks of literature. Similar battles are fought later in the period. In his commendatory verses to Brome's *A Jovial Crew* (1652) James Shirley takes aim at William Cartwright's 1651 *Works*, weighed down with over fifty epistles. In a poem prefixed to his own play *The Weeding of Covent Garden* (1658) Brome attacks the pomposity of Suckling's printing of *Aglaura* in Folio: "Give me the sociable pocket books. / These empty folios only please the cooks."[20]

This is what appears in print. There must have been plenty of carping and sniping in private. We have a glimpse of it in Ben Jonson's conversations with Drummond of Hawthornden: "that Sharpham, Day, Dicker, were all Rogues. . . . that Francis Beaumont loved too much himself & his own verses. . . . he had many quarrells with Marston beat him & took his Pistol from him." Since this is not only the fullest such record we have but virtually the only one, it has contributed to Jonson's reputation for arrogance and bad temper (though it should be noted that Drummond records praise as well, including a tribute to *The Faithful Shepherdess* that aligns Jonson's private opinion with his public one). Jonson, however, is not the only writer to turn curmudgeonly; he himself is attacked in two manuscript poems by his erstwhile friend George Chapman, one a long and vitriolic invective, the other a surly epigram. And of course we will never know what we have lost. If it were possible for us to wire certain rooms in Jacobean London, we might hear Fletcher complaining he's had it up to *here* with Heywood and his inverted snobbery, or Shakespeare declaring that if Jonson offers him one more pedantic correction he's going to drown him in a butt of Canary and then plead benefit of clergy.

In this survey of the self-presentation of the playwright there is one great presence and one great absence. The presence of course is Jonson; it has been impossible to discuss this subject without referring to him over and over again. To use Dryden's phrase, from another context, you track him everywhere in the snow. His presence is not just massive but detailed. Particular criticisms of him—his slowness of composition, his railing— become running gags. Jonson refutes both accusations in the Apologetical Dialogue appended to *Poetaster*, and refutes them again in the prologue to *Volpone*. Every time he refutes them he recalls them. In his commendatory verses to the Beaumont and Fletcher Folio, Brome can still get mileage out of the contro- versy surrounding the Jonson Folio thirty years earlier, and out of Jonson's reputation for labored composition:

> *While this of* Fletcher *and his* Works *I speake:*
> *His* Works *(says* Momus*) nay, his* Plays *you'd say:*
> *Thou hast said right, for that to him was Play*
> *Which was to others braines a toyle. . . .*[21]

Complimenting him, his colleagues adopt Jonsonian attitudes. This appears particularly in the commendatory verses to *Vol- pone*, where Beaumont, Fletcher, and Field dwell so much on the incompetent judgments of the audience that one would think the play had been a popular failure. In his contribution to *Jonsonius Virbius*, a collection of mostly turgid elegies pub- lished on Jonson's death, Jasper Mayne recalls, yet once more, the old accusation of slow composition (49–52). He goes on to reiterate, in terms Jonson himself might have used, the program of theatrical realism proclaimed in the *Every Man in* prologue:

> Thy *Scaene* was free from *Monsters*, no hard *Plot*
> Call'd downe a *God* t'untie th'unlikely *knot*.
> The *Stage* was still a *Stage*, two entrances
> Were not two *parts* o'th' *World*, disjoyn'd by *Seas*.
> Thine were *land-Tragedies*, no Prince was found
> To swim a whole *Scaene* out, then o'th' *Stage* drown'd.
>
> (79–84)

Among the possible targets of mockery in the last couplet one could list that moldy tale, *Pericles*.

Jonson cast a long shadow, and it lingered after his death. He is also virtually alone among playwrights of this period in making himself a recurring figure in his own work.[22] There are personal appearances, just offstage, by the belligerent author who kicks the stagekeeper around the tiring house for offering to rewrite *Bartholomew Fair*, and the more desperate figure who haunts the induction to *The Staple of News*, dealing with his opening-day nerves by pacing up and down, sweating profusely, tearing the playscript, and finally getting drunk, putting himself "*to silence in dead* Sacke"(72). Noel Coward again:

> if you lose hope
> Take dope
> And lock yourself in the John,
> Why must the show go on?[23]

It is Jonson who anticipates the later custom of calling the playwright before the curtain on opening night. There is no call (and no curtain) and so he brings himself forward as part of the script. In his later years he takes care to present his career as a whole, and to say to an audience that is in danger of forgetting him, "Here I am again." The prologue to *The New Inn* declares, "*We ha' the same Cooke, / Still, and the fat*" (3–4); the prologue to *The Sad Shepherd* introduces the author as "*He that hath feasted you these forty yeares*" (1). The induction to *The Magnetic Lady* presents the play as the summation of Jonson's career, closing up the circle that began with the humor comedies (99–106).

There was a private Jonson as well as a public one. The fat cook of the *New Inn* prologue is succeeded in the epilogue by a pathetic invalid: "*The maker is sick, and sad*" (4). Years earlier, Carlo Buffone, invading the induction to *Every Man Out of His Humour*, said of the wine he was drinking, "This is that our *Poet* calls *Castalian* liquor, when hee comes abroad (now and then) once in a fortnight, and makes a good meale among Players, where he has *Caninum appetitum:* mary, at home he keeps a good philosophicall diet, beanes and butter milke" (334–39). The private Jonson, writing alone in his study, appears most vividly in the Apologetical Dialogue appended to *Poetaster*, where the "Author" calls a writer's works "Things, that were borne, when none but the still night, / And his dumbe candle saw his pinching throes" (212–13), and describes the personal cost: "I, that spend halfe my nights, and all my dayes, / Here in a cell, to get a darke, pale face" (233–34). He claims, characteristically, that he can ignore the insults heaped on him, being one who "Doth yet so liue, although but to himselfe, / As he can safely scorne the tongues of slaues" (25–26). Just as characteristically, in claiming at length to be indifferent to criticism he shows he is really obsessed by it. In the end he commands,

> Leaue me. There's something come into my thought,
> That must, and shall be sung, high, and aloofe,
> Safe from the wolues black iaw, and the dull asses hoofe.

His interlocutor Nasutus creeps out (backwards, we imagine) with the words, "I reuerence these raptures, and obey 'hem" (237–40). Jonson's aloofness and his stoic indifference to opinion are put on public display in a naked appeal for admiration. Jonson is never so much a presence in the literary community as when he claims to be alone.

The great absence is Shakespeare. Aside from a brief, graceful reference to Marlowe in *As You Like It*, Shakespeare does not comment on other writers' work. He writes no commendatory verses, unless one counts *The Phoenix and the Turtle*, which shows him "in the unfamiliar role of nonce poet."[24] He gathers no commendatory verses for himself, and in fact seems to have taken no interest in the publication of his own plays. There was "no great outpouring of homage" at his death, and apart from Jonson's famous ode the commendatory verses to the 1616 Folio offer slim pickings, nothing like the flood of tributes that greeted the collected works of Beaumont and Fletcher and the now-forgotten William Cartwright.[25] The few contemporary hints about his personality describe a friendly, amiable man.[26] But when it comes to the public literary record, while Jonson proclaimed his aloofness Shakespeare remained genuinely aloof. When Greene attacked him he did not (so far as we know) spring to his own defense; it was Henry Chettle, who had prepared Greene's work for publication, who defended him, making a handsome public apology, praising Shakespeare's "uprightness of dealing, which argues his honesty, and his facetious grace in writing, that approves his art."[27]

We have seen a community of playwrights making themselves public figures, commenting on each other's work, creating a guild of artists self-conscious about their aims and ambitions. But when we look for the playwright who for us ought to be at the center of this community he vanishes like the Cheshire cat, leaving only the impression of a genial smile. What was his attitude to the business of being a playwright? Two of the sonnets, 110 with its lament, "I have gone here and there / And made myself a motley to the view" (1–2), and 111 with its complaint about depending on "public means which public manners breeds"(4), can be read as conveying a dislike of theatrical work, but the phrasing is just cryptic enough to prevent a decisive interpretation. Jonson makes a public show of his love of privacy; Shakespeare describes his in such a way as to preserve that privacy.

Are the plays any help? The practice of inferring Shakespeare's opinions from the statements of his characters is so thoroughly discredited it must be due for a revival; but until that happens we are left to see how authorship (dramatic authorship if we can find it, but also authorship in general) is presented in his plays, and to draw what speculative conclusions we can. In *Bartholomew Fair*, though he tries to hide his identity until he sees how the play takes (5.3.23–24), it is clear that Littlewit is the author of the puppet play, and Jonson characteristically holds him accountable for what he does to the Hero and Leander story. In Jonson, authors are public figures who have to take what is coming to them, be it praise or blame. With Shakespeare's plays within the play the situation is otherwise. The Hecuba play and *The Murder of Gonzago* are anonymous, and we never know what comes of Hamlet's plan to add a speech to the latter. The show of fairies in *The Merry Wives of Windsor*, Hymen's pageant in *As You Like It*, and *The Taming of the Shrew* in its capacity as an entertainment for Christopher Sly, are all anonymous. In *Love's Labor's Lost* we may imagine Berowne as the author of the masque of Russians, since he prompts Moth when the latter dries; but we are given no certain evidence. We may imagine Holofernes and Nathaniel as authors of show of the Nine Worthies, as they are of the closing songs. But they are never actually named as such. Is Peter Quince the author of *Pyramus and Thisbe?* Bottom expects him to write a ballad of his dream, and when they are struggling with rehearsal difficulties Bottom's command, "Write me a prologue, and let the prologue seem to say we will do no harm with our swords" (3.1.16–17), seems aimed at Quince. But the phrasing of Quince's reply is oddly evasive: "Well, we will have such a prologue; and it shall be written in eight and six" (3.1.23–24). It is as though Quince does not like to think of himself as an author, and retreats to the passive voice to conceal the notion of agency (as Macbeth does when he contemplates the killing of Duncan).

Even if Quince does the rewrites, we are still not certain that he wrote the original play. If he did, he seems oddly unfamiliar with his own script: he tangles the punctuation of the prologue, and it takes him a moment to realize that Flute is speaking all his part at once, cues and all. In fact the only play-within-the-play of whose authorship we can be absolutely certain is the Boar's Head tavern play, which has no script and is improvised by the actors.

These studies in authorial absence go along with a sense that writing itself is a private matter. The one author in Shakespeare who is a sociable being is the Poet in *Timon of Athens*, who engages in the chit-chat of the artistic salon—the Painter asks him, "When comes your book forth?" (1.1.26)—and who presents a theory of his art that sounds like a parody of Jonson's view of Shakespeare as flowing too freely, in need of restraint:

> A thing slipp'd idlely from me.
> Our poesy is as a gum which oozes
> From whence 'tis nourish'd. The fire i' th' flint
> Shows not till it be strook; our gentle flame
> Provokes itself and like the current flies
> Each bound it chases.
>
> (1.1.20–25)

Is this the closest Shakespeare comes to self-caricature? (Other possibilities, characteristically teasing, include William the slow-witted country boy of *As You Like It* and the William we find picking up a small bit of Latin in *Merry Wives*.) Among the shifting intentions of the *Timon* script, Shakespeare seems to have had some initial difficulty making up his mind about the Poet. There are two versions of the work he presents to Timon; one is straight flattery, the other a serious warning. But by the last act the Poet has clearly become one of the play's scoundrels. He is a writer with public manners, who makes himself a motley to the view; and the portrait is not flattering.

In *Titus Andronicus*, Tamora and her sons interrupt Titus in his study, invading the privacy of an author who is penning a revenge tragedy in which they will have leading roles:

> Who doth molest my contemplation?
> Is it your trick to make me ope the door
> That so my sad decrees may fly away,
> And all my study be to no effect?
> You are deceiv'd; for what I mean to do

See here in bloody lines I have set down:
And what is written shall be executed.

(5.2.9–15)

This may be the central image of authorship in Shakespeare: a study so private that only the startling word "molest" can describe the invasion of that privacy. And we may raise (though not answer) the question, Whose blood is Titus using? His own? If so, we may have the reason why writing is so private. It is acutely personal. We recall Ibsen's pronouncement that to write is to sit in doomsday judgment on oneself. (Ibsen was another writer who guarded his privacy and was notoriously evasive in answering questions about his work.) But we do not know if it is Titus's blood, and the image characteristically eludes final interpretation.

Another discredited critical practice is that of seeing *The Tempest* as Shakespeare's commentary on his own art; but this one has to be discredited over and over, because it keeps coming back. Suppose—just for a moment—that Prospero is Shakespeare, Miranda represents the people closest to him in his personal life, and Ariel is his art. Miranda has no relationship with Ariel, a point Shakespeare emphasizes by having Prospero put her to sleep before calling up the spirit. So far as we can tell, she does not even know that Ariel exists. Though Ariel appears to other characters, it is never in the form in which he appears to Prospero; and Prospero's surrender of Ariel seems to be a precondition for his final return to the human family. But while the play provokes such interpretations, it also resists them; enigmatic and elusive, it will not lock into a single shape and as we try to allegorize it we sense that we are betraying it. Shakespeare may have thought like this, it seems to say, but you won't catch him admitting it. He stands as aloof as the Antonio of Auden's *The Sea and the Mirror.* Jonson leaves his tracks everywhere; Shakespeare covers his.[28]

NOTES

1. Sheridan Morley, *A Talent to Amuse: A Biography of Noel Coward* (1969; reprint, Harmondsworth: Penguin Books, 1974), 138.

2. Fredson Bowers, ed., *The Dramatic Works of Thomas Dekker*, vol. 3 (Cambridge: Cambridge University Press, 1958).

3. *The Profession of Dramatist in Shakespeare's Time, 1590–1642* (Princeton: Princeton University Press, 1971), 60–61.

4. *Pierce Penniless his Supplication to the Devil*, cited in S. Schoenbaum, *William Shakespeare: A Compact Documentary Life*, rev. ed. (New York and Oxford: Oxford University Press, 1987), 160.

5. Figures are based on the information in volumes 3 and 4 of E. K. Chambers, *The Elizabethan Stage*, 4 vols. (Oxford: Clarendon Press, 1923). Not included in the count are masques, entertainments, Latin plays, translations, and editions whose dates are uncertain.

6. Bentley, *Profession*, 277, 287.

7. All references to Jonson and (except where otherwise noted) his literary record are to C. H. Herford and Percy and Evelyn Simpson, eds., *Ben Jonson*, 11 vols. (Oxford: Clarendon Press, 1925–52).

8. Bentley, *Profession*, 277.

9. Unless otherwise specified, references to material attached to the plays of Fletcher and his colleagues are to Fredson Bowers, ed., *The Dramatic Works in the Beaumont and Fletcher Canon*, 8 vols. (Cambridge: Cambridge University Press, 1966–92), in progress.

10. John Webster, *The White Devil*, ed. John Russell Brown (London: Methuen, 1960), 4.

11. John Webster, *The Duchess of Malfi*, ed. John Russell Brown (Cambridge: Harvard University Press, 1964), 4. Later references to the commendatory verses are to this edition.

12. Richard Brome, *The Northern Lasse*, ed. Harvey Fried (New York: Garland Publishing, 1980), 8–9.

13. Philip Edwards and Colin Gibson, eds., *The Plays and Poems of Philip Massinger* (Oxford: Clarendon Press, 1976), 3:19, 105.

14. Thomas Middleton, *Women Beware Women*, ed. J. R. Mulryne (London, Methuen, 1975), 3.

15. Arnold Glover and A. R. Waller, eds., *Beaumont and Fletcher* (Cambridge: Cambridge University Press, 1905), 1:xiv.

16. See Richard Brome's commendatory verses to the 1647 Folio (ibid., 1:lv), the prologue to *The Loyal Subject*, and the emotionally worded tribute by the actors John Lowin and Joseph Taylor in their dedicatory epistle to *The Wild-Goose Chase*.

17. Phoebe Sheavyn, *The Literary Profession in the Elizabethan Age*, 2d ed., rev. J. W. Sanders (Manchester: Manchester University Press, 1967), 141.

18. Macdonald P. Jackson and Michael Neill, eds., *The Selected Plays of John Marston* (Cambridge: Cambridge University Press, 1986), 401.

19. A. Wilson Verity, ed., *Thomas Heywood* (London, 1888), 154.

20. Richard Brome, *The Weeding of Covent-Garden and The Sparagus Garden*, ed. Donald S. McClure (New York: Garland Publishing, 1980), 43.

21. Glover and Waller, eds., *Beaumont and Fletcher*, 1:lv.

22. I have discussed Jonson's presence in his own work more extensively in *Ben Jonson: His Vision and His Art* (London and New York: Methuen, 1981), 199–232.

23. *The Lyrics of Noel Coward* (Woodstock, N.Y.: Overlook Press, 1973), 357.

24. Schoenbaum, *Life*, 328.

25. S. Schoenbaum, *Shakespeare's Lives: New Edition* (Oxford: Clarendon Press, 1991), 27, 29.

26. Schoenbaum, *Life*, 255.

27. Cited in ibid., p.154.

28. In constructing this picture of a Shakespeare who guards his privacy as an author, I am aware of the point reiterated throughout Schoenbaum, *Shakespeare's Lives*, that portraits of Shakespeare tend to be self-projections on the part of their creators. To say more would involve discussing my own attitude to authorship, and I would rather not do that.

"All Is True": Negotiating the Past in *Henry VIII*

ANNABEL PATTERSON

> Wherein we are to crave pardon that we may plainelie declare
> and tell the truth: for in all histories the perfect and full
> truth is to be alwaies opened, and without it the same wan-
> teth both authoritie and credit: . . . And yet the philosophers
> are of the opinion, that we ought to reverence so the higher
> powers in all maner of offices and dueties, as that we should
> not provoke nor moove them with anie sharpe speeches or
> disordered languages. . . . Wherfore it is a dangerous thing to
> speake evill against him, though the occasion be never so
> just, as who can foorthwith avenge the same. . . . It were
> surelie a verie happie thing, and that which I confesse pas-
> seth my reach, if a man intreating of princes causes might
> tell the truth in everie thing, and yet not offend them in
> anie thing.
>
> —"Holinshed's" *Chronicles* (1587), 2:29

LOOKING FOR "AN HONEST CHRONICLER"

Of all the half-truths about Shakespeare that have hardened
into dogma, one of the most misleading concerns the relation
of his history plays to the work known as "Holinshed's" *Chronicles*. This essay will set the record straight at least for the last
of Shakespeare's English histories, *Henry VIII* or *All Is True*.
This play has always been something of an embarrassment to
Shakespeareans, as is fully admitted and partly circumvented
by Samuel Schoenbaum's canny introduction to his Signet edition.[1] By virtue of its late date, *Henry VIII* denies to *The Tempest* chronological finality to add to its sense of symbolic
farewell. Because of its emphasis on pageantry and comparatively flat characterization, critics who find *Henry VIII* unworthy of Shakespeare invoke either the convenient theory of

collaboration (John Fletcher becomes responsible for the least interesting scenes), or that of time-serving (Shakespeare was drawn into the competition to celebrate the marriage of James's daughter Elizabeth to the Elector Palatine). Finally, the unusual dependence of the playtext on the actual words of the 1587 Chronicles[2] raises the frightening specter of creativity in abeyance, or other baser notions incompatible with the premise of genius. Shakespeareans therefore attempt to exorcise this specter by pointing to scenes for which the Chronicles give no mandate (such as Queen Katherine's intervention on behalf of the protesting clothworkers who have been put out of work by Cardinal Wolsey's unconstitutional new taxes), or claiming that the play condenses the disordered largesse of Holinshed into a tightly focused and causally satisfying drama.[3]

This orthodoxy has survived the discovery that Henry VIII is a cleverer play, more sophisticated and ironic in its approach to court politics and ceremonial, than the collaborationists or occasionalists believed. Since Geoffrey Bullough published his Narrative and Dramatic Sources of Shakespeare in the early 1960s, no one has reinvestigated the assumptions—indeed, the evidence—on which this defense of Shakespeare's inventiveness was constructed; and almost no one has seriously inspected the conceptual implications of that alternative title, All Is True. Stanley Wells and Gary Taylor print the play under the title All Is True and, on the basis of contemporary witnesses to the fatal performance of the play that resulted in the burning of the Globe, reject the Folio's solution that "transforms the play's subject matter into its title." They do not, however, venture any comment on what the title might mean, or how it might relate to Shakespeare's late return to the material of the chronicles.[4] Julia Gasper wisely aligns All Is True with a spate of plays about Tudor history that followed the Essex rebellion, Dekker and Webster's Sir Thomas Wyatt, Heywood's If You Know Not Me You Know Nobody, and Samuel Rowley's When You See Me You Know Me, and suggests that its title "may have been meant to suggest that it is less unhistorical than its predecessors." She notes, however, that "signs of the authors' creative license are visible in it everywhere."[5] But both these positions seem to me to be lacking in reach, implying a naiveté on the part of Shakespeare and his audiences on the subject of truth in general, and historiographical veracity in particular, that is most unlikely to have been sustainable by the second decade of the seventeenth century. In place of the Wells and Taylor position, I propose that in choosing "All Is True" as his title Shakespeare himself transformed its true subject matter—the nature of historical truth—into one of those proverbial sayings, like "All's Well That Ends Well," whose aphoristic status required interrogation. And whereas Julia Gasper disapproves of "unhistorical" elements in the play, especially because of the claims for superior veracity she sees in the title, I suggest that Shakespeare was not only mocking such claims, but selecting a subject that helped to explain, in historical terms, why historical objectivity was (both tragically and comically) hard to come by: that is to say, the coming of the Reformation to England.

There is, however, one significant precedent for thinking in this way. In 1984 Judith Anderson published a long essay entitled "Shakespeare's *Henry VIII:* The Changing Relation of Truth to Fiction," in which she observed that "thrice in thirty-two lines, the Prologue to the play mentions 'truth' explicitly," and in such a qualified way, including the phrase "chosen truth," as to render it suspect. Either, Anderson suggests, the Prologue is at variance with the title, or should the play that follows turn out to have ambiguous or contradictory contents, "the very notion of objective truth [will be] thereby subjected to examination." "In this last case," she added, "the claim that 'all is true' becomes not false, but ironic, as indeed I take it truly to be."[6] This essay, however, was published in her monograph on the art of biography in Tudor-Stuart writing, and seems to have missed the attention of Shakespeareans. Moreover, although our views of Shakespeare's intentions are very similar, the other heroes of Anderson's story are Cardinal Wolsey and his early biographers, especially, as we shall see, Cavendish and Stow; while mine are Raphael Holinshed and Abraham Fleming, the chroniclers most directly responsible for constructing the version of the Henrician Reformation that became *All Is True*, with all its ambiguities.

My epigraph itself derives from the 1587 *Chronicles*. Originally written by the medieval chronicler Giraldus Cambrensis in his *Expugnatio Hibernica*, which he presented to Henry II in 1188 and re-presented to King John, it was translated by the lawyer and constitutional historian John Hooker to form part of his continuation of the history of Ireland. Giraldus raises an issue that was no less critical for an Elizabethan chronicler, and its warnings were shown to be well taken in January 1587, when the second edition of the *Chronicles* was called in by the Privy Council on the grounds that it contained "reporte of matters of

later yeeres that concern the State, and are not therfore meete to be published in such sorte as they are delyvered."[7]

But that Shakespeare at the end of his career was meditating on problems of historiographical veracity that go beyond the merely prudential may be inferred from the conversation between Queen Katherine, now close to death, and her gentleman usher, Griffith, on the subject of Cardinal Wolsey's life and death. As Katherine admits, after she has allowed Griffith to rebalance her own hostile account of Wolsey with some of his virtues and genuine achievements:

> After my death I wish no other herald,
> No other speaker of my living actions
> To keep mine honour from corruption,
> But *such an honest chronicler* as Griffith.
> Whom I most hated living, thou hast made me,
> With thy religious *truth* and modesty,
> Now in his ashes honour: . . .
>
> (4.2.69–75; italics added)[8]

The *Chronicles* give no specific mandate for this statement of Katherine's, nor for this dramatic exchange between herself and Griffith. Yet conceptually they provide almost everything else necessary to the scene, its specific vocabulary being only one aspect of the dilemma there represented, in cogent if preanalytic form. For what Shakespeare had before him as he wrote was a lively representation of how historians diverge on the issue of evaluation, and how strenuous is the pull of ideological bias.

In their commentaries for the Arden and Cambridge editions respectively, Reginald Foakes and John Margeson refer to "Holinshed" as if Raphael Holinshed were the author or "writer" of all the material relating to Wolsey; whereas in fact the 1587 edition of the *Chronicles* that Shakespeare used is a far more complicated production, as a careful analysis of Katherine's exchange with Griffith will demonstrate. Katherine's negative account of Wolsey, which begins her debate with Griffith, is taken from a passage at the very end of the *Chronicles'* assessment of the cardinal's career:

> This cardinall (as you may perceive in this storie) was of a great stomach, for he compted himselfe equall with princes, & by craftie suggestion gat into his hands innumerable treasure: he forced little on simonie, and was not pittifull, and stood affectionate in his owne

opinion: in open presence he would lie and saie untruth, and was double both in speach and meaning: he would promise much & performe little: he was vicious of his bodie, & gave the clergie evill example.[9]

Katherine begins her tirade, "He was a man of unbounded stomach," and Foakes remarks that "stomach" is "Holinshed's word." Likewise, Margeson annotates "One that by *suggestion* tied all the kingdom," by stating that "Shakespeare uses Holinshed's word from the source passage." In fact, as the marginal note in the 1587 edition makes clear, this passage was imported by Abraham Fleming from Edward Hall's *Union of the Two Noble Families of Lancaster and York*, (194).

When Griffith moderates Katherine's opinion by citing the better aspects of Wolsey's record, he cites a passage for which Raphael Holinshed actually was responsible, secondarily. In the 1577 edition he had followed his brief account of Wolsey's death with an evaluation taken from Edmund Campion's history of Ireland:

I thinke (sayth he) some Princes basterd, no Butchers sonne, exceeding wise, faire spoken, high minded, full of revenge, vitious of his body, loftie to his enimies, were they never so bigge, to those that accepted and sought his friendship wonderfull courteous, a ripe scholeman, thrall to affections, brought a bedde with flatterie, insaciable to gette, and more princely in bestowing, as appeareth by hys two Colledges at Ipswich and Oxeford, the one overthrowen with his fall, the other unfinished, and yet it lyveth for an house of Studentes, considering all the appurtenances incomparable through Christendome, wherof Henry the eigth [sic] is now called founder, bycause he let it stand. ... *in commendum* a greate preferrer of his servauntes, an advauncer of learning, stout in every quarrell, never happy till this hys overthrow. Therein he shewed such moderation, and ended so perfectly, that the houre of his death did him more honour, than all the pomp of hys life passed. Thus farre Campion.[10]

This passage from Campion (via Holinshed) appears at the *beginning* of Abraham Fleming's summation of Wolsey's career in 1587, again clearly marked in the margin "The description of cardinal Wolseie, set downe by Edmund Campian" (3:917). And between the Jesuit Campion's positive assessment and the Protestant Edward Hall's hostile one,[11] Fleming had inserted a much longer passage about Wolsey, from what is perhaps the most important of all the "sources" of *Henry VIII*: George Cavendish's *Life and Death of Cardinal Wolsey*, which was originally

intended, in part, as a refutation of Hall's account of Wolsey.
Fleming did not know this early biography as such, however. For
immediately after the passage from Campion, he added: "Here it
is necessarie to adde that notable discourse, which I find in
John Stow . . ." and proceeded to give his source marginal credit:
"Abr. Fl. ex. I.S. pag. 904, 905, &c." (917)—that is to say, Stow's
*Chronicles of England, from Brute unto this present yeare of
Christ, 1580,* where the passage in question appears at the begin-
ning of a biographical account of Wolsey.

John Stow did not claim to be the "author" of this material.
In his own *Chronicles* for the year 1516, he wrote:

> And heere I thinke good to set downe some part of the proceedings
> of this so oft named Thomas Wolsey, Archbishop, his ascending
> unto honorious estate, and sodeine falling againe from the same, as
> I have bin enformed by persons of good credite. (904).

In the middle of his narrative, however, Stow slipped in a paren-
thesis ("sayeth myne Author," 939), which reveals him to have
been working from a written text.[12] But if one compares his
account with Cavendish's own version (of which an autograph
manuscript survives),[13] it is clear that Stow edited as he wrote,
omitting not only all traces of Cavendish's personal relationship
with Wolsey, but also anything inconvenient to his own stance
as the respectable citizen-chronicler of Elizabethan London.

When Richard Sylvester edited Cavendish's *Life* he noted
Stow's version in the *Chronicles,* but in terms that favor the
original and do Stow little credit:

> In order that his history might not meet with official censure, the
> tailor-historian showed himself to be quite adept at drawing a fine
> seam through the pages of Cavendish's story. Every time Cavendish
> mentions Anne Boleyn or manifests his dislike for the Protestant
> cause Stowe very carefully deletes the passage. The result is a some-
> what tatterdemalion version of the *Life,* a story with its core gone
> and its tragic motif suppressed.[14]

There may be another way of interpreting Stow's interventions,
however, than merely a desire to "omit anything that might be
construed as casting doubt on the good *mores* of [Elizabeth's]
ancestors." And there is certainly another way of understanding
why Stow's version, which retains Cavendish's unmistakable
respect for the *mores* of Katherine of Aragon, was incorporated
into the 1587 edition of the *Chronicles,* where it formed the

basis of three of the scenes most crucial to *Henry VIII*—at least to the theme of the divorce: the masque of shepherds at Wolsey's house, which Shakespeare appropriated from Cavendish, via Stow, via Fleming, and made into the moment where Henry first sees and becomes captivated by Anne Boleyn; the formal trial of Katherine's marriage; and the scene with the two cardinals in her chambers that follows.

Sylvester also remarked in a footnote that "a closer examination of the uses to which the play's author[s] put the *Life* (a subject which to my knowledge has never been fully investigated) might cast additional light on the composition of the play itself" (271). Since Sylvester wrote this note in 1959, nobody has accepted this invitation except Judith Anderson, who offered an extremely detailed account of what Stow took from Cavendish and what Shakespeare took from Stow.[15] Shakespeareans, however, have continued to speak of Shakespeare's use of "Holinshed" in these three scenes, two of which, in the collaborationist account, are usually assigned to Fletcher.[16]

There is, therefore, another point to be made about Katherine's debate with Griffith on the problem of historical fairness. The passage inserted by Fleming from Cavendish via Stow (which contains, among other material, the account of the masque of shepherds) separates by a full six pages in the *Chronicles* the positive evaluation of Wolsey by Campion and the negative one by Hall. Someone highly intelligent and experienced in reading the *Chronicles* reversed their order, dramatized their disagreements, and rendered that disagreement, in terms of the philosophy of history, theoretical. None of these conditions obtained for Fletcher.

Redefining "Authorship" in the Chronicles

Paradoxically, Shakespeareans who are willing to contemplate authorial collaboration in *Henry VIII* have imposed on the *Chronicles* retrospectively the anomalous idea of single authorship, with "Holinshed" standing in for the complex process of compilation, aggregation, and ideological negotiation that, as I have just illustrated, lies behind Cardinal Wolsey's historical postmortem. Still more paradoxically, this oversimplification derives from the entirely different status that Shakespeare's plays and the *Chronicles* have acquired in the twentieth century. As Stephen Booth wrote in 1968, "we care about *Holin-*

shed's Chronicles because Shakespeare read them."[17] In other words, knowledge of the *Chronicles* is merely ancillary to Shakespeare studies, since they were merely the raw material on which genius drew. This premise was formulated much earlier by a historian, C. L. Kingsford, who was not unhappy with the notion that the *Chronicles* have in this century basked in a reputation not their own:

> It is perhaps more due to the service which he rendered to Shakespeare than to any merit of his own that Holinshed has long overshadowed Hall and Stow as an historian of the fifteenth century . . . though his *Chronicles* were a meritorious compilation . . . their greatest interest now consists in their literary associations. . . . We may feel a just pride in realizing that so much of the rude material from which Shakespeare was to construct his chief historical plays was fashioned originally in our native English speech.[18]

As a historian of historiography, Kingsford was actually more appreciative of Holinshed than some of his colleagues have subsequently been. More common is the view that the *Chronicles* were an incompetently designed, incoherent mess. As F. J. Levy put it in 1967, in what is still our most important study of Tudor historiography:

> There was [then] no conception of history writing as selective: a historian did not remake the past in his own image or in any other but instead reported the events of the past in the order in which they occurred. The criterion by which a historian was judged was the quantity of information he managed to cram between the covers of his book. . . .[19]

As distinct from Hall and Stow, who showed some restraint, Holinshed "demonstrated most fully the idea that history could be written by agglomeration." This made him "the ideal source for the playwrights; everything needful (and a great deal more) was included, but the 'construction,' the ordering of events, was left to others."[20] Thus in a mirror image of Stephen Booth's assessment, Holinshed's *Chronicles* are considered useful only for literary purposes, since by the standards by which historians judge each other today they were sadly primitive. Levy was particularly distressed about what he saw as interpretive indecision by Holinshed, a stance that "came close to abdicating responsibility altogether." "This," he added, "was to leave the reader to be his own historian."[21] In fact, as I have argued at length elsewhere, Holinshed's encouragement of the 1577 reader to be his own historian was not negligence but part of a coherent agenda: to educate Elizabethan citizens in political and legal reality. Today we would align such a program with Enlightenment thought and certain versions of liberalism.[22]

As himself a reader of the *Chronicles*, Levy was, however, aware that they could not be attributed simply to Raphael Holinshed, who was dead by the time the second edition was under way. The story of the two editions, and of those who collaborated in them, is important enough for *Henry VIII* to deserve rehearsal here. The project originated with a printer, Reyner Wolfe, who had both Thomas Cranmer and Thomas Cromwell for patrons, and had been employed as royal printer by Edward VI. It scarcely needs saying that these were distinctly Protestant connections. Wolfe conceived the idea of publishing a universal history, to be illustrated with maps and other images, and to that end acquired a considerable collection of documents in manuscript. He employed Raphael Holinshed, who was university-educated and had taken clerical orders, as an assistant in the project, especially to work on translation, but Holinshed's role evidently expanded to that of major compiler and editor. Biographically we know remarkably little about him; but from the *Chronicles* themselves we can deduce that he was especially interested in legal and constitutional history. His handsoff historiography seems to have been part of a larger set of principles, which included religious toleration, parliamentary limits to monarchical power, and a generalized theory of justice as fairness, all of which were based on the clearly stated recognition that times and institutions change, thus depriving historians of a basis for evaluative certainty.

When Wolfe died in 1576 the financing of the project was taken over by his son-in-law, John Harrison, Lucas Harrison, who had leased his shop from Wolfe, and George Bishop. No relation to these was William Harrison, who was brought in to write the "Description of England" in some haste, and Richard Stanyhurst, who wrote the matching "Description of Ireland" and completed the history of Ireland on a foundation laid down by Edmund Campion, and who was also brought into the project late in the day. The first edition covered the history of England up to 1572, of Ireland to 1547, and Scotland to 1571. When Holinshed himself died in 1580, plans had already been made to produce a new edition that would bring all three histories up to the present moment: the publishers' team expanded to include Ralph Newberie, Henry Denham, and Thomas Woodcock, while the scholarly team consisted of Abraham Fleming, John Stow, Francis Thynne, and John Hooker. William Harrison's continuing presence is recorded in the substantial alterations he made to his "Description" for the 1587 edition.

Despite some confusion as to who was in charge of the second edition, the typographical practice of marginal attribution seems to support the claims of Fleming as the actual compiler; not only because there are so many insertions marked by his initials, but also because specific materials attributed to Hooker and Stow, the other two for whom editorial status has been claimed, are represented as if by a third party. Thus Fleming typically gives in the margin a page reference to Stow's *Chronicles* preceded by his own initials, a technique that fails to distinguish Stow from, say, Edward Hall. It is necessary to understand this process, however trivial the details may seem, for the second edition not only brought history up to date, it also carefully supplemented what Holinshed had produced ten years earlier. In some touchy areas, supplementation was also, evidently, a process of negotiation between the disagreements of previous historians and different members of the team. Since many of these disagreements reflected the divisive forces unleashed by the Reformation, no area of history was more dangerous (to use the term deployed by Giraldus via Hooker) for the historian than the reign of Henry VIII, in which Fleming, as editor, was particularly active.

The men who produced the *Chronicles* (in both editions) illustrate the idea of collaboration as an agreement to disagree. With the complex exception of John Stow, they were inarguably middle class. But they had different social connections, and, more surprisingly, could be found in widely different places on the religious spectrum. Whereas Holinshed himself was urbanely moderate on the subject of religion, William Harrison and Abraham Fleming were polemical Protestants, the former a Grindalian reformer, the latter aggressively anti-Catholic. One of the five booksellers who subsidized the project, Thomas Woodcock, had been imprisoned in 1578 for selling Cartwright's Puritan *Admonition to Parliament*.[23] He had also, interestingly, transcribed his own manuscript of Cavendish's *Life*, which suggests that he was rather more than a bookseller.[24] Richard Stanyhurst, on the other hand, had been a private pupil of Campion at Oxford, with whom he returned to Ireland, and whose influence undoubtedly affected his religion. On 26 November 1580 Stanyhurst was examined by Robert Beale, secretary to the Privy Council, about a purported plot for conveying Gerald Fitzgerald, Lord Offaley, into Spain at the instigation of a Catholic priest, and briefly imprisoned.[25] Shortly afterwards he left England for the Continent, converted explicitly to Catholicism, and conspired with Catholic exiles in Flanders. As for the brilliant Jesuit scholar Campion himself, his views on Wolsey were preserved by Fleming, although it was Fleming who enthusiastically recorded Campion's execution for treason in 1581.

Francis Thynne was the son of the famous editor of Chaucer and a friend of Sir Thomas Egerton, Elizabeth's solicitor-general in the 1580s and the chief prosecutor in the case of Campion. Thynne was essentially an antiquary, a member of the Society of Antiquaries formed around William Camden. Although he has been seen as the dullest and most cautious of the team,[26] Thynne was the contributor most directly embarrassed by the censorship of the 1587 edition, during which four of the several massive catalogues of office-holders he had contributed were all deleted. His catalogue of archbishops, though largely translated from Archbishop Matthew Parker's lives of seventy bishops in *De Antiquitate Britannicae Ecclesiae*, presumably fell prey to the Privy Council's sensitivity to religious dispute.[27] Ironically, one catalogue that escaped—Thynne's list of the constables of England—contains material that is quite as sensitive, not least because Thynne had prefaced it with the following provocative statement:

> The death of this duke of Buckingham, being the last constable of England, dooth present apt place to me wherein to insert the names of all such honorable persons as have beene invested with that title of the constableship of England, an office of great account, & such as sometime was the chefest place of a temporall subject in the relme the (high steward excepted) [sic] *whose power did extend to restreine some actions of the kings.* Wherefore being now no such office (for there was never anie advanced thereunto since the beheading of this duke) I thinke it not unmeet to make some memorie of those persons possessing so high place, least both they and their office might hereafter grow in utter oblivion. (3:865–66; italics added)

It has been shown that the ancient feudal office of Constable was recognized during the late sixteenth century as a constitutional tinderbox, one that had attracted the attention of Thomas Starkey, John Ponet, and Francis Legh, another member of the

Society of Antiquaries, and that can be linked to efforts by the second earl of Essex in the 1590s to establish the office of earl marshal in similarly dangerous terms.[28] But because Thynne's catalogue of the Constables was inserted into the reign of Henry VIII, and therefore not recognized as new material when the new edition was called in January 1587, it survived for the use of Shakespeare, who turned to it with scrupulous attention for Buckingham's farewell speech.[29]

Finally there was John Stow, who liked to be known as "Citizen," and who alone of the scholarly team began life below the middle class, as apprentice to a tailor. But he was a formidable autodidact, and soon acquired a reputation as an antiquarian and bibliophile, accepted by the Society of Antiquaries. His 1565 *Summarie of Englyshe Chronicles*, though addressed to a broad citizen audience, was dedicated to Leicester. On 8 March 1603 James I published Letters Patent commending Stow for his historical labors and authorizing him to "collect, amongst our loving Subjects, theyr voluntary contribution and kind gratuities . . . having already, in our owne person, of our speciall grace, begun the largesse, for the example of others."[30] On the other hand, Stow had some skeletons in his closet. In 1568 he had been examined by the Privy Council on the charge of possessing Roman Catholic propaganda against Elizabeth; and in February 1569 a search of his house revealed "old fantastical books" with papist tendencies and "a great Parcel of old M.S. Chronicles, both in Parchment and Paper."[31] Moreover, in the preface to his *Abridgement* (1570), and as an aspect of their rivalry as producers of condensed chronicles for wider audiences, Richard Grafton had complained that Stow's *Summarie* had contributed "to the defacing of Princes doinges," and that in his account of the past "the gates are rather opened for crooked subjectes to enter into the fielde of Rebellion, then the hedges or gaps of the same stopped."[32]

In fact, although Stow was suspected of Papist tendencies in the late 1560s, his work suggests a more evenhanded sympathy with the underdog, whoever he or she might be in the weathercock religion of the day. Stow was the owner of the manuscript diary now entitled the *Chronicle of Queen Jane*, now Harley MS 194, whose main focus is the rebellion of Sir Thomas Wyatt the younger against Mary Tudor, to which the diarist is noticeably sympathetic, and he had followed this in his 1580 *Chronicles*. Given the extent to which he edited Cavendish's *Life*, we can infer something of Stow's own sympathies from the fact that he retains, for example, the speech of the captain of the London militia sent to repulse Wyatt, and who instead turned to his support:

> We go about to fight against our native Countreymen of England and our native friends, in a quarrell unrightfull. . . . Wherefore I thinke no English heart ought to say against them, much lesse by fighting to withstande them. (1079)

This speech stood for the opinions of those who opposed Mary's plans to marry Philip II and hence, it was feared, to bring England under "the rule of the proude Spanyardes." Holinshed had similarly described how the whitecoats had rebelled, crying out as they did so, "We are all Englishmen, we are all Englishmen," (4:13); and this, I would argue, was the larger message of the *Chronicles* as a whole. Since the Reformation had been launched in England by Henry VIII as a political and marital expedient, the chroniclers wished to register how extraordinarily complicated, even dangerous, life had become for subsequent generations, when every change of regime initiated a change in the official religion. What at one moment was loyalty, obedience, and piety could at the next be redefined as treason or heresy. As Francis Thynne ironically summed up the situation from the perspective of 1587 in his (subsequently censored) catalogue of archbishops:

> King Edward the sixt being thus dead, his sister Marie obtained the crowne, made alteration of religion, set the before imprisoned bishops at libertie, restored them unto their see, and displaced other appointed thereunto in hir brothers time. Which bishops having now the sword in their hand, and full authoritie, stretched the same to the execution of their lawes, burning some, banishing others, and imprisoning the third sort: whereof, some were in life reserved untill the government of queene Elizabeth, and after advanced to places of great honor.[33]

This is, evidently, the world of *Henry VIII*, and in the early seventeenth century there was more of the same to follow.

ADDING SHAKESPEARE TO THE TEAM

These, then, were the authors, separate and combined, to whom Shakespeare owed the composite account there published

of the reign of Henry VIII. Is there any reason to suppose that
the dramatist, whose care in reading the *Chronicles* is generally
accepted, regarded himself as different ontologically (a great
Author) from those who had collaborated hitherto in constructing the complex profile of the reign? My rhetorical question is addressed both to those who have defended *Henry VIII*
on the grounds of its artistic improvements on the *Chronicles*
and also to those who, like Brian Vickers, have reacted with
alarm to Foucauldian attacks on the idea of authorship and the
literary ideals of "signification, originality, unity, creation."[34]

But I do not intend this essay to be mistaken for any of the
postmodern arguments against which Vickers erects his fortifications. My argument is restricted to Shakespeare's deployment
of the English chronicle tradition in *Henry VIII*, a topic that
Vickers omits. I propose that, in returning to that tradition at
the end of his career, Shakespeare saw himself as merely one of
a series of collaborators in a never-ending process of history
writing, whose goals were public education, as much freedom
of information as the chronicler dared to supply, and a definition
of what it meant to be English that was broader and more tolerant of difference than what he had himself imagined at the beginning of his career, in the three plays of *Henry VI*.

Hence his urbane skepticism (to balance the mysticism of *The
Tempest*) as to where historical truth resides. The word "truth"
or "true" is foregrounded not only in the Prologue, in sentences
ambiguous enough to require editorial assistance, but several
times thereafter in contexts that emphasize truth's elusiveness
in the arena of political reputation. So Buckingham, sentenced
to death, claims that he is "richer than [his] base accusers, /
That never knew what truth meant" (2.1.104–5). Other examples occur in the dispute between Katherine and Wolsey in
court, when the Queen accused Wolsey of lying and he defends
himself (2.4.88–90, 101–2); in Wolsey's defense of himself
against the dukes who come to deprive him of the Great Seal
(3.2.264–74); and, perhaps most significantly, in Henry's own
warning to Cranmer that "not ever / The justice and the truth o'
th' question carries / The due o' th' verdict with it" (5.1.129–31).
These instances, one for each of the four historical persons
tested by legal trial or accusation, acquire more potency if seen
against the background of the *Chronicles*. The truth of the accusations against Buckingham is left undecided in Shakespeare's
play, as it was by Raphael Holinshed, who remarked:

These were the speciall articles & points comprised in the indictment, and laid to his charge: *but how trulie, or in what sort prooved,*
I have not further to say, either in accusing or excusing him other
than as I find in Hall and Polydor, whose words in effect, I have
thought to impart to the reader, and without anie parciall wresting
of the same either to or for. . . . (3:864; italics added)

Shakespeare, surely, also assimilated the skepticism about
truth that was articulated during Katherine's trial, as told by
Cavendish via Stow via Fleming:

The kings councell alleaged the matrimonie not to be lawfull at the
beginning, bicause of the carnall copulation had betweene prince
Arthur and the queene. This matter was verie vehementlie touched
on that side, and to proove it, they alleaged manie reasons and si-
militudes of truth: and being answered negativelie againe on the
other side, it seemed that all their former allegations were doubtfull
to be tried, *and that no man knew the truth. (Chronicles,* 3:908;
italics added)

Because of this indeterminacy (a polite name for what happens
when the government has a case to make and somebody dis-
agrees), Henry, in frustration, sends the two cardinals to put
pressure on the queen privately to withdraw her opposition to
the divorce.

It is to Stow's edited version of Cavendish, we should remember, that we owe the highly sympathetic presentation of Queen
Katherine's trial and its sequel in Katherine's chambers. Shakespeareans have been so worried by the dependence of the corresponding scenes in *Henry VIII* on the text of the *Chronicles* that
they have downplayed how literary was the source here, how
much more than the vocabulary of Katherine's speeches Shakespeare inherited, how dramatic the details provided, including
the seating in Blackfriars, whereby the queen was symbolically
separated from her husband. Even the collaborationists assume
that Shakespeare wrote the following stage direction: "The
Queen makes no answer, rises out of her chair, goes about the
court, comes to the King, and kneels at his feet: then speaks."
Who, then, wrote the following sentence: "And because shee
could not come to the king alreadyie, for the distance severed
betweene them, shee went about by the court, and came to the
king, kneeling downe at his feet, to whom she said in effect as
followeth"? Well, Abraham Fleming inserted it and the speech
that follows into Holinshed's much briefer account of the trial.

He found these identical words in Stow's *Chronicles* (960), but Stow had edited what he found in his manuscript of Cavendish, where the autograph manuscript reads as follows:

> [She] rose uppe incontynent owt of hir chayer where as she satt / And bycause she cowld not come dyrectly to the kyng / for the distaunce whiche severed theme / she toke payn to goo abought unto the kyng knelyng down at his feete in the sight of all the Court & assemble / To whome she sayd in effect / in broken Englysshe, as folowythe / : . . .[35]

The disappearance of that phrase, "in broken Englysshe," seemingly so small an intervention, has the effect of rendering Katherine more English, more a part of the community that now wishes to exclude her.

Shakespeare could not have known of this aspect of Stow's intervention, though he clearly understood that the *Chronicles* saw Katherine as a sympathetic figure. And he certainly grasped the ideological significance of "English" in the scene that follows (which the collaborationists assign to Fletcher). Here, too, the dependence of the playtext on the narrative that has traveled from Cavendish via Stow via Fleming into the 1587 *Chronicles* is well known. What is not observed is the series of transformations that make "speaking English" a test of probity. What Cavendish wrote was simply this: "Than began my lord to speake / to hir in latten / Nay good my lord / quod she, speke to me in Englysshe I beseche you / allthoughe I understand latten," (88). What Stow wrote, and Fleming copied, was this: "Then began the Cardinall to speake to hir in Latine, nay good my Lord (quoth she) speake to me in English" (964). What Shakespeare wrote was this:

> *Wolsey. Tanta est erga te mentis integritas, regina serenissima—*
> [Such is the integrity of my mind towards you, most serene queen]
> *Katherine.* O, good my lord, no Latin;
> I am not such a truant since my coming,
> As not to know the language I have liv'd in.
> A strange tongue makes my cause more strange, suspicious;
> Pray speak in English. Here are some will thank you,
> *If you speak truth. . . .*
>
> (3.1.40–46; italics added)

As Shakespeare develops the Englishness of Katharine from the barest hint in the *Chronicles*, he brings to the surface and

extends their larger and more generous proposal: a true national-
ism will be able to value a Roman Catholic Spanish queen (and
one who, incidentally, adopts a most unfeminine unsubmissive-
ness in her own defense) as much or more as Cranmer, a Protestant archbishop. The English language comes to stand not for
Anglo-centrism, but for something close to its opposite: for can-
dor, openness, and fairness—all of which have been sorely
scanted in the series of trials on which the play is structured.

As Francis Thynne ironically summed up the end of
Cranmer's story in his censored catalogue of archbishops, in
Mary's reign "he was consumed to ashes": "a death not read
before to have happened to anie archbishop, who as he was the
first that publikelie impugned by established lawes the popes
authoritie in England, so was he the first metropolitane that was
burned for the same" (4:744). Shakespeare's decision to end his
play with the birth of Elizabeth and a prophecy of James I seems
a more optimistic version of the rule that history must continue
where fiction is free to end. As even Shakespeare's Cranmer
remarks as he ends his vision of Jacobean serenity, "Would I had
known no more."

But it is no coincidence that the one Caroline production of
the play for which we have a record was "bespoken of purpose"
by George Villiers, duke of Buckingham, Charles I's dangerous
favorite, in July 1628, in the context of parliamentary calls for
his indictment and a few days before his assassination. This
event belongs to the larger story of seventeenth-century struggles over politics and religion, struggles that also provoked the
1641 publication of Cavendish's *Life of Wolsey*, accompanied
by "A true Description or rather a Parallel betweene Cardinall
Woolsey . . . and William Laud."[36]

What, therefore, can we conclude, by the time that Shakespeare has completed his survey and analysis of the available
chronicle material, is included in the "All" of *All Is True?* First,
it is evidently true that there is more than one religion in England's recent past with claims to being the one true Church;
and that by the late 1630s, if not in 1613, the state religion more
resembles that of Wolsey than of Cranmer. Second, that all early
modern historians probably believed in, and several dutifully
pronounced, the requirement for truth at all costs defined in
Cicero's *De oratore* (2.15.62–63), which as rephrased by Giraldus Cambrensis at the beginning of his account of Henry II,
appears as my opening gambit also. But, third, because of the
difference in religious beliefs, the early modern historian's task

was harder still than that of the medieval one. He or she had, ideally, to represent diversity of opinion. It was not that nothing is true nor that truth is as you like it nor even that all's well that ends well, but that everybody does the best they can at the moment and from their own perspective. And for Shakespeare, who of dramatic necessity held multiple perspectives, returning to the English chronicles at the end of his own career led to the discovery of a title implying that he, at least, was not naive. Thereafter he abandoned the theater.

Notes

1. Samuel Schoenbaum, ed., *The Famous History of the Life of King Henry the Eighth* (New York: New American Library, 1967), xxii–xl.

2. It is well known that the scenes in act 5 that deal with Gardiner's enmity to Cranmer derive from John Foxe's *Acts and Monuments*. This essay deals only with Shakespeare's debt to "Holinshed's" *Chronicles*.

3. See, for example, John Margeson, ed., *King Henry VIII* (Cambridge: Cambridge University Press, 1990), 17.

4. Stanley Wells and Gary Taylor, eds. *William Shakespeare: A Textual Companion* (Oxford: Oxford University Press, 1987), 28–29, 618–19.

5. Julia Gasper, "The Reformation Plays on the Public Stage," in *Theatre and Government under the Early Stuarts*, ed. J. R. Mulryne and Margaret Shewring (Cambridge: Cambridge University Press, 1993), 207. While her reading of the play is far from unsympathetic, she points out that its "sunny picture of an Erastian solution is only arrived at by skirting the whole issue of persecution," that "the play gives the impression that there was a smooth transition from Henry's reign to that of Elizabeth." It is not clear whether she thinks that this and other examples of "tactful distortion" were intended to pull the wool over people's eyes or to be *noticed* as distortions, which would have the opposite effect.

6. Judith Anderson, *Biographical Truth: The Representation of Historical Persons in Tudor-Stuart Writing* (New Haven: Yale University Press, 1984), 126.

7. *Acts of the Privy Council, 1586–87*, ed. J. R. Dasent (London, 1901), 311–12. For a full discussion of this event and its consequences, see my *Reading Holinshed's Chronicles* (Chicago: University of Chicago Press, 1994), 237–39, 257–63.

8. Anderson also cites this speech. See *Biographical Truth*, 152.

9. *The Chronicles of England, Scotland, and Ireland* (London, 1587), 3:922.

10. *The Chronicles of England, Scotlande, and Irelande* (London, 1577), 3:1556. I assume that Shakespeareans will have the text of *Henry VIII* in front of them for comparison. It is worth noting that the one phrase notably omitted by Griffith from Campion's assessment, "vitious of his body," appears in Katherine's, with Hall's *Union* as its source. The praise and dispraise are therefore more clearly separated than they were in the *Chronicles*.

11. Edward Hall was the son of prominent Protestant reformers, and al-

though his loyalty to Henry VIII required considerable discretion, the tone of his *Union* with respect to the Reformation resulted in its being banned by Mary in 1555.

12. Stow's manuscript, now MS. Lambeth 179, was described by Richard Sylvester in his edition of the *Life*. It was owned by Sir Peter Manwood in 1598, and Stow recorded his role in the transcription on fol. 313v: "Wrytten by my man Rich. I borrowed ye originall of Mr. John Burrowes / John Stow." See Richard Sylvester, ed., *The Life and Death of Cardinal Wolsey* (Oxford: Oxford University Press, 1959; EETS, o.s., no. 243), 285.

13. British Library Egerton MS Egerton 2402. See Sylvester, ed., *Life and Death of Wolsey*, ix, xxvi. On the flyleaf of this manuscript Cavendish wrote that he finished his book on 24 June 1558. It was written, therefore, in Mary's reign, and Cavendish might have supposed that a biography so sympathetic to Wolsey could have seen publication, but Mary died in November of that same year. Cavendish had entered Wolsey's service as gentleman usher about 1522, and was therefore in an excellent position to give details about the cardinal's life style, with which the biography is overconcerned.

14. Ibid., 271; see also P. L. Wiley, "Renaissance Exploitation of Cavendish's *Life of Wolsey*," *Studies in Philology* 43 (1946): 130.

15. Anderson also believes that Shakespeare separately consulted Stow's 1592 edition of his chronicle, published under the title of *Annales*, a suggestion about which I am skeptical, given that it is not supported by the same kind of verbatim borrowing that marks Shakespeare's use of the 1587 *Chronicles*.

16. See, for example, R. A. Law, "The Double Authorship of *Henry VIII*," *Studies in Philology* 61 (1959): 471–88. Law's position, articulated in his earlier "Holinshed and *Henry the Eighth*," *Texas Studies in English* 36 (1957): 3–11, was that there is much greater dependence on Holinshed in the parts ascribed to Fletcher. I regard this account as untenable.

17. Stephen Booth, *The Book Called Holinshed's Chronicles* (San Francisco: Book Club of California, 1968), 72.

18. C. L. Kingsford, *English Historical Literature in the Fifteenth Century* (Oxford: Oxford University Press, 1913), 274.

19. See F. J. Levy, *Tudor Historical Thought* (San Marino, Calif.: Huntington Library, 1967), 168.

20. Ibid., 183–84.

21. F. J. Levy, "Holinshed in Context," paper delivered at the annual meeting of the Modern Language Association, December, 1986.

22. See my *Reading Holinshed's Chronicles*. In order to keep the documentation of this essay within the required limits, readers are requested to consult the *Chronicles*, especially for the biographies of the chroniclers.

23. See Ronald B. McKerrow, *A Dictionary of Printers and Booksellers in England, Scotland, and Ireland* . . . (London, 1910), 300.

24. The manuscript is now Bodleian MS Jones 14. Woodcock's signature appears on fol. 97. See Sylvester, ed. *Life and Death of Wolsey*, 280.

25. Colm Lennon, *Richard Stanihurst the Dubliner, 1547–1618* (Blackrock, County Dublin: Irish Academic Press, 1981), 40–41; See *Calendar of State Papers, Domestic, 1547–80*, 689.

26. Vernon Snow, *Holinshed's Chronicles* (1:ii) asserts, without giving a reference, that Thynne was "a controversial writer who had been in prison for suspected treason several years earlier." However attractive this statement

is to my thesis, I have been unable to corroborate it. Thynne was in prison for debt and appealed to Burghley for assistance, but this seems more like bad luck than bad judgment.

27. See Elizabeth Story Donno, "Some Aspects of Shakespeare's Holinshed," *Huntington Library Quarterly* 50 (1987): 238;

28. See Richard McCoy, *The Rites of Knighthood: The Literature and Politics of Elizabethan Chivalry* (Berkeley and Los Angeles: University of California Press, 1989), 90–95. McCoy also notes a connection between Essex and Thynne, who as soon as Essex became Lord Marshal prepared for him another of his catalogues defining the office and its previous holders (90). This catalogue now exists as BL Cotton MS, Vespasian 114.

29. Thynne's account ran as follows: "Henrie Stafford, whome our chronicles doo in manie places corruptlie terme Edward, was sonne to Humfrie earle Stafford, & was high constable of England, and duke of Buckingham. This man raising warre against Richard the third usurping the crowne, was in the first yeare of the reigne of the said Richard, being the yeare of Christ 1483, betraied by his man Humfrie Banaster (to whome being in distresse he fled for succour) and brought to Richard the third then lieng at Salisburie, where the said duke confessing all the conspiracie, was beheaded without arreignement or judgement" (869). *Henry VIII* 2.1.107–11 is a very close versification of this passage. We do not, of course, know whether Shakespeare used a complete or a "castrated" copy of the *Chronicles*, since some of the former escaped the censorship.

30. A copy of the printed Letters Patent is bound into Harley MS 367, fol. 10, #8. See also John Strype, ed., *A Survey of the Cities of London and Westminster . . . by John Stow* (London, 1720), 1:xi, xiii.

31. See *Tudor Royal Proclamations*, ed. Paul L. Hughes and James F. Larkin, 3 vols. (New Haven and London: Yale University Press, 1969), 2:312, where it is recorded that on 24 February 1569 the Bishop of London sent to the Privy Council a list of thirty-eight "unlawful books" found in Stow's possession, including recent recusant works by Thomas Dorman, Thomas Heskyns, Robert Pointz, John Rastell, Richard Shacklock, and Thomas Stapleton. For the "great Parcell" of chronicles, see *The Great Chronicle of London*, ed. A. H. Thomas and I. D. Thornley (London: G. W. Jones, 1938), xvi.

32. See C. L. Kingsford, ed., *A Survey of London by John Stow*, 2 vols. (Oxford, 1908), 1:ix–xii. Kingsford also provided a biography of Stow (1:vi–lxvii).

33. *Holinshed's Chronicles of England, Scotland and Ireland*, ed. Sir Henry Ellis (London, 1808), 4:742. Since unexpurgated copies of the 1587 edition are rare, I cite the nineteenth-century edition in which the castrated sections are restored.

34. Brian Vickers, *Appropriating Shakespeare* (New Haven: Yale University Press, 1993), 161–62.

35. Sylvester, ed., *The Life and Death of Wolsey*, 80.

36. See ibid., 272–73.

Part 3
The Playwright in the Play

Is There a Shakespeare after the *New* New Bibliography?

MEREDITH SKURA

> An author's individuality never exists as pure essence. . . .
> All plays . . . are in a sense collaborations.
> —Sam Schoenbaum, "Internal Evidence and the
> Attribution of Elizabethan Plays" (1960)

Few developments have so affected our sense of the author in the text as the recent reevaluation of Shakespeare's printed texts. For years Shakespeare's editors—the "new bibliographers"—had thought they were learning to identify and compensate for the distortions of acting companies, copyists, printers, and adapters, and were at last coming close to reconstructing Shakespeare's original text—just as we might reconstruct the original Rose Theater beneath layers of dust and later buildings. But now the effort of a new generation of "new bibliographers" has shown that there may never have been such a text, never have been a "single golden authorial manuscript," as Margreta de Grazia has called it.[1] We now know that Shakespeare was a reviser and even a collaborator; his text was always in process, always subject to intervention in the theater and printing house, always, as Stephen Orgel says, "unstable [and] infinitely revisable."[2] Shakespeare did not do it alone. The pressures from censorship and audiences, on the one hand, and the constraints of material production and economic distribution, on the other, have left their marks.

This is an important fact, and it has revolutionized the editing process. But its quite remarkable power over us noneditors—those of us who have not had to decide whether the last words in *King Lear* are spoken by Edgar, as in the Folio, or by Albany, as in the Quarto—invites comment. The wider disturbance

169

comes not so much from the fact of textual instability—unsettling as instability is—as from what that fact has prompted many Shakespeareans to conclude: namely that if we have no authorized text of *King Lear*, we have no *King Lear*, and, finally, no Shakespeare. Textual instability has come to mean that not only was Shakespeare a collaborator, but that he was himself a collaboration. "If the unity of a text goes," warns Gary Taylor, "so does the unity of the author. . . . Shakespeare had a plurality of incompatible intentions."[3] "There is no Shakespeare, no single Shakespeare," that is, says Jonathan Goldberg, "but only a divided kingdom."[4] Even the textual dividers, themselves once considered radicals, are no longer radical enough because they still believe in unified texts, only more of them, and all originating in Shakespeare's undivided mind. To unify the two texts of *King Lear* by referring them back to single author, says Paul Werstine, is "to substitute one fiction of origin for another."[5] In other words, we have by now slid from the instability of dramatic texts in early modern England to the instability of referential meaning in all discourse, and to the instability of the authorial self as Barthes and Foucault have seen it everywhere throughout history, even in seemingly stable texts.

Moreover, because we cannot untangle Shakespeare, at one end of the four hundred-year gap between him and us, from sixteenth-century censors, collaborators, acting companies, compositors, and booksellers, we know that any "Shakespeare" more coherent than the piecemeal collection of folios and quartos is artificially constructed by us, at our end of the gap, for our own contemporary purposes. Investigation, having detoured around Shakespeare, now aims at revealing those purposes. There have been several suggestions about what they are. Barthes and Foucault, in the two classic 1968 essays announcing the death of the author and the ubiquity of the author function, had originally suggested that one purpose was to protect us against a fear of signification gone wild once unleashed from the limitations of a single mind. "The author is the principle of thrift in the proliferation of meaning," said Foucault. "To give a text an Author," said Barthes, "is to impose a limit on that text, to furnish it with a final signified, to close the writing." Foucault in particular emphasized the tendentiousness of limiting a text to the historical figure said to have written it. If we really listen to the text, he said, there are a plurality of voices and therefore a plurality of "authors," which are functions of the text or of larger linguistic and social pressures, not of the supposed historical author. More recently critics have focused on one or another of these specific social pressures as motives for our construction of Shakespeare. "What is at stake in preserving the Complete Works from adaptation," says Michael Dobson in his study *The Making of the National Poet*, "is the integrity and indeed masculinity of Shakespeare himself."[6] We need a Bard of transcendent genius, universal wisdom, and unquestionable heterosexuality in order to shore up the empire—to reinforce "the ideological framework upon whose strength the persistence of our patriarchal, class-divided society depends."[7]

But today I want to talk about why it is nonetheless important to remember that there are other valid responses to the two texts of *King Lear* besides assuming that there is no *King Lear* or no Shakespeare—just as there are other responses to the two floor plans for the Rose Theater besides assuming that there was no Rose Theater. We know that a *King Lear* exists, if only to distinguish between "it" and the old *King Leir* play; the stationers' entries do not always distinguish among *Lear*s, but that does not mean that we cannot. And even if Shakespeare revised his *King Lear* or let others do it, he was nonetheless the play's author in a unique and useful sense. The story of a man who cannot make up his mind is not the story of a man who has no mind.

I think we may have been led nonstop from textual uncertainty to Foucauldian chaos by making two understandable but nonetheless questionable moves. First, we have exaggerated the degree of division within both play and author. Listening to the discussions that the two texts of *Lear* have generated, it sounds as if the "divided kingdoms" represented by two texts are as completely separate as Goneril's and Regan's kingdoms. But they are not; they overlap extensively. Much of the disturbance radiates from uncertainty about single words; and even some of biggest cracks in the façade, though they loom large to those of us caught inside the academic biosphere, entail relatively minor aspects of the play. I do not deny that details are vital—as someone interested in psychoanalysis, I in particular thrive on them—but they matter only in aggregates, only when they reinforce one another.

Second, and more troubling, where there is substantial textual division, we have exaggerated the importance of being certain about which version is more authentic. We have come to believe that if we cannot locate the text that Shakespeare wrote and approved once and for all, chaos is come again. No ocular proof, no Shakespeare. But it is important to remember that this is a long-standing philosophical argument, not about Shakespeare, but about the nature of all knowledge after attacks on it by radical skepticism. Apart from decisions about who "owns" the plays, there is no need to engage this argument. Let us assume instead that there is an "average expectable Shakespeare" or a Shakespeare with a probability value high enough for most purposes. I cannot justify such pragmatism, but neither can Foucault justify his skepticism; people who do this sort of thing for a living have been trying for years without much success. It is just that, as so many have already said in response to postmodern nihilism, if we do not assume certain things, there is no way of going about our business at all. (Interestingly enough, the philosopher Stanley Cavell has argued that Shakespearean tragedy itself is structured by a similar response to the argument of radical skepticism.)[8]

Of course all these pleas for pragmatism and common sense do not really address Barthes' main point. Neither he nor Foucault really meant there is no such thing as an author; I do not think they cared one way or the other in most cases. (Nor, probably, do the new "new bibliographers.") Neither of them, for example, ever thought to call Elizabeth Cary an author function, or doubted the existence of Christine de Pizan—but this does not mean that the likes of Cary and Pizan were the only authors who *really* existed in early modern Europe. It means that, as women, they were not important enough to attack. It is not the author whose death Barthes announced, but Authority, as arbitrarily created and idolized by us. Similarly the new "new bibliographers'" claims constitute an argument, not about Shakespeare, but about what we have done with him. And the point is well taken. Shakespeare has been used for purposes no one would want to endorse; and idolization of the Bard has distracted us from noticing the vital contributions made by forgotten laborers of the past—the copyists, compositors, and book sellers—all of whom were necessary to produce what we call "Shakespeare's" books. As Jerome McGann put it in *Critique of Modern "Textual Criticism"* (1983), we "so emphasize the autonomy of the isolated author as to distort our theoretical grasp of the 'mode of existence of a literary work of art' (a mode of existence which is fundamentally social rather than personal)."[9] What the new "new bibliographers" really mean is that literary hero worship is misplaced; the rest of their claim, we may assume, is just rhetoric. But the problem is that rhetoric, as we tend to believe lately, is seldom "just" rhetoric. Rhetorical overkill in a phrase like "the Death of the Author" does not merely make it sound better than "the Devaluation of Authority"; it has other effects as well. It transforms opinion into knowledge, a statement about value into a statement about fact. It naturalizes a particular ideological stance.

If the rhetoric is misleading, the entire move to replace the author with the material text has more serious, though perhaps unintended, problems. By getting rid of Shakespeare the new "new bibliographers" clear the way to an appreciation of his marginalized collaborators, but they thereby ignore marginal groups much closer to home (though still outside the academic elite) in the majority of colleges and libraries across the country. Recently, for example, one new "new bibliographical" critic, who has argued brilliantly to expose the inadequacies of our artfully constructed "Shakespeare," said (albeit perhaps jokingly) that he is "interested in what has been relegated to antiquarians, to the field of people who write books which only six people read, which are about spelling in Shakespeare."[10] I like to read about spelling in Shakespeare, too; but I cannot agree that uncertainty about the facts that six scholars study constitutes a crisis in Shakespeare studies at large.

Nor is that uncertainty necessary to persuade us that social process is as important as individual authors. It may in fact work the opposite way. Carlo Ginzburg, historian of early modern Europe, has argued that a concern for logical certainty in the first place can be elitist.[11] To give up on being able to know something (like the fact that the author Shakespeare existed) unless one can know it with logical or supposedly scientific certainty, Ginzburg argues, is to denigrate the popular pragmatic and "conjectural" ways of knowing (such as, "women's intuition") that have always been associated with powerless groups like peasants and women. Ginzburg cites the examples of connoisseurship and graphology, which search for an "author" by examining a painting's or a signature's scattered and trivial characteristics, beyond the conscious control of its painter or writer. He also cites the example of folk medicine, which guides diagnosis of diseases that, like the essential "Shakespeare," can never be observed apart from their scattered symptoms. Such conjectural knowledge derives from concrete experiences— from the experiences of an individual considering numerous individual cases. It gave way during the Enlightenment to the

more prestigious model of abstract scientific knowledge—a
knowledge supposedly purified of all anthropocentric, ethnocen-
tric, and other individual biases—like those to which we know
Shakespeare's early editors (like the rest of us) were subject.

But, taking Ginzburg's lead, rather than continuing to dispar-
age such impressionism, we might ourselves adopt a pragmatic
folk criticism in order to find the author of a text, just as we do
to find the author of a painting or of a crime. And we need not
always have imperialist motives in doing so. My effort to re-
claim subjectivity for Shakespeare-the-author is part of a more
comprehensive movement in which, for example, Carol Neely
has reclaimed individual subjectivity for early modern women
and Hortense Spillers has suggested reclaiming it for African-
Americans. I am not for a moment suggesting that the recent
attack on Shakespeare's individuality is in the same category as
the enduring erasure suffered by marginalized groups like
women and African-Americans. But I do think that the attack
on Shakespeare's subjectivity has helped make such defenses as
Neely's and Spillers's necessary.

Getting back to Shakespeare, once I discount the antiauthori-
tarian rhetoric and the radical skepticism behind recent textual
studies, what sort of "author" is left? For the most part, he is a
very familiar one. First, he is one who is an "originator," as
defined by Cotgrave in 1611: "An author, actor, causer, founder;
th'originall inventor, the first deviser, of a thing; also, an author,
or writer of bookes." In other words, though one of Barthes' and
Foucault's main points is that the concept of author is histori-
cally specific to the modern period, this is of course not true.
The concept of individually authored books is indeed far more
prevalent in the modern era (during which most such books
were produced) than it ever was before; but even so, the concept
of individual book authors has been around for a long time. In
fact one of Foucault's complaints is that we have not come
much further than Saint Jerome in knowing how to determine
a book's author. Second, this author is not an "author function"
only but a "person," as in the twentieth-century *Oxford English
Dictionary* definition of author, "a person who originates or
gives existence to anything." To decide that there is an "author
function" by definition insulated from the man from Stratford is
to beg the question. This author has Shakespeare-ish intentions
when writing, ranging from "I want this line to get a laugh" to
"I want to follow up on the dirt and stain imagery here." He has
a sense of himself as writer and knows what he wrote, though he

may not have valued the words he wrote as others have, may not have had legal rights of ownership to them, and may not have had what Joseph Loewenstein has so aptly termed a "bibliographic ego."[12] You or I may not be able to tell in all cases which lines Shakespeare contributed to *King Lear*, but I think Shakespeare could have told, even if he did not care. In other words, my Shakespeare is almost everything Foucault interrogates.

However, just because I believe in a Shakespeare whom I cannot directly observe does not mean I have not learned anything in the twenty-five years since Foucault's essay. Although, unlike his, my Shakespeare exists as an individual prior to the text, he is not necessarily not prior to everything else. He is not the mystified autonomous genius Foucault and others have caricatured. It is not (to quote Coriolanus) "as if a man were author of himself" (*Coriolanus* 5.3.36). Indeed he may be the uniquely unpredictable author he is only because of a unique set of prior determinants: political, social, economic, familial, psychological, or theatrical. Donald Forster, for example, has made a tantalizing suggestion that the roles Shakespeare played in the staging of his early plays influenced the vocabulary of the later plays.[13] Shakespeare was not necessarily conscious of all these influences at work in his writing, nor do they produce a completely consistent all-vanilla Shakespeare. But it still makes sense to see Shakespeare as a single subject encompassing many levels of consciousness and many kinds of conflict (a sort of fudge-ripple Shakespeare). By now, surely, the naive belief in a unified, autonomous, transcendent author has disappeared. (Indeed it already had in Sam Schoenbaum's 1960 assumptions, cited as epigraph to this paper, that "an author's individuality never exists as pure essence.... All plays ... are in a sense collaborations.") It is time to stop beating a dead author and to start working out the implications for authorship of the new discoveries about social process. Without the old certainties, all we have are differences in emphasis, which polemics do not help to explore.

In working out implications for authorship, then, the instability of the Shakespearean text need not paralyze me. Like the revisionists themselves, I do not privilege either text of *King Lear*, early or late, and each is useful so long as Shakespeare wrote it. In fact, drafts or unfinished texts such as *Timon of Athens*, like dreams, are the royal road to the unconscious. They show Shakespeare at work and suggest that, for example, he seems to have composed his characters' speeches piecemeal, from separate units of thought or imagery sometimes only half a line long, and only later to have added the narrative that linked the pieces.[14] As for the more serious problem of deciding which texts and what parts of them are Shakespeare's rather than his collaborators', if the only texts we had were *Pericles* and *The Two Noble Kinsmen*, I would give up, too. But there are lots of texts, and since I assume that collaboration in early modern theaters was as random and unpredictable a process as it is said to have been, I therefore also assume that the collaborators varied from play to play. Only Shakespeare's contribution remains constant. So long as we look for patterns that extend throughout the canon, the other contributions tend to cancel each other out. The main concern is to locate as many different kinds of patterns as possible, and never to base an argument on a detail that appears in only one of two disputed textual readings. Then—and here is the invaluable lesson the bibliographers have taught us—we just need to be careful. Not only did Shakespeare revise, but we must always be ready to revise too. In the end, exact details may be, as G. L. Kittredge said in trying to sort out Shakespeare's from Fletcher's contributions to *The Two Noble Kinsman*, "beyond the scope of sane criticism,"[15] but the general picture is clear enough.

Let me give an example of the sort of thing I do when constructing Shakespeare. Foucault begins with discourse, but before moving outward I look first for what Shakespeare says about himself, and for what Wayne Booth called the "implied author." Since Shakespeare "says" very little explicitly about himself as author, this means, among other things, looking at the way he represents authors generally. As I look, my interest is not so much in what Shakespeare consciously thought about writing. Instead, like a psychoanalyst, I want to ask Shakespeare not only what he thought about writing for the theater, but also what comes to mind when he thinks of theater—or, more strictly, to ask what turns up in the text when theater does come to mind.

And, rather surprisingly, I found that what turns up is the hunt—primarily the stag hunt, but others as well. We have long known how interested in hunting Shakespeare was, but I do not think we have realized how deeply implicated for him the sport was with theater. As we know, theatrical self-consciousness in Renaissance drama has been an abiding concern of critics, in one form or another, for many, many years. We used to talk about the metaphysics of plays-within-plays; lately we talk about the cultural poetics of theatricality, or "self-fashioning," but it is still theater we look at, and there are still a few Shakespearean plays at the core of the discussion: the plays that have plays inside them. My point is that nearly every one of these occurs near a hunting scene. If we look at Shakespeare's plots, the familiar Shakespearean play-within-a-play typically appears after an aristocratic patron has been out hunting; only then do the players provide their own sort of sport for him. The inner play in *Love's Labor's Lost*, for example, (the "Pageant of Worthies") turns up in the midst of two overarching metaphorical hunts, as well as a literal onstage hunt. The King's ambition in *Love's Labor's Lost*, announced in the play's first line, is a fame-hunt ("Let fame, that all hunt after in their lives, / Live regist'red upon our brazen tombs," he says, as he and his men retreat into a monastic academy, where they intend to learn the secrets of the gods). This quickly modulates into a love-hunt when a beautiful princess arrives and the men all forget their vows in order to become suitors [pronounced "shooters"]. The turning point of the play is a literal shooting party during act 4, where the princess shoots a deer while Berowne sees himself "toiling in a pitch" (punning on the phrase "pitching a toil," or setting up a hunting net). The inner play then follows as just another kind of sport.[16]

Each of Shakespeare's two other early inner plays also shares the stage with an aristocratic hunt. Amateur actors Christopher Sly in *The Taming of a Shrew* and Bottom in *A Midsummer Night's Dream* each wander into a forest preserve where an aristocratic lord is hunting, and each is then brought home with that lord to take part in a play. The lord in *Shrew* is hunting with his purebred dogs when he finds Sly out cold in front of a tavern and decides to bring the sleeping beggar home and teach him a lesson by dressing him up and pretending that he is a lord when he wakes. While this charade is in progress, a troupe of touring actors arrives to perform, for the lord and Sly, still bemusedly playing an aristocrat in the lord's amateur play, suddenly becomes an audience for the professional players. Similarly, in *A Midsummer Night's Dream*, Bottom goes into the forest to rehearse one play ("Pyramus and Thisbe"), and then becomes an unwitting actor in another play, which we might call "The Taming of Titania." The Duke does not notice when he almost trips over Bottom, but later he chooses Bottom's play for performance in the palace that evening. (When John Fletcher collaborated with Shakespeare in 1613 to retell the *Midsummer Night's Dream* story in *The Two Noble Kinsman*, he condensed the hunt and the play into one scene in the forest.)

The fourth Shakespearean inner play appears not long after *Dream*, in *The Merry Wives of Windsor*; and here hunting and playing coincide still more closely. Earlier, in the Henriad, Falstaff had already been a "harlotry player" (with Hal at the Boarshead tavern, *1 Henry IV* 2.4.395); and he had been a deer (Hal, seeing Falstaff's body on the battlefield, had quipped coolly that "death hath not strook so fat a deer to-day" [*1 Henry IV* 5.4.107] before promising to have him emboweled or dismembered like a dead stag). Now in *Merry Wives* Falstaff's two roles, player and deer, merge when he goes to the forest. There, disguised as Herne the Hunter for a secret adulterous tryst (wearing stag horns or possibly a whole deer's head), Falstaff also plays a second and quite unexpected role in the schoolboys' "Pageant of the Fairy Queen," which is being staged at the same time in the same part of the forest. Falstaff's costume marks him not only as an actor but also as the object of the hunt, a deer at bay; and a noise of hunting (*Merry Wives* 5.5.103 S.D.) is heard as he is surrounded by Evans's fairies, who pinch him like a circle of hunting dogs.

After such a pattern has been established, where else than in *As You Like It*, Shakespeare's one play about a community that lives by hunting, should we expect him to proclaim that "all the world's a stage and all the men and women in it merely players?" The entire action in *As You Like It* moves toward a happy resolution that begins with Jacques's solemn hunting ritual (4.2) and ends with a little inner play called the "Masque of Hymen" (5.4). Finally, hunting and masque actually collide in *The Tempest*, where Prospero, the last of Shakespeare's hunter-patrons, is in the midst of staging his Masque of Ceres for the young lovers when he suddenly remembers Caliban and the other would-be assassins who have been dressing up in his finery on their way to murder him. At once Prospero interrupts the masque, ends the revels, and sends out his spirit actors "in the shape of dogs and hounds" (*Tempest* 4.1.254 S.D.) to hunt down the three offenders. Instead of making players of the locals— like Sly and Bottom—who stumble into his hunt, he hunts the locals who stumble into his play. But the association between hunting and playing holds.

The association holds for Shakespeare in nondramatic texts

as well, like Sonnet 111, in which the poet seems to be talking about himself as playwright when he complains that Fortune

> . . . did not better for my life provide
> Than public means which public manners breeds

and goes on to confess that

> . . . almost thence my nature is subdu'd
> To what it works in, like the dyer's hand.

Here the connection between hunting and theater lies in the phrase "the dyer's hand," which suggests that the poet's work in the theater stains him permanently and taints his very nature. Where in this phrase is the allusion to hunting? It is not explicit, but because most dirty hands in Shakespeare's plays—like Lady Macbeth's—are stained with blood, it lies ready to be activated in the context of those plays. Listen, for example, to English Herald gloating in *King John*, when his troops return victorious:

> like a jolly troop of huntsmen come
> Our lusty English, all with purpled hands,
> Dy'd in the dying slaughter of their foes.
>
> (*King John* 2.1.321–23)

And listen to Antony in Shakespeare's *Julius Caesar* describing the men who have hunted Caesar down. After telling the assassins that "your purpled hands do reek and smoke" (3.1.158) and asking each to "render me his bloody hand" (184), Antony speaks to Caesar's corpse:

> Here wast thou bay'd, brave hart,
> Here didst thou fall, and here thy hunters stand,
> Sign'd in thy spoil, and crimson'd in thy lethe.
>
> (3.1.204–6)

For Shakespeare, I suggest, the playwright's hand, subdued to what it works in, is like the huntsman's and the assassin's hands, as well as like the dyer's. Perhaps we even hear in the sonnet's "dyer's hand" a fugitive allusion to hand as "unique style of penmanship," as if the indelible stain on the poet's hand becomes as much a sign of his identity as his handwriting, or as if he were writing in blood.[17]

I have left *Hamlet*—Shakespeare's most theatrically self-conscious play—out of this brief anthology of hunting/playing examples not because it does not fit, but because it is the seeming exception that proves the rule. *Hamlet*'s plot, unlike the others we have looked at, includes no hunt. But hunting appears in the play's language, especially in Hamlet's. Hamlet begins by worrying that he is a dull muddy mettled "rascal" or puny deer, and he asks the spies Rosencrantz and Gildenstern why "you go about to recover the *wind* of me, as if you would drive me into a *toil?*" (*Hamlet* 3.2.346–47; emphasis added). That is, he asks why they are trying to trap him in a hunting net (like Berowne's). But Hamlet also realizes that "the play's the thing / Wherein I'll catch the conscience of the King" (*Hamlet* 2.2.604–5) and decides to put on a play he calls "The Mouse-trap"; he himself changes from hunted to hunter and begins to sound like the other hunter-patrons. From this moment on Claudius in the audience becomes the prey. As Hamlet says,

> . . . If his occulted guilt
> Do not itself *unkennel* in one speech,
> It is a damned ghost that we have seen.
>
> (3.2.80–82; emphasis added)

That is, the "one speech" in the play is going to drive Claudius's guilt into the open, like a keeper driving a deer into the open to begin the hunt. Once Claudius takes the bait, as it were, and calls off Hamlet's play, Hamlet's manic crow of delight makes the analogy between playing and hunting explicit:

> "Why let the strooken deer go weep,
>   The hart ungalled play,
> For some must watch while some must sleep,
>   Thus runs the world away."
>
> (3.2.271–74)

Hamlet is the hunter who stalks deer with the players, and he boasts to Horatio that his efforts will get him a fellowship in "a cry of players" (3.2.277–78)—a "cry" being a canine hunting pack yelping after the scent, like Prospero's spirit dogs yelping after Caliban. Again, the association between playing and hunting holds. And it holds in all the *Hamlet* texts, folio and quarto.

Did Shakespeare invent this association between playing and hunting out of airy nothing? Is it a sign of his transcendent genius? His perfection? Of course not. In many ways he was speaking for the world he lived in—or letting it speak through him. The hunt was part of early modern culture in England. Shakespeare's forest was not just a collection of trees, but rather a specially identified aristocratic space; and the hunt was an elaborate ceremony with a specialized language that served more as a social marker than a source of meat. As such, it was a mixture of ritual and butchery mocked by Tudor humanists and Jacobean satirists alike. In particular it was already a complexly inflected sign of social relationships. Ordinary people did not hunt, though they might parody hunting rituals in their skimmingtons; when they went after animals it was called poaching. (This is an implication not lost on those biographers who readily reproduced the anecdote about Shakespeare's having been exiled from Stratford for poaching deer.) And on occasion hunting was elsewhere associated with theater, as in Antony Munday's Robin Hood plays, or in the inner play I mentioned earlier, in Fletcher's part of *The Two Noble Kinsmen*.[18]

But the persistent association between hunting and playing *is* Shakespeare's. Hunting, as D. H. Madden noted nearly a century ago, is more deeply embedded everywhere in Shakespeare's plays than in those of any other dramatist; and his cultural context cannot fully account for what use he makes of it. And Shakespeare's most characteristic elaboration of the hunt was to associate it with theater, linking the two in the figure of the great house lord whose status was defined partly by his hunting and his players. Shakespeare persisted in this association even though it was culturally outdated and practically irrelevant to his own London-centered career on the public stage. The association makes more sense in terms of Shakespeare's sensitivity to the idea of acting as a blood sport than it does in terms of a wider cultural discourse. Apparently for Shakespeare actor and audience are the hunter and hunted, as Michael Goldman says they are for twentieth-century actors.[19]

The hunt is even more pervasive in Shakespeare's language than in his plots. In fact one of the most reliable linguistic indications of Shakespeare's individuality is also an unmistakable symptom, to use Ginzburg's metaphor, of Shakespeare's fascination with the hunt. Hunting language helps constitute his most famous image cluster, which Caroline Spurgeon called "by far the clearest and most striking example" of his clusters: the "dog, licking, candy, melting group, called up . . . by the thought of . . . flatterers." The dog cluster proves to be only half of a larger cluster in which the fawning spaniel turns into a cur, or

circle of curs surrounding a central figure, pinching and at-
tacking him like hunting hounds circling a deer at bay—just as
Caesar was attacked by the fawning flatterers kneeling at his
feet in the Senate. Shakespeare's peculiar use of the hunt tells us
as much—if not more—about his own construction of warfare,
courtly politics, and the acting profession as it does about the
restraints that these institutions imposed on his plays.

I have been using an old-fashioned argument to justify main-
taining an old-fashioned Shakespeare alongside the new ways of
seeing his social context. The method I have used—tracing image clusters—is hardly original, or would not have been used
until just recently. But in the current critical climate, it may
not be so out of date. Think about Jorge Luis Borges's Pierre
Menard, who painfully composed sections of Cervantes' *Don
Quixote*, word for word, now in the twentieth century. As
Borges says,

> To compose *Don Quixote* at the beginning of the seventeenth cen-
> tury was a reasonable, necessary and perhaps inevitable undertak-
> ing; at the beginning of the twentieth it is almost impossible. . . .
> In spite of these . . . obstacles, the fragmentary *Don Quixote* of Men-
> ard is more subtle than that of Cervantes.[20]

So too, as Borges might say, to believe in an author at the beginning of the seventeenth century was a reasonable, necessary,
and perhaps inevitable undertaking; at the end of the twentieth
it is almost impossible. Terence Hawkes has said that we can
no longer approach any text (or author) with innocence, which,
for better or for worse, is true.[21] But we can try for what William
Blake called "organized innocence," somewhere between his
childish "songs of innocence" and jaded "songs of experience",
and hope that it may facilitate a subtler form of intervention
that avoids the extremes either of naive humanism or posthu-
manist nihilism.

NOTES

1. Margreta de Grazia, "The Essential Shakespeare and the Material
Book," *Textual Practice* 2.1 (1988): 69–86, 71.

2. Stephen Orgel, "The Authentic Shakespeare," *Representations* 21
(1988): 1–25, 24.

3. Gary Taylor, *Reinventing Shakespeare: A Cultural History from the
Restoration to the Present* (1989; New York: Oxford University Press, 1991),
357.

4. Jonathan Goldberg, "Textual Properties," *Shakespeare Quarterly* 37 (1986), 213–17, 214.

5. Paul Werstine, "The Textual Mystery of *Hamlet*," *Shakespeare Quarterly* 39 (1988): 1–26, 25.

6. Michael Dobson, *The Making of the National Poet: Shakespeare, Adaptation and Authorship* (Oxford: Clarendon Press, 1992).

7. Kiernan Ryan, *Shakespeare*, Harvester New Readings (Atlantic Highlands, N.J.: Humanities Press International, 1989), 2.

8. See Richard P. Wheeler, "Acknowledging Shakespeare: Cavell and the Claim of the Human," in *The Senses of Stanley Cavell*, ed. Richard Fleming and Michael Payne, a special issue of *Bucknell Review* 32.1 (1989): 132–60.

9. Jerome J. McGann, *A Critique of Modern "Textual Criticism"* (Chicago and London: University of Chicago Press, 1983), 8.

10. Peter Stallybrass, in the discussion following his "Shakespeare, the Individual, and the Text," in *Cultural Studies*, ed. Lawrence Grossberg, Cary Nelson, and Paula A. Treichler (New York and London: Routledge, 1992), 611.

11. Carlo Ginzburg, "Morelli, Freud and Sherlock Holmes: Clues and Scientific Method," *History Workshop* 9 (September 1980): 5–36. Ginzburg's essay explores the history of various relationships between "high" and "low" forms of knowledge; it does not argue for one or the other.

12. Joseph Loewenstein, "The Script in the Marketplace," *Representations* 12 (1985): 101–14; reprinted in *Representing the English Renaissance*, ed. Stephen Greenblatt (Berkeley and Los Angeles: University of California Press, 1988), 265–78.

13. Donald W. Forster, "Reconstructing Shakespeare," parts 1, 2, and 3, in *The Shakespeare Newsletter* 209 (1991): 16–17; 210 (1991): 26–27; 211 (1991) 58–59.

14. Una Ellis-Fermor, "*Timon of Athens*: An Unfinished Play," *RES* 18 (1942): 270–83, cited in H. J. Oliver, introduction to *Timon of Athens* (London: Methuen, 1969), xxv–xxvi.

15. Kittridge is cited in the introduction to *The Two Noble Kinsmen*, ed. G. R. Proudfoot (Lincoln: University of Nebraska Press, 1970), xvii.

16. Holofernes, one of its collaborative authors, also writes a poem about the death of the deer, as if the two events, hunt and theatrical performance, were equally in his purview.

17. For a different suggestion about implications of handwriting for Shakespeare, see Jonathan Goldberg, "Hamlet's Hand," *Shakespeare Quarterly* 39 (1988): 307–27.

18. See also John Webster's famous Character "Of an 'Excellent Actor'" (1615): "the flight of Hawkes and chase of wilde beastes, either of them are delights noble: but some think this sport [going to plays] of men the worthier, despight all *calumny*." Cited in E. K. Chambers, *The Elizabethan Stage* (Oxford: Clarendon Press, 1923), 4:258.

19. *The Actor's Freedom: Toward a Theory of Drama* (New York: Viking Press, 1975), 14–15. Actors often describe stage fright as "buck fever"—the paralysis that keeps a hunter from pulling the trigger when he sees his prey. Elsewhere I have argued that sixteenth-century playing conditions suggest that the experience may have been similar for Shakespearean actors, including Shakespeare himself. Meredith Anne Skura, *Shakespeare the Actor and the Purposes of Playing* (Chicago: Chicago University Press, 1993).

20. "Pierre Menard, Author of *Don Quixote*" (1939) in Jorge Luis Borges, *Ficciones*, translated by Anthony Kerrigan (New York: Grove Press, 1962), 51.

21. *That Shakespehearian Rag: Essays on a Critical Process* (London and New York: Methuen, 1986), 123.

Two Distincts, Division None: Shakespeare and Fletcher's *The Two Noble Kinsmen* of 1613

PHILIP J. FINKELPEARL

THE Two Noble Kinsmen, Shakespeare and Fletcher's adaptation of Chaucer's "The Knight's Tale," can be dated in 1613 with some precision.[1] The date is of some importance because several distinguished scholars have recently linked the play to the marriage of Princess Elizabeth and to other events of the same year.[2] Here, in an essay honoring the most rigorous biographer Shakespeare has ever had, I want to consider the precise sense in which *The Two Noble Kinsmen* can be related to topical matters.

This marriage of Elizabeth to Frederick V, Elector Palatine of the Rhine, was central to the plans of the recently deceased Henry, Prince of Wales, for creating a Protestant alliance to curb the Catholic Habsburgs' power. For the marriage the prince had devised, according to Roy Strong, "a splendid series of spectacles, expressly designed to establish the Stuart court in the eyes of Europe as the fount of revived Protestant chivalry."[3] Although the project never fully materialized because of the prince's death, Strong shows that the prince's aims can be detected in various surviving works. One of these was a wedding masque about Virginia by George Chapman for the Middle Temple and Lincoln's Inn that endorsed the anti-Spanish, anti-Catholic, and Protestant aspects of British imperialistic expansion. Another masque, commissioned for the same occasion by the Inner Temple and Gray's Inn and performed a few days after the wedding, was by Francis Beaumont. The preface Beaumont wrote for the published text of his masque indicates that his aims were similar to Chapman's. He designed the dance of mythological figures representing the Rhine and the Thames in the first antimasque and of "Common People" in the second antimasque (later adapted for *The Two Noble Kinsmen*) to register approval of the match. In the main masque Beaumont presented the political message of the prince through an elaborate fiction about the revival of the Olympic games since "The *Olympian* games portend to the Match, Celebritie, Victorie, and Felicitie."[4] "Victorie," it seems fair to say, is not a term normally associated with marriage. From the viewpoint of would-be heroes—young students at the Inns of Court were particularly critical of King James's pacific foreign policy—"Olympian games" on foreign fields, preferably battlefields, were in desperate need of revival and would be a highly desirable by-product of this match.[5]

Since *The Two Noble Kinsmen*, written after the princess's marriage, included a passage from Beaumont's marriage masque and opens with a masque celebrating the marriage of a prince and princess, it has spawned conjecture—there is no document specifically making the connection—that the play was one of the many dramatic celebrations of the courtly occasion. However, Beaumont, who would have been the natural continuator of the impulses behind the masque, had nothing to do with the play. Indeed, the astonishingly prolific, very young playwright—in 1613, twenty-eight years old but responsible for part or all of at least twelve plays over the past six years—produced no more work for the theater. It had been generally assumed that his marriage to an heiress in 1613 had obviated the need to write for a living, but recently I discovered that soon after the masque Beaumont suffered an incapacitating "apoplexe," or a stroke. He lingered until 1616, dying about a month before Shakespeare.[6]

This unexpected turn of events must have created a problem for the King's Men. That they were experiencing some kind of serious trouble seems to be confirmed by the last line of the prologue of *The Two Noble Kinsmen*, which speaks apprehensively about the possibility that if this play does not succeed, "Our losses fall so thick we must needs leave" (32).[7] After *The Tempest* in 1611 all evidence points to Shakespeare's spending most of his time in Stratford and curtailing, if not altogether stopping, his writing. His retirement would hardly have seemed financially disastrous to the company at a time when Beaumont and Fletcher were at the height of their popularity and capable of producing work at the same prodigious rate as Shakespeare. Now, suddenly, with Beaumont's stroke the production line was in danger of slowing down. This development may, perhaps, account for the reappearance in 1613 of shareholder Shakespeare as a writer, albeit in the new, reduced role of collaborator. Within the year his name is linked (with varying degrees of certainty) with Fletcher's in as many as three collaborative plays: the lost *Cardenio, Henry VIII,* and *The Two Noble Kinsmen.*

It is instructive to observe the nature of the product that emerges from the union of the greatest of all solo writers with the most successful of all dramatic collaborators. The seamless texture of a "Beaumont & Fletcher" production is a commonplace, occasioning Coleridge's confession, "I have never been able to distinguish the presence of Fletcher during the life of Beaumont, nor the absence of Beaumont during the survival of Fletcher."[8] This could never be said about *The Two Noble Kinsmen.* Whether it is the difference in spelling by Shakespeare and Fletcher of a character's name ("Pirithous" vs. "Perithous") or the repetition in a Shakespeare episode of what had already happened in one by Fletcher (cf. 4.1.23 and 5.6.36) or the rather arbitrary insertion of Beaumont's masque dance, there is evidence—and much more could be cited—of a product hastily cobbled together by partners as distant as Stratford and London.

Nonetheless, the final effect is of a hard-won unity. Initially *The Two Noble Kinsmen* seems as though it might become another vehicle for the propagation of Prince Henry's neochivalric activism. In the first act, allotted to Shakespeare, the legendary warrior Theseus, unlike the indecisive, humiliatingly pacific reigning King of England, demonstrates the validity of the constant praise he receives for his unrivaled military prowess. Like "a deity equal with Mars" (1.1.227) he decides to forsake his bride on their wedding day to perform a chivalric act. As in Chaucer, at the entreaty of some queens widowed by the cruel ruler Creon he wages a swift, successful war on Thebes. Unlike the amiable Theseus of *A Midsummer Night's Dream,* although sprung from the same source in Chaucer, here he is revered as a kind of Coriolanus: "O Jove, your actions, / Soon as they move, as aspreys do the fish, / Subdue before they touch" (1.1.137–39). Valor in the form of a remorseless brutality is for him the chiefest virtue, as we hear in his praise of the two noble kinsmen, Palamon and Arcite, whom he captured in the recent war:

By th' helm of Mars, I saw them in the war,
Like to a pair of lions smear'd with prey,

Make lanes in troops aghast. . . .

. . . .

The very lees of such millions of rates
Exceed the wine of others. . . .

. . . .

their lives concern us,
Much more than Thebes is worth.

(1.4.17–19, 29–30, 32–33)

As I have been describing this introductory section by Shakespeare, it sounds like an echo of Jonson's *Prince Henry's Barriers*
(1610), an event designed by the prince to announce to the world
what he hoped to stand for. There, England's greatest warrior
kings are extolled in terms like those lauding Theseus: Richard
Coeur de Lion "armed with wroth and fire / Ploughing whole
armies up with zealous ire," Edward the First, who "lets no less
rivers of blood," the Black Prince, "Mars indeed."[9] But despite
the glorification of a mortal Mars, Theseus the Slaughterer, in
The Two Noble Kinsmen certain passages make us wary about
Shakespeare's tone. When a weeping queen urges Hippolyta to
kneel for "no longer time / Than a dove's motion when the
head's pluck'd off" (1.1.97–98), we are uncertain whether this
new unit of time is meant as an admirably cold-blooded expression by a precursor of the Marquis de Sade or as the language
of a desperate widow whose sensibility has been corrupted by
the atrocities she has experienced. And how are we to feel about
the total immersion in barbaric military values of Theseus' recently conquered Amazonian queen, Hippolyta?

Hippolyta. . . . We have been soldiers, and we cannot weep
When our friends don their helms, or put to sea,
Or tell of babes broach'd on the lance, or women
That have sod their infants in (and after eat them)
The brine they wept at killing 'em.

(1.3.18–22)

In that same passage in which Theseus rates Palamon and Arcite's worth as exceeding that of millions of normal men, he
directs his surgeons to heal these paragons so that he can im-
prison them for life! By the fifth act we are so impressed by the
purity of Theseus' chivalric nature that Shakespeare can risk a
laugh at the expense of this tunnel-visioned warrior's terms of
commendation for a potential husband: "he is a good one / As
ever strook at head" (5.3.108–9). One passage encapsulates the

glorious defect in Theseus' values. When praised for having gone
to war in an honorable cause rather than spending his marriage
night with his wife, he responds, "As we are men / thus should
we do, being sensually subdu'd / We lose our human title"
(1.1.230–32). To be godlike, Martian, requires repression of natural instincts. Theseus is at once ponderous, holier than thou,
and a paragon.[10]

Through such shadings we realize that Shakespeare is constructing his usual complex dialectic. From the first Theseus'
sister-in-law Emilia tries to act as "a counter-reflect 'gainst /
My brother's heart, and warm it to some pity" (1.1.127–28). But
her function expands in 1.3, one of the most remarkable passages in Shakespeare's late work. She hears of the great friendship between Theseus and Perithous and without warning
breaks into an emotional, "high-speeded" (1.3.83) contrast between the mature love of two lifelong male friends and the love
she experienced at eleven with another girl of the same age.
The male relationship has been grounded in "judgment" and
responds to the friends' immediate personal needs. The two
girls, "things innocent"—they have scarcely acquired enough
identity to be called humans, as Emilia explains—

Lov'd for we did, and like the elements
That know no what nor why, yet do effect
Rare issues by their operance, our souls
Did so to one another.

(1.3.61–64)

Emilia then describes the identity, the fused oneness, of the two
lovers. Whether a flower, a hat, or a tune, if one of them owns
it, the other assimilates, imitates, or appropriates it:

Had mine ear
Stol'n some new air, or at adventure humm'd one
From musical coinage, why, it was a note
Whereon her spirits would sojourn (rather dwell on)
And sing it in her slumbers.

(1.3.74–78)

We are in the area of mystical love explored in the sonnets and
particularly in The Phoenix and the Turtle, where the lovers are
"two distincts, division none":

The flow'r that I would pluck
And put between my breasts (O then but beginning

To swell about the blossom), she would long
Till she had such another, and commit it
To the like innocent cradle, where phoenix-like
They died in perfume.

(1.3.66–71)

Emilia's friend Flavina died young, and the lovely equation of
the deaths of the girl and the roses, two "phoenixes," validates
by its eloquence Emilia's belief "That the true love 'tween maid
and maid may be / More than in sex dividual" (1.3.81–82); and
the seeming formlessness of Emilia's innocent outburst highlights the stiff artificiality of the world that surrounds her.

Emilia's passage sounds the keynote for a play that is structured around differences of age, gender, values, social class, and
ways of loving. This theme is explicitly stated in the bridge that
Shakespeare constructs in 2.1 to the contributions of Fletcher
that begin with 2.2 and continue through most of the play until
the fifth act. As we have seen, Theseus had been goaded into
fighting and defeating Creon's Thebes, in the process capturing
and imprisoning Palamon and Arcite. In 2.1 at Palamon and
Arcite's jail we hear praise of the two "noble sufferers" from
the daughter of their jailer. She exclaims—doubtless casting a
glance at her pedestrian if not ignoble wooer, who is also present—"It is a holiday to look on them. Lord, the diff'rence of
men!" (2.1.55–56). Shakespeare's Palamon and Arcite are angry,
idealistic moralists, proud of their purity yet wary of the inevitable corruption. In the prologue (generally ascribed to Fletcher)
the worry is expressed that Chaucer might find the play "witless
chaff" and resent the treatment "lighter / Than Robin Hood'"
that has been accorded to his "fam'd works" (19–21). There is
some justification for the prologue's concern because Fletcher's
portrayal of the kinsmen, in particular, shows a comic dimension to their chivalrous confrontations. Fletcher's Palamon and
Arcite are self-consciously noble rhetoricians, sentimentally lamenting their exile from a Thebes that Shakespeare's pure
knights had detested. When we view them alone together for the
first time, the cousins' despair gradually modulates to rapture at
the prospect of a life in prison, away from the corruption of this
world and the possible disruption of their great friendship:

Palamon.   Is there record of any two that lov'd
   Better than we do, Arcite?
Arcite.   Sure there cannot.

Palamon. I do not think it possible our friendship
    Should ever leave us.
Arcite.   Till our deaths it cannot.

(2.2.112–15)

At this moment the lovely Emilia appears in the courtyard below their cell. Palamon catches sight of her, as does Arcite a
moment later, they are both completely smitten by her image,
and their friendship immediately comes apart:

Palamon. I saw her first.
Arcite.   That's nothing.
Palamon.   But it shall be.
Arcite. I saw her too.
Palamon.   Yes, but you must not love her.

(2.2.158–62)

Here, without doubt is a broadly comic (*and* Fletcherian) moment that cuts through all the high-sounding talk, and it is not
an isolated one. In the ensuing exchange Arcite defends his right
to love Emilia, despite Palamon's microsecond priority in viewing her:

Arcite.   Because another
    First sees the enemy, shall I stand still,
    And let mine honor down, and never charge?
Palamon.   Yes, if he be but one.
Arcite.   But say that one
    Had rather combat me?
Palamon.   Let that one say so,
    And use thy freedom; else, if thou pursuest her,
    Be as that cursed man that hates his country,
    A branded villain.
Arcite.   You are mad.

(2.2.193–200)

Emilia as an enemy soldier, Arcite as a traitor to his country!
In the same scene Palamon has two other extravagant fantasies.
In the first he wishes he were an apricot tree that could supply
Emilia with fruit "Fit for the gods to feed on" (2.2.239). He
would "make her / So near the gods in nature, they should fear
her" (241–42). Then, Palamon concludes, "I am sure she would
love me" (243). When a few lines later he learns that Arcite has
been freed, he has another mad fantasy:

Were I at liberty, I would do things
Of such a virtuous greatness that this lady,
This blushing virgin, should take manhood to her
And seek to ravish me.

(2.2.56–59)

A virgin lady ravishing a man because she is so struck by his virtue! The inseparable partner of the author of *The Knight of the Burning Pestle* is beginning his portion of the play by shamelessly "camping up" the old, revered "Knight's Tale," in the process adding some surprising and amusing shadings to Shakespeare's "pair of lions."

Fletcher's treatment of Palamon and Arcite in the rest of the play continues to be two-edged but his tone is generally graver. As strict adherents of the chivalric code, their conduct is completely regulated for them. They *must* act as nobly and honorably as possible while pursuing Emilia to the exclusion of all else. Not surprisingly considering the emphasis of the play, "must" appears more frequently in *The Two Noble Kinsmen* than in any other play in Shakespeare's canon, almost twice his average.[11] Critics have attacked Fletcher for failing to differentiate the protagonists, but that is the point. Adherence to the code makes the two cousins nearly interchangeable automatons, and one may discern a deeper implication in their actions. Although the knightly code may originally have been designed to curb uncivilized instincts, here it sanctions and dignifies the urge for revenge, murder, and suicide. In 3.6 the cousins arm each other for single combat with extravagant, "noble" courtesy, and each tries to cede advantages in the combat to the other. Then they fight with a "mad" (122) impulse to annihilate each other—all this, we must recall, for a girl whom Palamon, at least, has never met. When separated by Theseus, who happens upon them in combat, they now try to outdo each other in a show of indifference for their lives, each pleading to be punished if the other is, each refusing freedom if it means abandoning the quest for Emilia, each eager to be killed if Emilia prefers the other. To Theseus and his court with their identical values this fanatical commitment to love or death appears magnificent. "These are men!" (3.6.265) exclaims Pirithous, and we must agree with all this implies, with the full spectrum from admiration of their purity of commitment to revulsion at their exhibitionistic machismo.

It is left to Theseus, the legendary embodiment of the heroic life, to sanction the kinsmen's noble values by the solution he ordains for their dilemma. Of course, they must engage in a chivalric encounter, but they must find "three fair knights" to fight along with them. The winner "shall enjoy her; the other lose his head, / And all his friends" will also be executed (3.6.296–97). The Spartan harshness of the *four* executions does not, significantly, derive from Chaucer: its invention is one of the clearest signs that the play is viewing the honor code skeptically and, perhaps, is supporting King James's recent decree (1613) against dueling. When Emilia hears the admiring descriptions of the cavaliers, whose extravagant sense of noblesse oblige has made them partners in her lovers' fight, she underlines the outlandish stringency of the conditions: "Must these men die too?" (4.2.112). Fletcher's Emilia is consistent with Shakespeare's portrayal—soft-hearted, gently questioning the harsh tenets of her civilization—but even her sister, the Amazonian warrior Hippolyta, notes the disproportion between the stakes and the penalty. Such a group of men as those pledged to fight, she says, "would show / Bravely about the titles of two kingdoms. / 'Tis pity love should be so tyrannous" (4.2.144–46). Both love and her husband are pitiless and tyrannous, and thus in their world of "must's," she acknowledges, "It must be" (148). A comment in the subplot wryly makes the same point about courtly values. Asked whether Theseus' conditions for settling Palamon and Arcite's differences are "good," someone comments, "They are honorable, / How good they'll prove, I know not" (4.1.29–31). Honorable behavior is not automatically "good."

This is not the only connection between the subplot and the main plot. Comprising about 20 percent of the play, with no basis in "The Knight's Tale" and attributed almost completely to Fletcher, this nearly independent story of the pathetic fortunes of the Jailer's Daughter makes a powerful judgment about heroes who live their lives on the high wire. Like her father's captives, she, too, has contracted a passion—a hopeless one in her case because of her social position—for Palamon. In a succession of soliloquies alternating with the main plot, we hear that her love is an unquenchable sexual hunger: "O for a prick now, like a nightingale, / To put my breast against" (3.4.25–26). Eventually she goes mad out of sexual frustration. After much Victorian prudery about the sort of "trash" we would expect of the lubricious Fletcher, this subplot and particularly the character of the Daughter have come to be appreciated in recent years as stageworthy and moving: "Infinitely more interesting than

Ophelia. A terribly credible character for us, now," according to the distinguished British actress Imogen Stubbs who played the Daughter in the 1986 Royal Shakespeare Company production at the Swan Theatre.[12]

The Daughter's scenes are counterpointed to ones showing Palamon and Arcite's rivalry, the mad helplessness of animalistic love being set against the mad automatism of courtly love. It is unclear which is worse for humans: to be subdued by one's senses or by one's "godlike" aspirations. But Fletcher exploits the contrast in another way by showing the world of difference between the treatment of love madness in the cousins' heroic, and the Daughter's pastoral, worlds. In 3.5, just before Theseus' harsh but equable solution to the noble kinsmen's problem, we are shown the Daughter's humane return to society and her family. She has been aimlessly wandering around the countryside in search of Palamon and is suddenly spotted by a troop of country folk—they call themselves "mad boys" (3.5.24)—who in the manner of A Midsummer Night's Dream are preparing a morris dance to entertain Theseus and his court. They are in desperate need of another woman because "Cicely the sempster's daughter" has not appeared. Suddenly they see the Daughter, obviously mad:

> *First Countryman.* A mad woman? We are made, boys!
> *Schoolmaster.* And are you mad, good woman?
> *Jailer's Daughter.* I would be sorry else.
>
> (3.5.76–78)

In her sorry state, madness has been her only protection, but now in an open, unquestioning manner, the Countrymen, mad boys that they are, incorporate her madness into theirs. The morris dance in The Inner Temple Masque was so admired by the king that he "called for it againe at the end"; Beaumont intended it to create "a spirit of Countrey jollitie."[13] Perhaps the motive in inserting the dance into the play may have been merely commercial, a much-needed added attraction for the King's Men, reeling from their recent "losses." However, the effect is similar to that of the "bergomask" in A Midsummer Night's Dream, its "Countrey jollitie" a healthy madness that momentarily clears the air.

The Jailer's Daughter had seemed destined to play the mad Ophelia, but while we hear of her further sufferings, we never see her alone again and can no longer imagine her destined for a tragic fate. In her next appearance (4.1), just after Theseus has established the bloody conditions that will cure the cousins' madness and after we hear her "Wooer" describe how he saved the Daughter from drowning, she enters, as obsessed by Palamon as ever. Now, however, she is back in a warm family circle that literally "humors" her by pretending to be on a ship taking her to Palamon:

> *All.* Owgh, owgh, owgh! 'Tis up! The wind's fair.
>   Top the bowling! Out with the mainsail!
>   Where's your whistle, master?
> *Brother.*   Let's get her in.
> *Jailer.* Up to the top, boy!
> *Brother.*   Where's the pilot?
> *First Friend.*   Here.
> *Jailer's Daughter.* What ken'st thou?
> *Second Friend.*   A fair wood.
> *Jailer's Daughter.*   Bear for it, master.
>   Tack about!   *Sings.*
>   "When Cynthia with her borrowed light," etc.
>   (4.1.147–53)

The family's frantic, desperate "play therapy" offers a uniquely moving moment in Jacobean drama.

But it is the manner in which Fletcher has the Daughter's madness cured that best distinguishes two rhythms of life, two kinds of civilization. The family's doctor sees that the Daughter's trouble is "not an engraff'd madness, but a most thick and profound melancholy" (4.3.48–50). The symptom being a kind of schizophrenia, he prescribes a form of therapy that has adherents today. The family must enter her fantasy world and act the parts she assigns them: "It is a falsehood she is in, which is with falsehoods to be combated" (4.3.93–4). This may involve actions that under ordinary circumstances would be considered immoral. Her old "wooer" must *play* the part of Palamon:

> *Doctor.* . . . do any thing,
>   Lie with her, if she ask you.
> *Jailer.*   Ho there, doctor!
> *Doctor.* Yes, in the way of cure.
> *Jailer.*   But first, by your leave,
>   I'th' way of honesty.
> *Doctor.*   That's but a niceness.
>   Nev'r cast your child away for honesty.

Cure her first this way, then if she will be honest,
She has the path before her.

(5.2.17–23)

After the father leaves, this amoral medical empiricist repeats
his contempt for the Jailer's unscientific, moralistic qualms:
"You fathers are fine fools. Her honesty! / And we should give
her physic till we find that—" (5.4.28–29). At the very moment
when the climactic battle between the forces of Palamon and
Arcite is in preparation—"the noblest sight / That ev'r was
seen" (5.2.99–100)—the Wooer, pretending to be Palamon, is
preparing to take the Daughter to bed. The "therapy" works,
and we hear that the cured Daughter is planning to marry her
faithful lover. "Honesty," meaning (as often for Beaumont and
Fletcher) unthinking adherence to unnatural precepts, is a
"niceness" like love unto death; it is a concern of the heroic
world.[14] For the rest, those who do not aspire to "nobility" or
godhead, it is enough to satisfy natural appetites and keep the
noiseless tenor of their way.

The structure of *The Two Noble Kinsmen* is unusual in that
a double plot, largely Fletcher's, is enfolded by Shakespeare's
contribution. Only rarely is he concerned with plot or character
development. While Fletcher dramatized a contrast between
"kinds" of humans, Shakespeare wrapped the human predica-
ments in broader, cosmological implications. At the opening
of the play he establishes the martial, chivalric atmosphere of
Athens, but he also keeps reminding us of the higher forces that
master our destinies, such as, "Th' impartial gods, who from
the mounted heavens / View us their mortal herd, behold who
err / And in their time chastise" (1.4.4–6), "This world's a city
full of straying streets, / And death's the market-place, where
each one meets" (1.5.15–16). When Shakespeare resumes control of the action in the fifth act, he once again raises matters
to a higher power, particularly in the magniloquent prayers by
the combatants to their tutelary deities before the battle. Arcite's to Mars is as spine-tingling as it is bone-chilling. One
thrills to the evocation of a power "whose breath blows down /
The teeming Ceres' foison; who dost pluck / With hand armipo-
tent from forth blue clouds / The mason'd turrets" (5.1.52–55).
Yet intermixed with the rousing tribute to militarism are passages that may seem less attractive to us than they do to Arcite.
The god he unreservedly admires "makes the camp a cestron /
Brimm'd with the blood of men" (46–47); he "heal'st with

blood / The earth when it is sick, and cur'st the world / O' th' plurisy of people" (64–66). Palamon's great prayer to Venus describes her as even more powerful: "What godlike power / Hast thou not power upon?" (5.1.89–90), but (again in seemingly unconscious derogation) what this love goddess inspires in men is behavior that is humiliating, horrid, or disgusting: "sovereign queen of secrets, who has power / To call the fiercest tyrant from his rage / And weep unto a girl" (5.1.77–79); "thy yoke / [is] . . . heavier / Than lead itself, stings more than nettles" (95–97). Finally, Emilia's exquisite prayer is to a Diana whose purity makes her utterly ineffectual amid such brutal powers: "O sacred, shadowy, cold, and constant queen, / Abandoner of revels, mute, contemplative" (5.1.137–38). Emilia desires to remain outside the sexual world (with much good reason, we are made to feel), but against the two supreme powers, she hopelessly realizes, Diana is impotent: "I shall be gather'd" (170). The bleak conclusion to the play is thus a natural development from the stress Shakespeare has been placing in act 5 on the role of the gods:

> *Theseus.* . . . O you heavenly charmers,
>   What things you make of us! For what we lack
>   We laugh, for what we have are sorry, still
>   Are children in some kind.
>
> (5.4.131–34)

However different the members of the "mortal herd" (1.4.4–6) may appear from ground level, we are all alike, ludicrous, helpless "things." The somber conclusion by Theseus is apparently Shakespeare's last written utterance. Of course, we have no more right to identify Shakespeare with Theseus than we do with Prospero or Leontes, but at this concluding moment the sentiment sounds ominously closer to Gloucester's view of us as "flies to wanton boys" than to that of the Victorian Bard on the heights bidding a serene farewell to us as "precious winners all."

In any case, *The Two Noble Kinsmen* was a collaboration based upon complementarity. Throughout his career Fletcher laughed at mad lovers and overly rhetorical poseurs; questioned the implications of some of the most prominent cant terms of the time, especially "noble"; and viewed critically the inflexibility of the honor code and hence of the duel. Shakespeare, too, had treated such matters, particularly in *Coriolanus*, where his fifty-eight uses of "noble" remorselessly anatomize the entire spectrum of its meanings from "large-spirited" to "fascistic." Here, however, Shakespeare primarily viewed this play about mad lovers from perspectives we expect in his late plays: on earth that of the idealized love of the Emilia-Flavina relationship and above, virtually from their eighth sphere, that of the marble-hearted "heavenly charmers."

Thus we are left with my initial problem, how this play fits into the theatrical offerings of 1613. It was a play produced at the Blackfriars with an "upscale" audience ready to leap upon any possible contemporary allusion and written by the two most prominent playwrights of the time. It was also a play that began with a masque celebrating a royal marriage, that included a much-admired dance from an actual marriage masque for the princess, and that stressed Prince Henry's favorite topics—honor and chivalric values—written amid other theatrical works that directly celebrated the marriage. Such a play obviously has connections to its time and place, to the topics of the day. But what does it say about them? Certainly it is not a clear endorsement nor is it a criticism of Prince Henry, the king, the princess, or the Protestant political agenda. On the other hand, subtly, tangentially, complexly, it does deal with such topics.[15] We are made to thrill at the magnificence and purity of purpose of the worshipers of Venus and Mars in their various manifestations both high and low while laughing at their confusions, their superficiality, and their ultimate impotency. In part, the richness of the play is made possible by the generous inclusiveness of the Elizabethan dramatic form that can contain divergent but overlapping artistic impulses from dissimilar artists. With a clear opportunity to write something that could cater to power, that could flatter and support official doctrine, Shakespeare and Fletcher demonstrated (as was frequently the case in Jacobean drama, *pace* some New Historicists!) the essential independence of the greatest dramatists.[16] With utter indifference to external pressures they sniffed their way all around the issues with no "irritable reaching after fact and reason." Even at the end of his career Shakespeare with much support from his new partner made his old players, as always, "tell all."

NOTES

1. It adapts a dance from a masque of 20 February 1613 by Beaumont, and Jonson alludes to it in 1614. Despite Paul Bertram's powerfully argued claims

for Shakespeare's unassisted authorship in *Shakespeare and The Two Noble Kinsmen* (New Brunswick: Rutgers University Press, 1965), I accept the traditional ascription of joint authorship (for which there is much corroboration) first registered in the Stationers' Register in 1634 and on the title page of the quarto of the same year. There is remarkable unanimity of agreement about the authorship of individual scenes: here I follow the Riverside Shakespeare.

2. See Eugene Waith, ed., *The Two Noble Kinsmen* (Oxford: Clarendon Press, 1989); Glynn Wickham, "The Two Noble Kinsmen, or A Midsummer Night's Dream, Part II?," in *The Elizabethan Theatre VII*, ed. G. R. Hibbard (Papers given at the Seventh International Conference on Elizabethan Theatre, Waterloo, 1977) (Hamden, Conn.: Archon Books, 1980), 167–96; M. C. Bradbrook, "Shakespeare as Collaborator," *The Living Monument* (Cambridge: Cambridge University Press, 1976), 227–41.

3. *Henry, Prince Of Wales* (London: Thames and Hudson, 1986), 175. Further page references to this book are in the text.

4. *The Maske of the Inner Temple and Grayes Inne*, ed. Fredson Bowers in Bowers, gen.ed., *The Dramatic Works in the Beaumont and Fletcher Canon* (Cambridge: Cambridge University Press, 1966), 1:128, lines 36–38.

5. See my *Court and Country Politics in the Plays of Beaumont and Fletcher* (Princeton: Princeton University Press, 1990), 206–11, for a more detailed discussion of the masque and Beaumont's politics.

6. Ibid., 41–42, 255–58.

7. All quotations are from Stanley Wells and Gary Taylor, eds., *William Shakespeare: The Complete Works* (Oxford: Oxford University Press, 1986). I insert without notice some readings from the Quarto (notably 4.1.145) where the Oxford edition's emendation is unnecessary. Some have guessed that "losses" refers to the fire of 1613 that leveled the Globe during a production of *Henry VIII*. Some have suggested that the plural "losses" makes possible a reference to Prince Henry's death; or, I would add, to Beaumont's stroke or to the 1613 death of Shakespeare's last surviving brother Richard.

8. *Coleridge on the Seventeenth Century*, ed. Roberta F. Brinkley (Durham, N.C.: Duke University Press, 1955), 650.

9. I have been quoting and paraphrasing from Strong, *Henry, Prince of Wales*, 141, 143–44.

10. See Talbot Donaldson, *The Swan at the Well: Shakespeare Reading Chaucer* (New Haven: Yale University Press, 1985), 67, for a view of Theseus as "untouchable by human feelings." For a radically different view see Waith, *Two Noble Kinsmen*, "the emphasis on pity in the play supports the idealism of the principal characters."

11. My figures derive from Marvin Spevack, *A Complete and Systematic Concordance to the Works of Shakespeare* (Hildesheim: Georg Olms, 1968–80). The nearest rival, *The Winter's Tale*, has 16 percent fewer "must's." In the 2,350 lines of "The Knight's Tale" "must" occurs only five times.

12. Ronnie Mulryne, *This Golden Round: The Royal Shakespeare Company at the Swan* (Stratford-upon-Avon: Mulryne and Shewring Ltd., 1989), 110.

13. "The Maske of the Inner Temple," ed. Bowers, 134.

14. For an extended justification of this generalization about Beaumont and Fletcher, see my *Court and Country Politics*, esp. chap. 10 on *The Maid's Tragedy*.

15. The same may be said of the other Shakespeare-Fletcher collaboration

sometimes linked, such as in the Arden edition, to the princess's marriage, *Henry VIII*. Balanced against the rehabilitation of Henry VIII at the end and the nostalgic tribute to Queen Elizabeth is pervasive criticism of the governance of a despotic king, an evil counselor, and a corrupt clergy.

16. I am asserting a position that I argue at length in "The 'Comedians' Liberty': Censorship of the Jacobean Stage Reconsidered," *English Literary Renaissance* 16 (1986): 123–38.

"The Norwegians are Coming!"
Shakespearean Misleadings

SUSAN SNYDER

To explore what seems to me a characteristic Shakespearean strategy, I want to consider two battles that don't happen: the Turkish attack against Cyprus in *Othello* and the invasion of Danish lands by Fortinbras and his Norwegian force in *Hamlet*. Both of these loom large in the early action of their respective plays. The upcoming wars are the focus for agitated discussion, diplomatic maneuver, and (especially) martial preparation. For a few scenes at least, we have every reason to believe that the Turks/Norwegians will attack and that the ensuing wars will be the main substance of the dramas we are watching. Yet early in act 2 of *Hamlet*, the ambassadors Voltemand and Cornelius report back to Claudius that Fortinbras has been diverted to Poland. By this time, in any case, we have heard the Ghost's tale of fratricide and know that Denmark's malaise has nothing to do with Norwegians. At a similar point in *Othello*, the Turkish peril and the expectations it arouses are even more cleanly cut off when a storm demolishes the enemy's fleet. Speculation, anxiety, and mobilization end abruptly with "News, lads! Our wars are done."[1] Why so much ado about these wars if they are to be "done" so quickly, in fact never to happen at all?

Of course these lines of action, even unfulfilled, have some secondary functions in their respective dramatic designs. Fortinbras's mission to recover the lands Old Hamlet took from his father introduces the repeated motif of the revenger-son in *Hamlet*. And the shrewd move by which Claudius forestalls this danger begins the buildup of the King into a suitably mighty opposite for the hero-prince. In a similar way, the formidable threat posed by the Turks affirms Othello's stature by showing how much the state depends on his generalship. It also occasions a significant move of the action from civilized Venice to the demonic green world of Cyprus. Even so, what is the structural point of these abortive wars? What does Shakespeare accomplish by raising expectations he is not going to fulfill?

Something is already deeply wrong in Denmark when *Hamlet* opens. We are immediately introduced to a jumpy, apprehensive watch and fragmentary reports of a supernatural presence. "This thing," "this dreaded sight," "this apparition," as the watchers call it, is perhaps only "fantasy,"[2] but in any case it is not yet described or named. Then the Ghost appears—fully armed and holding the truncheon that marks the military commander (1.2.200–204). The audience has not been prepared for anything beyond the fact of the Ghost: when it appears, its martial accoutrements thus have greater impact for being unexpected. Now "this thing" is identified with the dead King Hamlet, and specifically the King as leader in battle. This is what Horatio registers in saluting "that fair and *warlike* form / In which the majesty of buried Denmark / Did sometimes *march*" (1.1.45–47, emphasis added). Later remarks add to the military emphasis. Old Hamlet's Ghost moves with "martial stalk" (1.1.65), he frowns (1.1.61, 1.2.229–30).[3] A generally bad omen, the King who walks abroad after death instead of lying in suitable repose, is thus apparently specified in its import, directing the mind to his role as defender of Denmark against foreign adversaries. Specificity pinpoints the adversary, too: the Ghost appears in the same armor he wore long ago in combat with "th'ambitious Norway."

It is natural that the frightened onlookers should look immediately to Norway as the source of the current trouble. When the Ghost disappears, Horatio predicts from it "some strange eruption to our state," and at once the talk turns to the warlike vigilance and preparation that are already present as signs of trouble, in addition to the armed specter. The strange eruption on the horizon is young Fortinbras's mission of revenge against Denmark, occasioned by that long-ago fight between Old Hamlet and "ambitious Norway," Fortinbras's father. The elder Fortinbras was defeated and killed, and now his son wants to refight the battle. It all fits: the strict watch, the munitions-makers and shipwrights working overtime, and now this ghost in the likeness of the original combatant. Barnardo adds it up:

Well may it sort that this portentous figure
Comes armed through our watch so like the king
That was and is the question of these wars.[4]

Horatio the scholar seeks parallels in history, especially the unnatural events before Julius Caesar's fall. Viewers who were familiar with Roman history, perhaps through Shakespeare's own
recent dramatization in *Julius Caesar*, might be subconsciously
troubled by the parallel—it was, after all, his closest friends who
destroyed Caesar, not a foreign force[5]—but the main emphasis
is consistent, as Horatio points to similar, more recent harbin-
gers of disaster in Denmark's own past. Frank Kermode observes, "So far as plot goes, this might be the opening scene of
a play about a Caesar-like Hamlet now dead but still posthumously interested in empire."[6]

In the next scene we leave the midnight watch on the battlements for a formal court gathering, but the signs seem to go on
pointing the same way. The threat of Fortinbras and his lawless
resolutes is the first business of the new king. Only after taking
steps against that threat does Claudius turn to other concerns,
the petitions of Laertes and Hamlet to leave the court and especially the embarrassment of Hamlet's prolonged grief. Claudius
with characteristic wiliness speculates on what has prompted
the belligerent boldness of young Fortinbras: perhaps contempt
for the new king himself as not the equal of his mighty brother,
or perhaps conjecture that a state in transition between rulers
will be "disjoint and out of frame" (1.2.20). Since we suspect
that both these propositions are true, however Claudius tries to
dismiss them, the false signal continues, reinforced: beware the
Norwegians, ready on the horizon to take advantage of internal
disruptions in Denmark.

Claudius counters Hamlet's grief with platitudes, and, having
given Laertes leave to travel to Paris, refuses his nephew-son's
request to go back to Wittenberg. I have observed elsewhere
that this play is full of young men coming and going on foreign
expeditions. Only Hamlet is, until late in act 4, confined to his
Danish "prison,"[7] thus enacting physically the claustrophobic
quality of the play's central action. When the false lead of the
Norwegian invasion fizzles out after attracting such attention
in the opening scenes, this claustrophobic inwardness is reinforced. The threat is not the visible foreign one but a hidden
one at home, not even a serpent slithering from somewhere else
into the secluded royal retreat. The enemy is not outside at all,
but inside the kingdom, inside the family—"The serpent that
did sting thy father's life / Now wears his crown" (1.5.39–40).
And perhaps inside Hamlet's own self as well.

The Turks in *Othello* are similarly clear as outside enemies.

Their intentions and strategies may occasionally be in doubt, but their status as alien adversaries is not. To understand their role, I would like to examine a general perspective on war and peace that colors several of Shakespeare's plays. Though he is no particular friend to bloodshed, at times he presents war as having certain advantages over peace. It offers clearcut action, more or less publicly sanctioned, against known enemies: something straightforward—that is, as opposed to the temptations, complications, and evasions characteristic of society's peacetime practices. In *All's Well That Ends Well* Bertram gladly goes off to war in Italy to escape from married life with Helen, a situation in which personal dislike strains against obligation to his patron the King. By comparison, doing battle in a foreign land looks easy and desirable. "Wars is no strife / To the dark house and the detested wife." The dying Henry IV recommends to his son and successor a campaign abroad as a way out of intrigue and dissension at home. The "giddy minds" Henry fears have in the past turned all too readily against himself and each other, and "daily grew to quarrel and to bloodshed, / Wounding supposed peace." In counseling Hal to occupy those unstable minds in *foreign* quarrels, Henry makes a different but relevant distinction: not war as opposed to peace, but overt war against a sharply defined Other as an alternative to the tragic muddles of internecine struggle. Henry's strategy is successful. *Henry V* shows us the new king leading an army away from England against an outside enemy—if not the absolute Other his father had dreamed of fighting, the Muslim infidel, still the notably foreign French, who go far beyond the variant versions of English that divide Henry's Irish, Scots, and Welsh contingents to speak another language entirely. (Or rather, they necessarily speak the same tongue as the English most of the time so that London audiences can understand them, but even apart from Princess Catherine's language lesson Shakespeare colors the defending army's discourse with enough incidental French to keep their differentness constantly before us.) And the "English," after the treason of Cambridge, Scrope, and Grey is disposed of, are indeed more or less united against this obvious foe, their internal differences submerged in the common cause, in the manner of those heterogeneous U.S. bomber crews in World War II films.[8]

Several plays present war as a kind of prologue to the main action. *Much Ado About Nothing* opens just after a war has ended. Don Pedro and his officers are unsuspicious, ready to relax and play. During the war, Don John's hostility was clear when he "stood out" against his brother.[9] Now, the defeated John dissembles malice under apparent accord—and becomes twice as dangerous in the intricate pastimes of peace: dances with masked partners, the merry wars of courtship. Destructive forces are present still, but concealed: in the bastard brother, and even in the unthinking assumptions of Pedro himself and his callow protégé Claudio. The troubles of Titus Andronicus also begin after open battle has ended. Titus goes by the rules. The principle of primogeniture rather than personal merit dictates his choice for emperor, the requirements of ritual lead him to sacrifice Tamora's son and thus set her against him, and an oversimple idea of honor bids him kill his own son. The straightforward, rigid code that served Titus well enough in the field fails miserably in the tangle of passion and ambition that he encounters at home. What Aufidius criticizes in Coriolanus marks Titus's limitations as well: "Not to be other than one thing, not moving / From th' casque to th' cushion, but commanding peace / Even with the same austerity and garb / As he controlled the war" (Coriolanus 4.7.42–45). Coriolanus himself can conquer a whole city singlehanded, but he finds civil life as unnegotiable a maze as Titus finds personal relationships. The corresponding prologue-battle in Macbeth is over almost before we hear of it. Seventy-five lines into the play, the bleeding captain and Ross have given their report and Duncan is rejoicing in total victory. Even before Macbeth makes his first entrance, their glowing accounts call attention to his sphere of achievement—and then cut it off. Macbeth is a highly effective warrior, but there are no more wars in prospect. Though he is not as unused to civil life as Coriolanus is, the shift to peace opens him to more complex imperatives of self-fulfillment, as it brings to Coriolanus a different, more perplexing duty. It is women who promote these new roles, Volumnia the mother and Lady Macbeth the wife, domestic counselors with their own devious agendas who replace the male companions of the straightforward combat. Different from each other as these plays are—the comedy, the early and late Roman plays, the tragedy—they all use the war-prologue to make us conscious of the transition from the loud clash of armies to more oblique and subtle encounters.

So does Othello, another play about a professional soldier. From this perspective the jubilant cheer that greets the perdition of the Turkish fleet, "Our wars are done," is as ominous for the hero's future as any of Iago's sneers. The play has begun with concerns of peacetime like intrigues for professional advancement, courtship, and marriage. In the second scene, however, the war threat breaks into these preoccupations with disruptive force. The danger is at first unnamed, as in *Hamlet:* Cassio and the officers arrive with breathless tidings of "something from Cyprus," "a business of some heat" in which the Duke has urgent need of his general. "The galleys / Have sent a dozen sequent messengers / This very night at one another's heels." Othello is "hotly called for," must come "haste-post-haste" (1.2.37–44). Great national events are clearly in the making. As the summons to the Venetian council interrupts Othello's conversation with Iago about his recent marriage, the dynamic of action suggests that the public emergency will displace this private matter. In the council scene that follows, there are almost fifty lines of agitated speculation about the numbers and intentions of the enemy, now identified as the Turks, punctuated by two more of those sequent messengers arriving with fresh news. Only after all this does Brabantio enter to plead his personal grievance against the Moor for marrying his daughter. But Brabantio's cause makes little headway amid pressing affairs of state. After hearing the defenses of Othello and Desdemona, the Duke turns quickly back to his overriding concern and orders the Moor at once to Cyprus.

Not only does the imperative of war seem to put parentheses around Othello's new marital relationship—he himself exits telling his bride, "We must obey the time" (1.3.300)—but even his long lyrical account of their courtship has served to remind us that Othello's proper scene is war. We have already learned that from the age of seven his home has been the tented field, his experience all "feats of broil and battle" (1.3.83–87). This is what Othello knows. There is a sense in which, when the Turkish fleet is suddenly blown to destruction early in act 2, Othello's occupation is already gone, even before Iago poisons his mind against Desdemona. The end of hostilities is the signal for revelry; and, as in *Much Ado*, revelry is a good cover for the insidious attack. The Otherness to be feared now shifts from the defeated Turks to the concealed enemy, Iago, who wears his honesty like a mask and is all the more dangerous for being the trusted battle-companion *as well as* the domestic counselor who acts, ostensibly, out of love.

> *(To Cassio)* Good lieutenant, I think you think I love you. . . . I protest, in the sincerity of love and honest kindness.

(To Othello) My lord, you know I love you

. . . .
I humbly do beseech you of your pardon
For too much loving you.[10]

The Turks were a convenient manifestation of the Other in Shakespeare's time. They were foreign. They zealously followed and promulgated an alien, inimical religion. Powerful in battle, they were a real and continuing threat at the gates of southern and eastern Europe. "Not-us" in race, nation, and religion, Turks were also traditionally imaged as the epitome of rampant, unchecked sexuality. Edgar as Poor Tom, claiming that he "in women out-paramoured the Turk" (Lear 3.4.85–86), invokes that stereotype, which perhaps was based on Europeans' knowledge that Muslim men were allowed four wives as well as additional concubines.[11] When the Other in *Othello* is relocated to the familar and close-at-hand, it is Iago who manifests the Turk's malevolence and formidable power, and his foreignness as well: though Venetian and nominally Christian, Iago is alien to all human community. The dialogue slyly links him with the missing Turk. Challenged in banter with Desdemona for a wholesale slander of wives that anticipates the later, greater deception, he protests, "Nay, it is true, or else I am a Turk." It is not true. Later when Othello surveys the drunken brawl that has interrupted his wedding night and caused Cassio's disgrace, he asks, "Are we turned Turks, and to ourselves do that / Which heaven hath forbid the Ottomites?"[12] The answer, at least for Iago as sole architect of the recent disaster, is yes.

Iago is somewhat like Don John of *Much Ado* in his urge to sabotage whatever is attractive and admirable and in his closeness to the people he means to harm. If not trusted as much as Iago, John at any rate attracts no suspicion from Claudio, or even the brother he has betrayed once already, Don Pedro. Indeed, these two siblings are close in another sense, both meddlers in the affairs of others who back off from real human engagement. Pedro has more surface charm, but the bastard brother at his elbow reminds us that his drive to control has its dark underside.[13] There is a shadow side to Othello as well, which Iago makes manifest. He could not have succeeded without the Moor's self-doubts, his sexual and social insecurities, and his defensive pride, all of which Iago helps bring into full articulation in order to play on them.

In the same shake of the kaleidoscope pattern brought about

by the disappearance of the external enemy, the Turk's raging sexuality finds a new but different home: not in actuality with Iago and Othello but in fantasy, projected by Othello onto Desdemona. Such imaginations of female desire as out of control and insatiable are as old as stories of Eve, part of the more general male impulse to construct the woman as feared Other. Othello discovers the "curse of marriage" almost by reflex: "That we can call these delicate creatures ours / But not their appetites!" (3.3.272–74). Only after Desdemona is dead does he finally recognize the enemy in himself. In timing his own death blow to coincide with that earlier stroke in his story, by which he punished the Turk who did harm to Venice and its native citizen, Othello identifies with that "malignant" felon—*malignant* gathering in not only "rebellious," but "contagious," like a disease, poisonous.[14]

In both *Hamlet* and *Othello*, the relocation of the Other is a destabilizing shift from out there to right here: in someone or something close at hand, in one's own being. My uncle (O my prophetic soul!), my brother, my self. Inevitably this brings with it a displacement like that in *Much Ado* and *Titus*, from the prospect of marching out against a declared foe, with the battle lines clearly drawn, to the confusions inherent in the concealed enmity of one's own kind. This distinction comes through well in the second scene of *Macbeth*, where the enemies detailed in the complicated battle report are of both kinds. On the one hand are the foreigners, the Norwegians (again!)[15] who come on like obvious adversaries, defiantly showing their banners (*Macbeth* 1.2.49). To these we might add the Hebridean soldiers whose label of "kerns and gallowglasses" links them with the alien Irish.[16] These, the official Other, present a hard fight but no particular confusion or ambiguity. But there are inside enemies too, the rebels Macdonwald and Cawdor. In these cases of Scot against Scot, as reported by the Captain and Ross, ambiguities abound. When the Captain describes Macbeth's confrontation with Macdonwald, the signifying pronouns "he" and "his" slide about so loosely as to leave us unsure for a moment just who was killing whom when Macbeth

Carved out his passage till he faced the slave,
Which ne'er shook hands nor bade farewell to him
Till he unseamed him from the nave to th' chops,
And fixed his head upon our battlements.

(1.2.20–23)

If it is hard at this point to sort out Macbeth grammatically from the enemy Macdonwald, the later account of Macbeth's fight with the traitorous Thane of Cawdor seems designed to muddle rebel and loyalist even more thoroughly: "Bellona's bridegroom . . . Confronted him with self-comparisons, / Point against point, rebellious arm 'gainst arm" (34–36). The Scots Macdonwald and Cawdor bring with them the tensions and confusions of the Other as "we," beginning the more radical relocation in this play that will find in the hero himself the King's worst enemy and his own.

How does this redirection of our expectations work on us? If the road we thought we were traveling turns out to be a dead end, if the signs keep saying "this way . . . this way" only to pull us up short with "no, *this* way," the result should be that we are now paying closer attention to the new road on which we find ourselves. What are its landmarks and what do they mean? How will this new journey both substitute for the aborted one and differ from it? Since the first frustration of expectation has shaken our passive, easy acquiescence in the playwright's guidance, we should become more alert, more actively focused on the new, subtler markers of our progress. Or, to change the metaphor, think of a sleight-of-hand artist, who keeps us focused on one hand while performing his magic with the other: when we see the result, we concentrate with special force on the hand newly identified as powerful. This spotlighting of the real tragic arena, by presenting an alternative and then leaving it in darkness, need be no less effective for operating below the level of consciousness.

I have used "should be" rather than "is" about this effect because I am trying to recover at least theoretically an experience that was far more available to Shakespeare's original audiences than to most of us. Playgoers at productions of *Hamlet* nowadays usually *know* that the Norwegians are not the real menace: they studied the play in high school, they saw the Olivier film or the Mel Gibson one, or they just absorbed the outlines of the dramatic action through cultural osmosis. Test this on your students. Even if they have never read the play, they probably know the Ghost's mission is not to alert the Danes to danger from Norway but to lay a burden of revenge on his son. Since the plots of Shakespeare's great tragedies are the common currency of our English-speaking culture, lay audiences as well as professional Shakespeareans experience the plays in ways that might have surprised Shakespeare. They have no hope that

King Lear or *Romeo and Juliet* will end happily, they are confident that the Ghost of Old Hamlet is telling the truth about his murder and Claudius's guilt—and they are probably not taken in by the Norwegian decoy. The same osmosis deprives *Othello* of its novelty too. Even if the plot is somewhat less familiar than that of *Hamlet,* people know enough about what is coming to focus on Iago as the important destructive force rather than on the Turks.

But the Globe audiences had no such certainties. Unfamiliar with the stories of Othello and Hamlet, they could be made to watch the wrong hand first, to follow the ignis fatuus, and then in reassessment to be jolted into superawareness. In several of his sonnets, where Shakespeare uses a similar strategy to develop lyric material that is less familiar in our culture than the major plays, the experience is still available to modern readers. In Sonnet 129, for example, "Th'expense of spirit in a waste of shame," the whole body of the poem is given over to sexual nausea. The couplet starts out still on this tack, summarizing "all this," but then turns aside with "yet" to find a radically new direction.

> All this the world well knows, yet none knows well
> To shun the heaven that leads men to this hell.

The climactic point is not disgust but ecstasy, a "heaven" of pleasure so intense that it can effortlessly sweep away the weight of denunciation of the first twelve lines. The "in spite of" or "nevertheless" structure intensifies the affirmation. "Nevertheless" also drives home with extra force the point of Sonnet 130, "My mistress' eyes are nothing like the sun." One quatrain after another presents a clear-eyed, judicious view of the mistress as an ordinary woman, nothing special, not living up to the extravagant analogies of the sonnet convention. Again the couplet changes direction, continuing the satiric gaze at traditional love poetry with its shopworn conceits ("false compare"), but now celebrating the mistress as very special indeed. She is not only as "rare" as other sonnet heroines, but by implication even rarer than these, in that she has not been degraded by impossible analogies.

The three-quatrains-and-a-couplet format lends itself to this kind of italicizing reversal in the last two lines. Sonnet 66, however, "Tired with all these, for restful death I cry," keeps its reversal for the very last line. The first thirteen lines enact deep

disgust with a society that disdains virtue and skill while ex-
alting worldly power and gaudy show. The basic structural unit
here is not the quatrain but the single line, one following another in parallel grammatical form to create the cumulative effect of one injustice after another:

> And purest faith unhappily forsworn,
> And gilded honour shamefully misplaced,
> And maiden honour rudely strumpeted,
> And right perfection wrongfully disgraced,
> And strength by limping sway disabled,
> And art made tongue-tied by authority . . .

(lines 4–9)

The catalogue of wrongs ends with a climactic summing-up and
conclusion in line 13: "Tired with all these, from these I would
be gone." Only the final line enters a telling reservation, turns
the "would" from the simple wish we heard first to a conditional: "Save that to die I leave my love alone." "My love" gains
extraordinary power through placement. Just the simple two-
word allusion counters the whole negative accumulation of
abuses and affronts, and in effect cancels them—if not as realities, at least as grounds for despair.

World-weariness is the keynote of Sonnet 30 as well, "When
to the sessions of sweet silent thought." Since the poem is about
griefs remembered and reexperienced, there is seemingly no end
to its sorrow. Repetition and alliteration enact endless recapitu-
lation: "old woes new wail. . . . grieve at grievances foregone . . .
woe to woe tell o'er . . . fore-bemoaned moan." How can a poem
so bound up with recurrence ever end? But the couplet breaks
the circle, leads us quickly out of the maze. A simple appeal to
the beloved friend allows poem and speaker to find their place
of rest, appropriately, on the word "end":

> But if the while I think on thee, dear friend,
> All losses are restored, and sorrows end.

Sonnet 84, part of the "Rival Poet" group, is especially unpredictable. The body of the sonnet offers apparently straightforward praise of the friend, who is so excellent that those who
write of him need only copy what is there. Rhetorical embellishment is unnecessary, even detrimental ("making worse what
nature made so clear"). But then without warning the couplet
turns on the friend himself, accusing him of being "too fond on

praise": perhaps "too indiscriminate in commending tributes" to himself, but chiefly "too greedy for compliments of any kind." Because of this "curse," the friend encourages embellishment whether it is needed or not, and thus cheapens praises of himself.[17] The battle lines between ally and enemy have apparently been clearly drawn in Sonnet 84. On the one hand are the bad poets with their too-elaborate meretricious praises, and on the other are the poet-speaker and his exemplary young friend. The couplet, however, transfers those meretricious impulses to the friend himself. As in *Hamlet* and *Othello*, the enemy is no longer out there but right inside the circle of intimacy. As an italicizing relocation of the Other, this sonnet returns us from this excursus to our main concern.

Though the changes of direction in the plays are less patterned than those appropriate to the highly formalized sonnet, they are just as deliberate. In fact, the plays themselves call attention to the strategy they employ. They make it a matter for comment and show us characters who make use of it for their own ends. In *Othello*, it is the Turks themselves who borrow Shakespeare's device of the false direction. First they seem to be making for Cyprus (1.3.8), but then according to a new message they are heading for Rhodes (14). The self-reflexive dimension is accentuated when Shakespeare has a Venetian senator analyze the Rhodes maneuver as sleight-of-hand: "'tis a pageant / To keep us in false gaze" (19–20). Iago, of course, takes over the trickery of the false gaze along with other aspects of the Turkish Other. In *Hamlet*, the hero has his own devious strategies to approach Claudius on the bias, but the one who articulates the basic theory of false leading to underline the truth is—perhaps unexpectedly—not Hamlet but Polonius. His elaborate instructions to Reynaldo on how to check up on Laertes' behavior in Paris (2.1) are themselves a kind of dramatic false lead, since we never see their result. More important, Polonius assumes that the true report he wants on his son cannot be got at by any direct question but must be evoked at one remove, by hypothesis and conjecture. True, Reynaldo is to focus on his real topic, Laertes, and not start by asking about some other young man. Still, he is ordered to be consciously deceptive in order to jolt the people he questions into a truth they would otherwise not have given up so readily.

> See you now,
> Your bait of falsehood takes this carp of truth;

And thus do we of wisdom and of reach
With windlasses and with assays of bias
By indirections find directions out.

Polonius's summary suggests his own skill in plotting, and in a different register Shakespeare's as well. Norwegians and Turks are bait; by such pageants that detain us in false gaze he refocuses that gaze with special intensity.

NOTES

1. *Othello* 2.1.20. Here and elsewhere in this essay the plays and poems are cited from *William Shakespeare: The Complete Works*, ed. Stanley Wells et al. (Oxford: Oxford University Press, 1986).

2. 1.1.19, 23, 26, 21.

3. Old Hamlet's frown is linked to a specific occasion, of an "angry parley," but Harold Jenkins notes that the frown is generally appropriate for the warrior, citing *Merchant* 3.2.85 and *Cymbeline* 2.4.23: *Hamlet*, Arden ed. (London: Methuen, 1982), 169, 195.

4. Additional Passages, A. 2–4. These lines, like the discussion of Julius Caesar immediately following, are in Q2 but not in F.

5. Similarly, *eruption*, "violent outbreak," suggests trouble within rather than without.

6. Introduction to *Hamlet, Riverside Shakespeare*, ed. G. Blakemore Evans (Boston: Houghton Mifflin, 1974), 1138.

7. 2.2.241–48; see Snyder, *The Comic Matrix of Shakespeare's Tragedies* (Princeton: Princeton University Press, 1979), 115.

8. *All's Well* 2.3.288–89; *2 Henry IV* 4.3.323–24. Michael Neill considers the varieties of English in *Henry V* as on a continuum with the more foreign French, all ultimately playing out linguistically England's forcible colonization: "Broken English and Broken Irish: Nation, Language, and the Optic of Power in Shakespeare's Histories," *Shakespeare Quarterly* 45 (1994): 18–22.

9. *Much Ado* 1.3.20. *Stood out* means "mounted a rebellion," but the phrase also functions in its modern sense of "was conspicuous."

10. 2.3.304, 320; 3.3.121, 216–17.

11. Bernard Lewis, *Islam and the West* (New York: Oxford University Press, 1993), 82–83.

12. 2.1.117; 2.3.163–64.

13. Jean E. Howard, in an excellent essay, shows how both brothers use "theatrical deceptions" that call on cultural stereotypes to manipulate others: "Renaissance Antitheatricality and the Politics of Gender and Rank in *Much Ado About Nothing*," in *Shakespeare Reproduced: The Text in History and Ideology*, ed. Jean E. Howard and Marion O'Connor (New York and London: Methuen, 1987), 172–83. While her sociological argument emphasizes the contest between Don Pedro and Don John for control of an aristocratic male prerogative, the two brothers in their close parallelism can also be seen as different angles on a single problematic activity, two versions of the same thing.

14. *OED*, s.v., "malignant," *a*.1, 2, and 3.

15. The Viking marauders of medieval history and legend are a far cry from the cheerful ski fans of the 1994 Winter Olympics, let alone the repressed good citizens chronicled by Garrison Keillor. In any case, Holinshed's account of the incursion used by Shakespeare in *Macbeth* assigns it to the Danes.

16. Kenneth Muir, ed., Arden *Macbeth* (London: Methuen, 1953), note to 1.2.13.

17. In certain sonnets reversals like these feel strained and unconvincing, as the speaker tries to accommodate the inequalities of devotion, his own great dependency and the friend's waywardness and shallowness. In Sonnet 34, for instance, "Why didst thou promise such a beauteous day," the couplet cannot entirely blot out the effect of the preceding three quatrains of anguished question and reproach. The young man's "tears of pearl," which are set up to "ransom all ill deeds," seem merely decorative against the earlier blunt pain of "Though thou repent, yet have I still the loss."

Remembering and Forgetting in Shakespeare

JONAS BARISH

THE act 1 battle scenes in *Coriolanus* conclude with a curious episode. Caius Martius, scourge of Rome's enemies, has returned to Rome in triumph after defeating the Volscians. With great reluctance he has listened to his general, Cominius, praise him for his exploits, has refused the official gifts decreed him as reward, but accepted the more personal offer of Cominius's own horse, as well as the honorary title of "Coriolanus." Before leaving to clean up he begs a favor, that a Volscian prisoner captured in the recent battle, a certain poor man at whose house he was once hospitably received, be set free. The order given, however, the newly named Coriolanus suddenly realizes he is "weary," his "memory is tir'd" (1.9.91), and he has forgotten his benefactor's name. Rather than tax himself further he asks for wine, and the benefactor's fate falls into oblivion. A recent editor of the play cites an earlier editor to the effect that his forgetfulness is due "not to an affectation of magnanimity, but to 'the amnesia of an exhausted man.'"[1]

There may well be a grain of truth in this, but I find it unsatisfying. Exhausted or not, Martius has had the energy to spurn the eulogies, decline most of the gifts, denounce the empty flattery of the instruments trumpeting his victory, and then, still unwearied, to reject for a second time the "acclamations hyperbolical" being heaped on him (1.9.51)—all in his most vehement and highly charged rhetorical style. The lapse of memory, in short, occurs at a moment when we have no inkling of his having run out of steam. Moreover, it is Shakespeare who has added the detail of the memory lapse to the account in Plutarch, as well as having transformed the Volscian host from "an olde friende and hoste of mine, an honest wealthie man," who has lived "in great wealth in his owne countrie"[2] into a "poor man," at whose house "I sometime lay" (82–83) (that is, presumably on a single occasion).

Why does Shakespeare make these changes? Perhaps the reason lies in rhythmic balance, his desire to round off the battle sequence on a quieter note, end it in a less hectic key. Once the discord between the general and his most brilliant subordinate has been resolved, once Martius has accepted Cominius's steed and his own new title, he momentarily becomes more peaceable, more tractable. He can think less rigidly, feel more freely, and so recall the pity he felt for his beleaguered Volscian acquaintance, a pity then stifled by rage at the sight of Aufidius.

But he has forgotten the friend's name! There is now no way he can follow through on his generous impulse. Is it possible that in making the friend poor rather than wealthy, Shakespeare means to insinuate a motive for his lapse of memory? As a poor man, after all, whatever his excellent private and personal qualities, the erstwhile host belongs to the despised lower orders, for whose sufferings Martius has shown such harsh contempt in the opening scene, and who therefore makes a much more equivocal candidate for his sympathy than had he been a patrician.

It would seem that the surge of positive feeling experienced at this juncture runs against a counterimpulse towards self-removal and self-sufficiency. Even when he wishes to, Coriolanus cannot quite let himself go enough to bring to mind the name of a plebeian who once succored him, but must let him sink back into the undifferentiated mass of scorned commoners. The incident would seem to reflect not merely a momentary numbness brought on by fatigue, but an underlying ambivalence, the hero's half-expressed desire for mutuality with his fellows colliding with a self-absorption that drives him away from them, hampering and distorting the positive impulse, and so turning it ultimately into part of a self-defeating mechanism.

This is probably as close as Shakespeare ever comes to depicting the kind of memory lapse that interested Freud, the tendentious forgetfulness motivated by repression.[3] If my guess is at all correct, Coriolanus's lapse is indeed motivated by repression, and in that respect conforms to the Freudian model, even if it does not, like Freud's examples, involve the involuntary blurting out of a wrong name in place of the right one.

But Coriolanus has, at least, genuinely failed to call to mind the name he was seeking. There can be no doubt that it has eluded him, and in that respect the episode is virtually unique.

I can find no other instance in Shakespeare in which such an unmistakable, unequivocal failure of recollection takes place. The wool-gathering Hotspur, in *1 Henry IV*, may think he has neglected to bring the map with which he and his fellow conspirators expect to carve up the country for themselves, but this is mere distraction. It takes the magician and dreamer, Glyndwr, to be levelheaded and produce the missing document: "No, here it is" (3.1.6–7), he announces calmly. In most cases, forgetting comes down to a refusal to remember, a conscious act of denial, often a self-serving shutting out of something inconvenient or unwelcome, as in Proteus's abandonment of his sweetheart, "One Julia, that his changing thoughts forget" (*Two Gentlemen* 4.4.119). Frequently it is associated with ingratitude, as the exiled courtiers remind us in *As You Like It:* "Blow, blow, thou winter wind, / Thou art not so unkind / As man's ingratitude . . . Freeze, freeze, thou bitter sky, / Thou dost not bite so nigh / As benefits forgot" (2.7.174–90).

"Benefits forgot," indeed, along with obligations ignored, might serve as rubric for most Shakespearean forgetting. Richard II demands of the still-standing Northumberland, acting as messenger from the newly returned Bullingbrook, "how dare thy joints forget / To pay their aweful duty to our presence?" (3.3.75–76), thus construing the forgetting (correctly) as open flouting and mutinous repudiation of a solemn oath. The rebellious Hotspur in his turn burns to unseat, if he can, "this unthankful king, / . . . this ingrate and cank'red Bullingbrook," "this forgetful man" (*1 Henry IV* 1.3.136–37, 161), just as his uncle Worcester, cataloguing Henry's misdeeds, charges him with having "Forgot your oath to us at Doncaster," of using him and his family "As that ungentle gull, the cuckoo's bird, / Useth the sparrow" (5.1.58, 60–61). Lear cannot believe that his own daughter will prove a cuckoo bird: "Thy half o'th' kingdom hast thou not forgot," he implores Regan, "wherein I thee endowed" (*Lear F* 2.2.353–54).

Similar disbelief assails the snubbed and baffled Achilles. "What, are my deeds forgot?" he demands, and receives a memorable answer, concerning a mythic "monster of ingratitudes" that "devour[s]" good deeds and consigns them to oblivion "as fast as they are made," forgetting them "as soon as done" (*Troilus* 3.3.144–50). In simple fact, of course, no one has forgotten Achilles' deeds. The generals have simply chosen, for their own politic reasons, to pretend so. Nor does Achilles himself really believe it. Similarly Coriolanus, nerving himself to dismiss

Menenius and so break definitively with Rome, declares himself ready to bear the stigma of ingratitude—"That we have been familiar, / Ingrate forgetfulness shall poison rather / Than pity note how much" (5.2.85–87)—thus consciously preparing to tamper with his own memory, so as to kill the fellow-feeling he still harbors for his old friend in order to cleave to newer and (as he supposes) more urgent commitments.

In nearly all these these cases, forgetfulness can only be viewed as pseudoforgetfulness, or feigned forgetfulness, a willed amnesia masquerading, or half-masquerading, as an inability to possess one's past. The term itself comes to seem little more than a handy euphemism to excuse a dereliction by making it appear beyond the reach of conscious choice. It is only retrospectively that Edward IV, lamenting the death of his brother, ordered by himself, can ascribe it to "brutish wrath" that "Sinfully plucked" from him the "remembrance" of Clarence's love (*Richard III* 2.1.119–20). It is only retrospectively, also, that the Senators of Athens, striving to placate the alienated Timon, can attempt to atone for their ingratitude by confessing "forgetfulness too general gross" towards him (*Timon* 5.1.144)—where the very plea amounts to a self-extenuating effort to shift the burden from their own past inhumanity onto a subterranean psychic process out of the reach of their conscious control.

A further form of forgetfulness involves *self*-forgetting. In *Richard III*, Queen Elizabeth, vacillating (or pretending to vacillate) in the face of Richard's plea to her to woo her daughter on his behalf, demands rhetorically, "Shall I forget myself to be myself? / *King Richard.* Ay, if yourself's remembrance wrong yourself" (*Richard III* 4.4.420–21). That is, should she overlook her overwhelming maternal grievances, set aside her passionate resentments, in order to obey the religious injunction by which she believes she lives and certainly wishes to live—to forgive, to "do good"? In *King John*, the distraught Constance, learning of Arthur's capture, rejects the suggestion that she is losing her wits. "I am not mad, I would to heaven I were! / For then 'tis like I should forget myself. / O, if I could, what grief should I forget!" (3.4.48–50) Here forgetfulness is imagined as a longed-for release from the intolerable pressure of an unbearable reality, under which pressure Constance will sink, until by the time she leaves the stage for the last time, she is hopelessly crazed. And in the fourth-act quarrel between Brutus and Cassius, in *Julius Caesar*, Cassius sharply taxes his one-time intimate: "Brutus, bait not me, / I'll not endure it. You forget yourself /

To hedge me in." A moment later he presses him further: "Urge me no more, I shall forget myself; / Have mind upon your health" (4.3.28–36). For Cassius to warn, "I shall forget myself" in this instance would seem to mean something like "I shall be driven to do things utterly foreign to my nature, things my normal self could never even have contemplated, let alone executed"—including, presumably, a murderous physical attack on Brutus. In all these instances, forgetfulness of self seems to spell, or to threaten, a loss of identity, transforming the self-forgetter into something unpredictable, unrecognizable, and therefore frightening.

However shallow, sophistical, and self-interested these alleged instances of forgetting may be, or however rooted in the speaker's troubled sense of self, it is plain that Shakespeare is nothing if not deeply preoccupied with memory and its pitfalls. *Hamlet*, notoriously, seems obsessed with it. The Ghost concludes the act 1 interview between himself and Hamlet with the solemn injunction "Remember me," to which Hamlet, alone on stage a moment later, responds with fervent acquiescence,

> Remember thee!
> Ay, thou poor ghost, while memory holds a seat
> In this distracted globe. Remember thee!
> Yea, from the table of my memory
> I'll wipe away all trivial fond records,
> All saws of books, all forms, all pressures past
> That youth and observation copied there,
> And thy commandment all alone shall live
> Within the book and volume of my brain,
> Unmix'd with baser matter.
>
> (1.5.95–104)

One thing these lines convey is the immense effort Hamlet expects it to cost him to remember, as well as his sense that remembrance henceforth constitutes a sacred duty, neglect of which would be a shameful betrayal.

Such total erasure of all that has previously engrossed him, however, is more easily promised than practiced. Hamlet, we know, has a capacious and well-stored memory. He demonstrates as much when, "with good accent and good discretion" and only a momentary false start, he declaims—on the spur of the moment—the first fifteen lines of the speech about "The rugged Pyrrhus," so as to prompt the Player to recite the rest (2.2.452–69). Yet it shortly becomes clear that he has not kept his newly prescribed mission so immovably in the forefront of his consciousness as he has vowed, or else that he has (cunningly?) allowed other "baser" matters like the arrival of the Players to crowd it out, since the Ghost soon reappears to chide him for his slackness: "Do not forget! This visitation / Is but to whet thy almost blunted purpose" (3.4.110–11). Hamlet's delay is accompanied, or the Ghost thinks it is accompanied, by a fading of memory. Uncertainty and unwillingness to act have induced an inability to keep the Ghost's command fresh in mind and allowed nearly to crumble altogether the purpose once so fervently espoused. For, as the Player King has already lucidly explained to his fearful Queen,

> Purpose is but the slave to memory,
> Of violent birth but poor validity,
> Which now, like fruit unripe, sticks on the tree,
> But fall unshaken when they mellow be.
> . . . .
> What to ourselves in passion we propose,
> The passion ending, doth the purpose lose.
>
> (3.2.188–95)

Thus action—meaningful, purposeful activity—does not hinge alone on stated intention, but rather on memory, which in turn depends on passion, and, for its continuance, on the durability of that passion. Claudius, spurring Laertes to revenge against Hamlet, speaks in similar terms, pointing out the likely fragility of Laertes' indignation, owing to the mythic monster, Time, which "qualifies the spark and fire of it" so that "That we would do, / We should do when we would; for this 'would' changes, / And hath abatements and delays" (4.7.113–20). Laertes, that is, must strike while the iron is hot, not allowing Time to dull the edge of love, memory, and purpose and so disable him for action.

To say, through the Player King, that "Purpose is but the slave to memory" is to accord a crucial role to memory as a key to action in the world. Memory had from ancient times been recognized as a precious but vulnerable faculty, subject to assaults from age, accidents, and mental disturbance. But Shakespeare shows no interest in pigeonholing it or classifying it as a separable psychological datum, nor does he show any curiosity about the so-called *artes memorativae*, that weird melange of mnemotechnics and occultism that dazzled so many Renaissance philosophers and scientists. He is, however, keenly interested in the dynamics of memory, in how it weaves itself into the intimate texture of our lives. Above all, as these examples attest, he is interested in our shameful proneness to blame it for our own evil actions, to use it to plead diminished responsibility, as though such a plea could absolve us at one stroke of all guilt and nullify all possible penalty.

So much for the negative side of forgetting and its implications of perfidy, perjury, and ingratitude. It has a more benign aspect when it means the casting out from the mind not of the benefits one has received from others but the injuries. To "forget," in such a context, is to forgive, and Shakespeare often brackets the two. The bracketing, of course, may be more or less perfunctory or meaningful depending on the circumstances. Richard II advises Bullingbrook and Mowbray to bury their differences: "Forget, forgive, conclude and be agreed, / Our doctors say this is no month to bleed" (1.1.156–57) he counsels, but the patly chiming couplet, with its frivolous second line, robs the plea of all urgency. The earl of Warwick, receiving the unwelcome news of his king's marriage to Lady Grey, upbraids himself for having ignored other affronts: "Did I forget that by the house of York / My father came untimely to his death?" (3 Henry VI 3.3.186–87). Queen Margaret, receiving the same news in the same moment, is so overjoyed to lose a dangerous enemy and gain such a redoubtable ally as Warwick that she instantly vows to sweep from her mind all traces of the rancor between them: "Warwick, these words have turn'd my hate to love, / And I forgive and quite forget old faults" (199–200). Failure of memory here is unabashedly being offered, promised for political advantage, with the clear implication that the offerer has the power to decide for herself what she will remember and forget. Memory for her is but the slave to expediency, a device to be controlled and manipulated as convenience dictates.

In a less self-serving vein, the King of France assures the Countess of Roussillon that he has set aside his wrath at Bertram's trespasses: "My honor'd lady, / I have forgiven and forgotten all, / Though my revenges were high bent upon him" (All's Well 5.3.8–10). Once again "forgetting" has little to do with actual failure of memory. The King remembers well enough— no doubt painfully, stingingly—how Bertram has misbehaved, yet he proposes to proceed as if he has truly forgotten: "The nature of his great offense is dead, / And deeper than oblivion we do bury / Th' incensing relics of it" (23–25)—oblivion thus signaling not a literal loss of remembrance so much as the deliberate casting out of a long-smoldering anger. King Leontes, for his part, after sixteen years of "saint-like sorrow," is implored by his attendant Cleomines to punish himself no longer, but "At the last [to] / Do as the heavens have done, forget your evil, / With them, forgive yourself" (*The Winter's Tale* 5.1.2–6). The penitent monarch, however, cannot rid his mind of the memory of what he has lost through his crazed jealousy: "Whilest I remember / Her and her virtues, I cannot forget / My blemishes in them, and so still think of / The wrong I did myself" (6–9). Remembrance here constitutes a form of piety, and Leontes' stubborn refusal to forget becomes the badge of an authentic conversion.

Memory, then, it would seem, carries an inescapable moral dimension for Shakespeare, and its supposed failures must be understood according to the circumstances in which they occur. Being so crucial to action, it cannot be divorced from conscious choice: it stems from willed or half-willed decision and must be judged accordingly. As our current vocabulary would have it, it is "constructed," sometimes out of whole cloth. At the same time, to remember the good one has received from others is in itself a good: it bespeaks a recognition of the claims of others, fosters the mutual bestowal of benefits, and so reinforces the links that bind us one to another, whereas to cling doggedly to the memory of past offenses is to perpetuate them, to forswear the one form of change capable of sweetening our relations with each other, and so block the road to reciprocity and full community. If conditions point to it, therefore—if the provocation has ceased or if forgiveness has been duly requested—forgetfulness can become a moral imperative. But what we see in the majority of cases is a disheartening resort to the mere word as a miraculous talisman to lift the onus of misdeeds, to demote malicious actions to the less culpable level of venial faults, excusable because the author of them, precisely, lay helpless at the mercy of his own buried self.

NOTES

1. Philip Brockbank, ed., *Coriolanus*, The [New] Arden Shakespeare (London: Methuen, 1976), 148, citing the earlier Arden edition of R. H.Case.
2. From Plutarch's *Lives of Noble Grecians and Romanes*, 1579, "The Life of Caius Martius Coriolanus," cited in Brockbank, ed., *Coriolanus*, 326.
3. See, for example, Chapter 1 in *The Psychopathology of Everyday Life*, entitled "The Forgetting of Proper Names," *Standard Edition*, trans. James Strachey et al. (London: 1960), 6:1–7, and "The Forgetting of Names and Sets of Words," 15–42.

Two Versions of *Romeo and Juliet* 2.6 and *Merry Wives of Windsor* 5.5.215–45: An Invitation to the Pleasures of Textual/ Sexual Di(Per)versity

STEVEN URKOWITZ

Sᴀᴍ Schoenbaum taught our community the delights of watching how stories about Shakespeare grew and changed over time. Close study of the tales, the tellers, and their changing contexts unraveled histories and offered insight into the concerns and projects of their authors. We looked fresh-eyed into old volumes, and we have been fascinated. Today, many similar enticements beckon us to read Shakespeare's texts in their earliest available forms rather than in modern editions, and, if we would only elect to use it, the technology of photocopying throws into our hands the variant quarto and Folio versions. For many no doubt practical reasons, few of us read alternative texts of these plays, nor do many of us suggest that our students consult them. But I suggest that we should, and I do so for reasons fundamental to my perception of Shakespeare's artistic project.

In performance plays seem to work, to fascinate, because as we watch players go through their rehearsed actions we perceive surprising relationships and juxtapositions among fictional characters, their language, their movements, the objects and settings in their playing space, and even with ourselves as the audience. To achieve at least some of the pleasure attainable from energetic performances, the reading of a script rather than the witnessing of a performance is best accomplished by someone who knows and who can recognize the patterns of expectation and surprise coded in the text. Over the past decade, as a teacher and lecturer addressing both naive and experienced play-readers, I have found that the substantially variant versions of Shakespeare's plays, laid side by side, disclose theatrically interesting patterns not readily discernable when only a single text is examined.

By comparing the earliest printed scripts of Shakespeare's multiple-text plays, we can recover for ourselves, for performers, and for our students dimensions of artistic experience and details suggesting real or imagined theatrical presentation inaccessible or aesthetically quite different in modern edited texts of the plays. Exemplary passages from those early alternative scripts—two versions of *Romeo and Juliet* 2.6 and two versions of the last thirty-odd lines of *The Merry Wives of Windsor*—illustrate textual resources unexpectedly available to, for example, discussions and performances of Shakespeare's ways of imaging gender.

Flower Power vs. Loathsome Deliciousness

In the earliest printed text of *Romeo and Juliet*, the 1597 First Quarto, speeches by Romeo and Friar Lawrence opening 2.6 ring with exuberance and with hopeful predictions of forthcoming joy as they await Juliet's arrival:

> *Rom:* Now Father Laurence, in thy holy grant
>   Consists the good of me and Juliet.
> *Fr:* Without more words I will doo all I may,
>   To make you happie if in me it lye.[1]

This first pair of speeches initiates a rhythm of concord: Romeo barely voices his request and the Friar accedes. Then Romeo forecasts Juliet's arrival in a rhyming couplet, and Friar Laurence affirms this expectation, matching rhyme for rhyme.

> *Rom:* This morning here she pointed we should meet,
>   And consumate those never parting bands,
>   Witnes of our harts love by joyning hands,
>   And come she will.
> *Fr:* I gesse she will indeed,
>   Youths love is quicke, swifter than swiftest speed.

The lexicon of this exchange resonates with positive virtue: words like "holy" and "good," "happy" and "morning," "never-parting," "love," "youth," "quick," "swifter," and "swiftest" build a local language of unrelieved cheer. The two characters are engaged in complementary verbal activities, and one might hope that a player enacting the Friar's physical presentation of the role here—through his postures, his gestures, his dynamic spatial relationship to Romeo—would be kinesthetically sympathetic and supportive of the youthful bounce suggested by Romeo's language. An old hand on a boy's shoulder, an arthritic skip-step echoing a romantic leap, or an affirmative smile or upraised countenance—any appropriate body move from the local nonverbal vocabulary would do the trick. A youth and an old counselor look forward to a young girl's presence as a wonderful fulfillment.

At this point in the 1597 script a stage direction and Laurence's continuing speech seem to call for a further extravagantly joyful eruption: words and indicated action signal additional emotional harmony.

> *Enter Juliet somewhat fast, and embraceth Romeo,*
> See where she comes.
> So light of foote nere hurts the troden flower:
> Of love and joy, see see the soveraigne power.

The incantatory rhyme of "flower-power," the three repetitions of "see" and of other "s" sounds, and the "o"s of "troden," "love," "joy," "soveraigne," and "power" build a celebratory music during Juliet's "somewhat fast" approach to Romeo, accompanying their first embrace. I imagine that the Friar's words calling attention to Juliet's movement across the stage could be spoken as he himself moves away from Romeo in order to give the pair emotional and visual "stage center" for the following exchange, but any number of choreographic possibilities may be suggested by local stage conditions. In any case, the following dialogue focuses attention on the young people:

> *Jul:* Romeo.
> *Rom:* My Juliet welcome. As doo waking eyes
>   (Cloasd in Nights mysts) attend the frolicke Day,
>   So Romeo hath expected Juliet,
>   And thou art come.
> *Jul:* I am (if I be Day)
>   Come to my Sunne: shine foorth, and make me faire.
> *Rom:* All beauteous fairnes dwelleth in thine eyes.
> *Jul:* Romeo from thine all brightnes doth arise.

At her entry, Friar Laurence celebrates Juliet as a queen of love and joy, and then the lovers transfigure one another as "Day" and the "Sunne"; their physical embrace signaled in the stage direction extends verbally to their coupling rhymes, "in thine eyes" and "doth arise." The script dictates only minimal action and words; the performers are invited to invent specific gestures, movements about the stage, and vocal tones to realize the recipe.

Laurence next separates the boy and girl in order to bring them more quickly to the sacramental joining of marriage. Because commands need not be repeated if obeyed at once, the Friar's repeated calls, "Come . . . come, . . . Defer . . . Part . . .," and his short, declarative sentences should indicate to the actors playing Romeo and Juliet that they ignore his first efforts at parting their embrace:

> Fr: Come wantons, come, the stealing houres do passe
>   Defer imbracements till some fitter time,
>   Part for a while, you shall not be alone,
>   Till holy Church have joynd ye both in one.

He urges the "wantons" to follow him from the stage. When Romeo and Juliet indicate their enthusiastic acceptance of his invitation, he promises as if in recompense that the "soft and faire" delay of the marital rite will make their marriage "sweetest worke" where simple haste would hinder their pleasures:

> Rom: Lead holy Father, all delay seemes long.
> Jul: Make hast, make hast, this lingring doth us wrong.
> Fr: O, soft and faire makes sweetest worke they say.
>   Hast is a common hindrer in crosse way. *Exeunt Omnes.*

All three players are generating the energy of this exit, as the script calls for one after the next to display delighted movement toward the exit, life-affirming sanctification between a boy, a girl, and a totally supportive father-substitute. If performed by actors sensitive to the elegant possibilities of theatrical coding, the emotional exclamations and celebratory dramatic trajectories traced by this scene might be recognizable even by a witness who did not comprehend the language.

The corresponding version of this scene from the 1599 Second Quarto instead tolls with equally recognizable language and gestures signaling dark, driving discords of sex and death, patriarchal cynicism, compulsion, and ominous forebodings. Physical cues suggest hierarchy and distance rather than proximity, conflict rather than concord. Repeatedly we find each verbal expression and many actions countered with a contending opposite: for example, as Friar Laurence enters with Romeo he invokes heaven, perhaps with an imploring gesture, to oppose his ominous reference to "after houres" and "sorrow." Then Romeo follows with a pair of seemingly obedient "amen"s before he strongly states his rejection of the Friar's concerns.

> *Enter Frier and Romeo.*
> *Fri.* So smile the heavens upon this holy act,
>   That after houres, with sorrow chide us not.
> *Ro.* Amen, amen, but come what sorrow can,
>   It cannot countervaile the exchange of joy
>   That one short minute gives me in her sight:

Romeo's "Amen, amen" may also be read as an impatiently doubled affirmative equivalent to a negation, "yes, yes, but . . .," indicating disagreement, not assent. Heavens' smile is countered by sorrow's chiding; "sorrow" is heard twice against a single utterance of "joy"; "after houres" weigh against "one short minute." Rhetorically, Juliet and joy seem balanced against the weight and authority of heaven and time.

Then Juliet's femaleness is held in opposition to death's masculinity as Romeo values even the momentary speaking of the marriage vow equal to "love-devouring death":

> Do thou but close our hands with holy words,
> Then love-devouring death do what he dare,
> It is inough I may but call her mine.
> *Fri.* These violent delights have violent endes,
>   And in their triumph die like fier and powder:
>   Which as they kisse consume. The sweetest honey
>   Is loathsome in his owne deliciousnesse,
>   And in the taste confoundes the appetite.
>   Therefore love moderately, long love doth so,
>   Too swift arrives, as tardie as too slowe.

In the earlier version Friar Laurence matched Romeo's sense of good will; here he meets and exceeds the boy's rhetoric of confrontation. "Violent delights" are topped by "violent ends," "in their triumph die" is doubled by another combative phrase, "as they kisse consume." The different lexicon of the Second Quarto's opening exchange between Romeo and the Friar registers these negatively affective words with no equivalents in the earlier text of this scene: "sorrow," "love-devouring death," "dare," "violent," "die," "consume," "loathsome," "confoundes," "tardie," and "too slowe." Both men's language places them in opposition to one another; a semiotically effective realization of the dialogue would have them stand or move in opposition as well, so when Friar Laurence says, "The sweetest honey / Is loathsome in his owne deliciousnesse," challenging rather than supporting Romeo's most ardent wishes, he could move away or upbraid, or express physical disgust in reaction to Romeo's imaginative evocation of matrimonially closed hands and exchanged joy.

Then Juliet enters. Friar Laurence's greeting crackles with ironic criticism rather than praise:

> *Enter Juliet.*
> Here comes the Lady, Oh so light a foote
> Will nere weare out the everlasting flint,
> A lover may bestride the gossamours,
> That ydeles in the wanton sommer ayre,
> And yet not fall, so light is vanitie.

Where in the earlier text he matched a line ending "so light a foote" with a following line ending with an image of an unbruised flower, the Friar in the Second Quarto text completes the second line of his greeting to Juliet by calling to mind the gloomy heaviness of "everlasting flint." Rather than the earlier version's sovereignty over love and joy, Juliet now exemplifies idle, wanton vanity, and the Friar here draws on commonplaces of antiromantic critical rationality. He ridicules rather than praises her.

With such a greeting, as she moves from the stage entrance towards Romeo and the Friar, Juliet's pace could be measured, rather than "somewhat fast." Or a player could enter rapidly for a few paces and pause for a moment to assume some sacred dignity in a holy place. Or perhaps she could pause at the entry, absorb the Friar's tone, and move in a manner to contest his characterization of her lightness. But the Second Quarto stage direction suggests no exuberant embrace. In the presence of this father-substitute who bristles with denigrating barbs, rather than speaking to her lover Juliet twice addresses the Friar with decorous restraint. Pointedly, in contrast to the earlier text, she says nothing directly to Romeo:

> *Fri.* . . . so light is vanitie.
> *Ju.* Good euen to my ghostly confessor.

> *Fri.* Romeo shall thanke thee daughter for us both.
> *Ju.* As much to him, else is his thankes too much.

Crucial to an understanding of the action and dialogue here, we must recognize that the Friar's and then Juliet's lines about "thanks" are *not* prompted by a passionate exchange of kisses between the lovers, usually indicated in modern editions by interpolated stage directions. (Evans, for example, follows Juliet's speech here with *"Romeo kisses Juliet,"* and the Friar's next speech is followed by *"Juliet returns his kiss."*[2]) Instead, the lines about thanks are triggered by Juliet's invocation of God's gift, "Good even" (short for "God give you good evening"). Scores of instances in the canon of Shakespeare's plays show that social invocations of "good day" or "farewell" or "Greetings, my lord" will prompt a reply of "thank you." Today's pale vestige of this Renaissance verbal habit may be found in "God bless you," "Thank you," when we sneeze. "As much to him," indirectly, obscurely (perhaps shyly?) extends the same "Good even" to Romeo without directly addressing him.

Instead of the childlike, uncontrolled whoops of "Romeo" and "My Juliet welcome" after her twice-distanced nongreeting, Romeo in the Second Quarto gingerly and with densely ornamented mannerisms conditionally asks merely that Juliet turn from Friar Laurence to speak to *him*, and he then asks that she discourse specifically about her image of their happiness:

> *Ro.* Ah Juliet, if the measure of thy joy
>   Be heapt like mine, and that thy skill be more
>   To blason it, then sweeten with thy breath
>   This neighbour ayre and let rich musicke tongue,
>   Unfold the imagin'd happines that both
>   Receive in either, by this deare encounter.

Romeo is painfully self-aware, fluently tongue-tied, rhetorically implorative for the gifts of rhetoric. He asks for reassurance about her feelings; if she had already demonstrated them in embraces, the request would not be needed. But Juliet at first seems still to refuse him. We cannot tell that she will accede in any way until the third and fourth lines of her speech gradually reveal that she has been spinning out an elegantly delineated "inexpressibility" commonplace.

> *Ju.* Conceit more rich in matter then in words,
>   Brags of his substance, not of ornament,

They are but beggers that can count their worth,
But my true love is growne to such excesse,
I cannot sum up sum of halfe my wealth.

At first she sounds like Marc Antony: "There's beggary in love that can be counted." The beginning of this speech and her two earlier lines addressed to Friar Laurence fit a wary observer deeply sensitive to the linguistic and physical codes of reticence and control that regulate Verona's social interactions. Juliet and Romeo in this text here and elsewhere both fully participate in those codes rather than appear simply as innocent victims of them, as seems to be the case in the 1597 version.

Rather than in happy concert with the two lovers as in Q1, here in Q2 Friar Laurence alone drives the scene to a darker conclusion:

Fri. Come, come with me, and we will make short worke,
For by your leaves, you shall not stay alone,
Till holy Church incorporate two in one.

The Friar promises only "short worke" rather than "sweetest worke," and he strives only to make their bonds swiftly legal rather than deliciously soft and fair. Here he represents the authority of the Church, not a friendly escort to the greater pleasures of marriage, and he speaks with the cautionary voice of experience. Romeo and Juliet obey him silently; no dancing rhymes here at their exit (nor elsewhere in the exchange). We have, it appears, two radically different conceptions of this scene in the two earliest printed texts of *Romeo and Juliet.* One rings exuberantly, one tolls ominously.

Some editors of this passage insert into Q2 the bubbly stage direction for Juliet's entry from Q1, and then they cordially but without warrant explain "Romeo shall thank thee daughter for us both" and Juliet's modest reply as some cryptic reference to an exchange of embraces. The Arden edition, for example, suggests, "Romeo shall return Juliet's greeting with a kiss on behalf of the Friar," and "Juliet considers that Romeo exceeded his brief and included a kiss from himself; she restores the balance by giving him one back."[3] (Evans rejects the Q1 stage direction because it "suggests a wanton quality to Juliet's entrance that is more suitable to Q1's almost wholly different version of this scene than to Shakespeare's," but he includes the kisses.)

It seems as if the editorial conflation purposefully or inadvertently recuperates the bouncy Juliet from the 1597 text and allows her momentarily to dance in the harsher confines of the 1599 version. Such directorial or choreographic potentialities need not be eliminated from a repertory of imagined or actualized performances. But when incongruously spliced into a context replete with loathsome deliciousness, "fier and powder," and "love-devouring death," the interpolated joyful entry and embrace transform the two early versions of the exchange into an odd theatrical oxymoron: the modern text asks the player of Juliet to act with unconstrained exuberance while speaking with mannered reticence. And in the conflated version, Romeo asks Juliet for affirmation of her love immediately after he receives physical evidence of it. Superimposing the idea of an effervescent Juliet onto a text calling for more visible control, the editors generate a Juliet who, I feel, fits stereotypes of feminine instability. In contrast, the 1597 text offers Juliet as an innocent victim of Veronese social codes and the 1599 text shows her as a full participant in their subtlety.

PLUMS AND PARDONS IN *THE MERRY WIVES OF WINDSOR* 5.2

The alternative final thirty-odd lines of *The Merry Wives of Windsor* present a similarly striking change in visual and psycholinguistic registers of a complex figured scene. In the first printed version, the 1602 Quarto, when she enters with her new husband, Anne Page is harshly challenged by her apprehensive mother and father.

> *Pa.* O I am vext at hart, what shal I do?
>   *Enter Fenton and Anne.*
> *Mis.Pa.* Here comes the man that hath deceived us all:
>   How now daughter, where have you bin?
> *An.* At Curch forsooth.
> *Pa.* At Church, what have you done there?

"At C[h]urch" may perhaps be spoken as a calm confession, as a gleeful assertion, or as a bride's proud triumph over her parents' mercenary schemes. The actor playing Anne may pace onto the stage abashed or calm or exultant, twined about Fenton or removed from him, but her simple answer to her mother's question reveals through its witty compression that she no longer is to be controlled by her parents.

Anne's husband, Fenton, steps figuratively or literally "between the dragon and his wrath." By his interposition he brings attention to himself, possibly by moving towards Anne, or perhaps by drawing away from her, or by advancing towards her parents, or even simply by raising Anne's hand in his own.

> *Pa.* . . . what have you done there?
> *Fen.* Married to me, nay sir never storme,
> Tis done sir now, and cannot be undone.
> *Ford:* Ifaith M.Page never chafe your selfe,
> She hath made her choise wheras her hart was fixt,
> Then tis in vaine for you to storme or fret.
> *Fal.* I am glad yet that your arrow hath glanced
> *Mi.For.* Come mistris Page, Ile be bold with you,
> 'Tis pitie to part love that is so true.

Fenton's repeated use of "Sir" to address Page insistently generates a new dynamic of formal status and power, signaling Anne's translation from daughter to wife. The player acting Page, I imagine, should somehow be erupting in "storme" and then "chafe" himself in order that Fenton and Ford's lines may have appropriate references. Page's neighbors Master and Mistress Ford both intervene to counsel a gentle reconciliation, and Falstaff seems to place the Pages' disappointments into the context of their triumph over his machinations.

In this text, of the two parents, first Mistress Page accedes to the *fait accompli* and gives her belated permission for Fenton to "take her."

> *Mis.Pa.* Altho that I have missed in my intent,
> Yet I am glad my husbands match was crossed,
> Here M.Fenton, take her, and God give thee joy.

Imagining this moment as a theatrical director, I would suggest that Mistress Page cross to her daughter and bring or offer or direct Anne towards Fenton at "Here M.Fenton, take her." While these are only three of many possible ways to enact such a line, "Here . . . , take her" implies some kind of movement and gesture of joining.

With a little further prompting, Anne's father also changes into a model of benevolence and reconciliation:

> *Sir Hu.:* Come M. Page, you must needs agree.
> *Fo.* I yfaith sir come, you see your wife is wel pleased:

> *Pa.* I cannot tel, and yet my hart's wel eased,
>   An yet it doth me good the Doctor missed.
>   Come hither Fenton, and come hither daughter,
>   Go too you might have stai'd for my good will,
>   But since your choise is made of one you love,
>   Here take her Fenton, & both happie prove.

Again, Master Page directly addresses both Fenton and his daughter, and his words imply joining the new couple in a circuit of arms at "Come hither Fenton, and come hither daughter" when he repeats his wife's parental grant, "Here take her." As in the 1597 version of *Romeo and Juliet* 2.6, we have a momentary tableau of concord including the affectionate figure of a father and a nuptial couple.

The play concludes in this 1602 text with two silly and joyful speeches by Sir Hugh and Master Ford, both predicting celebratory rituals forthcoming:

> *Sir Hu.* I wil also dance & eat plums at your weddings.
> *Ford.* All parties pleased, now let us in to feast,
>   And laugh at Slender, and the Doctors jeast.
>   He hath got the maiden, each of you a boy
>   To waite upon you, so God give you joy . . .

As he initiates the common exit to feasting and laughter, Ford stresses the ameliorative delights of the play's resolution. He mollifies any painful sense of ridicule for Slender and the Doctor by granting them their *faux*-brides as pages, perhaps to serve them during the ensuing feast. The final moment gives each of the subsidiary figures attention and a token of grace.

The 1623 version of this denouement follows a very different trajectory. At her equivalent entry in the 1623 Folio version, in response to her father's challenge to Fenton (where the Quarto had her mother challenge Anne), Anne moves to take the stage with a compelling appeal for reconciliation:

> *Page.* My heart misgives me, here comes Mr. Fenton.
>   How now Mr Fenton?
> *Anne.* Pardon good father, good my mother pardon
> *Page.* Now Mistris:

If perhaps she kneels, or if the other performers on stage clear space for her verbal gesture of appeasement to be seen, or simply if time, vocal energy, and emotional verisimilitude have been harnessed for this moment, we may have in performance a striking visual display and an abrupt emotional shift from laughter to intense family stress generated here by Anne herself rather than by her parents. In the 1602 text, Anne's plot and its successful execution seem to protect her from parental manipulation; her witty "at C[h]urch forsooth" signals an achievement of institutional certification of an independently achieved marriage. But here in the equivalent moment from the Folio she yet seeks a further step, familial reintegration and reconciliation, the healing of violated relationships where parents treated their child as chattel and child wrested independence through subterfuge.

Although Master Page shifts his direction of address from Fenton to his daughter—"How now Mr Fenton?" deflects to "Now Mistris" after Anne's plea—as far as we can tell, both parents pointedly ignore her striking imploratives as if the words she spoke had no meaningful content:

> *Anne.* Pardon good father, good my mother pardon
> *Page.* Now Mistris:
> How chance you went not with Mr Slender?
> *M.Page.* Why went you not with Mr Doctor, maid?

They fail to acknowledge her appeal for pardon, and according to Fenton their questions apparently strike her dumb:

> *Fen.* You do amaze her: heare the truth of it,
> You would have married her most shamefully,
> Where there was no proportion held in love ...

Fenton's lecture on the miseries of an enforced marriage seems to produce the same effect on the Pages as they had on Anne:

> *Ford.* Stand not amaz'd, here is no remedie:
> In Love, the heavens themselves do guide the state,
> Money buyes Lands, and wives are sold by fate.

In this text, the angry father is the first of the parents to turn from anger to acceptance:

> *Page.* Well, what remedy? Fenton, heaven give thee
> joy, what cannot be eschew'd, must be embrac'd.

Then Mistress Page has her turn to accept Fenton as her son-in-law:

Mist.Page. Well, I will muse no further: Mr Fenton,
 Heaven give you many, many merry dayes:

But in the Folio version Master and Mistress Page say nothing
whatsoever conciliatory to their daughter Anne. Although as I
imagine the stage action here, Anne seizes the audience's attention when she takes the stage at her entrance appealing for pardon, in the Folio text neither parent grants her the forgiveness
she asks. In the speeches subsequent to their initial challenges
to her, they both address only Fenton. As far as we can tell,
they direct their blessings to him alone: Master Page's "Fenton,
heaven give thee joy" uses the second person singular "thee,"
and thus (at least linguistically) excludes Anne, and then Mistress Page omits any reference to Anne in a speech explicitly
identifying "Mr Fenton" and "Good husband."

Instead of the Quarto's explicitly inclusive and ameliorative
festival, the final tableau of the Folio reasserts social hierarchies
of patriarchy, gender, and class. Mistress Page addresses her social superiors, Fenton, her husband, and Falstaff, lumping the
rest together as "every one" and "all":

                               . . . Mr Fenton
 Heaven give you many, many merry dayes:
 Good husband, let us every one go home,
 And laugh this sport ore by a Countrie fire,
 Sir John and all.

Ford ends the play, "Let it be so," followed with roughly the
same final couplet from the Quarto: "To Master Broome, you
yet shall hold your word, / For he, to night, shall lye with Mistris Ford:"

But gone from the Folio are the boys to wait upon the losers,
gone the widespread invocations to joy, gone the giddy enthusi-
asm for dancing and wedding plums, gone the repeated parental
gestures of handing bride to groom, and gone the individual
invitations to the celebratory feast. Instead Sir John and Fenton
dominate the parents' attention; other players in the drama are
subsumed into the omnibus, anonymous "and all." They are
promised only laughter and ridicule rather than feasting. In
sharp juxtaposition to the action called for in Q1, no parent ever
answers Anne's ingratiating plea for pardon, no one embraces
her with good wishes, and no one other than her husband, not
momma nor poppa nor neighbor nor pedagogue nor prowling fat
fool nor even postmaster's boy, lends her a kind word of affir-

mation for her daring revolt. I am puzzled and disturbed by this "reading" of the play's ending, and I am not at all sure how it might be performed. Of course, unscripted action could easily sweep Anne into the warmth of a reconciled family. But, as with the scene from *Romeo and Juliet*, the theatrical experiences prescribed by these alternative *Merry Wives* texts seem to be differentially encoded. In the Folio, Anne risks more as she shows herself vulnerable by asking for forgiveness, and she wins less. Perhaps we are all brought together by witnessing the Page family in amazement. From that confusion, perhaps the best we can expect, at least in this Windsor, is measured rather than unconditional reconciliation.

When Mistress Page hands Mistress Ford the letter she receives from Falstaff in Q1 *Merry Wives*, she says, "I prethie looke on that Letter." Mistress Ford invites her to collate it with a second exemplar of nearly the same text:

> Ile match your letter just with the like,
> Line for line, word for word. Only the name
> Of misteris Page, and misteris Foord disagrees:
> Do me the kindnes to looke upon this.

In the Folio version Mistress Ford rather than Mistress Page makes the first presentation, and she offers the text far more urgently: "Wee burne day-light: heere, read, read." The earlier text is more polite, constrained, and regular; the later pounds with urgency, broken decorum and abrupt rhythms.

Following the modern paradigm for producing single reading versions from texts with divergent earlier exemplars, editors withhold from readers what I submit are real pleasures of reading and comparing alternative versions of Shakespeare's multiple-text plays. I suggest that rich insights, otherwise obscured, into staging, "meaning," and theatrical experience may be gained when the alternative versions are compared.

In our contemporary texts we are warned that in contrast to Q2, Q1 *Romeo and Juliet* for example is "dramatically, not simply verbally, shoddy" and contains "vulgarizations, interpolations, and additions very characteristic of actors who alter details to suit their interpretation."[4] And that it "is a detestable text, probably a reconstruction of the play from the imperfect memories of one or two of the actors. . . . It is confused, often ungrammatical; much of the poetry has gone or been spoilt by the corrupting of the lines."[5] Again we are cautioned, "This entire scene [2.6 in Q1], however, is non-Shakespearean (perhaps by Chettle) and its evidence must be viewed with suspicion."[6] More generally, we are told that for any Shakespearean text we must not

> fix the origins of the early printed versions upon single agents, when these texts were open to penetration and alteration not only by Shakespeare himself but also by multiple theatrical and extra-theatrical scriveners, by theatrical annotators, adapters and revisers (who might cut or add), by censors, and by compositors and proofreaders.[7]

In just this way, Iago was able to parlay Desdemona's spotted handkerchief into ugly fantasies of degradation involving the whole camp, pioneers and all. Describing essentially common-place literary phenomena of several hands contributing to textual revision in theatrical or purely literary contexts, such charged imagery has effectively discouraged readers from looking at the documents and evidently excuses Shakespearean editors from presenting the textual alternatives in readable formats.[8] The wider community of textual scholars working with bibliographic problems presented by other authors or composite author-groups whose works exist in multiple versions have for some time been more comfortable about displaying alternatives and discussing what we may learn by examining them.[9]

Suppose for a moment that, rather than "Shakespeare himself," the clever boy playing Anne Page and the actor playing the Host invented one or even both of the versions of that final tableau in *Merry Wives*. Or suppose that an apprentice play-adapter wrote one and an overreaching censor sketched in the other of the *Romeo and Juliet* 2.6 texts, and then adapters cut and revisers added and compositors composed and proofreaders miscorrected them. Or suppose that Shakespeare wrote one version and his experience watching the script develop in rehearsal or in performance led him to write the other, and then after many other adventures the texts we know were set into print with all the transformations that manuscripts suffer in those journeys. Whatever their underlying origins, I invite you to consider that we may yet think creatively about Q1's *Romeo and Juliet* and about Q2's *Romeo and Juliet*. We may yet justifiably analyze all those merry wives and their daughters, whoever wrote them. We may yet benefit when we try out the alternative versions in rehearsals or in productions or in our critical discourses. Our students may yet grasp the dynamic energies of theatrical imaginations "working" dramatic possibilities. What is to be lost if we "privilege" such diverse texts by raising them up to visibility? We gain space for imaginative play; we lose only that false security of unverifiable authenticity championed by one "authoritative" edition after the next.

Instead of "penetration and alteration," we could call that process of change witnessed by the extant versions the "nurturing" of a theatrical script. We may want to give up the quasi-legal fiction of a sole father-author and possible interloping male inseminators penetrating a manuscript at different stages of its conception in order to recognize instead the accomplishments of a revising mother (or a diverse community of mothers) bringing along a script through a series of conditional, transitional stages.[10] Why don't we do this? The reason is that we have not sat down to read the alternative texts.

With only ridiculously few exceptions, modern editors insist on providing only singular texts of Shakespeare's plays. So we learn of one Romeo, one Juliet, one Friar, one momma, and one poppa for one Anne Page. Perhaps it is time to confront the grotesque texts—unwieldy, out-of-bounds, and impolite in their old typography, occasional gross blunders, and testimony to the irrational existence of multiple mommas and poppas, Annes, Romeos, Juliets, friars, and schoolmasters. With the two merry wives, indignant over having been targets for a bloated, self-important good-ol'-boy who assumed his victims would be restricted to a single text, I prithee, do me the kindnes to looke vpon these earliest printed versions of Shakespeare's plays as sources of delight and critical empowerment. "We burn daylight. Heere, read, read!"

NOTES

1. Quotations of Quarto texts are taken from Allen and Muir, eds., *Shakespeare's Plays in Quarto: A Facsimile Edition of Copies Primarily from the Henry E. Huntington Library* (Berkeley and Los Angeles: University of California Press, 1981); Folio texts are from Charlton Hinman, *The First Folio of Shakespeare: The Norton Facsimile* (New York: Norton, 1968). Typographic conventions such as *u* and *v*, *i*, and *j* have been modernized, turned up or turned under lines regularized, and italicized proper nouns in dialogue printed in roman font.

2. G. Blakemore Evans, ed., *Romeo and Juliet: The New Cambridge Shakespeare* (Cambridge: Cambridge University Press, 1984), 120.

3. Brian Gibbons, ed., *Romeo and Juliet: The Arden Edition* (London and New York: Methuen, 1980), 158. See also Stanley Wells and Gary Taylor, eds., *William Shakespeare: The Complete Works* (Oxford: Clarendon Press, 1986), 394.

4. Gibbons, ed., *Romeo and Juliet*, 9.

5. T. J. B. Spencer, ed., *Romeo and Juliet: The New Penguin Shakespeare* (London: Penguin Books, 1967), 284.

6. George Walton Williams, ed., *The Most Excellent and Lamentable Tragedie of Romeo and Juliet: A Critical Edition* (Durham, N.C.: Duke University Press, 1964), 145.

7. Paul Werstine, "Narratives About Printed Shakespearean Texts: 'Foul Papers' and 'Bad Quartos.'" *Shakespeare Quarterly* 41 (1990): 65–86, p. 86.

8. Werstine calls for "a narrative that includes post-structuralist differential readings of multiple texts [which] would keep in play not only multiple readings and versions but also the multiple and dispersed agencies that could have produced the variants" ("Narratives," 86). Oddly, the New Folger Library Shakespeare edition of *Romeo and Juliet* omits listing any modern source where a playful reader interested in multiple versions might find either of the Quarter texts reproduced. See Barbara Mowat and Paul Werstine, eds., *The Tragedy of Romeo and Juliet: The New Folger Library Shakespeare* (New York: Washington Square Press, Pocket Books, 1992), 277–78.

9. See Jack Stillinger, "Multiple Authorship and the Question of Authority," *Text: Transactions of the Society for Textual Scholarship* 5 (1991): 285–96; G. Thomas Tanselle, "Textual Criticism and Literary Sociology," *Studies in Bibliography* 43 (1990): 83–145; and James Thorpe, "The Aesthetics of Textual Criticism," *PMLA* 80 (1965): 465–82.

10. For further discussions of the possibilities of revision and editorial responsibilities in both single and multiple-text plays, see for example Fredson Bowers, "Mixed Texts and Multiple Authority," *Text: Transactions of the Society for Textual Scholarship* 3 (1987): 63–90, and Gary Taylor, "Revising Shakespeare," *Text: Transactions of the Society for Textual Scholarship* 5 (1987): 285–96. For an admirably flexible negotiation between the conflicting discourses of literary and performance criticism parallel to my own analysis, see Anthony Dawson "The Impasse over the Stage," *English Literary Renaissance* 21 (1991): 309–27.

Part 4
Playwrights and Contexts

Theatrical Politics and Shakespeare's Comedies, 1590–1600

GEORGE K. HUNTER

Let me begin with some facts that are, I believe, uncontested:

1. In 1584 Sir William More recovered possession of the playhouse in the Blackfriars that Richard Farrant had set up in 1576 (with the aim of putting on paid performances by boys of the Chapel Royal). A legal prevarication allowed John Lyly to show plays there in the 1584/85 season, but thereafter there were no more performances in this playhouse.

2. In 1590 the other well-established boys' playhouse "in Paul's" was closed, presumably because the company had been meddling in the Martin Marprelate controversy. (It follows that between 1590 and 1599/1600 there was no theatrical repertory by boys' troupes available in London.)

3. In 1596 James Burbage, actor, joiner, builder of the Theatre, and landlord to the Chamberlain's Men, leased the old Parliament Chamber in the Blackfriars, intending to use it as a playhouse for his company, the Chamberlain's Men. In the same year this enterprise was stopped by a petition to the Privy Council; the other inhabitants of the Blackfriars did not want a rowdy public playhouse in their vicinity, though they had accepted a small private playhouse in previous years.

4. In 1599 the Burbages dismantled the timbers of the Theatre, shipped them across to the Bankside, and erected The Globe.

5. In 1599 or so the Boys of Paul's began to show plays once again.

6. In 1600 Burbage's heirs leased the Blackfriars playhouse to the managers of a revived troupe of the Children of the Chapel, and the children played there till 1608, when the Burbages reacquired the Blackfriars.

7. Between 1595 (approximately) and 1600 (approximately)

Shakespeare wrote six "romantic comedies" (*Love's Labor's Lost, A Midsummer Night's Dream, The Merchant of Venice, Much Ado about Nothing, As You Like It,* and *Twelfth Night.*[1])

The facts contained in this recital are all well known. Nevertheless, much that is consequential remains open to speculation and discussion. We may ask, for example, if there is any relation between the aesthetic documents in item 7 and the documentary material in the preceding items. Did the theatrical politics of the capital have a direct effect on the kinds of plays that were performed in particular theaters?

One obvious point is that Shakespeare's romantic comedies were all written when the boys' theaters were closed, their audiences footloose and open to bids for their favor. Presumably Burbage was thinking about this well-paying and prestigious audience when he made his bid for the Blackfriars.[2] Did he talk to his fellow Shakespeare about his plans? We cannot know, of course, but it seems possible to suppose that he had in mind a repertory of plays that would appeal to private as well as public theater customers and an idea that Shakespeare might supply some such plays. Certainly we must allow that Shakespeare, like other Elizabethan dramatists, was tied to the purposes of his company. He wrote plays for their approval; if they were not approved they would not be produced. As a sharer (from 1595) he was himself part of the management and must have been anxious to promote its success. We may also note that the comedies Shakespeare wrote after *Twelfth Night* (that is, after 1600,[3] when the boys' theaters were open again) are much more like the plays being written by other authors and performed in other theaters than the 1595–1600 comedies. Thus *Measure for Measure* (1604) appears as only one of a set of disguised ruler plays, *The Malcontent,* also of 1604, (apparently "stolen" by the King's Men from the boys), *Parasitaster, or The Fawn* (1604), *The Phoenix* (1604), and *The Fleer* (1606). Thus *All's Well That Ends Well* (1602) joins *How a Man May Choose a Good Wife* (1602), *The Fair Maid of Bristowe* (1604), *The London Prodigal* (1604), *The Wise Woman of Hogsden* (1604), and *The Second Part of the Honest Whore* (1605) as yet another story of a prodigal husband saved at the last moment by a saintly wife. Thus *The Merry Wives of Windsor* (1600) looks like a bid to satisfy a taste for topographical nostalgia elsewhere represented by *The Merry Devil of Edmonton* (1602), *The Tale of a Tub* (1598), and *Two Angry Women of Abingdon* (1588).[4]

Moreover, when Shakespeare turned in 1608 to yet another

kind of comedy in his so-called romances we can see again a symmetry between change in theatrical politics and change in genre. The connection between the King's Men's recovery of the Blackfriars playhouse and the new line in "romance" has been frequently discussed[5] and widely accepted. The hiring of Beaumont and Fletcher (formerly playwrights for the boys' companies) at the same time, gives us another sign of a deliberate shift in dramaturgy to accommodate a new theater (and potentially a new audience). Are we to assume that this move to the private theater had consequences in playwriting, where the earlier episode, discussed above, had none?

If we look at the whole history of Shakespeare's comic writing in the nineties we can understand why the Burbages might think him just the man for the job in hand. He had begun writing comedies close to the time when the boys shut down, and his repertory[6] demarcates a mode in comedy obviously nearer to that of the boys than that of the other major adult company, the Admiral's Men.[7] Unlike Henslowe's dramatists, most of whom come to our attention in the mid- to late nineties, Shakespeare was rooted, in life as in art, in the era of the "University Wits," Greene, Lyly, Marlowe, and Kyd. He was already twenty when Lyly's first comedies were performed and printed and was twenty-five when Greene's *Friar Bacon and Friar Bungay* appeared on the stage. It is entirely proper that Ben Jonson, in the memorial verses he contributed to the First Folio should name Lyly, "sporting Kyd," and Marlowe as Shakespeare's coevals. From the beginning his comedy followed in their footsteps, setting the cool, neat, Terence-based[8] drama that Lyly wrote for the boys against the sprawling romantic narratives Greene wrote for the men (eventually turning into the historical adventure comedies that formed the staple of the Admiral's repertory). Shakespeare's early attempts to combine his models are, however, exercises in balance rather than fusion. The "love story" of Luciana and Antipholus in *The Comedy of Errors* (1592) complements the hard-headed tale of exploitation that we meet elsewhere in the play, but neither aspect throws much light on the other. The violent realism of the taming plot in *The Taming of the Shrew* (1594) stands with equal unease against the formal chess-game wooing of the lovers in the Ariosto plot of Lucentio and Bianca. Neither of these plays gives particular scope to the detached quality of boy acting, which exploits an ironic relationship between actor and role. In *Two Gentlemen of Verona* (1593) we meet the first example of what was to become the characteristic Shakespearean role of the boy pretending to be a girl pretending to be a boy. But there is too much Greenian pathos and too little Lylian irony in the presentation of the disguised Julia to offer us more than a hint of the compound form we find eventually in *Twelfth Night*. And this is true in spite of the fact that this part of the story comes eventually from the same source as *Twelfth Night*—from the anonymous Sienese play of *Gl'Ingannati*. In *Two Gentlemen* the story appears in the version found in Montemayor's sprawling pastoral romance, the *Diana*. As there, it is focused for our attention as a tale of female victimization. Julia follows her lover with ardent hope. He has forgotten her, but she can stay close to him disguised as a page. He will employ her to carry love tokens to his new beloved. She bewails her unfortunate destiny.

The dramaturgy of these earlier comedies shows the boy heroine as essentially passive, as reacting to male initiatives rather than making her own moves. But she can survive and achieve happiness without having to sojourn with a hermit in a forest cave or else become a saint (as so often happens in the Elizabethan repertory). Shakespeare's comic worlds are controlled by civil discourse, so that justice can be recovered by eloquence (as in Portia's speech), by appeal to the rules of the highly structured worlds depicted, and so do not need the masculine violence that the Henslowe plays use for their denouements. Indeed, one might say that Shakespeare, if compared with his adult theater contemporaries, appears as a restrictive and unindulgent playwright, holding within controlled environments the geographical and chronological spread of his stories and continually cutting off the romantic intensity of particular situations by introducing contrast and creating objective balance.[9] His fables of loss and recovery (*The Merchant of Venice, Twelfth Night*) do not involve whole societies in chaos, nor do they give us any sense of souls adrift in an inexplicable deprivation such as we find, for example, in Henslowe's *The Weakest Goeth to the Wall* or *A Knack to Know an Honest Man*. The dukes who control Shakespeare's comedies provide a boundary that delimits the range of disorder that can occur. In the plays that (like so many of Henslowe's) involve banishment (*A Midsummer Night's Dream, As You Like It*), even the world of exile turns out to be under benign control and indeed has curative qualities.

The potential to give the boys in the Chamberlain's company something like the control of tone that we find in all-boy plays could only be indulged so far in Shakespeare's early comedies. There the demands of overarching narrative and of emotional realism tend to infringe the comic assurance of the boy actors that precocious self-confidence and intelligent trickery will solve all the problems presented. In *Gallathea*, the one Lyly play in which we meet boys pretending to be girls pretending to be boys, the effect achieved is not romantic pathos but rather a gay insouciance in the face of the bizarre situation that gods and fathers have devised for them. And the insouciance is not misplaced, for the formal language in which these characters live can describe disaster but hardly enact it. Distanced by this, we are free to laugh at the comic inventiveness that Lyly's two maidens, Phillida and Gallathea, bring to their dilemma. They convince us they can combine adventurousness with innocence or, we might say, can control both male and female stereotypes.

It is obvious that the disguising of "girls" as men is one of the principal devices in Shakespeare's comic dramaturgy in the second half of the 1590s.[10] The effect achieved, and presumably aimed at, is different from that found in Lyly, for the irruptions into male (and adult) life that we find in *The Merchant of Venice*, *As You Like It*, and *Twelfth Night* are not circumscribed by the actions of men; men's actions, we might say, are only there to provide the problems that the boys/women can exercise their wits on and solve for themselves. After a scene or two to establish femininity, the boys playing Portia, Rosalind, and Viola take charge of the plot, move situations in the direction they require, and become responsible for the comic ending. The men around them are reduced to conformity and applause. But of course these women are not simply automata of efficiency. Like the boys of the children's theater, they handle their plots with a gleeful sense of fun (in *The Merchant of Venice* this is only fully apparent in act 5). The pleasure taken in collusion with the audience, the teasing of the other characters, replicate qualities that the boys' theater imposed on its audience as a general effect.

We can see this power gradually emerging in Shakespeare's handling of his principal female characters, whether disguised or not—think of the princess and her ladies in their response to the Navarrese courtiers, especially in the "Muscovite" scene. Characteristically these ladies are found in a society that gives them the power and freedom that comes from an easy command of courtly social forms (often defined as "wit"), imposing defer-ence and courtesy and then sharing amusement with one another and with us when they get it.

   In his adaptation of plot to give scope to such characteristics Shakespeare found a useful model in the Italian *commedia erudita*. This offered him a dramaturgy poised between social realism and stage convention, the whole carried by a romantic longing for emotional satisfaction and completed by impeccably Plautine discoveries, recognitions, reconciliations of parents and children, brothers and sisters.[11] It is a drama that assumes a degree of social or political breakdown, of characters who have lost their identity in the wars, sieges, invasions of Renaissance Italy. To survive in that context, masters have to become servants, boys become girls, and girls become boys; they have no alternative but to negotiate their way back into social integration by wit and a sharp sense of what will be believed (in this resembling New Comedy's figure of the clever slave). The emotionally tense and often desperate situations in which these characters find themselves do not, however, deprive their plays of the buoyant optimism of love. But it is clear that the search for true love can be completed only by the cleverness and energy of the lovers. The *commedia erudita* offered Shakespeare an image of the desiring woman as capable (even outside the protected environment offered by Lyly) of turning her frustration into a commanding power and a free ability to manipulate everyone around her.

   Shakespeare's relation to this body of drama can only be sketched in outline here[12] by considering his response to one play—the anonymous *Gl'Ingannati*, performed first in Siena in 1531 at the Academy of the Intronati (the thunderstruck). *Gl'Ingannati* was one of the great successes of European dramaturgy, translated and adapted across the Continent and in various genres. To make contact with this play is to meet a central current in Renaissance theater, one acknowledged even in remote and backward England. When *Twelfth Night* was performed in the Middle Temple on 2 February 1602, the lawyer John Manningham called it in his diary "a play much like *The Comedy of Errors* or *Menaechmi* in Plautus, but most like and near to that in Italian called *Inganni*." What is surprising in this comment is not that Manningham got the wrong one out of the collection of plays about *inganni* (deceptions) but that he knew enough to get it almost right.[13] Deceptions by disguise and deceptions by girls dressed as boys abound in this repertory. The turn of the screw that *Gl'Ingannati* provides (the turn that caught the taste of Europe) is that not simply does the disguised girl (Lelia), yearning to be close to her former lover (Flamineo), seek employment as his page, but that she is then sent to carry messages of love to his new mistress (Isabella), who then falls in love with "him." It is clear that what attracted Shakespeare to this story in *Twelfth Night* was the opportunity it gave to combine a romantic exploration of female longing, frustration, and hope—the material of Ovid's ever-popular *Heroides*[14]— with a fast-moving and intricate plot, full of clever manipulations, of twists and turns and surprises. What the *Diana* and *Two Gentlemen* took out of it was the romance. But this left much of the source untouched, for in *Gl'Ingannati* (and in Italian comedy in general) there is little romance. Lelia is a beleaguered and resourceful woman in the Boccaccian mode, not given to introspection. She keeps her gaze firmly fixed on her goal, the repossession of her lover. When Isabella makes it clear that she is more interested in the page than the master, Lelia (unlike Julia or Viola) wastes no sympathy on emotions so like her own, but immediately grasps at the power given her. She promises to satisfy Isabella's desires, but not before Flamineo has been summarily dismissed. Then, she supposes, she herself will be able to catch him on the rebound.

Here, as in other Italian plays involving cross-dressing, the assumption of male dress seems to convert socially protected and conventionally demure girls into stereotypes of the sex they are mimicking, into macho adventurers capable of imposing themselves on society and demanding satisfaction under threat. In the highly popular *Alessandro* of Alessandro Piccolomini, Lucrezia (disguised as Fortunio) falls passionately in love with Aloisio (disguised as Lampridia) and becomes so much "a real man" (as one might say) that she breaks into her beloved's bedroom and tries to seduce her. She is only satisfied by the eventually not-unwelcome discovery that Lampridia is in fact Aloisio, her old sweetheart.

Shakespeare uses these characteristics not as models but as counterweights to the romantic stress that had hitherto dominated his presentation of shrinking female love. The effect of his later disguised boy heroines depends on the simultaneous and self-conscious deployment of male role together with female sensibility, so that "a swashing and a martial outside" (*As You Like It* 1.3.120) is managed with ironic awareness that it cannot lead to a "doublet and hose . . . in disposition" (3.2.206). As in Italian comedy, the disguise creates dramatic tension by the ever-present danger of discovery, but in Shakespeare the most important developments are not in the plot twists to avoid this but rather in the opportunities provided to present wit not simply as a plot resource but as an aspect of the romantic personality, a means of self-discovery in a "dialogue of one" between female and male, powerlessness and power, alienation and fulfillment,[15] as in Viola's attempt to woo Orsino by telling him the tale of her sister who

> never told her love,
> But let concealment like a worm i' th' bud
> Feed on her damask cheek; she pin'd in thought,
> And with a green and yellow melancholy
> She sate like Patience on a monument,
> Smiling at grief.
>
> (*Twelfth Night* 2.4.110–15)

The direct question that follows, "Was not this love indeed?" is aimed at Orsino, but it is only we, the ultimate auditors, who can respond to it fully, registering concealment as revelation, silence as a claim for recognition.

The play between presentation and concealment allows sympathy and comedy, involvement and detachment, to coexist between female characters. In *Two Gentlemen* Julia and Sylvia share the sadness of love's betrayal; the "boy" achieves identification with the lovelorn lady both as differentiated witness and as identical participant. In Viola's case, even more specifically, we can watch her growth into definition both in terms of the empathy created with Olivia and by her differentiation from Orsino's male love, supposedly identical. We watch the self-discovery of Rosalind in the playlets she organizes to parody and betray her real love and in the unwitting self-revelation that appears in her "objective" handling of the Sylvius-Phoebe affair. In all these devices, the crosscurrents of emotion ("between a sob and a giggle," as George Hibbard calls it[16]), fill the space at the center of the comedy to a degree that could not be tolerated in Italian drama, where the extraordinarily complex web of circumstances leaves no space for contemplative stasis.

The capacity to "answer back" in boy's disguise, however deviously, is a capacity that Shakespeare extends to the women in his comedies, even when no disguise is involved. It gives them a status that comically infringes the superiority of the adult actors and so recreates in some degree the gleefully subversive comedy of the boys' theater. In *Love's Labor's Lost* the Princess of France and her ladies are more than a match for their male suitors. The doubleness of their roles as political envoys and as objects of love allows them to manage their love-game comedy with an ambiguous power of "play" that permits the woman's imagination of possibilities to outstrip all male attempts to privilege "real" expressions of unified feeling, sincerity, and faithfulness. This works wonderfully well in this highly artificial drama. But as soon as social relations come into sharper focus, the free power of wit begins to dissipate. Thus the deromanticized world of Kate the Shrew keeps us so uneasily close to everyday ideas of shrewishness that it becomes difficult to preserve a balance, unless we read shrewishness as itself a self-conscious form of wit, as a social game played to win. Beatrice, in *Much Ado*, is kept more clearly free of any explanation in terms of mind-set. Laughter, "a merry soul," happy integration into a close-knit family group, allow us to respond to her as a person whose acerbity is never more than one aspect of her witty control of the world around her, designed to tease and avoid definition, and therefore easy to reverse when society makes it clear that it no longer approves. However, here too critics find it difficult to handle the situation without imagining a secret agenda: the "merry war" between Beatrice and Benedick is "merry" because it is only the negative image of a declaration of love.

Such arguments are, I take it, symptoms of the difficulty we are bound to experience in these mature comedies, whose "something-for-everybody" quality, simultaneously romantic and antiromantic, character-driven and plot-controlled, cannot be resolved into any single paradigm. In a boys' play no such efforts are required, for there it is the *raison d'être* of the characters to fulfill the pattern. And if the issue is present in the swashbuckling romances of the Admiral's Men, it certainly is not highlighted in terms of the analytical self-consciousness that Shakespeare learned from Lyly.

Shakespeare's position between these repertories, his capacity to play one against the other in this segment of his *oeuvre*, and in particular his boy-heroine's command of the plot so as to replicate the boys' theater's effect of serious playfulness—these undoubted characteristics cannot be proved to be a result of commercial calculation, even though such commercial calculation was going on all around. We find it virtually impossible to suppose that transcendent genius can be used to fulfill monetary purposes. Yet we must acknowledge that the monetary purposes were in fact fulfilled. The King's Men made the Blackfriars the most successful theater in London and the Blackfriars made the King's Men the wealthiest and longest lived of the London companies.

NOTES

1. I have chosen these dates, thus excluding *The Comedy of Errors, The Taming of the Shrew*, and *Two Gentlemen of Verona*, because these are the years when The Chamberlain's Men are likely to have been caught up in the idea of the Blackfriars project. The company first comes to notice as a clearly demarcated entity in 1594.

2. The most obvious question is one to which there can be no answer: what were James Burbage's intentions in negotiating the purchase of a playhouse in the Blackfriars? Was he planning something like the post-1608 arrangement whereby the company ran both a public and a private playhouse, one for the summer and one for the winter? This was to prove a very profitable arrangement, and the canny James may have foreseen this as early as 1596. On the other hand, the fact that the company dismantled the Theatre and moved to the Globe, only three years after the Blackfriars venture was blocked, may suggest that Burbage's intention in 1596 was to abandon the Theatre and take over the Blackfriars as the sole acting venue for his company. In this case The Chamberlain's Men would then have become an up-market adult company, and the socially stratified theatrical situation of the 1630s would have come into being some forty years earlier.

3. I am using the dates of plays found in the Harbage-Schoenbaum *Annals of English Drama* (Philadelphia: University of Pennsylvania Press, 1964).

4. Also dated, equally plausibly, 1598.

5. The basic argument is given in G. E. Bentley, "Shakespeare and the Blackfriars Theatre," *Shakespeare Survey* 1 (1948): 38–50, and often repeated since then.

6. This is not to say the company's repertory, which is unknown.

7. The estimate is that *Love's Labor's Lost* and *A Midsummer Night's Dream* were produced in the same year as *A Knack to Know an Honest Man*, that *The Merchant of Venice* was the contemporary of *The Blind Beggar of Alexandria*, *Much Ado about Nothing* of *Look About You*, *As You Like It* of *The Four Prentices of London*, and *Twelfth Night* of *The Blind Beggar of Bednal Green* and *The Weakest Goeth to the Wall*.

8. See T. W. Baldwin, *Shakspere's Five-Act Structure* (Urbana: University of Illinois Press, 1947).

9. See J. R. Brown, "The Presentation of Comedy: The First Ten Plays", in *Stratford on Avon Studies* 4, *Shakespearian Comedy* Stratford upon Avon Studies 14, ed. Malcolm Bradbury and David Palmer. London: Edward Arnold (1972); New York: Crane Russak (1972).

10. Among thirty-five surviving adult comedies between 1595 and 1606 there are only two page-boy disguises outside Shakespeare (in *The Four Prentices of London* and *The Wise Woman of Hogsden*), though there are fifteen plays with male disguise: father disguised as servant, lover as porter, gentleman as friar, and so forth.

11. It might be argued that Plautus's *Rudens* (for example) already has combined all these romantic-classic characteristics (it even has a shipwreck). But both the shipwreck and the union of the lover and the girl are primarily commercial issues in the play. What is central is the restoring of legal rights to the girl (who has already been paid for), to the long-lost father, to Gripus his servant, and to the Temple of Venus, all of them equally violated by the improprieties of the *leno.*

12. See Leo Salingar, *Shakespeare and the Traditions of Comedy* (Cambridge: Cambridge University Press, 1974), for a full and lucid exploration of the relationship.

13. *Gl'Ingannati* had already appeared in England in the translation into Latin called *Laelia* and was performed in Cambridge in 1595 (and also perhaps in 1546).

14. They seem to be remembered in Julia's story of playing the abandoned Ariadne in a pageant (4.4.167).

15. Some premonitions can be discovered in romance narrative. In Montemayor's *Diana* the lovelorn heroine tells her hearers how she "dissembled one emotion while showing another." In Shakespeare, of course, neither emotion is "dissembled."

16. *Shakespeare, Man of the Theater*, ed. Kenneth Muir, Jay Halio, and D. J. Palmer (Newark: University of Delaware Press, 1983), 122.

Speculating Shakespeare, 1605–1606

ARTHUR F. KINNEY

In his exacting and eloquent biographies of Shakespeare, *William Shakespeare: A Documentary Life* (1975) and *William Shakespeare: A Compact Documentary Life* with its somewhat enlarged text (1977), S. Schoenbaum has relatively little to say about the years in which Shakespeare wrote the great tragedies. Because of the scarcity of documentation available for that period, we learn only that on 28 September 1602 Shakespeare "acquired the copyhold title to a quarter-acre of land, comprising a garden with cottage, on the south side of Chapel Lane"; that on 24 October 1604 and on 1 August 1606 he is listed as paying an annual rent and taking up customary tenancy in Rowington Manor; that on 24 July 1605 he "made his most ambitious investment" of £440 for a half-interest in certain tithes in three hamlets neighboring Stratford; and that in London he was named part of the King's Men in a royal warrant of 17 May 1603, which, according to Sir Edmund Tilney, Master of the Revels, played eleven times between 1 November 1604 and 31 October 1605 and 187 times, according to another reckoning, between the time of the patent and the playwright's death. *King Lear* was presented before the king on 26 December 1606, some months after the death that spring of another member of the company, Augustine Phillips.[1]

This is the fullest and most authoritative account we have, representing both Schoenbaum's superior sleuthing and his scrupulous judgment. Still we yearn to know more, to go beyond what the compilation of legal, religious, and economic documents can tell us. We tend to let the plays themselves supplement the biographical data, searching for thematic or imagistic clues to understanding the writer; we look more broadly at events concurrent with the plays; we conjecture. Since "all events become part of the conditions for producing texts," as Meredith Anne Skura has recently written,[2] and since texts

252

share such conditions with the authors and audiences of those texts, we can perhaps speculate about Shakespeare by looking at data that a reliable biographer like Schoenbaum could, by the very nature of his task, not permit himself to investigate. We can, that is, look at the text of a play—*Macbeth*, for instance— in connection with the cultural moment that first produced it and, in seeing connections, infer, if only obliquely (and speculatively), what may have captured Shakespeare's attention during a part of 1605–06.

Much of the most significant literary criticism of Tudor and Stuart texts in recent years has done just that. "Considering literary texts not as autonomous utterances out of history, but as illustrations of a Renaissance culture whose forms of representation are conditioned by the social, political world they participate in," Thomas Healy observes, "has prompted readings of texts which seek to restore their former agencies and original discursive energies."[3] Such a semiotic practice of reading literary texts, customs, and actions all as cultural documents, as signs of a cultural moment that mutually illuminate each other as well as writers such as Shakespeare, is for me even more firmly rooted in the theory of the *Annales* school represented in the work of Marc Bloch.[4] The powerfully influential argument of that school—that history must extend beyond conventional archival resources to include all kinds of evidence, so that even extraverbal or nonverbal pieces of evidence such as a landscape are "read" as texts—has helped to provide a fuller sense of history and consequently may contribute to an understanding of biography and of Shakespeare. The method supplies multiple viewpoints, often irreconcilable, which locate facets of a past moment or period that both extend and enrich our knowledge of it. While Bloch argues that all knowledge is indirect and must necessarily operate to reconstruct rather than to recover or reidentify the past, his further insistence that understanding the past always means interrogating it by asking what evidence it can yield has been especially useful. Bloch proposes a field theory of examination by which any single work or life is always seen in the wider context of which it is and always has necessarily been a part. While such an inquiry of *Macbeth* and the period 1605–06 must now rely on extant written evidence, it will also take us along different but complementary paths from those of Schoenbaum's pioneering work, helping us to speculate further what, heightened by representation in *Macbeth*, the playwright and his audiences of that time were considering.[5]

Macbeth opens with *"Thunder and lightning"* and with "hurly-burly" and "battle" announced by the weird sisters (1.1. S.D.; 1.1.3–4). In January 1605 Sir Dudley Carleton wrote Ralph Winwood of other apparitions and battles: "There was lately an apparition near Barwick of armies and fighting-men on Holydown-hills, which gave the alarm to the town, and frighted those of the Scottish Border,"[6] suggesting a connection between Scotland—and especially Berwick—and evil spirits that James I had already described in his *Daemonologie* of 1597.[7] The following summer, according to a later report (dated 14 September 1605) by the Venetian Ambassador Nicolo Molyno, the boys of Christ Church entertained King James by debating on 29 August as a question in philosophy, "An imaginatio possit producere reales effectus." The question was accompanied by explanatory verses:

Qualia monstra parit, quot vis phantastica formas,
Quam vaga fert Proteus, quam nova Nilus habet.
Concipit Aethiopem dum foemina mente nigellum,
Ventre simul foetum concipit alba nigrum.

(The force of the imagination brings forth such monsters
and as many shapes
As Proteus makes changes, or the Nile new things.
When a white woman conceives in her mind a dusky Ethiopian,
Straightway she conceives in her belly a black foetus.[8])

The king's imagination, like Macbeth's, was much occupied with witchcraft. The earl of Mar wrote Robert Cecil from Royston on 26 January 1605, "We are here continually busied either at hunting or examining of witches, and although I like the first better than the last, yet I must confess both uncertain sports."[9] A year earlier Sir John Harington had written to Sir Amyas Paulet, "His Majestie did much presse for my opinion touchinge the power of Satane in matter of witchcraft; and askede me with much gravity,—'If I did trulie understande, why the devil did worke more with anciente women than others?',"[10] while during the summer of 1605, when in Oxford, James took particular interest in calling before him a young girl from Abingdon, Anne Gunter, who had been accused of witchcraft and examining her himself, later taking her father, whom he suspected of encouraging her, to trial before Coke in Star Chamber.

Whether James wished to pursue such matters as only scientific inquiry, or whether as for Macbeth they became matters troublesome to the mind, they must be understood alongside James's stern attempts to establish his authority with statements of absolutism. In his *Trew Lawe of Free Monarchies* published in Scotland in 1598 and widely distributed in England in 1603, he declared,

> The Kings . . . in Scotland were before any estates or ranks of men within the same, before any Parliaments were holden or laws made, and by them was the land distributed (which at the first was wholly theirs), states erected and decerned, and forms of government devised and established. And it follows of necessity that the Kings were the authors and makers of the laws and not the laws of the Kings. . . . And according to these fundamental laws already alleged, we daily see that in the Parliament (which is nothing else but the head court of the King and his vassals) the laws are but craved by his subjects, and only made by him at their rogation and with their advice. For albeit the King makes daily statutes and ordinances, enjoining such pains thereto as he thinks meet, without any advice of Parliament or Estates, yet it lies in the power of no Parliament to make any kind of law or statute without his sceptre be to it for giving it the force of law. . . . And as ye see it manifest that the King is overlord of the whole land, so is he master over every person that inhabiteth the same, having power over the life and death of every one of them.[11]

John Nichols records that by January 1606 James was securing his authority further by making an inventory of "The Imperiall Diadem and Crowne, and other Roill and Princely ornaments and Jewells," which registered his leadership of an empire inherited from Elizabeth I to which he was adding Scotland in his plan of union: not, then, as "happy prologues" but for James already "the swelling act / Of the imperial theme" (1.3.128–29):

> Imprimis, the Imperiall Crowne of this Realme, of gould, the border garnished with seaven ballaces, eight saphiers, five pointed diamonds, twenty rubies (two of them being crased), nineteen pearles; and one of the crosses of the same Crown garnished with a great sapphire, an emoralde crased, four ballaces and nyne pearles not all of one sort. . . .

> Item, a Crown Imperiall of gould, set about the nether border with nyne pointed diamonds, and betwene every diamond a knot of pearl, set by five pearls in a knot; in the upper border eight rock-rubies and twenty round pearlees; the foure arches being set each of them with a table diamond, a table ruby, an emerald; and upon two of

the arches eighteen pearls, and uppon the other two arches seventeen pearles; and betweene every arch a great ballace sett in a collett of gould, and uppon the toppe a very great ballace pierced, and a little crosse of goulde upon the toppe, enamelled blewe.[12]

James had already made use publicly of the imperial crown by substituting it, without precedent, for the words "By the King" in the proclamation of 5 November 1605, "A Proclamation for the search and apprehension of Thomas Percy," announcing the Gunpowder Plot. In a subsequent speech to Parliament his anxiety drew analogies to the death of his father by an explosion during his first year of life: "these wretches," James told Parliament, "thought to have blown up, in a manner, the whole world of this Island."[13] Correspondence once again helps us to capture that cultural moment most authentically, this time in a letter from John Chamberlain:

> I cannot but remember what you have diverse times told me touching Thomas Percy, that you suspected him to be a subtle, flattering, dangerous knave. He hath not only verified your judgment but exceeded all degrees of comparison and gone beyond Nero and Caligula, that wished all Rome but one head that they might cut it off at a stroke; for he at one blow would have ruined the whole realm.
>
> He had hired the house or lodging next to the Parliament, together with the cellar or vault under the Upper House, into which by the means of one Johnson, his man—a superstitious papist, or rather a priest as is thought—he hath conveyed any time this twelvemonth as much powder in satchels, as four or five and thirty barrels, hogsheads and firkins could contain, with intent the first day of the Parliament, when the King should be in his speech, to blow them all up; and had so cunningly covered them with billets, faggots, and such trash that without long search they could not be discovered. And but that God blinded him or some of his to send this enclosed, without name or date, to the Lord Monteagle, it was very like to take effect.[14]

William Hubbard, one of the king's chaplains, made the point even more tellingly: "O thou most noble Prince Henry, the staffe of thy fathers strength . . . whose innocent life these bloodthirstie Babilonians longed for, equally with thy Princely fathers: to destroy roote, and branch: and fruite, parent, and childe in one day: to kill damme and young in one nest,"[15] rather like Lady Macduff: "Poor bird, thou'dst never fear the net nor lime, / The pitfall nor the gin" (4.2.34–35).

After the discovery of the plot, anxiety spread. Molyno writes on 21 November 1605:

> The King is in terror; he does not appear nor does he take his meals in public as usual. He lives in the innermost rooms with only Scotchmen about him. . . . Catholics fear heretics and vice versa . . . both are armed; foreigners live in terror of their houses being sacked by the mob which is convinced that some, if not all foreign princes, are at the bottom of the plot. . . . The conduct of the French Ambassador is much criticised, not only on the ground of what I have already reported but because he would not wait for the letters that the Queen was writing for France. He insisted on crossing on Monday evening though the weather was bad.[16]

On 22 March 1606—two months after Anne Gunter's father had gone to trial and half a year after the attempt to blow up Parliament, Arthur Wilson still records this climate of fear, recalling the near-death of James at the hands of the Gowries in Perth in 1600 and focusing on an instrument very pertinent to the imaginative world of *Macbeth*:

> A rumour was spread (by what strange means unknown) that the King was stabbed . . . with a poysoned knife: The *Court* at *Whitehall*, the *Parliament* and *City* took the *Alarum*, mustering up their Old Fears, every man standing at *gaze* as if some new *Prodigie* had seized them; such a Terrour had this late *monstrous* intended *mischief* imprinted in the *spirits* of the People, that they took Fire from every little Train of *Rumour*, and were ready to grapple with their own *Destruction* before it came,[17]

while in other contemporary plays in 1605–06 the dagger was associated with Rome and with regicide.

James's Macbeth-like fear of superstition also caused him to have considerable difficulties early in his reign in reinforcing his royal authority with the King's Touch for scrofula, which Malcolm attributed to Edward the Confessor in Shakespeare's play: "How he solicits heaven, / Himself best knows; but strangely-visited people, / All swoll'n and ulcerous, pitiful to the eye, / The mere despair of surgery, he cures" (4.3.149–52). A letter sent to Rome from London on 8 October 1603 shows James faltering in this regard:

> At this time the King began to take interest in the practice pertaining to certain ancient customs of the Kings of England respecting the cure of persons suffering from the King's Evil. So when some

of these patients were presented to him in his antechamber, he first
had a prayer offered by a Calvinist minister, and then remarked that
he was puzzled how to act. From one point of view he did not see
how the patient could be cured without a miracle, and nowadays
miracles had ceased and no longer happened: so he was afraid of
committing a superstitious act. From another point of view however
inasmuch as it was an ancient usage and for the good of his subjects,
he resolved to give it a trial, but only by way of prayer, in which he
begged all present to join him and then he touched the sick folk. It
was observed that when the King made this speech, he several times
turned his eyes toward the Scotch ministers around him, as tho he
expected their approval of what he was saying, having first conferred
with them.[18]

Such insecurity, fear, and superstition together may account
for the savagery that both Scottish kings share. But where Macbeth knows "They have tied me to a stake; I cannot fly, / But
bear-like I must fight the course" (5.7.1–2), James is content for
Coke to act, following torture, in the name of justice. Thus,
proclaims Coke, with the same explicit physical brutality as
darkens Shakespeare's play:

after a traitor hath had his just trial and is convicted and attainted,
he shall have his judgment to be drawn to the place of execution
from his prison as being not worthy any more to tread upon the
face of the earth whereof he was made; also for that he hath been
retrograde to nature, therefore is he drawn backward at a horsetail
. . . he must be drawn with his head declining downward, and lying
so near the ground as may be, being thought unfit to take benefit
of the common air. For which cause also shall he be strangled, being
hanged up by the neck between heaven and earth, as deemed unworthy of both, or either . . . then he is to be cut down alive, and to
have his privy parts cut off and burnt before his face. . . . His bowels
and inlaid parts taken out and burnt, . . . After, to have his head cut
off, which had imagined the mischief. And, lastly, his body to be
quartered, and the quarters to be set up in some high and eminent
place, to the view and detestation of men, and to become a prey for
the fowls of the air.[19]

The heads of the four traitors were carried, like Macbeth's head,
and placed on the spikes of London Bridge, treated so that they
would rot for years rather than months. As John Rhodes Minister recorded in doggerel in 1606, "Heads of *Catesby*, and of
Piercy, / they were sent: / And sette vpon, the vpper house, / of
Parlyment." This, then, was fitting conclusion to an event that

began with "*Fawkes* at midnight, and by torch light, / there was found: With long matches and deuises, / vnderground":[20] a situation that may well have influenced the imagery of Shakespeare's "Out, out, brief candle! / Life's but a walking shadow" (5.5.23–24). Such a complex, charged, prolonged atmosphere of suspicion and fear of the supernatural is the particular marking mood in Macbeth.

Dominant events of the cultural moment thus permeate *Macbeth*. But so do writings of the moment, writings of all kinds. Anticipating the 1605 debate of the boys at Christ Church, John Florio's 1603 translation of Montaigne Englishes his essay on the imagination in phrases that seem to have planted themselves in Shakespeare and, later, become a part of his play. "*Fortis imaginatio generat casum,*" writes Montaigne in Book I of the *Essayes*. "*A strong imagination begetteth chance*. . . . I am one of those that feele a very great conflict and power of imagination. All men are shockt therewith, and some overthrowne by it. The impression of it pierceth me, and for want of strength to resist her, my endevour is to avoid it."[21] Macbeth thinks of the forceful imagination as "A dagger of the mind, a false creation, / Proceeding from the heat-oppressed brain" (2.1.38–39), but the problem is more critical when, enlarged and projected first onto his wife and then onto his entire country, imagination turns into a fixed state of illness: "If thou couldst, doctor, cast / The water of my land, find her disease, / And purge it to a sound and pristine health" (5.3.50–52). "It is very likely," writes Montaigne through Florio, "that the principall credit of visions, of enchantments, and such extraordinary effects, proceedeth from the power of imaginations, working especially in the mindes of the vulgar sort, as the weakest and seeliest, whose conceit and beleefe is so seized upon, that they imagine to see what they see not."[22]

Florio's translation of Montaigne was followed in 1605 by an English translation of Pierre Le Loier's *Treatise of Specters or straunge Sights, Visions, and Apparitions appearing sensibly unto men*, printed in London by Valentine Sims, who had by then also printed several of Shakespeare's plays. "A Specter or Apparition," Le Loier writes, "is an Imagination of a substance without a Bodie, the which presenteth itself sensible unto men, against the order and course of nature, and maketh them afraid. . . . So that the severall and speciall kindes of the Imagination are, the Specter or strange sight, the Phantosme, the vision & the fantasie. . . . Suydas saith, That a Phantosme is an imagination of thinges which are not indeed, and doth proceede of the senses being corrupted." Later on he adds, most appositely:

> Now amongst the manifold numbers of those that have their consciences troubled, by reason of their wicked and lewd lives, and are perplexed and terrified with a million feares; we may well account those tyrants, who by unlawfull and indirect meanes, have usurped a tyrannicall authoritie over their own native countries, or in some strange estate, and have changed a good forme of common-wealth and government, into an unjust and tyrannicall power; putting to death thousands of persons, whom they suspected to bee men of noted vertue and honestie, and who might be able to resist their damnable attempts and usurpations. How often have we seene, that these men have bin troubled and tormented with most horrible phantosmes & imaginations, which do com into their heads both sleeping & waking: . . . . How often have they supposed and imagined, that they have seene sundry visions and apparitions of those whom they have murthered, or of some others whome they have feared?[23]

Such texts may well have resonated for Shakespeare's audience, and the playwright himself might also have heard echoes of still a third Englishing—Sir Thomas North's translation from Jacques Amyot's French of Plutarch's "Life of Marcus Brutus," to which he had turned a few years earlier in writing *Julius Caesar:* "In our sect, Brutus, we have an opinion that we do not always feel or see that which we suppose we do both see and feel: but that our senses being credulous, and therefore easily abused (when they are idle and unoccupied in their own objects), are induced to imagine they see and conjecture that which they in truth do not."[24] Moreover, another current sense of the imagination, biblical in origin, was that it was the primary agent of evil. In a Protestant Bible published in 1605, this passage is found in Genesis: "When the Lord sawe that the wickednesse of man was great in the earth, and all the imaginations of the thoughts of his heart were onely euill continually, Then it repented the Lord, that hee had made man in the earth, and he was sorie in his heart. . . . and the Lord sayd in his heart, I will hencefoorth curse the ground no more for mans cause: for the imagination of mans heart is euill, euen from his youth: neither will I smite any more all things liuing, as I haue done" (Genesis

6:5–6, 21). The idea of man's corrupting imagination is repeated in Genesis 8:21, Numbers 15:39, and Galatians 6:3.

Turning to James's *Trew Lawe,* an anonymous report in 1606 argues that James must be "an absolute and perpetuall power, to exercise the highest actions and affaires in some certaine state. These are the proper qualities of Soueraigne or Maiesticall power; that it be both absolute and also perpetuall. If it be absolute but not perpetuall, then it is not soueraigne,"[25] raising for the Scottish James the twin chief concerns of the Scottish Macbeth. The *Essayes* of Sir William Cornwallis, published in 1606, provided various apposite warnings in essay 4 on suspicion, essay 10 on ambition, essay 18 on sleep, and essay 25 on "fantastickenesse,"[26] while the anonymous *Falshood in Freindship. or vnions VIZARD: OR Wolues in Lambskins* (1606) holds up as antitype to James the tyranny of Tarquin: "So the Romaines chased out of the Kingdome *Tarquine,* the proude, whome they had receiued as their King: but because of the tyranny of him and his sonne, they subiected theselues to a lesser authoritie, namely of Consuls" (cf. *Macbeth* 2.1.55–56). Still other pamphlets constituting the cultural moment of *Macbeth* give recipes for the King's Evil, provide directions for hosting a banquet, and give remedies for spots and stains.[27] And, varying on this last, the 1606 Englishing of a French translation of Artimodorus's *Ivdgement, Or exposition of Dreames,* published earlier in Greek and Latin, finds special meaning in the repetitious act to make clothes clean in dreams: "To dreame to wash ones clothes, or an other bodies, is to stayne, and loose, or escape some hurt, & danger about the body, or life, for clothes being washed, loose their vncleanesse. This dreame also shewes, that some body, shall learne and perceaue our secrets, for to wash, is to take, and amend, or correct, and therefore it is an ill dreame, for them which are in doubt to be reprooued or surprised."[28] Lady Macbeth's perpetual "washing her hands. I have known her continue in this a quarter of an hour" and her "damn'd spot!" (5.1.29–30, 35) have been traced to no precise source and are not in Holinshed.

Since the work by Albert H. Tricomi,[29] students of the drama of early modern England have recognized a vogue for disguised-duke plays in the period under consideration. These often focus on tyranny and rebellion, making Shakespeare's theater the site of political commentary often scrutinized by the Revels Office. Familiar too are Ben Jonson's recurrent difficulties with the censor: Herford and Simpson sum them in part as "Imprisoned for his share in *The Isle of Dogs*, 1597; cited before Lord Chief Justice Popham for *Poetaster*, 1601; summoned before the Privy Council . . . for *Sejanus*, 1603; imprisoned for his share in *Eastward Ho*, 1605."[30] In fact, *Macbeth* comes at a cultural moment of anticourt plays that all portray a ruler whose obvious abuses with the court and with society would at the very least have alerted the new King James to a widespread feeling of grievance and "to quickening expectations for redress."[31] Marston's *The Malcontent* (1602–3; revised 1604) and *The Fawn* (1604; revised 1606), Shakespeare's own *Measure for Measure* (1603–4), Middleton's *The Phoenix* (1603–4) and Sharpham's *The Fleer* (1606) all come long before the more notorious *Game at Chess* (1625). Take, for example, *The Malcontent*: originally produced by Blackfriars, it was later augmented by Marston, in 1603 stolen by the King's Men, given an induction by Webster and produced again in 1604. The motto pointedly reads, *"Vexat censura columbas":* Censorship disturbs the doves.[32] The anonymous *Tragedie of Caesar and Pompey or Caesars Reuenge* (1606) is unique among a clutch of Caesar plays in this period by offsetting Caesar's assassination with the preceding bloody slaughter of Pompey and with the equally bloody death of Brutus that followed. Edward Sharpham's *The Fleer* transfers its anatomy of tyranny from Italy to London, and Samuel Daniel even had to apologize and withdraw his *Tragedie of Philotas* (1605), dedicated to Prince Henry, because the protagonist, "noted of vaineglory," suspected of plotting the death of Alexander and "arraigned for the same fact, which hee stoutly denying, was afterward put to torture, and then confest his treason,"[33] was widely believed to be based on the last days of the rebellious earl of Essex.

In the random survival of texts from this cultural moment, comedy is also relevant. Chapman's *The Widdowes Teares* (1604) can be read as a general burlesque of James's court and ministers; his *Monsieur d'Olive* (1605) specifically ridicules the earl of Nottingham, whom James had just appointed to sign a peace treaty with Spain; while the *Eastward Ho!* (1605) of Chapman, Marston, and Jonson lampoons James's Scots courtiers newly arrived in London and recently given titles. The Arcadia and Lacedominia of *The Ile of Gvls* by John Day (1606) are thinly disguised portraits of England and Scotland, and the play contains a personal attack on James, despite an assurance in the prologue that it does not "figure anie certaine state, or private government: farre be that supposition from the thought of any indifferent Auditor," a disclaimer that merely raises that very possibility.[34] Most notorious of all is the tragedy of *Sejanus*, written by Chapman and Jonson in 1603, then revised by Jonson alone in 1605 and published despite its concentrated analysis of the tyranny of Tiberius, which was immediately interpreted as an attack on James. In such an environment, we are not surprised to learn that in 1604 Beaumont, the French ambassador, is recorded as asking, "What must be the situation of a state and of a Prince . . . whom the actors represent upon the stage, whose wife goes to see these representations in order to laugh at him, who is defied and despised by his parliament and universally hated by his whole people?"—rhetorical questions confirmed by one Mr. Calvert, who confides in his friend Winwood that "players do not forbear to present upon the stage the whole course of this present time, not sparing either the King, State or Religion, in so great absurdity and with such liberty, as any would be afraid to hear them."[35]

Although no commentary on early Stuart drama has taken into account the republication of earlier plays—and while such republication may not establish renewed performances, although this is likely—such dramas are also constituents in the cultural moment of *Macbeth*, and some of them seem now to provide verbal anticipations of Shakespeare's play whether heard or read. Tamburlaine's grief at the death of Zenocrate in Marlowe's *Tamburlaine the Greate: The second part* (reprinted 1606; the first part was reprinted in 1605) contrasts with Macbeth's terse "She should have died hereafter" at 5.5.17, but his ensuing rage anticipates Macbeth's final courage of despair:

Behold me heere diuine *Zenocrate*,
Rauing, impatient, desperate and mad,
Breaking my steeled Launce, with which I burst,
The rusty beames of *Ianus* Temple doores,
Leeting out death and tyrannizing war,
To march with me vnder this bloody flag,
and if thou pittiest *Tamburlain* the great,
Come downe from heauen, and liue with me againe.[36]

So also does the later death of the Captain: "I cannot liue. / I feele my liuer pierc'd, and all my vaines, / That there begin and nourish euerie part, / Mangled and torne, and all my entrals bath'd / In blood that straineth from their orifex."[37] The treachery and slaughter that characterize Kyd's *Spanish Tragedie* also mark an earlier part of the story that was published in a short-ened, presumably acting, version as *The First Part of Ieronimo: With the Warres of Portugall, and the life and death of Don Andraea* in 1605. The plays by Marlowe and Kyd were by then theatrical staples in Southwark and in the provinces.

Two other plays reprinted in 1605 have more direct connections with Shakespeare. Ragan's late soliloquy in *The True Chronicle History of King LEIR*, which Shakespeare had just consulted for his own play on Lear, sounds like a model for the opening soliloquy of Lady Macbeth (1.5.38ff.):

A shame on these white-liuerd slaues, say I,
That with fayre words so soone are ouercome.
O God, that I had bin but made a man;
Or that my strength were equall with my will!
These foolish men are nothing but meere pity,
And melt as butter doth against the Sun,
Why should they haue preeminence ouer vs,
Since we are creatures of more braue resolue?
I sweare, I am quite out of charity
With all the heartlesse men in Christendome,
A poxe vpon them, when they are affrayd
To giue a stab, or slit a paltry Wind-pipe,
Which are so easy matters to be done.
Well, had I thought the slaue would serue me so,
My selfe would haue bin executioner:
Tis now vndone, and if that it be knowne,
Ile make as good shift as I can for one,
He that repines at me, how ere it stands,
'Twere best for him to keepe him from my hands,[38]

and there are other striking resonances in the discussion between Ragan and the Messenger about regicide, the Messenger's own thoughts of killing the king while asleep, and Cambria's thoughts of witchcraft.[39] *The Tragedie of King Richard the third*, "Newly augmented, By *William Shakespeare . . . As it hath bin lately Acted by the Right Honourable the Lord Chamberlaine his seruants*" (and so before 1603), was reprinted in 1605 with telling anticipatory echoes in speeches by Richard such as "Plots haue *I* laid, inductions dangerous, / By drunken prophesies, libels and dreames," and in Clarence's account of his guilty nightmare ("I haue past a miserable night, / So full of vgly sights, of gastly dreames") and the confession of remorse to Brokenburie ("O then began the tempest to my soule").[40] Such sights and sounds constituted a main part of the imaginative climate of 1605–6, in life as well as in literature.

There were other sights and sounds too in 1605 and 1606 far less familiar to us now than they were then. Speculating on Shakespeare's possible experience during the cultural moment he was composing *Macbeth*, we find a show of kings in the streets of London, although such a show is absent from the 1577 Holinshed that was most probably his source,[41] which contains no second visit by Macbeth to the witches. This show is not where we might first look for it: it is the 1604 Lord Mayor's Show, entitled *The Trimphs of Re-United Brittania*, printed in 1605, for which Anthony Munday received two pounds but which Jonson apparently wrote. According to the records of the Merchant Taylors guild, which sponsored the show, it was to honor the installation of Sir Leonard Halliday of their guild as the new Lord Mayor. David M. Bergeron calls *The Triumphs of Re-United Brittania* "unique in at least two respects. It contains the only full-scale treatment of the popular Brutus-in-Albion myth of English history to be found in civic pageantry down to the closing of the threatres. The pageant has the further distinction of having been readied twice for performance, but the scheduled day, 29 October, was the occasion of a storm which did much damage to the preparations; thus upon request of the company "the same shewes were newe repaired, and caried alreade upon *All Saincts day* . . . ' . . . which partially accounts for the total expense of £710 2s.5d."[42] "The Pageant" as it is printed in 1605 relies for its most dramatic effect on the presence of James himself in the audience:

> On a Mount triangular, as the Island of *Britayne* it selfe is described to bee, we seate in the Supreame place, vnder the shape of a fayre and beautifull Nymph, *Britania* hir selfe accosted with *Brutes* deuided kingdoms, in the like female representations, *Leegria*, *Cambria*, and *Albania*. *Brytania* speaking to *Brute* her Conqueror, (who is seated somwhat lower, in the habite of an aduenturous warlike *Troyan*) tels him, that she had still continued her name of *Albion*, but for his conquest of her virgine honour, which since it was by heauen so appointed, she reckons it to be the very best of her fortunes, *Brute* shewes her what height of happinesse she hath attained vnto by his victorie, being before a vast Wildernes, inhabited by Giantes, and a meere den of Monsters: *Goemagot* and his barbarous brood, being quite subdued, his ciuill followers, first taught her modest meanners, and the meanes how to raigne as an Imperial

lady, building his *Troya noua* by the riuer *Thamesis*, and beautifeing his land with other Citties beside. But then the three *Virgin* king-domes seeme to reproue him, for his ouermuch fond loue to his sons, and deuiding her (who was one sole Monarchy) into three seueral estates, the hurt and inconuenience whereon ensuing, each one of them modestly deliuered vnto him. He staies their further progres in reproofe, by his and their now present reuyued condition, beeing raised againe by the powerfull vertue of Poesie (after such length of time) to behold *Britaniaes* former Felicity againe, and that the same *Albania*, where *Humber* slew his son *Albanact*, had bred a second *Brute*, by the blessed mariage of *Margaret*, eldest daughter to king *Henrie* the seauenth, to *Iames* the fourth king of *Scotland*, of whom our second *Brute* (Royall king *Iames*) is truely and rightfully descended: by whose happye comming to the Crowne, *England*, *Wales*, & *Scotland*, by the first *Brute* seuered and diuidied, is in our second *Brute* re-united, and made one happy *Britania* again.⁴³

Verbal or visual memory of this show may also have played a part in Shakespeare's *King Lear*, but here the sweep of history, with its striking parallel to that of Holinshed (whose sole disrup-tion of chronology in the history of Scotland comes just here in the linkage of Banquo to James I and VI), is the ideational back-drop to the show of eight kings in *Macbeth*, another chronologi-cal disruption that brings the play of ancient Scotland into Shakepeare's own time. And there are other connections are well. "The Chariot" that follows, which Bergeron thinks was carried along in the progress rather than stationary, presents seven kings (not eight)—Edward III, Richard II, Henry IV, Henry V, Henry VI, Edward IV, and Henry VII⁴⁴—with individual speeches about their contributions to the history of the Mer-chant Taylors, but a vacant place is left in the chariot for James, just as the eighth king in *Macbeth* holds a mirror to reflect James at a royal performance, suggesting that there too, without James, there are only seven kings, not eight after all. The pres-ence of the actual monarch is thus essential to complete both "shows," but the distinction between them is deeply ironic: the honorable guild is paying tribute to the king; the demonic witches are warning Macbeth.

Another popular show, both seen and heard before being printed in 1606, is the overlooked *No-Body, and Some-Body* "With the true Chronicle Historie of Elydure, *who was fortu-nately three seuerall times crowned King of England . . . as it hath beene acted by the Queens Maijesties Seruants*," ac-cording to the title page. Like the Lord Mayor's show, this is not a piece of high art, and its weak comedy resembles more than anything else a pastiche of lines and situations better represented (or reconstructed) in *Lear, Hamlet,* and *Macbeth.*[45] The overplot is about long-suffering Nobody, whose service and charity go unrecognized because he announces his good works are those of Nobody, until Somebody attempts to take the credit—an extended trope of a single, obvious joke. The underplot, however, in which the bookish Elydure is given the crown three times, examines kingship as tyranny: first in the hands of his father, the absolutist tyrant Archigallo; then in the hands of his two tyrannical uncles, Peridure and Vigenius, who slay each other in an act of double regicide. Whether or not this play by a company rivaling the King's Men was a deliberate parody of Shakespeare, and especially of *Macbeth,* here too there seem to be notable echoes. The desire to rebel, which Cornwell shares with Martianus, is reminiscent of the colloquy between Malcolm and Macduff (4.3):

> *Mart.* Alls nought already, yet these vnripe ills
>   Haue not their full growth, and their next degree
>   Must needes be worse then nought, and by what name
>   Doe you call that?
> *Cornw.* I know none bad enough:
>   Base, vild, notorious, vgly monstrous, slauish;
>   Intollerable, abhorred, demnable;
>   Tis worse then bad, Ile be no longer vassaile
>   To such a tirannous rule, nor accessarie
>   To the base sufferance of such out-rages.
> *Mart.* Youle not indure it, how can you remedie
>   A mayme so dangerous and incurable?
> *Corn.* There is a way; but walls haue eares and eyes
>   Your eare my Lord, and counsell.[46]

Elydure's wife, known only as Lady, shares Lady Macbeth's passion for power: "let him be straight waies Crownd, / That I may triumphe whilst the trumpets sound"; "you are too mild, iudgment belongs to me."[47] Both the secrecy and the suddenness of regicide—and its dominance throughout the play, even when it turns to comedy—unite *No-Body, and Some-Body* with *Macbeth,* as they also dominated the sights and sounds of the cultural moment the two plays shared.

Schoenbaum brings the new edition of *Shakespeare's Lives* (1991) to a close by echoing Thomas Hardy:

What would we not give for a single personal letter, one page of diary! Hardy expressed what many have felt when he wrote [of Shakespeare]:
Bright baffling Soul, least capturable of themes,
Thou, who display'dst a life of commonplace,
Leaving no intimate word or personal trace
Of high design outside the artistry
　　　　　Of thy penned dreams,
Still shalt remain at heart unread eternally.

A certain kind of literary biography, rich in detail about (in Yeats's phrase) the momentary self, is clearly impossible.[48]

Strictly speaking, of course, this remains true, like so very many of Schoenbaum's pronouncements. We do not know, for instance, if *The Most royall and Honourable entertainement, of the famous and renowmed King, CHRISTIERN the fourth, King of* Denmarke *&c.* (1606) by H. R. (Henry Robarts), which was rushed to press before the Danish king left English soil and is so much more diffuse and generally inferior to the slightly later account of *The King of Denmarkes welcome* (also 1606), which remains anonymous, was written before or after *Macbeth* was completed and staged, although Henry Paul has argued that it came afterwards.[49] Either way, however, its opening concentration on "the Imperiall crown" and its repetition of "mirrour" in connection with James, [50] recalling James's own wish in his speech to Parliament concerning the Gunpowder Plot that "there was a crystal window in my breast, wherein all my people might see the secretest thoughts of my heart,"[51] also find their distinct and telling parallels in *Macbeth*. The dominant ideas of the time shared a topical vocabulary and imagery, and together they define the cultural moment of Shakespeare's play, making it a definable part of that moment.

Again, strictly speaking, this does not so much isolate Shakespeare, as we speculate on him at a distance, as make him a part of his age as well as for all time. Yet the many, perhaps infinite, ways in which *Macbeth* registers its own time also capture those ideas, values, attitudes, and words that Shakespeare held and sent forth, consciously or not. So, in their way, they provide a kind of biography, too.[52]

NOTES

1. S. Schoenbaum, *William Shakespeare: A Compact Documentary Life* (New York: Oxford University Press, 1977), 246, 250–54.

2. Meredith Anne Skura, *Shakespeare the Actor and the Purposes of Playing* (Chicago: University of Chicago Press, 1994), 128.

3. Thomas Healy, *New Latitudes: Theory and English Renaissance Literature* (London: E. Arnold, 1992), 60.

4. Marc Bloch, *The Historian's Craft*, trans. Peter Putnam (New York: Knopf, 1953).

5. We have only the F1 text, but clearly its inconsistencies, lacunae, and later additions (such as Thomas Middleton's) suggest it is imperfect. The initial script, doubtless an acting script, seems beyond recovery.

6. Quoted in John Nichols, *The Progresses, Processions, and Magnificent Festivities, of King James the First, His Royal Consort, Family, and Court*, 4 vols. (London, 1828), 1:474.

7. Entered in the Stationers' Register in England in 1598.

8. In Henry N. Paul, *The Royal Play of "Macbeth"* (New York: Macmillan, 1950), 54–55.

9. Quoted in ibid., 114.

10. Sir John Harington, *Nugae Antiquae*, 2 vols. (London, 1804), 1:368.

11. Quoted in J. R. Tanner, *Constitutional Documents of the Reign of James I, A.D. 1603–1625* (Cambridge: Cambridge University Press, 1952), 9.

12. Nichols, *Progresses*, 2:45.

13. *Harleian Miscellany*, 15 vols. (London, 1809), 4:249.

14. *The Chamberlain Letters*, ed. Elizabeth McClure Thomson (London: Murray, 1966) 57–58.

15. William Hubbard, *Great Britaines Resvrrection* (1606), sig. B2r.

16. Quoted in Lilian Winstanley, *Macbeth, King Lear & Contemporary History* (Cambridge: Cambridge University Press, 1922), 55.

17. Paul, *Royal Play of "Macbeth,"* 231.

18. Ibid., 373–74.

19. Henry Garnett, *Portrait of Guy Fawkes* (London: Hale, 1962), 145.

20. John Rhodes, *A Briefe Summe of The Treason* (1606), sigs A4v; A4r.

21. *The Essayes of Michael Lord of Montaigne done into English by John Florio*, ed. Thomas Seecombe (New York, 1908), Book I, chap. 20; p. 96.

22. Ibid., 99.

23. Paul, *Royal Play of "Macbeth,"* 57–58.

24. Ibid., 50.

25. Sig. B2v.

26. William Cornewallys, *Essayes* (1606).

27. *Rams little Dodeon* (1606), sig. O6v; R. F., *The Schoole of Slovenrie* (1605), fols. 9r, 13r, 21r, 52r; L. M., *A Profitable Booke, declaring diuers approoued Remedies to take out spots and staines* (1605), sigs. A4v, B1v.

28. Sigs. F2r–F2v.

29. Albert H. Tricomi, *Anticourt Drama in England, 1603–1642* (Charlottesville: University Presses of Virginia, 1989), 9.

30. *Ben Jonson*, ed. C. H. Herford and Percy and Evelyn Simpson, 11 vols. (Oxford: Clarendon Press, 1952), 11:253.

31. Tricomi, *Anticourt Drama*, 13.

32. Lines 25–26.

33. "The Argvment," in *The Tragedy of Philotas By Samuel Daniel*, ed. Laurence Michel (New Haven: Yale University Press, 1949), 101.

34. Tricomi, *Anticourt Drama* 35; the prologue is not in my copy of the 1606 Q.

35. Beaumont and Calvert are quoted in E. M. Albright, *Dramatic Publications in England, 1580–1640* (Oxford: Oxford University Press, 1927), 117, 118.

36. Sig. D1v; cf. *Macbeth* 5.5.50–51.

37. Sigs. E2v–E3r; cf. *Macbeth* 5.7.1.

38. Sig. I1r; cf. also Lady Macbeth at 1.7.47ff.; 2.2.1ff.

39. Sigs. E3r–E3v; F1r; F3r; G3r.

40. Sigs. A2r–A2v; C4r: cf. *Macbeth* 2.4; sig. C4v.

41. "And surely heerevpon had he put Makduffe to death, but that a certaine witch whom he had in great trust, had told that he should neuer be slain with man borne of any woman, nor vanquished till the wood of Bernane, came to the Castell of Dunsinnane" (London, 1577), sig. Q5r. I have made the case for Shakespeare's use of the 1577 folio of *The Historie of Scotland* in "Scottish History, the Union of the Crowns and the Issue of Right Rule: The Case of Shakespeare's *Macbeth*," in *Renaissance Culture in Context: Theory and Practice*, ed. Jean R. Brink and William F. Gentrup (London: Scolar Press, 1993), 18–35.

42. David M. Bergeron, *Venetian State Papers and English Civic Pageantry, 1558–1642* (Columbia: University of South Carolina Press, 1971), 141.

43. Sigs. B1r–B2r.

44. Sigs. C1r–C2r.

45. *Lear*, sigs. A4v, B3r, D2r, G1v–G3r, G4v–H1r; *Hamlet*, sigs. C4v, I3r; *Macbeth*, sigs. A3v, B1v, B2r, C4r, D1r, D1v, G2r.

46. Sig. B1v; see also D1r. Cf. Macbeth 3.4.130–31.

47. Sigs. D1r, D1v.

48. S. Schoenbaum, *Shakespeare's Lives: New Edition* (Oxford: Clarendon Press, 1991), 568.

49. Paul, *Royal Play of "Macbeth"* 402.

50. Sigs. A4r, B2v, B4v.

51. *Harleian Miscellany*, 4:249.

52. I am grateful to the staffs of the Bodleian Library, Folger Shakespeare Library, and Huntington Library (especially Barbara Quinn and Alan Jutzi) for supplying me with original texts used here, and to R. B. Parker and Sheldon P. Zitner, the kindest and gentlest of editors, for their helpful suggestions.

King Lear: Monarch or Senior Citizen?

R. A. FOAKES

In recent years we have heard a good deal about transgression in the theater of Shakespeare and the subversive implications of his drama. These subversive implications are exemplified in the idea that *King Lear* undermines the social hierarchy, offers an image of "social inversion" in the idea of feeling what wretches feel, and retreats at the end from radical analysis of the economic structure of society into "the domestic and familial, as a shelter from sociopolitical awareness."[1] Such a view can find support in many modern productions of the play, which have transformed *King Lear* into something Shakespeare would hardly have recognized as his own. They have shown us from the start an old pensioner with nothing royal about him, white-haired, rather decrepit, fitter to play shuffleboard than to rule a kingdom, losing the last shreds of his uncertain dignity in the opening scene. The setting tends to be vague, the costumes of no particular time. Lear may appear in a kind of military greatcoat (Donald Sinden in 1976 and Michael Gambon, 1982), as if he were a superannuated army officer, or in shirt and braces, like Robert Stephens (1993), more like a contemporary wino than a king driven mad, or in something like a Ph.D. gown with an open-necked shirt underneath (Nicholas Hytner's production, 1990). When Lear is so presented, the stage business with the map suggests not so much a royal king dividing what Lear calls "our fair kingdom" as an old fool unwisely sharing out his property among his children—rather like the midwestern farmer of Jane Smiley's novel *A Thousand Acres* (1991) making a hash of things by transferring land to his daughters.

In eighteenth- and nineteenth-century productions Lear was discovered sitting on a throne, or he entered and ascended a chair of state in regal pomp. This sense of pomp, royal robes, and all the addition of a king, has in recent times been abandoned. It survived through the nineteenth century, but was qualified by other aspects of productions. Some actors, like Philip Kemble and Henry Irving, chose to make Lear from the first somewhat decrepit or palsied, and those, like Edwin Forrest, Werner Kraus, and John Gielgud as recently as 1940, who presented a grand figure of regal authority, did so in a particular way,[2] for the most kingly figures were generally associated with a remote past. The Victorian urge to historicize Shakespeare's plays, which had led William Macready in 1838 and later producers to locate *King Lear* in ancient Britain, usually with Saxon or Romano-British suggestions and often with hints of stone circles or megaliths recalling Stonehenge,[3] has continued to influence productions in the twentieth century, right down to the Granada television production of 1983 with Laurence Olivier in the title role.

So if Lear was still dressed regally and given symbols of authority in the opening scene, the overall effect was to distance the play in time and detach it from any connection with Shakespeare's own age, allowing Lear, typically, to be identified with figures like the biblical Job. Such treatment gave scope both on the stage and in criticism for Lear to be privatized and sentimentalized into a display of the pathos "of an old man humbled and petted, disarmed and then restored to peace and gratitude."[4] Indeed, the immensely influential essay of A. C. Bradley converted the play into "The Redemption of Lear" and emphasized the "effect of suffering in reviving the greatness and eliciting the sweetness of Lear's nature."[5] Kenneth Tynan was belated when, in his review of Peter Brook's production in 1962, he wrote, "Lay him to rest, the royal Lear with whom generations of star actors have made us reverently familiar; the majestic ancient"; for Brook, he said, had discovered a new protagonist, "an edgy, capricious old man, intensely difficult to live with."[6]

So if some effort was made on stage to give Lear the trappings of royalty, it was not in such a way as to connect him with monarchs like James I, of Shakespeare's time, or with monarchs of the twentieth century. For instance, in productions like those in which John Gielgud (1950, 1955), Michael Redgrave (1953), Eric Porter (1968), or Laurence Olivier starred (1983), the appearance of the stage continued to suggest a primitive Lear with settings that conjured up an ancient world, the stage being strewn with standing stones or offering hints of Saxon England. Lear might be strikingly differentiated from everyone else by being costumed in special robes and coronet or crown (as in Trevor Nunn's 1968 production, in which Eric Porter wore an enormous coronet with a double row of spikes sticking up from it), but not with reference to the familiar emblems of British royalty.

Gloucester at one point refers to Lear's "anointed flesh" (3.7.58), which shows that Shakespeare had the familiar English monarchy in mind, since the practice of anointing kings with holy oil at their coronation began only in the Middle Ages and has continued ever since as the focal point of the ritual. The opening court scene centers on an idea of majesty that relates more to James I than to ancient kings. It is shown in the way, for instance, Kent addresses Lear:

> Royal Lear,
> Whom I have ever honor'd as my king . . .
>
> (1.1.139–40)

The keynote of more recent productions, however, has not been taken from such references to Lear's majesty, but rather from Kent's words a little later, when he breaches all decorum in his anxiety about Lear's division of the land to cry, "What wouldest thou do, old man?" (1.1.146). If Lear is already no more than an "old man," Kent's words lose their point; throughout the scene Lear demands to be perceived as "royal," or as Burgundy addresses him, "Most royal Majesty" (1.1.193, Folio).

At the present time there are hardly any kings left, and none in Western democracies who have any significant power. Kings are no longer part of our world, and it was perhaps inevitable that in productions of the play a shift would take place, so that Lear from the beginning would be presented as a rather cuddly if crusty old man in vaguely modern dress rather than a powerful king. So J. S. Bratton remarks on "attempts to make *King Lear* less a play about grandeur—the falling monolith—and instead a portrayal of the king as common man, his tragedy that of everyman."[7] If, however, we seek to recover an idea of the play as it was performed before James I on 26 December 1606, or for that matter as any audience in Shakespeare's age would have understood it, we have to retrieve a much stronger sense of what it meant to be a king. Shakespeare and his audience were familiar with the idea of power as embodied in royal authority, in the figures of Queen Elizabeth and James I, who told his parliament, "Kings are justly called Gods, for that they exercise a manner or resemblance of Divine power upon earth."[8] The audience would have noticed the way Lear asserts his authority by speaking in the royal plural in addressing his court and in the shattering of decorum as Kent calls Lear an old man in an attempt that fails to shock him into the recognition that he is behaving foolishly.

Lear's costume when he enters in the opening scene is therefore a matter of importance. If he is a bare-headed senior citizen warming his hands at a fire or a cantankerous retired Ruritanian army officer in a greatcoat or not distinguished except by age from those around him, then we are bound to react to him primarily in terms of his seniority, if not senility. The entry, however, both in the Quarto and in the Folio, calls for a sennet, or flourish, on wind instruments to signal a ceremonial entrance; in the Quarto a processional entry is led by "one bearing a coronet," and though this phrase is not present in the Folio, a property coronet is required in the scene since Lear hands one to Cornwall and Albany at line 139: "This coronet part between you." It has been argued that Lear refers here to his crown, but Shakespeare and his audience knew well the difference between a coronet and an imperial crown:[9] coronets were appropriate to dukes or princes, crowns to kings. The Duke of Albany and the Duke of Cornwall in the opening scene of *King Lear* may be presumed in the first performances of the play to have worn their ducal coronets; in his anger with Cordelia, Lear then gives them a third coronet, the one apparently intended for Cordelia, who was to be invested with her share of the kingdom.[10]

The scene presents a formal ceremony officially publishing the division of the kingdom Lear has planned. It is also a state occasion in which Lear intends to determine a husband for his youngest daughter and announce formally the result of what becomes something like a public auction, as she is offered to the Duke of Burgundy and the King of France.[11] For such an important state ceremonial business, it would have been proper for Lear to be wearing his crown and seated initially on a throne or chair of state. The date of the play's action is not fixed by any reference in the text. Although the many versions of the story of Lear and his daughters are set in a remote past, and although there has been a long tradition of stage productions evoking in their settings a primitive and barbaric world, the text allows a whole range of possibilities, and Cordelia's suitors, representative of "The vines of France and milk of Burgundy" (1.1.84), seem to belong to Shakespeare's own age, or some period within fairly recent history, just as Cornwall and Albany relate in some way to Prince Henry, created duke of Cornwall, on James's accession to the English throne, and Prince Charles, named duke of Albany at his baptism in 1600. In many other ways, not least the disguise of Edgar as a bedlam beggar, the use of the Bible, and of Samuel Harsnett's account of recent exorcisms, the play speaks to and of Shakespeare's own age.

Those productions of the 1950s and 1960s that gave us a more kingly Lear costumed him in some sort of regalia, but almost invariably with a form of coronet rather than an imperial crown. The distinction is important for the play. A coronet (the word is, of course, a diminutive of "crown," that is, "crownet") is a form of circlet, worn originally by relatives of the sovereign and by peers of the realm on state occasions, and sometimes ornamented with small crosses or fleurs-de-lys. A crown is differentiated often by having raised sides, and always by being "archée," or having between four and eight arches over the circlet, topped with an emblem such as a large jewel or other symbol of power.[12] James I had his portrait painted by Paul van Somer showing the imperial crown, which had four arches surmounted by an orb (this painting is in the Royal Collections, Windsor Castle), and his *Works* (1616) contains a frontispiece showing him wearing a four-arched crown and sitting in a chair of state.

It makes dramatic sense if Lear wears such a crown in the opening scene of the play.[13] The title of *King Lear* emphasizes the royal image, and Kent is "unmannerly" in the first scene when he sees "majesty" stooping to folly. Majesty there should be in a scene of such ceremonial importance and some sense of the "large effects" that go with it, and, since Lear continues to act imperiously throughout it, until his departure at line 266, I would suggest that, as originally played, he would have continued as King, with the crown on his head, in spite of having in effect renounced his power and shared his kingdom between Cornwall and Albany. Visually this would highlight the irony of the scene, in which Lear announces his intent "To shake all cares and business from our age," yet wants to retain "The name and all th' addition to a king." His folly is to imagine that he can give away power and responsibility, and hang on to his royal prerogatives; and his visible retention of the crown in this scene would bring this belief home to an audience who would in the reign of James I naturally identify a king with absolute authority. When Lear returns to the stage in 1.4 he no longer has the crown, as the Fool shows in his acerbic joke about the crowns of an egg:

BEATI PACIFICI

Crounes haue their compasse, length of dayes their date,
Triumphes their tombes, felicitie her fate:
Of more then earth, can earth make, none partakers,
But knowledge makes the KING most like his maker.

Simon Passæus sculp: Lond.   Ioh: Bill excudit.

James I, *Works*, 1616, frontispiece portrait. By permission of the Folger Shakespeare Library.

Fool. . . .Nuncle, give me an egg, and I'll give thee two crowns.
Lear. What two crowns shall they be?
Fool. Why, after I have cut the egg i' th' middle and eat up the meat,
the two crowns of the egg. When thou clovest thy crown i' th'
middle, and gav'st away both parts, thou bor'st thine ass on thy
back o'er the dirt. Thou hadst little wit in thy bald crown when
thou gav'st thy golden one away. . . .

(1.4.155–63)

In some productions of the opening scene the coronet, brought
on by an attendant according to the Quarto stage direction, has
instead been worn by Lear, who hands it to Cornwall and Albany. This way of staging is based on the Fool's bitter joke about
the egg and its two crowns, but ignores the difference between
crowns and coronets. The Fool, as the Cambridge editor notes,
is really commenting on Lear's division of his lands, but at the
same time he does make clear that Lear has had a golden crown,
and that in 1.4 he is no longer wearing it.

In dividing his kingdom Lear gives away his power; the Fool's
joke about the egg clarifies what this means, as it follows from
his question, "Can you make no use of nothing, nuncle?":

Lear. Why, no boy, nothing can be made out of nothing.
Fool. Prithee tell him, so much the rent of his land comes to. He
will not believe a fool.

(1.4.130–35)

Lear has given away his land, the source of his revenues and
power. In drawing attention to this, the Fool may have reminded
the audience at the Globe, and certainly that at court in 1606,
that the behavior of Lear in dividing the kingdom was not only
foolish, but improper. In an age when the queen or king had
vast estates and enormous power, the ability of the monarch to
give away land was a matter of great importance. Queen Elizabeth herself sought clarification on this point in 1561–62, in
relation to some property leased out by her predecessor, Edward
VI.[14] Her counsel advised that any property belonging to a monarch, whether it comes by descent from royal ancestors or from
other sources, must be regarded as part of the royal estate and
not as owned by the king as an individual. They appealed to the
doctrine of the king's two bodies, and wrote, "although he has
or takes the land in his natural body, yet to this natural body is
conjoined the body politic, which contains his royal estate and
dignity, and the body politic includes the body natural, but the

body natural is the lesser, and with this the body politic is con-
solidated." They referred to the case of Henry IV, who was in
possession of the Duchy of Lancaster when he became king.
Once he sat on the throne he could not give away any of the
property belonging to the Duchy except by letters patent. Thus
Henry in fact asked Parliament to authorize a charter that segre-
gated the Duchy of Lancaster from the royal estate and freed
him from this restriction. In normal circumstances, however,
the king could not part with land, even land inherited from
his mother or acquired by some other means, as if he were a
private person.

The Queen's Counsel thus determined that the king (they
always refer to the head of state as king, even though they are
advising Queen Elizabeth) cannot give away property by "livery
of seisin," or delivery of the property directly into the corporal
possession of another person. In the case of the transfer of land,
this would be signaled by handing over a twig, a piece of turf,
or some other token. So the Counsel ruled.

> that, if the King will part with land in fee which he has by descent
> on the part of his mother, or by some other ancestor who was not
> King, this shall pass by his letters patent only without other matter,
> and without livery of seisin, for he cannot make livery of seisin in
> his body natural, distinct from the body politic, because they are
> the one same body and not divers. So that he cannot do it without
> doing it as King, and . . . livery of seisin is a matter of fact, which
> the King cannot do, for his acts ought to pass by matter of record,
> which is suitable to His Majesty. Therefore, the land shall pass by
> the King's letters patent only by the course of the common law.[15]

What this means is that the king could not transfer land except by an open letter of authorization conferring the title, written on parchment and with the great seal attached, according
to the common law. Whether the usual audience at the Globe
were familiar with such matters it is impossible to say, but the
lawyers and Inns of Court men among them, and certainly many
in the audience at court in 1606, would have been aware of what
was a matter of considerable importance.[16] When Lear comes
on stage in the opening scene, he takes a map of England, or
perhaps of Britain, and invites his daughters to express their
love for him. Ironically, Goneril does so by referring to land,
saying she loves him "Dearer than eyesight, space, and liberty";
Lear picks up the word "space" in giving to Regan her third,

No less in space, validity and pleasure,
Than that conferr'd on Goneril.

(1.1.81–82)

Lear marks out on the map the shares of Goneril (Scotland) and
then Regan (Cornwall and Wales). His words indicate his action
and show that the map is simply a token representing space:

Of all these bounds, even from this line to this,
With shadowy forests and with champaigns rich'd,
With plenteous rivers and wide-skirted meads,
We make thee lady.

(1.1.63–66)

In some productions Lear actually tears off a third of the map
and hands it to Goneril at this point, an action that would confirm the illegality of what he is about, in effect handing over
his lands by a form of "livery of seisin," or direct delivery by
token into the hands of the new possessor. The king thus
breaches the law, for he could only transfer property by the formal authorization of letters patent, required by common law.

To argue so is, of course, to treat the play as relating directly
to Jacobean England, rather than to the ancient history that gave
us the Lear story. But, as Peter Brook put it, "*Lear* is barbaric and
Renaissance; it's those two contradictory things."[17] The play
connects in some way with the ambition of James I to unite the
kingdoms of England and Scotland into Great Britain, and it
seems likely that many in the audience would have known that
the king was barred by law from giving away his lands in the
way Lear does. When he hands the coronet apparently intended
for Cordelia to Cornwall and Albany and says, "This coronet
part between you," he again in effect may be handing over
through this token part of his lands to the two dukes by livery
of seisin.

Lear's giving away of his lands is thus both foolish and illegal.
It strips him of the source of his wealth and his power and
makes him dependent on the good will of his daughters. That
is one way of putting it, and Edmund points up his folly in the
second scene, for his plot against Edgar has as its aim to win
Edgar's inheritance; he goes off saying, "Let me, if not by birth,
have lands by wit" (1.2.183), for lands give him status and rank.
Another way would be to say that what Lear has done is impossible for a king to do, because, as the Queen's Counsel advised
Elizabeth, "the body politic includes the body natural, but the

body natural is the lesser, and with this the body politic is con-
solidated. So that ... he has not a body natural distinct and
divided by itself from the office and dignity royal, but a body
natural and a body politic together indivisible, and these two
bodies are incorporated in one person. . . ." Lear divides what is
"indivisible," which is to say that in dividing the kingdom he
acts in the body natural, doing what in the body politic is not
allowed, and so divides not only his lands but himself. This
contradiction Shakespeare exploits with superb dramatic effect.
Lear is forced to sense the split in himself without understanding it, as soon as Goneril complains about the behavior of him
and his retinue:

> Does any here know me? This is not Lear.
> Does Lear walk thus? speak thus? Where are his eyes?
> Either his notion weakens, his discernings
> Are lethargied—Ha! waking? 'Tis not so.
> Who is it that can tell me who I am?
>
> (1.4.226–30)

In the Quarto, Lear answers this question himself, and continues, in prose, "Lear's shadow? I would learn that, for by the
marks of sovereignty, knowledge, and reason, I should be false
persuaded I had daughters." The effect of his devastating rhetorical question "Who is it that can tell me who I am?" is dissipated
as he returns to harping on his daughters. In the revised version
in the Folio, the Fool answers Lear's question by saying "Lear's
shadow," and the rest is cut. Thus in the Folio Lear's question
gains much greater weight and the Fool's response sufficiently
stresses his loss of sway. The question resonates, however, precisely because it highlights at once both the rift in Lear himself
that is a result of his dividing the kingdom and that will lead
to madness, and also his failure to perceive the true nature of
what he has done.

So while Goneril and Regan force him to acknowledge his
impotence, at the same time Lear cannot stop being the king.
Regan focuses on his age:

> O, sir, you are old,
> Nature in you stands on the very verge
> Of his confine. You should be rul'd and led
> By some discretion that discerns your state
> Better than you yourself.
>
> (2.4.146–50)

It is true that he has not been able to "discern his state," his condition of mind and body, or his loss of "state" or power, at all clearly, and his response, which is to kneel in what is a deliberate piece of play-acting, ironically expresses a truth he has been unwilling to face:

> "Dear daughter, I confess that I am old;
> Age is unnecessary. On my knees I beg
> That you'll vouchsafe me raiment, bed, and food."[18]
>
> (2.4.154–56)

It is a truth he is driven to realize more fully when both Regan and Goneril join to strip him of his retainers:

> You see me here, you gods, a poor old man,
> As full of grief as age, wretched in both.
>
> (2.4.272–73)

If Lear in his natural body is "a poor old man," at the same time he remains the king, and not only those loyal to him, like Kent, but even his enemies frequently refer to him as such throughout the rest of the play. This is perhaps the most surprising feature of the text, for the first part of the action, to the end of act 2, builds up to the point where Goneril and Regan seek to strip away from Lear all his followers and reduce him to nothing more than a hanger-on in their courts, completely powerless and at their mercy. In so doing they force upon him a recognition that he is indeed no longer an all-powerful ruler, and Regan refers to him scornfully late in the scene as "the old man" (line 288), yet the power of this scene, culminating in Lear's "reason not the need" speech, lies in the way it dramatizes the transfer of power from father to daughters, rather than in a reduction of Lear to nothing.

For earlier in act 2, Regan seems naturally to refer to her father still as "the King," as at 2.2.50, and later on, in 3.7, where she and her husband Cornwall are grilling Gloucester, they both continue to speak of "the King" and of the country as the kingdom. The dialogue runs:

> Cornwall. And what confederacy have you with the traitors
> Late footed in the kingdom?
> Regan. To whose hands you have sent the lunatic King—
> Speak.
> Gloucester. I have a letter guessingly set down,

> Which came from one that's of a neutral heart,
> And not from one oppos'd.
> *Cornwall.*   Cunning.
> *Regan.*   And false.
> *Cornwall.* Where hast thou sent the King?

(3.7.44–50)

We might expect Kent, Albany, and Cordelia to continue to think of Lear as king, but it is striking that Oswald, Edmund, Regan, and Cornwall do so as well.

The point is that Lear cannot shed his royalty, but remains King Lear, every inch a king, even when powerless, not only because he cannot stop behaving like a king ("Let me not stay a jot for dinner"), but because assuming the country of Britain is a kingdom ruled by a king appears to be the mental habit of all the characters, ingrained, as it no doubt was taken for granted by a Globe audience that England, or Britain (James was proclaimed King of Great Britain at Westminster in October 1604), was essentially a monarchy. In the light of this we should not be surprised that stage tradition well into the nineteenth century presented a Lear dressed in contemporary royal robes—some kind of scarlet decorated with ermine—throughout most of the play, which is the way, for example, Garrick, Kean, Macready, and Edwin Forrest played the role. When in the storm scenes he cries "Off, off, you lendings," it was his regal gown, symbol of royalty, that he tried to tear off, and was prevented from doing so by the Fool and Kent. Thus, although Lear is stripped of power and cast out into the storm, in some sense he remains throughout still king. Nineteenth-century productions continued the tradition of clothing Lear in regal attire even in the mad scenes, as is shown in the print of Forrest in costume in 4.6, crying "Ay, every inch a king!"; he wears a robe trimmed with ermine, a crown made of flowers, and holds a sceptre of straw.[19] It contrasts notably with John Wood's costume in 1990, an open-necked shirt hanging outside old jeans, a crumpled jacket, and a hat with bits of straw on it, altogether lacking any hint of majesty.

When Cordelia returns in 4.4—having been offstage since the opening scene—she describes her father as seen

> Crown'd with rank fermiter and furrow-weeds,
> With hardocks, hemlock, nettles, cuckoo-flow'rs,
> Darnel, and all the idle weeds that grow
> In our sustaining corn.

(4.4.3–6)

Edwin Forrest in 1871 as the mad Lear, in Gabriel Harrison, *Edwin Forrest; The Actor and the Man*, 1889, facing p. 114. By permission of the Folger Shakespeare Library.

Often in 4.6, when Lear next appears, as in the Royal Shakespeare Theatre production in 1990, he is not so much crowned as decorated with what look like bits of straw. The Arden edition calls for him to be *"fantastically dressed"* in wild flowers, and the recent Cambridge edition merely has *"enter Lear mad"*; I am glad to see that the Oxford and Riverside editions have *"Enter Lear mad, crowned with weeds and flowers,"* for the image of the mock-crown here is very important. It parodies Lear's entrance in the opening scene wearing his crown, and through all the pathos of his madness it reminds us that he still is king.

Thus the stage direction in the Folio for the entry of Lear in 4.7 is signficant: *"Enter Lear in a chaire carried by Seruants."* "Fresh garments" have been put upon him while he has been unconscious, and often in productions he is dressed in white, or informally in shirt and trousers, but older stage traditions suggest that he was once again arrayed in royal robes. Cordelia is fighting to put him back on the throne, and it is notable that once Lear comes to consciousness she addresses him only as king, not as father. Moreover, this episode echoes visually the opening scene, when Lear sat in his chair of state, and the dramatic irony of the scene would be enhanced if, as some productions have shown, Goneril and Regan kneel in the opening scene to deliver their flattering speeches, while Cordelia stands to confront her father with the outrageous word "Nothing." For in 4.7. Cordelia kneels to Lear, and he tries to kneel to her, both in mutual forgiveness. The visual connections are important, not only the business with the chair, which may also remind us of Gloucester bound to a chair, but also the kneeling, for Lear had mockingly knelt to Regan in 2.2. If Lear has his royal robes returned to him in 4.7, the scene becomes that much more poignant, for his thoughts center upon his acquired humility and on dying, while Cordelia, for all her love, insists on engaging in a war to restore him to the monarchy. Her mission in invading England is to return to him his "right"; the feebler he is, the more she treats him with reverence: "How does my royal lord? How fares your majesty?" (4.7.43, Folio). Ironically, it is a role he would shed when he comes to consciousness, kneels to Cordelia, and acknowledges that he is "a very foolish, fond old man," but Cordelia seems unable to release him from it.

Then in the battle scenes at the beginning of act 5, after the English armies led by Edmund and by Albany have appeared on stage, we see, preceded by "Drumme and Colours," according to F, Lear, Cordelia and soldiers pass over the stage. The direc-

John Wood as Lear in 4.6 in the 1990 production by the Royal Shakespeare Theatre, directed by Nicholas Hytner; Gloucester (Norman Rodway) and Edgar (Linus Roache) are with him. Joe Cocks Studio Collection, Shakespeare Centre Library.

tion in Q calls for the powers of France to pass "ouer the stage, Cordelia with her father in her hand," and the Cambridge editor suggests that the change in F is designed to show Lear's defiance and strength rather than his weakness. In Q the army is led by Cordelia, in F by Lear, and if the change is deliberate, it would be appropriate for Lear again to wear the crown here. Then, when he is taken prisoner, Edmund seizes it, only for Albany to take it from him when he is given his death wound by Edgar. This would make possible a tableau at the end of the play. Albany there calls for the dead bodies of Lear, Cordelia, Goneril, and Regan to be removed from the stage ("Bear them from hence"); he then calls on Kent and Edgar to share the rule with him, but Kent declines, "My master calls me; I must not say no." Edgar and Albany are thus left to rule jointly, and perhaps stand holding the crown, each with a hand on it, recalling Albany and Cornwall parting a coronet between them in the opening scene.[20]

To sum up, on the stage, and often enough in criticism, Lear
is portrayed as a senior citizen bullied and humiliated by a cruel
state, denied the welfare he is entitled to, and eventually rescued
and comforted, or even "redeemed," by a loving daughter. I suggest that Shakespeare's audience would have been puzzled by
such interpretations. The king had two bodies, one subject to
infirmities, including madness, the other, the body politic, a
body "utterly void of infancy and old age, and other natural
defects and imbecilities, which the body natural is subject to."[21]
There is no hint that the king might retire, as Lear proposes to
do in the opening scene,[22] nor can he simply give away his lands.
Goneril and Regan may take advantage of what Goneril calls
"the imperfections of long-ingraff'd condition" (1.1.296) in their
father, but it is striking that they, as well as other characters,
continue to think of Lear as king and of the country as a kingdom. It is natural that, in bringing Lear to his senses, Cordelia,
and later Albany, should want to restore the monarchy and
make him king again, even if in his natural body he is no longer
competent. Once a king, always a king; this is what the play is
about, and the title, *King Lear* alerts us to this theme. The visual
contrast between the crown worn by Lear in the opening scene
and the coronets bestowed on his daughters emphasizes the illegality of Lear's actions: in giving away his land and power he
creates a self-division, a split between the body natural and body
politic, that leads to his madness. But it is in his madness that,
ironically, he realizes that he is still the king he always was,
"every inch a king," or, as he says to Cordelia's servants who
seek him out, "Come, come, I am a king. Masters, know you
that?" A gentleman replies, "You are a royal one, and we obey
you" (4.6.201). The tragedy is that this realization comes too
late, and only after he has instigated the civil and foreign wars
that lead to the deaths of all three of his daughters and finally
to his own death. But even at the end, when he no longer seems
fully aware of those around him, it is entirely appropriate on
one level, if ironic on another, that Albany should still perceive
Lear as king, and propose to

> resign,
> During the life of this old majesty,
> To him our absolute power.
>
> (5.3.299–301)

The wheel comes full circle, not just for Edmund (5.3.151), but
for Lear too, who at the last, when he can no longer comprehend

what it means, has for his final moments restored to him the "absolute power" as king that he gave away at the beginning of the play. The pathos of the ending involves both the sense we have of Lear's suffering at the death of his now-beloved daughter, and our desire to see him released from a world that offers him no reason to live longer. This pathos would, for Shakespeare's audience, have been compounded by the further dimension of a king who can no longer sustain the image of royalty when it is restored to him, a dimension modern productions and critical accounts of the play generally ignore. Richard Helgerson has recently argued against those who find subversion and the advocation of the welfare state in *Lear* that "Shakespeare's history plays are concerned above all with the consolidation and maintenance of royal power."[23] I do not think this large generalization can be applied to *King Lear*, but an image of royal splendor surely is at the heart of this play too, and perhaps we might recover a sense of it in criticism and on the stage.

NOTES

1. Annabel Patterson, *Shakespeare and the Popular Voice* (Cambridge: Harvard University Press, 1989), 111, 116.

2. See Marvin Rosenberg, *The Masks of King Lear* (1972; reprint, Newark: University of Delaware Press, 1992), 22–32.

3. 3. See *King Lear*, ed. J. S.Bratton, Plays in Performance (Bristol: Bristol Classical Press, 1987), 35, 43. The 1983 Granada television production invoked Stonehenge and presented Lear as a crowned king in an ancient world; the BBC version in 1982 by contrast made the play contemporary with James I, but omitted the crown and coronet to minimize the idea of royalty and dwelled on Lear as father. The two productions are symptomatic of modern treatments. See James P. Lusardi and June Schlueter, *Reading Shakespeare in Performance: King Lear* (Rutherford, N.J.: Fairleigh Dickinson University Press, 1991), 42–60.

4. Bratton, *Lear*, 41. For a wider perspective on presentations of Lear, see ibid., 60–63 and Rosenberg, *Masks of Lear*, 22–32.

5. A. C. Bradley, *Shakespearean Tragedy* (London: Macmillan, 1904), 284–85.

6. *A View of the English Stage, 1944–1963* (London: Davis-Poynter, 1975), 343.

7. Bratton, *Lear*, 46.

8. Speech to Parliament, 21 March 1609, in *The Political Works of James I*. Reprinted fom the edition of 1616, with an introduction by Charles Howard McIlwain (Cambridge: Harvard University Press, 1918), 307.

9. See, for example, *The Tempest* 1.2.111–16.

10. See Lusardi and Schlueter, *Reading Shakespeare in Performance*, 36–37, who note that we cannot be sure for whom the coronet was intended, and are

"placed in the position of attempting to understand what would have happened had Cordelia professed she loved her father all."

11. Lynda Boose, in "The Father and the Bride in Shakespeare," *PMLA* 97 (1982): 332–35, has argued that Lear's demand that she declare her total love for him is actually a contrivance to keep her, since she cannot marry if she loves her father all and will lose her dowry unless she does. This is an ingenious perception of a possible suppressed incestuous motif in the play, but is from a modern perspective that sees Lear as father, not as absolute monarch.

12. See Major-General H. D. W. Sitwell, *The Crown Jewels and Other Regalia in the Tower of London* (London: Dropmore Press, 1953), esp. 16–32. Since at least the reign of Henry IV crowns had been worn by English kings for state occasions, such as the opening scene in *King Lear*.

13. So G. B. Shand argued in "Lear's Coronet. Playing the Moment," *Shakespeare Quarterly* 38 (1987): 78–82: "His own crown is central to his retention of the perquisites of kingship" (81). He thought the coronet to be intended for the King of France, as equivalent to Cordelia's dowry.

14. This case is considered by Ernst H. Kantorowicz in *The King's Two Bodies: A Study in Medieval Political Theology* (Princeton: Princeton University Press, 1957), but only in relation to the doctrine of the king's two bodies; see 9ff. and 405–9.

15. *All England Law Reports Reprint, 1558–1774* 36 vols. (London: Butterworth, 1968), 1:148.

16. Edmund Plowden's law reports, from which I have been quoting, were not published at this time, but there was widespread interest in the law, and his fame was such that the proverb "The case is altered, quoth Plowden" was in common use.

17. *The Shifting Point . . . 1946–1987* (New York: Harper and Row, 1987), 89.

18. These lines are usually seen as reflecting on Goneril and Regan, as in the note by Jay Halio in the Cambridge edition (1992), 164: "Lear aptly summarises Gonerill's and Regan's Darwinian outlook, in which survival of the fittest rules and the elderly are superfluous." But the topsy-turvy image of a father/king kneeling to his daughter is a striking stage emblem of what Lear has brought about by his division of the kingdom and a recognition on his part that he has indeed succeeded in making himself superfluous.

19. This is reproduced from Gabriel Harrison, *Edwin Forrest: The Actor and the Man* (New York, 1889), facing 114. Forrest played the role most seasons for forty years until 1871, with "imposing majesty" (Alger, 781), and in the storm scenes he was seen "exulting as the monarch of a new realm" (2:788). He was followed on the New York stage by Tommaso Salvini, whose realist Lear by contrast "emphasized the human attributes of *old man*"; see Charles H. Shattuck, *Shakespeare on the American Stage*, 2 vols. (Washington, D.C.: Folger Shakespeare Library, 1987), 2:155.

20. Rosenberg, *Masks of Lear*, 322, suggests some such byplay with the crown as a possibility.

21. *All England Law Reports 1558–1774*, 1:147.

22. In *New Readings vs. Old Plays* (Chicago: University of Chicago Press, 1979), 149–51, Richard Levin, pointing to the abdication of David in favor of Solomon and to the retirement of the Emperor Charles V in 1555, argues that Lear's abdication would not have been regarded as a violation or sin in Shakespeare's age. He also notes that James, in his *Defence of the Right of*

Kings (1615), "raises no objection" to the idea that kings might renounce their royalty. In fact, James is there citing the argument of a Catholic apologist, William Barclay; and in his *The Trew Law of Free Monarchies* (1598), he insists on the king's right by birth, and that "at the very moment of the expiring of the king reigning, the nearest and lawful heire entreth in his place" (*Political Works*, 69). James simply does not consider the idea of abdication as possible for himself or his heirs.

23. Richard Helgerson, in *Forms of Nationhood: The Elizabethan Writing of England* (Chicago and London: University of Chicago Press, 1992), 234, contrasts the Royalist histories performed at The Theatre and the Globe with the plays staged by the Henslowe companies at the Rose and Fortune; the latter put much greater emphasis on the common people and the ruled than on the rulers, and their heroes and heroines are often victims of power.

The World Beyond: Shakespeare and the Tropes of Translation

MICHAEL NEILL

> Having been borne across the world, we are translated men.
> It is normally supposed that something always gets lost in
> translation; I cling, obstinately, to the notion that something
> can also be gained.
>
> —Salman Rushdie, *Imaginary Homelands*

"THERE is a world elsewhere," declares Coriolanus as he turns
his back on Rome (*Cor.* 3.3.135). For seventeenth-century audiences tuned to the images of New World discovery, his line, like
Antony's "Then must thou needs find out new heaven, new
earth" (*A&C* 1.1.17), must have had a potent anachronistic resonance. Coriolanus, however, is constitutionally incapable of
imagining, let alone inhabiting, a world that is anything more
than a poor mirror of the one he has left behind. He crosses into
the domain of the Volsces, but the translation is purely physical;
and the fantasy of "a world elsewhere" serves only to express
the pathos of an impossible transformation. It is a small detail,
but its effect is symptomatic; for, while Shakespeare's writing
can often seem almost perversely indifferent to the geographic
excitements of his age, it betrays at its margins, like so much
literature of the period, a haunting awareness of worlds elsewhere. Only one of his plays makes significant use of discovery
literature (and even then the approach to New World encounters
is puzzlingly oblique), yet the experience of crossing over into
the space of the Other is figured in play after play.

Shakespeare's fascination with such crossings was necessarily
bound up with the role of his own theater as a place of miraculous translations—advertised, in the case of the Globe, by a
name and sign that proclaimed its capacity to carry the audience

to any quarter of the newly discovered world. The English, one foreign visitor observed, while generally not much given to actual travel, flocked to the theater as an imaginative surrogate for its excitements.[1] It was precisely to this desire for vicarious transport that Marlowe vauntingly appealed in the prologue to *Tamburlaine*, a theatrical manifesto that promised to lead his audience to the hero's "stately tent of war"; and the same intoxicated sense of theater's translative capacity informs the high rhetoric and mock-disclaimers of Shakespeare's *Henry V* choruses. Unlike the medieval theater of communal self-realization, "[t]his scene," in Peter Womack's words, "is not part of any community, but takes you *out of it* . . . as if the price of admission bought a ticket to Asia Minor," to France, to the Caribbean, to the very Antipodes.[2]

"Translation" seems a particularly convenient term for such crossings because of its broad range of meanings: deriving from the Latin *transfero* ("bear across"), it has as much to do with changing places as with shifting speech; it embraces the negotiation of all sorts of boundaries—physical, linguistic, and cultural—while its Elizabethan connotations include forced transportation and theft[3] at one extreme and rapture at another; and, of course, it is a standard term for metaphor: Puttenham's "Figure of transporte,"[4] by which the proper is "translated" into the improper, the strange into the familiar. Something of the rich ambivalence of its processes can be illustrated from an essay of Montaigne's that was to provide the essential pre-text for the greatest of all Shakespearean dramas of crossing and translation, *The Tempest*.

"Of the Caniballes" anecdotalizes the same paradoxes of cultural relativity that Montaigne famously articulated in a wry pun on his own name: "What truth is that which these Mountaines bound, and is a lie in the World beyond them?"[5] It was a question to which Shakespeare and his contemporaries would return again and again: whether that "world beyond" is called America, Illyria, Egypt, Mauritania, "a wood near Athens," or simply "the island," it is always conceived as a kind of epistemological or moral antipodes in which the supposed absolutes of European civilization are exposed as mere accidents of language and location. In "Of the Caniballes" Montaigne makes a partial crossing into one such world, that of the Tupinamba people of northeastern Brazil. A double translation is involved in this encounter: like so many other inhabitants of the New World, the Tupinamba (whom Montaigne interrogates) have

themselves been subjected to violent translation from the South
American rain forest to the streets of Rouen. Montaigne, offering himself as a species of go-between, will complete that process of appropriation by rendering them comprehensible—
through translation—to his European readers. To bring this
about he must negotiate the "wondrous distance betweene their
forme and ours";[6] and through this attempt at imaginative self-
translation, he discovers a perspective from which the *mores* of
his own culture emerge as more barbarous and unnatural than
anthropophagy itself. As it turns out, however, Montaigne's investigations grant him only fragmentary and unreliable
glimpses of this other mentality, for his cultural translation is
itself ironically dependent upon the mediation of an incompetent interpreter, "who through his foolishnesse was so troubled
to conceive my imaginations, that I could draw no great matter
from him."[7] Given the radically unsettling potential of his discoveries, this is perhaps fortunate; and it is possible to sense a
certain relief behind the abruptness with which the essay is cut
short ("but what of that? They wear no kinde of breeches nor
hosen"[8]); for however it may mock the complacencies of the
essay's implied reader, this odd, ironic shrug also has the convenient effect of returning the Indians to the symbolic indeci-
pherability of the naked condition in which they were first
encountered.

Translation, Montaigne's essay suggests, is always a two-
edged sword: it is both an instrument of power, mastery, and
expropriation and a vehicle of self-transformation entailing disorientation and even the threat of self-loss. In its aggressive
mode translation is the process described by Eric Cheyfitz that
brings together the various forms of discursive and physical violence on which the creation of empire depends: "the imperialist
mission," he writes, "is [essentially] one of translation: the
translation of the 'other' into the terms of empire."[9] Significantly enough, "translation" became a term of art in the discourse of colonization, with men like Richard Beacon and
Edmund Spenser arguing that the problems of Ireland could be
resolved by the "translating of colonies" on the one hand and
the "translating" of the native Irish out of their lands and language on the other.[10] Yet the recurrent nightmare of "degeneration" that permeates such texts serves as a reminder that the
appropriative drive of translation was always liable to unac-
countable reversal, producing what their authors saw as a dangerous kind of alienation—an "unnatural" transformation in

which the civil self was drawn into the orbit of the barbarous Other.[11]

The aggressive face of translation, as I have argued elsewhere,[12] is most obviously displayed in Shakespeare's history cycles. The negotiation of linguistic boundaries plays an especially crucial role in these plays, where imperial aggrandizement and the fashioning of national identity are seen as two sides of a single coin. In *1 Henry VI* the straightforward Talbot is confronted by the treacherous stratagems of a French witch whose name punningly translates as "puzzel/puzzle" and whose magically persuasive speech is marked by all the duplicity supposedly native to her tongue. It is entirely characteristic that the only line of actual French spoken by Pucelle in the play should occur at the point when she and her soldiers gain entry to Rouen disguised as simple countryfolk coming to market (*"Paysans, la pauvre gens de France,"* 3.2.14)—as if the language itself were the sign of national deceitfulness. Similarly in *Richard II*, to repudiate the ambiguous sleights of translation, as the Duchess York does ("Speak 'pardon' as 'tis current in our land, / The chopping French we do not understand," 5.3.123–24)—is to claim community with the same fellowship of honest, plain-spoken souls who are assumed to make up the audience—the nation to whose sympathy Mowbray appeals when he laments his exile from the linguistic home of "native English." To yield to the siren music of alterity, as Mortimer surrenders to the untranslated Welsh song of Glendower's daughter in *1 Henry IV*, on the other hand, is to degenerate from kind in a way that compromises one's nationality and masculinity together.

In *Henry V*, which presciently anticipates James I's creation of the "Empire of Great Britain" by insisting that, more than anything else, the possession of a common speech is what defines a nation, language and translation become all-important. But here, as in Spenser's Ireland, it is the conquered Other who is subjected to forcible translation. Englishness is consistently imagined as the not-French, and no play is more insistent upon the physical barrier that symbolically divides "two mighty monarchies, / Whose high, upreared, and abutting fronts / The perilous narrow ocean parts asunder" (*Prol.* 20–22). Elsewhere the channel may be invoked as a symbol of separateness and defensive strength, but only in *Henry V* does crossing it seem to constitute a real difficulty. The audience are summoned to vicarious participation in Henry's enterprise by the rhetorical transports of the chorus; and all the force of their straining imaginations, together with the fierce rhetorical insistence of three choric orations, is required simply to "transport the scene," "convey" the spectators , and "carry" Henry to France for the first time; while the fifth chorus, which has to get the king over the channel twice (and Essex across the Irish Sea for good measure), wryly attempts to overcome the improbability of this triplicated translation with a punning appeal to the viewers' indulgence: "Then brook *abridgement*, and your eyes advance, / After your thoughts, straight back again to France" (5 *Chor.*, 44–45; italics added).

Once conveyed to France the hero himself becomes a "conveyor" in the sense used by Richard II (4.1.317), dispossessing the French of their lands in a process that is represented not merely in scenes of military violence, but through metaphors of linguistic translation. Not for nothing is Henry presented as a master of all discourses (1.1.38–52), with a gift for histrionic self-translation carried over from his Eastcheap past. Not for nothing does he turn these very attributes into the instruments of imperial expropriation. In a scene (3.4) that immediately follows Henry's first victory on French soil, the French Princess is shown preparing herself for an occupation that, like the entering of Harfleur's "maiden walls" (5.2.322), is also a defloration. She enacts her surrender by systematically Englishing her body, translating it into the conqueror's language, as Henry himself will convey the body of the land into his own power—an equation that is made perfectly explicit in the scene of lingusitic enforcement that ends the play where *"le possession de France"* translates as the possession of its princess, and where French Katherine is translated to English "Kate." Behind the playful bullying of this thinly masked rape, with its talk of tongues and hearts, lies the assumption brutally articulated by Spenser in his *View of the Present State of Ireland* that identity and loyalty are substantially determined by linguistic allegiance—the speech being English, Henry assumes, the heart must needs be English too.[13]

Although the patriotic stage history of *Henry V* is enough to show how profoundly Shakespeare's writing was implicated in the Empire-building translations it describes, the play far from simply endorses the imperial propaganda on which it draws, and its reservations are nicely epitomized in the scene of comic mistranslation that parodies Henry's victory at Agincourt. Pistol's capture of Monsieur le Fer stands in much the same relation to the King's heroics as does Katherine's self-blazoning to the surrender of Harfleur. It also asks to be read as a parodic prolepsis of Henry's wooing, for if Katherine submits to Henry as *"mon très puissant seigneur"* (5.2.256), Le Fer (almost certainly with the same gesture of handkissing) capitulates to Pistol as *"le plus brave, vaillant, et très distingué seigneur d'Angleterre"* (4.4.56–57); and if Katherine's dowry is the promise of a crown, Le Fer's ransom is the promise of two hundred crowns, while Pistol's mercenary concession ("Tell him my fury shall abate, and I / The crowns will take" 4.4.47–48) accurately parodies Henry's show of conquering magnanimity—just as his broken French, in the Quarto version of 4.6, brutally translates Henry's order to kill the prisoners: "Coup le gorge." These scenes remind us that if the King is master of several languages, so too is the play; and the burlesque idiom of the Pistol scenes repeatedly demonstrates how different Henry's patriotic rhetoric or the imaginative transports of the Chorus can sound when translated into Eastcheap dialect:

Then forth, dear countrymen!. . .

. . . .
Cheerly to sea! The signs of war advance!
No king of England, if not king of France!

> Yoke-fellows in arms,
Let us to France, like horse-leeches, my boys,
To suck, to suck, the very blood to suck!

> (2.2.189–93; 2.3.54–56)

The function of such restless switches of dialect is to expose the audience itself to unexpected forms of translation, bearing it across from point of view to another. It is just this translative capacity, it might be argued, that renders Shakespeare's plays so resistant to univocal reading, and it is something upon which they themselves repeatedly reflect.

If *Henry V* plays off the discourse of colonization in which translation figures as a one-sided agent of imperial incorporation, other plays reach back to the discourse of wonder generated by the earliest encounters with the "world elsewhere"—to its moments of weird disorientation and to the experience of rapture that (as Stephen Greenblatt has argued) habitually precedes the rape of possession.[14]

A marvelous illustration of the disorienting potential of such encounters is to be found in a contemporary text from the New

World—Pedro de Quiroga's *Coloquios de la verdad* (1555).[15] The principal figure in these "Colloquies of Truth" is a pentitent conquistador and defender of the Peruvian natives named Barchilon. In the first dialogue he accosts a newly arrived soldier of fortune, Justino, whom he rouses from an exemplary colonial dream in which he has become "the most powerful and the richest man of the world." Having instructed his friend in the symbolic truth of this fantasy ("That for certain will be the dream of the wealth of this land, and of this century, all of which is a dream and a mockery"), Barchilon goes on to warn him against a land where "everything is the reverse of what it is in Castile" and where apparent resemblance is only a temptation to misrecognition: "Have nothing to do with the things of this land until you understand them, because they are different matters, and another language." Far from urging Justino to master this other language, however, Barchilon warns him that to understand it will involve him in a self-confounding cultural translation from which there can be no return: "Do not learn the language of this land. Nor even listen to it, for I tell you that if you do, one of two ends will befall you, for it will either drive you mad or you will wander restlessly for the rest of your life." (pp. 40–41)

The fear of derangement that attends such encounters with the "world beyond" is refracted in the confusion, halfway between "wonder" and "madness," that settles on Sebastian and Viola in Illyria *(Twelfth Night* 4.3.1–4) or in the self-estrangement that renders the transported Syracusans of *The Comedy of Errors* "transformed . . . both in mind and . . . shape," as if "disguised" from themselves (2.2.195–214), or in the bizarre psychic metamorphoses that afflict the Athenians of *A Midsummer Night's Dream* when they cross so carelessly into Oberon's domain—a "wood" whose very name, the play punningly suggests, is madness (2.1.192). The pattern of all these metamorphoses is supplied by Bottom, whose appearance in an ass's head fills his fellow performers with the panic always threatened by the Wild, but whose own experience of translation anticipates the sense of mysterious transfiguration felt by the play's awakened lovers—a benign lunacy in which Hippolita discerns the lineaments of wonder ("But howsoever, strange and admirable," 5.1.27).

"Bless thee, Bottom! Bless thee! thou art translated!" (3.1.118–119) Peter Quince's cry of alarm responds only to the weaver's grotesque physical appearance, but this bestial transformation turns out to be the sign of a much more radical translation—one that exemplifies the pattern of a comedy whose whole plot turns on the "bearing across" of characters from one world to another. The play begins, after all, with the spectacle of Theseus and the conquered Queen whom he has forcibly brought to Athens to become his bride; and the violent translation of Hippolyta from the Amazonian wild to the civil world of Athens is matched by the equally abrupt translation of the young Athenian lovers from the city to a "desert place" (2.1.218), the estranging wilderness that renders them "woode within this wood" (2.1.192). Theseus' wooing of his captive Amazon is paralleled in Titania's dalliance with "A lovely boy stolen from an Indian king" (2.1.22)—the "changeling" whom Oberon in turn plans to carry off. And all of these rapes are parodically replayed in Bottom's abduction by the Fairy Queen.

If the world into which Bottom is translated nostalgically reinvents the realm of "faery," onto which medieval fantasies of nature's wild otherness were projected, it belongs also with the play's dreamlike variations upon much more contemporary notions of alterity. Linked to a remote, unspecified Indies, not simply through their competing desire for the changeling child but through a shared familiarity with "the farthest steep of India" and its "spiced Indian air" (2.1.69, 124), the Fairy King and Queen share with Oberon's "buskin'd mistress" an association with barbaric exoticism. Thus the action of the play not only resonates, as Margo Hendricks has demonstrated, with the mercantile exoticism of East and West Indian voyaging,[16] but recalls the radically unsettling transpositions that would put a John Smith at the mercy of a Powhatan, bring a Pocahontas (in the guise of a Stuart courtier) to the court of King James, or reduce a Cabeza de Vaca to the "naked" condition of the Florida Indians among whom he was cast away.

Of all the translated characters in *A Midsummer Night's Dream*, it is Bottom whose experience of being borne across into another world is most absolute and defamiliarizing. It is as if the playful self-translation of theatrical performance is made disconcertingly real by Puck's ironic whimsy: "I led them on in this distracted fear, / And left sweet Pyramus translated there" (3.2.31–32). Like one of those heroes of sixteenth-century bourgeois romance who are picked out to become the lovers of foreign princesses—figures whose narratives refract the self-transforming ambitions typically associated with voyaging enterprise—the weaver undergoes a translation that allows him

miraculously to escape the confines of birth and rank. Shakespeare mocks such fantasies, for the same transformation that
renders Bottom "gentle" in Titania's eyes (3.1.137, 164) bemon-
sters him in the eyes of his compatriots (in a fashion that recalls
not merely the Mandevillean freaks of discovery literature, but
the bestial "degeneration" thought to await those who surrendered to the seductions of the Wild). Yet Bottom rises above
such easy satire to the extent that he alone, of all the characters
in the play, fully enters the alien world of the wood and is privileged to hear and understand its speech; and it is essential to
the play's effect that he should not appear simply as a comic
victim, for he is also a kind of explorer—one who crosses to the
other side and returns—however confused the language in
which his experience is conveyed.

Bottom, like many a returned traveler, faces the problem of
authorizing an inconceivable narrative whose truth will not
readily translate back to the world from which he came. As
Anthony Pagden has shown, if the chronicler of such a crossing
into the unfamiliar wished to be believed, he could only fall
back upon the appeal to "autopsy" (the incontrovertible witness
of the I/eye who has seen)—the one claim that might distinguish
his traveler's tale from the improbable romances which it otherwise so embarrassingly resembled. Since such self-sufficient authority emulates that of Scripture, it is perhaps not surprising
that Bottom's stumbling attempt to articulate his dream should
paraphrase a celebrated passage from 1 Corinthians (2.9): "the
eye of man hath not heard, the ear of man hath not seen, man's
hand is not able to taste, his tongue to conceive, nor his heart
to report what my dream was" (4.1.209–12). The original passage
refers to the "hidden wisdom" of "the deep things of God"
whose "mystery" is apprehensible only through spirtual revelation; and Bottom, whose dream "hath no bottom," conceives it
as a secular epiphany. He has, as Starveling sagely remarks, been
"transported" (4.2.3–4); and the effect produced by his subli-
mated rape is strikingly close to that sense of "wonder" and
"ravishment" that Greenblatt finds expressed in the more ec-
static moments of discovery. The problem with such rapturous
transports, however, is that they typically involve a crossing
into the inexpressible. "I am to discourse wonders; but ask me
not what," warns Bottom, faced with interpreting his experience, "for if I tell you, I am no true Athenian" (4.2.29–31). To
tell the truth would render him untrue to the experience of his

auditors, would make him something Other than true Athenian, and would require another language:

> I have had a most rare vision. I have had a dream, past the wit of man to say what dream it was. Man is but an ass, if he go about t'expound this dream. Methought I was—there is no man can tell what. Methought I was, and methought I had—but man is but a patch'd fool, if he will offer to say what methought I had.
>
> *(MSND* 4.1.204–11)

Like Enobarbus struggling to evoke an oriental exoticism that "beggar'd all description" *(Antony and Cleopatra,* 2.2.198), or like Columbus driven to his sterile repetitions of the phrase "that it was a wonder"—the weaver is baffled by the sheer intractability of language to descriptions of the unfamiliar. What he faces, then, is exactly the recurrent crisis of "incommensurability" described by Pagden, a crisis produced by a place "filled with things for which there was no adequate classification, no known terms"—in short, an untranslatable world. Bottom plans to compose a ballad of his dream, a traveler's tale to amuse the Duke, but the performance never comes to pass because he, like Barchilon, knows only too well that in the last analysis "it is incommensurability itself which is ultimately the *only* certainty, the only possible context in which America [or Fairyland] can be made at all intelligible" and that "[i]n a world where no translation is possible, silence is the necessary condition of speech."[17]

In its mixture of the poignant and the grotesque, the rapture of ass-headed Bottom is a neat emblematic reminder of how close the marvelous stands to the monstrous, and, as the woeful history of discovery from Columbus onwards repeatedly illustrates, it is an equally short step from the wonder of discovery's primal moment to the expropriative brutality of colonization. Thus, as Peter Hulme and others have shown, the paradigmatic move of colonizing discourse is to redefine the naked innocents of first encounters as monstrous cannibals.[18] If Montaigne seeks to reverse this move through a translative maneuver of his own that makes the ethics of cannibalism themselves an occasion for admiration,[19] Shakespeare's *The Tempest* reasserts the colonial paradigm, but does so in full consciousness of the discursive violence on which its translations depend. The ideal community of the Tupinamba has here been reduced to a mere flourish of

Gonzalo's fancy (2.1.144–69), as remote from possibility as the "imaginarie commonwealth" of Plato,[20] while Montaigne's noble cannibals are metamorphosed into the "salvage and deformed" Caliban, a creature whose incorrigibly "bastard" condition is the reverse of their "originall naturalitie." On Prospero's island, moreover, the wonder that in "Of the Caniballes" and *A Midsummer Night's Dream* is the defining attribute of the "world elsewhere" has become an effect of the colonizer's power. The only marvels that Bottom's clownish counterparts dream of carrying back to their city are monsters and dead Indians—the loot of fairgrounds and *wunderkammern*, objects to be possessed and translated at will.

If the physical transportation of island exotics appears a quite unproblematic prospect to these voyagers, the same goes for the more sophisticated translations to which the island and its denizens are subjected by Prospero. Under his aegis this other world, in contrast to the almost impenetrable strangeness of Barchilon's Peru, is made to seem so filled with lucid meanings that even the billows, wind, and thunder appear to "speak" to Alonzo (3.3.96–99); while the "people of the island," when they do not simply communicate with the courtiers in mysteriously perspicuous speech, have recourse to "a kind / Of excellent dumb discourse" (3.3.38–39) exhibiting the universal eloquence attributed to the human body by so many early explorers. Prior to the arrival of Prospero and Miranda, however, the island is said to have been languageless: like those Arawaks who, Columbus proclaimed, must "learn to speak" under Spanish tutelage, Caliban, whose brutish gabble supposedly barred him even from knowledge of his own meaning, has been "made to speak" by Miranda. It is as if he needed the intervention of his enslavers to translate him to himself: as if, miraculously, it is not they who are out of place, but he; not they who have been "carried across" to this strange world, but Caliban who has needed rescue from the isolation of his primitive self-estrangement.

The obverse of Bottom's delicious vertigo, the feeling that the new is beyond naming, untranslatable, is this belief that it only requires the transforming touch of the colonizer's language to spring into meaning: "This isle is mute without me" as Prospero disdainfully puts it in Aimé Césaire's satiric postcolonial reworking of *The Tempest*.[21] The physical translation that brings the Italian courtiers (like their colonizing counterparts in the Virginia pamphlets) to this still-unbraved new world, necessarily entails a further translation through which the "salvage" Caliban (like Columbus's Indians) is salvaged—brought into the civil fold of Prospero's language, learning "how / To name the bigger light, and how the less, / That burn by day and night" (1.2.334–36). In the process the very topography of the island is transformed; for, no less than the obscure "purposes" of Caliban's inner world, "The fresh springs, brine pits, barren place and fertile" of his supposedly preverbal habitat have been "endow'd ... with words that made them known" (1.2.338, 357–58).

If language is the play's principal instrument of cultural translation, clothing is another. Indeed the two are closely related, for as denizens of a culture in which dress was organized by codes of signification, Europeans, as Cheyfitz observes, "typically ... equated ... nakedness with either absence of or a deficiency in language."[22] Thus, as the troping of nakedness in *King Lear* persistently suggests, to be bare of clothes was to be relegated to the unintelligible chaos of nature, so that it is more than simply a figurative association that links the nakedness of "poor Tom" with his gibberish and both with the wildness of the heath. In the same way the routine denigration of the "wild Irish" as a "naked" people (even while so much attention was given to their "improper" mode of dress) was entirely of a piece with the denigration of their language as barbarous non-speech."[23] One reason why peoples of the New World and sub-Saharan Africa proved so difficult to assimilate into the mental universe of early modern Europe (and why, in consequence, their bodies could be treated with such savagery) was that they too were perceived as "naked peoples," located not merely by virtue of their barbarous speech, but by fundamental bodily habit outside the domain of culture and therefore of meaning.

So it is that on Prospero's island costume is what effectively determines the legibility, the visibility—in effect, the *reality* of bodies. As surely as Prospero's "magic garment" renders him invisible, it is Antonio's stolen costume that makes visible his ducal person ("look how well my garments sit upon me, / Much feater than before," 2.1.272–73). Antonio is translated into the role he usurps precisely as costume translated the actor. So too Prospero's reassumption of the "hat and rapier" of "sometime Milan" (5.1.84–86) not only renders him visible to the enchanted Neapolitans, but allows a wonder-filled Caliban to perceive his "actual" princely identity the first time ("How fine my master is!" 5.1.262). Similarly the awakening of the Boatswain and crew from their deathlike sleep is experienced as a mysterious self-restoration figured in the recovery of "all our trim" (5.1.236), the proper attire of their seamen's calling. If bodies are formed only from "such stuff as dreams are made on," it is "stuff" (the material of costume), the play keeps insisting, that bodies forth those dreams and makes them appear substantial. Thus it is not merely Antonio's usurpation but Prospero's restoration that is parodied in the entry of Stephano and Trinculo tricked out in the glistering apparel filched from Prospero's line.

By contrast, the natives of what Prospero will call "this bare island" (Epil., line 8) are understood as being in one way or another naked, with bodies that in consequence are either illegible or invisible. Caliban's virtual nakedness, like his disdain for the costumes of fake authority, is a part of his "salvage" condition—the bodily equivalent of the languageless state in which Prospero supposedly found him. The only clothing attributed to him is the shapeless "gaberdine" that renders his body virtually indecipherable to his clownish discoverers, who read onto him the predictable signs of Mandevillean monstrosity (2.2.27–34, 57–70), Trinculo discovering fins even where he plainly sees arms. Thus Caliban's much-stressed but curiously ill-defined "deformity" seems to be as much an effect of undress as of any actual physical malformation—just as Ferdinand's "brave form" and "goodly person," or the beauty that Miranda discovers in the "goodly creatures" of her "brave new world," like the "fine" appearance of the restored Prospero (1.2.412, 417; 5.1.181–84, 262), are primarily effects of dress.

If Caliban's virtual nakedness appears to unform his body, laying it open to the autoptic invention of old and new masters, the other inhabitants of the island are presented as essentially bodiless—invisible except when dressed by Prospero's magic in the guises that allow them to appear as harpies, goddesses, nymphs, and "REAPERS, properly habited" (4.1.138.0); or as those "strange SHAPES," whose "living drollery" seems to confirm the wildest inventions of travelers—unicorns, phoenixes, "mountaineers, / Dewlapp'd, like bulls. . . . [and] men / Whose heads stood in their breasts" (3.3.22–47). Just as Caliban must be taught to "know his own meaning," so it is only after Prospero brings culture to this bare island, it would seem, that its denizens, under his colonizing gaze, acquire bodies and become capable of meaning—though these bodies and meanings (like those of the actors who perform their parts) will never be "properly" their own.

The insistent analogy between these corporeal transformations and the translations wrought by the theater itself is foregrounded not only by the histrionics of the masque, but by the
witty reflexivity of an epilogue that makes Prospero's crossing
back to Italy a figure for the actor's return from his "translated"
condition—as well as (traditionally) a metaphor for the dramatist's own retreat to the bourgeois solidities of his Stratford life.
In a different context such analogies might appear subversive,
and there are certainly moments in Shakespeare—Henry V's
"ceremony" speech, for example, or Lear's discovery that "robes
and furr'd gowns hide all"—where the translative power of costume and personation suggests the hollow fictiveness of all social identity. But perhaps such moments can be staged only
because of the more powerful persistence of a belief in the meta-
morphic efficacy of translation, including the conviction that
at some very deep level clothes really do make the man—ironically the same belief that inspired many of the most ferocious
denunciations of theatrical pretense. Caliban's "How fine my
master is" (where he might have said "looks") registers the sub-
stantive nature of Prospero's change: what he acknowledges is
not so much a shifting of shape as a secular epiphany.

The translations experienced by those who are really "borne
across" to the island—as opposed to those who, like Antonio,
Sebastian, Stephano, and Trinculo, have in effect never left
home—are real transformations, experiences from which they
emerge, even as they cross back to their former selves, changed.
For all of them (as for Bottom) something is gained in the translation ("in one voyage / Did Claribel her husband find at Tunis, /
And Ferdinand, her brother, found a wife / Where he himself
was lost; Prospero his dukedom / In a poor isle; and all of us,
ourselves, / When no man was his own," 5.1.208–13). But these
transformations are no longer conceived as produced by
the shock of an unmediated encounter with the Other, for
the "world elsewhere" is now recognized as always already
reformed/deformed by the colonizer's translations.

Stephen Greenblatt has made much of the possibility that a
single, apparently untranslatable word—"scamel"—stubbornly
survives from Caliban's pristine tongue. But the truth of this
nostalgic supposition is probably irrelevant,[24] for once Caliban
has been translated, all he can do is repeat the history of his
transformation, either in the key of farce—as when Stephano
offers to "give language to him" and he responds exactly as he
had to his first master ("I'll show thee every fertile inch o' th'

island; / And I will kiss thy foot; I prithee, be my god. . . . Thou wondrous man," 2.2.148–64)—or in the key of abject pathos— as in his resubmission to Prospero ("I will be wise hereafter, / And seek for grace," 5.1.295–96). By Prospero's act of naming, Caliban's island has been changed as surely and irremediably as the newly mapped Irish landscape of Brian Friel's play *Translations* is altered by the surveyor's Name-Book. Even when his oppressor is gone, Caliban will have to live in a translated world, like Friel's Hugh Mor O'Donnell: "We must learn those new names. . . . We must learn where we live. We must learn to make them our own. We must *make* them our new home."[25]

But how far the victims of translation can learn to truly inhabit the new tongue, as Friel insists is necessary, remains highly questionable; and what is arguably missing from Shakespeare's play is anything resembling Friel's defiant sense that cultural translation might, after all, become a creative two-way process of the kind that the anthropologist Marshall Sahlins celebrates in his studies of early Pacific contact[26]—any hint that for Caliban the trappings of Prospero's culture could ever amount to more than the borrowed frippery, the "glistering apparel" that hangs seductively on Prospero's "line." Everything depends, perhaps, on what one makes of the speech with which the dramatist endowed Caliban, that powerfully individualized dialect of cursing and lyrical ecstasy that so impressed the play's earliest recorded critics, moving them to marvel that "Shakespear *had not only found out a new character in his* Caliban *but had also devis'd and adapted a new manner of Language for that character.*"[27]

Yet over and above the play's apparent confirmation of the interpretive authority asserted by the European gaze are hints that the island itself remains, in the last analysis, as resistant to real translation as Barchilon's Peru or Bottom's Fairyland. These arise partly from the recurrent demonstrations of the arbitrariness of the intruders' translative moves, for the basic physical realities of the island seem absurdly dependent on the interpretive impulses of those who observe it, rendering it alternately a desert filled with the "confused noise" that signs its unredeemed condition and a verdant landscape infused with the mysterious transcendental harmonies that mark it as an earthly paradise. By the same token the "monstrous shape" of Ariel's companions inspires dread in the King's party, even while Gonzalo hails them as *"people of the island . . . more gentle, kind, than of / Our human generation you shall find"* (3.3.31–33; emphases added), thus opening to question the whole matter of "kind" and "likeness" upon which the last scene lays so much emotional stress. In much the same way Caliban is simultaneously repudiated as a deformed and bestial monster, "a freckled whelp, hag-born" and acknowledged as a "man" with "a human shape" (1.2.283–84, 446): from one perspective (established in the play by his pairing with Ferdinand, as log-bearer, suitor, and potential rapist of Miranda) he is a man exactly like the Neapolitans; from another he seems so unimaginably different from them as to be almost beyond satisfactory description.

Nor is even Prospero's power sufficient to effect a lasting translation of this wild place, with its resistance to containing definition, into the civil domain of European empire. Indeed the very fact that Prospero's own mastery of the island's "strangeness" is dependent upon the arcana of "magic" is a sign of how much this place belongs to the realm of the inexpressible, the untranslatable. It is true that the books which are the reputed source of his control have come from Italy, but in Milan they were merely the source of bookish impotence, the occasion of his downfall. The power they confer is in every sense insular, something Prospero must bury or drown before, like the other Italians, he can be "himself" again, re-translate himself from the estrangement of exile to the familiar world of Milan. For Prospero, as for Barchilon, the crossing over into another world exacts its price; its very incompleteness means that in Milan, where "every third thought shall be my grave," he will be haunted by an even bleaker version of the Spaniard's displacement, a sense of fretful imperfection that only death can assuage. In this playing out of the colonizer's self-defeating dream of triumphant return, as in so many other ways, *The Tempest* seems prophetic. No wonder that the epilogue gives us a Prospero still pleading for release from the "bare island" to which Shakespeare's uncharacteristic refusal of the theatre's translative magic has kept him confined.

It is perhaps *The Tempest's* very hesitancy about the ultimate possibilities of translation which requires that its dream of empire be in the end surrendered—even if it can never be forgotten. In this, like Fletcher's parasitic *The Sea-Voyage*, where the island colony is once again gratefully abandoned, Shakespeare's play no doubt reflected the uncertain fluctuations of English colonizing ambition in the New World. But the dream of theater remains intact. When Miranda speaks her distress at the destructive spectacle of the tempest ("I have suffered with those that I saw suffer") she is made to describe an experience of emotional translation that Shakespeare seems to have seen theater as uniquely equipped to produce—an experience that she has in fact just shared with the theater audience. The even more intense challenge that Lear issues in another tempest—"Expose thyself to feel what wretches feel"—is to just such a displacing of the self (one which the audience is at that very moment being forced to experience). Such translation is itself a kind of exploration and (in a way that perfectly accords with the Renaissance rewriting of Aristotle that made "wonder" an essential component of theatrical experience) it is always, even in its most forlorn moments, infused with a sense of the marvelous, for it creates the illusion (which the discovery literature of the period never manages to supply) that it may after all be possible to cross over into the space of the Other, whether its name is Caliban or Shylock or Othello or even la Pucelle.

It is partly because Shakespeare more than any other writer of his period is capable of glimpsing how it might feel to inhabit the other side of Montaigne's mountains that he himself seems worth the labor of translation—the unending task of carrying him across to the present. But to make such a claim is emphatically not to place his work outside history, to smuggle in a new version of the universal Shakespeare through the backdoor. Indeed, as I have tried to suggest, it is not because he stands above history, but because he was so intensely embroiled in it that Shakespeare still translates. Translation, he shows us, is always an ambiguous process. It can be either active or passive, empathic or aggressive, an instrument of conquest, a vehicle of trade, or a passport to wonder. A translator is, according to the punning Italian proverb always a traitor—*traduttore vuol dire traditore*—but translation is also the process by which (as Bottom discovers in the Athenian woods) one may become a "translated man"—one who is borne across into the "world beyond." Translation is never innocent and its motives are usually mixed; but only through its uncertain operations, Shakespeare suggests, can human beings stretch their fragile pontoons into the unknown.

NOTES

1. Thomas Platter, *Travels in England*, trans. Clare Williams (London: J. Cape, 1937), 170.

2. Peter Womack, "Imagining Communities: Theatres and the English Nation in the Sixteenth Century," in *Culture and History 1350–1600: Essays on English Communities, Identities and Writing*, ed. David Aers (Brighton: Harvester Wheatsheaf, 1992), 91–145, 108.

3. Patricia Parker, "*The Merry Wives of Windsor* and Shakespearean Translation," *MLQ* 52 (1991): 225–61.

4. George Puttenham, *The Arte of English Poesie*, ed. Gladys Doidge Willcock and Alice Walker (Cambridge, Cambridge University Press, 1936), 178.

5. John Florio, trans., *Montaigne's Essays*, 3 vols. (London: Dent, 1965), 2:xii, 297.

6. Ibid., 1:xxx, 227.

7. Ibid., 1:xxx, 229.

8. Ibid., 1:xxx, 229.

9. Eric Cheyfitz, *The Poetics of Imperialism: Translation and Colonization from "The Tempest" to Tarzan* (New York: Oxford University Press, 1991), 15.

10. See Richard Beacon, *Solon his Follie, or A Politique Discovrse, touching the Reformation of common-weales conquered, declined or corrupted* (Oxford, 1594), 110, and Edmund Spenser, *A View of the Present State of Ireland*, ed. W. L. Renwick (London: Scholartis Press, 1934), 197.

11. Even Spenser, whose project of translation is sometimes disturbingly close to genocide, seems to have experienced the seductive pull of alterity through his efforts to have the poetry of Irish bards translated; and the disturbance that resulted from his discovery of "sweet witt ... good grace and Comelynesse" directed (as it seemed) "to the gracing of Wickednes and vice" (*View*, 97–98) is reflected in *The Faerie Queene's* obsessive fascination with the Circe motif and its associated bouts of antiaesthetic violence.

12. Michael Neill, "Broken English and Broken Irish: Nation, Language, and the Optic of Power in Shakespeare's Histories," *Shakespeare Quarterly* 45 (1994): 1–32.

13. Edmund Spenser, *View of the Present State of Ireland*, 88.

14. Stephen Greenblatt, *Marvelous Possessions: The Wonder of the New World* (Chicago: University of Chicago Press, 1991), 16 and passim.

15. See Anthony Pagden, *European Encounters with the New World* (New Haven and London: Yale University Press, 1993), 38–41. All citations from Quiroga are from his text.

16. See her so-far unpublished "Obscured by Dreams: Race, Empire and Shakespeare's *A Midsummer Night's Dream*."

17. Pagden, *European Encounters*, 41.

18. Peter Hulme, *Colonial Encounters: Europe and the Native Caribbean, 1492–1797)* (London: Methuen, 1986).

19. *Essays*, 1:xxx, 227.

20. Ibid., 220.

21. Aimé Césaire, *A Tempest (Une Tempête)*, trans. Richard Miller (New York: Ubu Repertory Theater, 1985), 73.

22. Cheyfitz, *Poetics of Imperialism*, 120.

23. See, e.g., *The Famous History of the Life and Death of Captain Thomas Stukely* (1605) (Oxford: Oxford University Press, 1975), lines 1179–80.

24. See Greenblatt, "Learning to Curse," p. 31; and Cheyfitz, pp. 107–8.

25. Brian Friel, *Translations* (London: Faber and Faber, 1981), 66.

26. Marshall Sahlins, "Goodbye to Tristes Tropes: the Anthropology of History in Polynesia," The Robb Lectures, University of Auckland, 1992.

27. A conversation between Lucius Cary, John Hales of Eton, Chief Justice Henry Vaughan and others, reported by Nicholas Rowe; cited in Alden T. Vaughan and Virginia Mason Vaughan, *Shakespeare's Caliban: A Cultural History* (Cambridge: Cambridge University Press, 1991), 95–96.

A Checklist
S. Schoenbaum, 1927–
Director, Center for Renaissance and
Baroque Studies
University of Maryland

Compiled by NANCY KLEIN MAGUIRE

Principal Books and Honors

Internal Evidence and Elizabethan Dramatic Authorship: An Essay in Literary History and Method. Evanston, Ill.: Northwestern University Press, 1966; London: Edward Arnold, 1966.

Shakespeare's Lives. Oxford: Clarendon Press, 1970; revised edition, 1991.

William Shakespeare: A Documentary Life. Oxford: Clarendon Press, 1975.

William Shakespeare: A Compact Documentary Life. New York and Oxford: Oxford University Press, 1978; revised with new postscript, 1987.

Shakespeare: The Globe and the World. New York: Oxford University Press, 1979.

William Shakespeare: Records and Images. London: Scolar Press, 1981; New York: Oxford University Press, 1981.

Shakespeare and Others. Washington, D.C.: Folger Books, 1985; London: Scolar Press, 1985.

Shakespeare: His Life, His Language, His Theater. New York: Penguin USA, 1990.

Shakespeare's Lives: New Edition. Oxford: Clarendon Press, 1991.

Founding Editor. *Renaissance Drama* (1964–73)

Revision of Alfred Harbage's *Annals of English Drama, 975–1700*. Philadelphia: University of Pennsylvania Press, 1964.

Co-editer, with Kenneth Muir. *A New Companion to Shakespeare Studies*, the Cambridge University Press, 1971.

Twenty-five articles and chapters in books as well as approximately fifty book reviews, mainly in the *Times Literary Supplement* and *The Washington Post*.

Guggenheim Fellowship (1956–57, 1969–70)

National Endowment for the Humanities Senior Fellowship (1973–74)

Newberry Library Grant (1958)

Huntington Library Grant (1959, 1967)

The Friends of Literature nonfiction award for *Shakespeare's Lives* (1971)

The Distinguished Service Award of the Society of Midland Authors for *William Shakespeare: A Documentary Life* (1976)

Fellow of the Royal Society of Literature of the United Kingdom (1984)

Life Trustee of the Shakespeare Birthplace Trust in Stratford-upon-Avon (1984)

Honorary D. Litt., Susquehanna University (1986)

Honorary D. Litt., the University of Colorado at Boulder (1987)

Contributors

JONAS BARISH is Professor of English at the University of California at Berkeley. Since his *Ben Jonson and the Language of Prose Comedy* (1960), he has written extensively on Jonson and on other topics in Renaissance drama and edited *Volpone* (1962) and *Sejanus* (1987).

IAN DONALDSON is Professor of English and Fellow of King's College, Cambridge. He is currently completing a biography of Ben Jonson. He has edited Jonson's poetry and other writings for the Oxford University Press (1975, 1985, 1995).

RICHARD DUTTON is Professor of English at Lancaster University, where he has taught since 1974. Recent publications include *William Shakespeare: A Literary Life*, in the *Macmillan Literary Lives* series (of which he is general editor), and *Mastering the Revels: The Regulations and Censorship of English Renaissance Drama* (Macmillan and Iowa University Press). Forthcoming works include an edition of *Jacobean Civic Pageants* (Keele University Press) and *Ben Jonson, Authority, Criticism* (Macmillan).

MARY EDMOND is an independent scholar based in London. Since her *Rare Sir William Davenant* (1987), she has published articles in *Shakespeare Survey, Shakespeare Quarterly*, and elsewhere on the builders of Elizabethan theaters and on other Elizabethan subjects.

PHILIP FINKELPEARL is the Anne Pierce Rogers Professor of English, Wellesley College. Aside from notes and reviews, his most recent publication is a study of Beaumont and Fletcher (1990). An article is "forthcoming" in *RES:* "The Fairies' Farewell: *The Coleorton Masque* (1618)." His contribution is part of a book project: "Fletcher, Shakespeare, and 1613."

R. A. FOAKES, Professor of English in the University of California at Los Angeles has written, most recently, *Illustrations of the English Stage, 1580–1642* and *"Hamlet" versus "Lear": Cultural Politics and Shakespeare's Art.*

BRIAN GIBBONS is Professor of English Literature, University of Münster, Germany. He is the General Editor of the New Cambridge Shakespeare and of The New Mermaid Drama Series. Among his books are *Shakespeare and Multiplicity* (1993) and *Jacobean City Comedy* (2d ed. 1980), and recent editions of *Measure for Measure* (1991) and *Romeo and Juliet* (1980).

GEORGE K. HUNTER is Emily Sanford Professor Emeritus, Yale University. He has recently edited Lyly's *Campaspe,* and is now preparing an edition of *Gallathea.* His volume 6 of the *Oxford History of English Literature* ("The Age of Shakespeare") should be published in 1996.

ARTHUR KINNEY is Thomas W. Copeland Professor of Literary History in the University of Massachusetts at Amherst and the editor of *English Literary Renaissance.* He has written on *Humanist Poetics, John Skelton,* and other Renaissance topics.

ALEXANDER LEGGATT is Professor of English at University College, University of Toronto. His recent publications include *Shakespeare's Political Drama, Shakespeare in Performance: King Lear,* and *Jacobean Public Theatre.*

NANCY KLEIN MAGUIRE, a Scholar-in-Residence at the Folger Library, is the author of *Regicide and Restoration: English Tragicomedy, 1660–1671* and is currently engaged in a study of French politics in England from 1660 to 1688.

BARBARA A. MOWAT, the Director of Academic Programs at the Folger Library and editor of *Shakespeare Quarterly,* is also co-editing the New Folger Shakespeare with Paul Werstine. Her integration of criticism and scholarship is typical of her *Dramaturgy of Shakespeare's Romances* (1967).

MICHAEL NEILL is Associate Professor of English at the University of Auckland, New Zealand. His more recent publications include an edition of *Anthony and Cleopatra* for the Oxford Shakespeare (1994), "Broken English and Broken Irish: Language, Nation and the Optic of Power in Shakespeare's Histories," (*Shakespeare Quarterly* 45, 1994), and "Putting History to the Question: An Episode of Torture at Bantam in Java, 1604," (ELR, 1995).

ANNABEL PATTERSON is the Karl Young Professor of English at Yale University. Among her publications are *Censorship and Interpretation* (1984, 1990), *Shakespeare and the Popular Voice* (1989), *Reading between the Lines* (1992), and *Reading Holin-*

shed's Chronicles (1994). She has edited *The Merchant of Venice* for the *Shakespearean Originals* series.

MEREDITH SKURA is Professor of English at Rice University. Her most recent work, *Shakespeare the Actor and the Purposes of Playing* (1994), carries on the concerns of her earlier *The Literary Uses of the Psychoanalytic Process.*

SUSAN SNYDER is Gil and Frank Mustin Professor Emerita of English at Swarthmore College. Her edition of *All's Well That Ends Well* for the Oxford Shakespeare was published in 1993.

STEVEN URKOWITZ is Professor and Chairman of English at the City College of New York. His *Shakespeare's Revision of King Lear* (1980) was among the earliest works to examine the implications of revised or multiple texts. He has further explored these implications through subsequent publications and activity in the theater.

STANLEY WELLS is Professor of Shakespeare Studies and Director of the Shakespeare Institute of the University of Birmingham. He is General Editor of the Oxford Shakespeare and editor of *Shakespeare Survey,* and his most recent book is *Shakespeare: A Dramatic Life* (1994).

The editors, BRIAN PARKER and SHELDON P. ZITNER, are Professors of English at Trinity College, Toronto and have written extensively on Elizabethan drama. Professor Parker's most recent books are a Revels Series edition of *Volpone* and an edition of *Coriolanus* for Oxford. Professor Zitner has recently published a study of *All's Well that Ends Well* (Harvester) and an edition of *Much Ado About Nothing* for Oxford.

Index